THOMSON
NELSON

Nelson Mathematics 3
Western Edition

Series Authors and Senior Consultants:
Marian Small, Mary Lou Kestell

Senior Authors:
Heather Kelleher,
Kathy Kubota-Zarivnij, Pat Milot,
Betty Morris, Doug Super

Authors:
Carole Adam, Jennifer Brown,
Carol Brydon, Catharine Gilmour,
Elizabeth Grill-Donovan, Jack Hope,
Wendy Klassen, David Leach,
Ian Stackhouse, Stella Tossell,
Rosita Tseng Tam

Assessment Consultant:
Damian Cooper

Director of Publishing:
David Steele

Publisher, Mathematics:
Beverley Buxton

Senior Program Manager:
Shirley Barrett

Program Managers:
Lynda Cowan
Mary Reeve

Developmental Editors:
Brenda McLoughlin
Linda Nigro
Michael Tabor
Robert Templeton
Susan Woollam

Developmental Consultants:
Jackie Williams
Colin Bisset
David Hamilton

Editorial Assistants:
Christi Davis
Darren McDonald
Megan Robinson
Matthew Sheehan
Christine Szentgyorgyi

Executive Managing Editor, Development & Testing:
Cheryl Turner

Executive Managing Editor, Production:
Nicola Balfour

Senior Production Editor:
Linh Vu

Production Editor:
Sheila Stephenson

Copy Editor:
Julia Cochrane
Margot Miller

Senior Production Coordinator:
Sharon Latta Paterson

Production Coordinator:
Franca Mandarino

Creative Director:
Angela Cluer

Art Director:
Ken Phipps

Art Management:
ArtPlus Ltd., Suzanne Peden

Illustrators:
ArtPlus Ltd., Andrew Breithaupt,
Steven Corrigan, Deborah Crowle,
Jock MacRae, Sharon Matthews

Interior and Cover Design:
Suzanne Peden

ArtPlus Ltd. Production Coordinator:
Dana Lloyd

ArtPlus Ltd. Composition:
Valerie Bateman, Miriam Semple

Photo Research and Permissions:
Vicki Gould

Photo Shoot Coordinators:
ArtPlus Ltd., Trent Photographics

Printer:
Transcontinental Printing Inc.

Printed and bound in Canada
1 2 3 4 06 05 04

For more information contact Nelson, 1120 Birchmount Road, Toronto, Ontario, M1K 5G4. Or you can visit our Internet site at http://www.nelson.com

National Library of Canada Cataloguing in Publication

Nelson mathematics 3 / Marian Small ... [et al.].—Western ed.

Includes index.
For use in grade 3.
ISBN 0-17-627241-0

1. Mathematics—Textbooks.
I. Small, Marian
II. Title: Nelson mathematics three.

QA135.6.N443 2004
510 C2003-907068-9

Nelson Mathematics 3

Western Edition

Series Authors and Senior Consultants

Marian Small • Mary Lou Kestell

Senior Authors

Heather Kelleher • Kathy Kubota-Zarivnij • Pat Milot
Betty Morris • Doug Super

Authors

Carole Adam • Jennifer Brown • Carol Brydon • Catharine Gilmour
Elizabeth Grill-Donovan • Jack Hope • Wendy Klassen • David Leach
Ian Stackhouse • Stella Tossell • Rosita Tseng Tam

Assessment Consultant

Damian Cooper

THOMSON NELSON

Australia Canada Mexico Singapore Spain United Kingdom United States

Advisory Panel

Senior Advisor

Doug Duff
Learning Supervisor
Thames Valley District School Board
London, Ontario

Advisors

Donna Anderson
Coal Tyee Elementary School
Nanaimo, British Columbia

Keith Chong
Principal
School District #41
Burnaby, British Columbia

Anne Cirillo
Consultant
Toronto Catholic District
School Board
Toronto, Ontario

Attila Csiszar
Math Helping Teacher
Surrey School District #36
Surrey, British Columbia

David P. Curto
Principal
Hamilton-Wentworth Catholic
District School Board
Hamilton, Ontario

Marg Curto
Principal of Programs, Elementary
Hamilton-Wentworth Catholic
District School Board
Hamilton, Ontario

Edna Dach
Director Instructional Services
Elk Island Public Schools
Alberta

Wendy Dowling
Peel District School Board
Mississauga, Ontario

Lillian Forsythe, B.Ed., B.A., M.Ed.
Regina, Saskatchewan

Peggy Gerrard
Dr. Morris Gibson
Foothills School Division
Okotoks, Alberta

Mary Gervais
Durham Catholic District
School Board

C. Marie Hauk, Ph.D.
Consultant
Edmonton, Alberta

Rebecca Kozol
Maple Ridge School District #42
Maple Ridge, British Columbia

A. Craig Loewen, Ph.D.
Mathematics Education
University of Lethbridge
Lethbridge, Alberta

Frank Maggio
Mathematics Curriculum Consultant
Halton Catholic District
School Board
Burlington, Ontario

Moyra Martin
Principal
Msgr. O'Brien School
Calgary Catholic School District
Calgary, Alberta

Janet Millar Grant
Ontario

Meagan Mutchmor
Consultant
Winnipeg School District #1
Winnipeg, Manitoba

Mary Anne Nissen
Consultant
Elk Island Public Schools
Sherwood Park, Alberta

Darlene Peckford, B.Ed., M.A.
Principal
Taber, Alberta

Kathryn Perry
Peel District School Board
Brampton, Ontario

Susan Perry
Consultant
Durham Catholic District
School Board
Oshawa, Ontario

Bryan A. Quinn
Consultant
Edmonton Public District
School Board
Edmonton, Alberta

Ann Louise Revells
Vice-Principal/Teacher
Ottawa-Carleton Catholic
School Board
Ottawa, Ontario

Evelyn Sawicki
Mathematics Consultant
Calgary, Alberta

Lorraine Schroetter-LaPointe
Program Facilitator
Durham District School Board
Whitby, Ontario

Nathalie Sinclair, Ph.D.
Simon Fraser University
Faculty of Education

Susan Stuart
Professor
Nipissing University
North Bay, Ontario

Joyce Tonner
Learning Coordinator
Thames Valley District School
Board
London, Ontario

Stella Tossell
Mathematics Consultant
North Vancouver, British Columbia

Sandra Unrau
Principal
Calgary Board of Education
Calgary, Alberta

Gerry Varty
Math Coordinator
Wolf Creek School Division #72
Ponoka, Alberta

Michèle Wills
Calgary Board of Education
Calgary, Alberta

Reviewers

Mary Adams
Thames Valley District School Board

Wilda Audet
Ottawa-Carleton District
School Board

Michael L. Babcock
Limestone District School Board

Anne Boyd
Campbell River School District 72
British Columbia

Kelly Buske
Upper Canada District
School Board

Maralee Chambers
Peel District School Board

Catherine Chau
Toronto District School Board

Deborah Colvin-MacDormand
Edmonton Public District
School Board

Anna Dutfield
Toronto District School Board

Heather Dymond
Peel District School Board

Susannah Howick
North Vancouver School District

Heather Kelleher
University of British Columbia

Gowa Kong
North Vancouver School District

Joanne Languay
Hamilton-Wentworth District
School Board

Joan McDuff
Faculty of Education
Queen's University

Ken Mendes
Ottawa, Ontario

Joanne Simmons
Toronto District School Board

Lindy Smith
Peel District School Board

Jennifer Peacocke
Ottawa-Carleton District
School Board

Mary Wallace
Peel District School Board

Aboriginal Content Reviewers

Brenda Davis
Education Consultant
Six Nations

Moneca Sinclaire, M.Sc.
Doctoral Candidate
Manitoba

Laura Smith
School District #34
Abbotsford, British Columbia

Equity Reviewer

Arlene Campbell
Toronto District School Board
Educator
York University Doctoral Candidate

Literacy Reviewer

Dr. Roslyn Doctorow
Educational Consultant

Thank you to the following teachers for testing the Chapter Tasks.

Mary Adams
Thames Valley District
School Board

Sue Bergen
Central Okanagan School
District #23

Jennifer Bryan-Pulham
Avon Maitland District
School Board

Maralee Chambers
Peel District School Board

Stefanie De Angelis
Peel District School Board

Heather Dymond
Peel District School Board

Jessica Fairley
Peel District School Board

Julie Fowlie
Durham District School Board

Sonya Gould
Peel District School Board

Carol Kurtz
Algoma District School Board

Christine Novak
Thames Valley District
School Board

Contents

- Guided Activity
- Direct Instruction
- Exploration

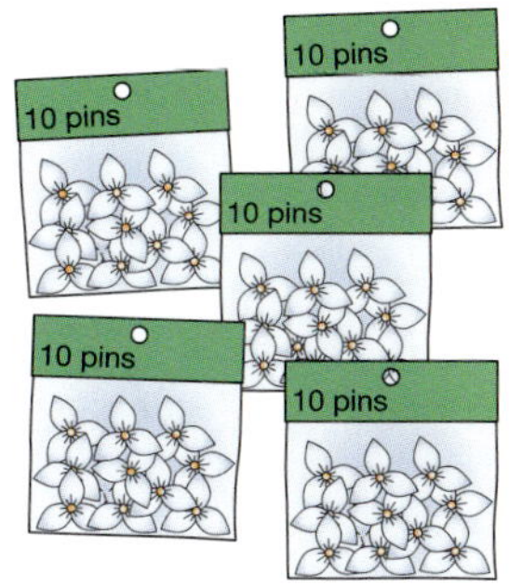

CHAPTER 4 Addition and Subtraction 83

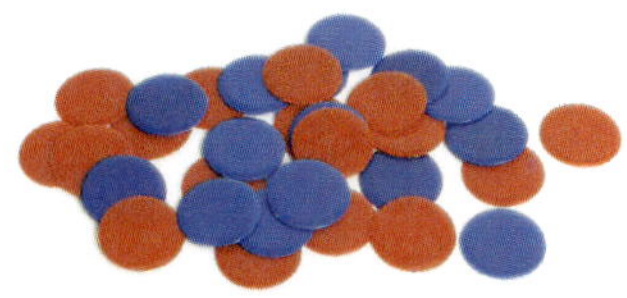

CHAPTER 5 Measuring Length, Time, and Temperature 111

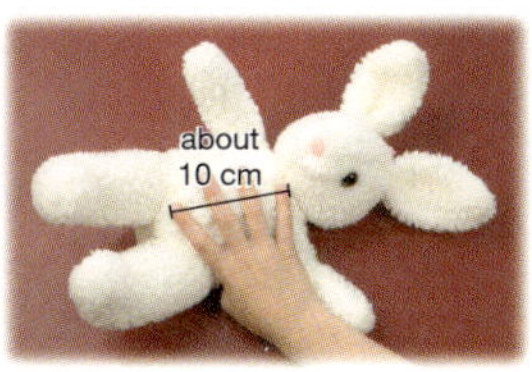

- Guided Activity
- Direct Instruction
- Exploration

CHAPTER 6 Adding and Subtracting with Greater Numbers 145

- Guided Activity
- Direct Instruction
- Exploration

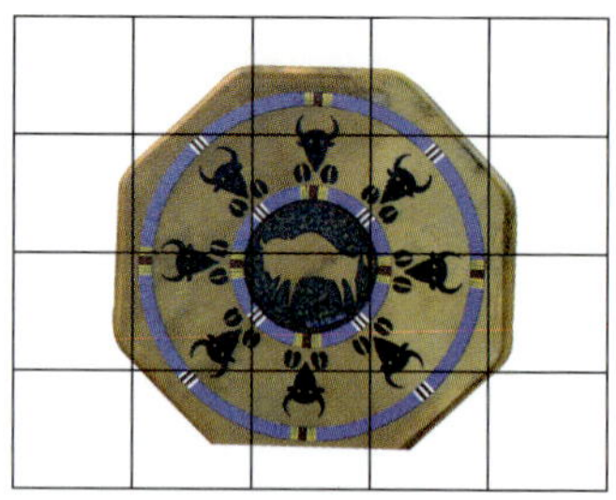

CHAPTER 9 Multiplication

CHAPTER 10 Division

- Guided Activity
- Direct Instruction
- Exploration

CHAPTER 11 3-D Geometry and 3-D Measurement 269

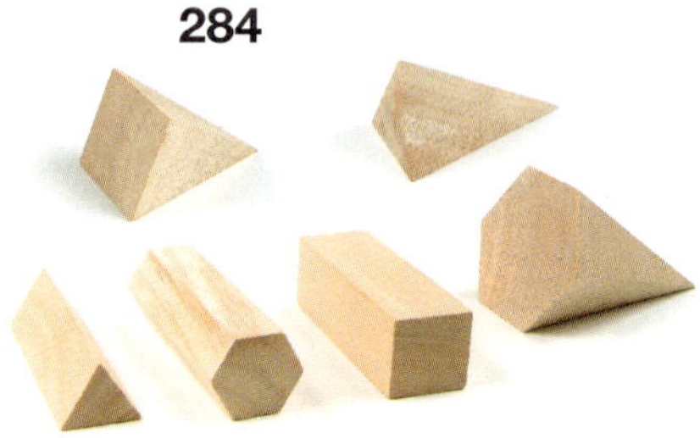

CHAPTER 12 Fractions 301

- Guided Activity
- Direct Instruction
- Exploration

- Guided Activity
- Direct Instruction
- Exploration

CHAPTER 1

Patterns in Mathematics

Goals

You will be able to

- **identify, describe, extend, and create patterns**
- **use pattern rules to make predictions**
- **use charts and grids to represent and extend patterns**
- **communicate about patterns**

Playground patterns

Getting Started

Patterns All Around

Some grade 3 students are lining up.

? What patterns do you see?

A. Choose 1 student. Tell what the student is wearing.

B. Look at the next student in line.
Tell what this student is wearing.

C. Compare what the 2 students are wearing.
What is the same? What is different?

D. Look for patterns in what all of the students are wearing. Describe 3 patterns that you see.

E. Choose 1 pattern from the picture.
Imagine that 3 new students join the line.
Describe what each new student will be wearing.

Do You Remember?

1. Look for the pattern. Write the part that repeats.
   a) 2, 4, 6, 2, 4, 6, 2, 4, 6, …
   b) **red**, **blue**, **orange**, **orange**, **red**, **blue**, **orange**, **orange**, **red**, **blue**, **orange**, **orange**, **red**, **blue**, …
   c) 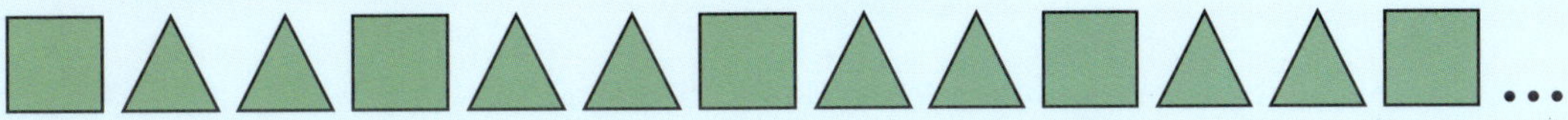

2. Write the next 3 numbers or draw the next 3 pictures in each pattern.
   a) 20, 19, 18, 17, 20, 19, 18, 17, 20, 19, 18, 17, …
   b) 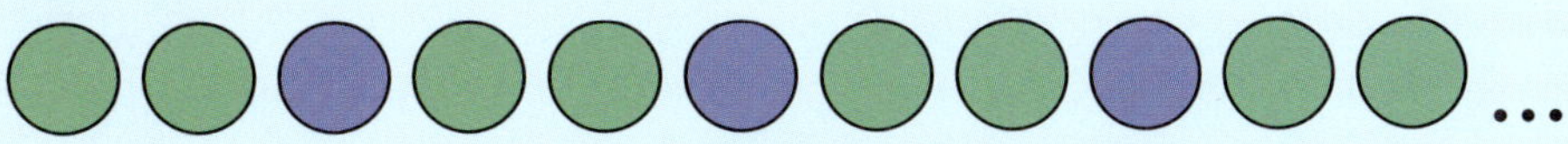

3. Use these words to name each type of pattern.
   repeating pattern   growing pattern
   a) 4, 6, 8, 10, …
   b) 35, 40, 45, 50, …
   c) 3, 1, 4, 3, 1, 4, 3, 1, 4, …

1 Repeating Shape Patterns

Goal **Extend and create shape patterns.**

You will need

- pattern blocks

- pencil crayons

Sukan is making wrapping paper patterns.

? How can you use pattern blocks to make patterns?

Sukan's Pattern

I started my pattern with 2 green triangles and a red **trapezoid**.

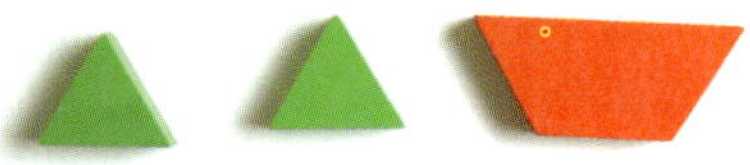

I extended my pattern by repeating my starting shapes.

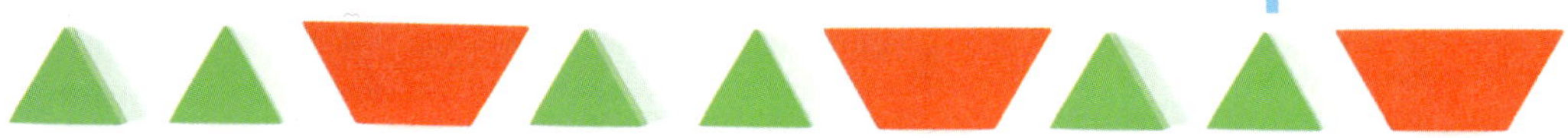

2 of the **attributes** that change in my pattern are shape and number of shapes. This is how the attributes change:

Number of shapes: 2 triangles, 1 trapezoid, . . .
Shape: triangle, triangle, trapezoid, . . .

attribute
A feature that you can use to describe and compare things (e.g., colour, shape, size, number, texture, position)

A. Predict the 12th block in Sukan's pattern.

B. Extend Sukan's pattern to check your prediction.

C. Make a different block pattern.
Use the yellow **hexagon** and the blue **rhombus**.
How do the attributes change?

D. Make a new pattern that repeats at least 3 times.
Trace your pattern. How do the attributes change?

Reflecting

1. How can repeating patterns be the same?
   How can they be different?
2. What do you need to know to extend a pattern?

Checking

3. Lee made this pattern.

   a) What attribute is changing?
      How is the attribute changing?
   b) Show the part of the pattern that repeats.
      Use pictures or words.

Practising

4. a) Tell how the attributes change for the pattern.
   b) Sketch the part that repeats to extend the pattern.
   c) Predict the 18th block in the pattern.
   d) Extend the pattern to check your prediction.

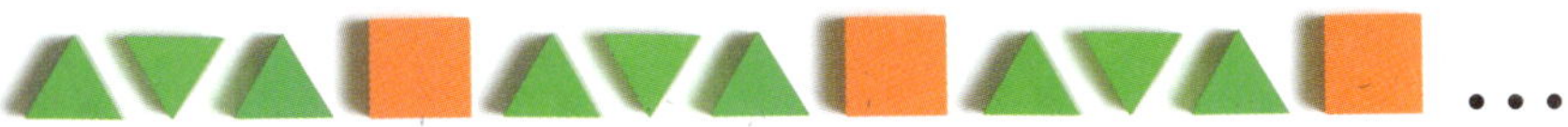

5. Tell how the attributes change for each pattern.
   Sketch the part that repeats to extend the pattern.

   a) 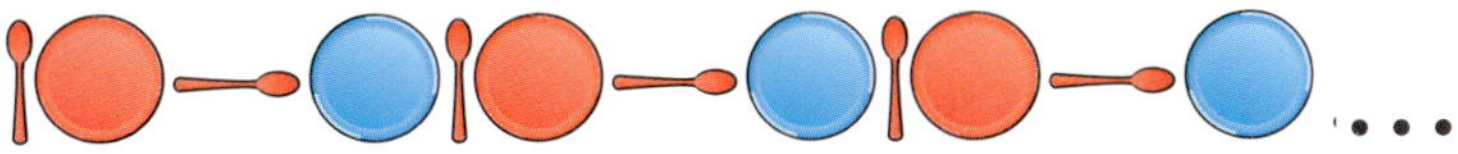

   b) 

   c) 

6. a) Sketch a pattern with 2 changing attributes.
      Make your pattern repeat 3 times.
   b) Tell how the attributes change.

CHAPTER 1

2 Exploring Patterns

Goal **Create and explore patterns that change in more than one way.**

You will need

- grid paper

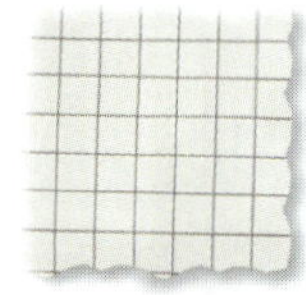

- pencil crayons

? How can you make repeating name patterns?

A. List the attributes that change in these name patterns. How does each attribute change?

SHARLEENSHARLEEN…

AMITAMITAMITAMIT…

MiChAeLmIcHaEl…

B. Plan a pattern with your own name. Decide on 2 changing attributes.

C. Make a pattern that repeats at least 6 times. Use your name over and over.

D. Write your name pattern over and over on a 4-by-4 grid. What new patterns do you see?

E. Write your name pattern over and over on a 5-by-5 grid. What new patterns do you see?

F. Create a new pattern with a classmate's name. Repeat parts B, C, D, and E with that name.

N	i	S	h
A	n	I	s
H	a	N	i
S	h	A	n

Reflecting

1. Describe the name patterns you made. How do the attributes change?

Mental Math

Addition Patterns

Amit used a number pattern to add 2 numbers.

A. Explain Amit's addition pattern.

B. Use Amit's addition pattern to calculate the other sums.

Amit's Addition Pattern

I know 9 + 6 = 15.
So 19 + 6 = 25.
And 29 + 6 = 35.

9 + 6 = 15
19 + 6 = 25
29 + 6 = 35
39 + 6 = ■
49 + 6 = ■
59 + 6 = ■

Try These

1. Use a pattern to add.

a)	b)
9 + 4 = ■	18 + 5 = ■
19 + 4 = ■	38 + 5 = ■
29 + 4 = ■	78 + 5 = ■
39 + 4 = ■	88 + 5 = ■

Curious Math

Dance Patterns

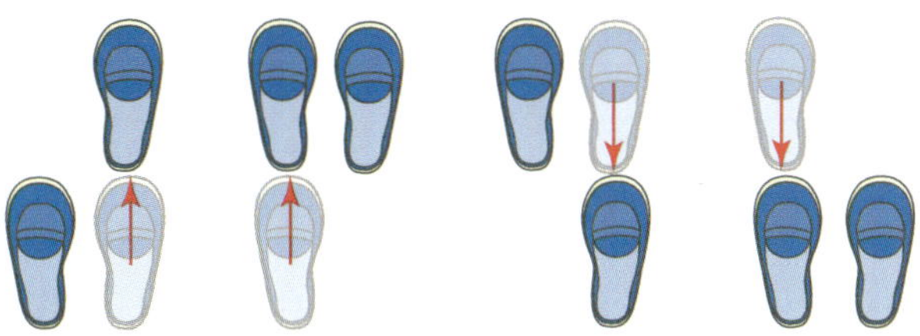

Dancers follow patterns in their steps.
This is a pattern for a 4-step dance.
By repeating the pattern, you can do the dance.

1 Describe the dance. How is it a pattern? Try the dance.

2 Make up your own dance pattern and record it.

3 Patterns in a 100 Chart

Goal **Represent adding and subtracting patterns on a 100 chart.**

Tiffany's Pattern

I will make an adding number pattern with this **pattern rule**: Start with 3 and add 5 each time.

When I press 3 [+] 5 [=] [=] [=]…, my calculator **skip counts** by 5s.

I put a counter on each number on a 100 chart that is in the pattern.

? What do adding and subtracting number patterns look like on a 100 chart?

A. Use counters on a 100 chart to make Tiffany's pattern. Extend the pattern to 98.

B. Describe the pattern made by the counters.

C. Write the pattern rule for the numbers.

D. Make a different adding number pattern. Use a calculator. Pick an odd start number between 1 and 10. Skip count by 10s from your start number. What is your pattern rule?

E. Circle the numbers of your pattern on a 100 chart. Use red. Describe the red circle pattern.

You will need

- a calculator

- 100 charts

1	2	3	4
11	12	13	14
21	22	23	24

- pencil crayons

- clear counters

pattern rule

A description of how a pattern starts and how it can be extended

skip count

To count forward or backward by the same number each time

F. Make a subtracting number pattern. Skip count backward from 100 by 2s. Press 100 [−] 2 [=] [=] [=]....
What is your pattern rule?

G. Circle the numbers in the pattern on the same 100 chart. Use **blue**. Describe the **blue** circle pattern.
Describe the number pattern.

Reflecting

1. Look at your **red** and **blue** patterns.
Which pattern is a growing or increasing pattern?
Which pattern is a shrinking or decreasing pattern?

2. Look at the subtracting number pattern. What adding number pattern would look the same?

Checking

3. Use a 100 chart. Place a counter on all the squares where the number contains a 5.
   a) Describe the pattern made by the counters.
   b) Describe one of the number patterns.

1	2	3	4	5	6	7	8	9	10
11	12	13	14	15	16	17	18	19	20
21	22	23	24	25	26	27	28	29	30
31	32	33	34	35	36	37	38	39	40
41	42	43	44	45	46	47	48	49	50
51	52	53	54	55	56	57	58	59	60
61	62	63	64	65	66	67	68	69	70
71	72	73	74	75	76	77	78	79	80
81	82	83	84	85	86	87	88	89	90
91	92	93	94	95	96	97	98	99	100

Practising

4. Place counters on a 100 chart to make each pattern. Describe the pattern made by the counters.
   a) Start at 40 and skip count backward by 2s.
   40 [−] 2 [=] [=] [=]...
   b) Start at 4 and skip count forward by 5s.
   c) Start at 100 and skip count backward by 10s.

5. Extend each pattern for 10 more numbers.
Place counters on a 100 chart to make each pattern.
Write each pattern rule.
   a) 1, 3, 5, 7, ...   b) 95, 90, 85, 80, ...   c) 7, 12, 17, 22, ...

LESSON

Mid-Chapter Review

1

1. Draw the part that repeats to extend the pattern.
List the attributes that change. Tell how they change.

 ...

2. Predict the 15th block in this pattern.
Extend the pattern to check your prediction.

 ...

3. Draw the part that repeats to extend each pattern.
Tell how the attributes change.

a) 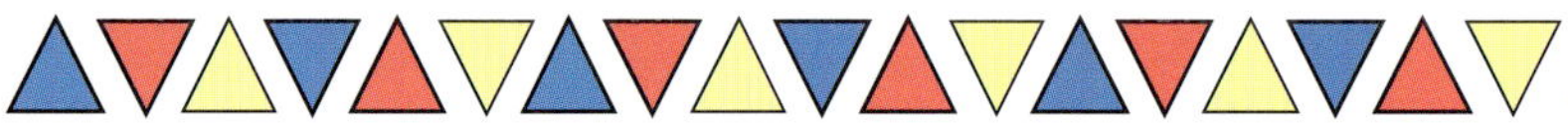 ...

b) 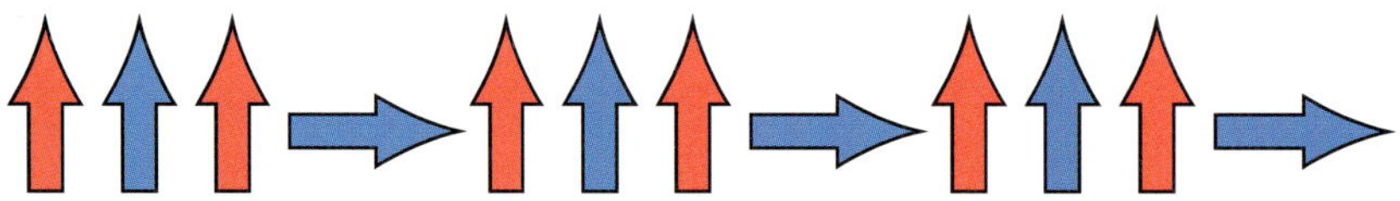 ...

c) A B B C A B B C A B B C ...

2

4. Tell how the attributes change in each name pattern.

a) jeSsicajeSsiCajeSsica... **b)** *RaShAdRaShAdRaShAd*...

3

5. Describe each pattern as increasing, decreasing, or repeating. Write a pattern rule for each.

a) 70, 60, 50, 40, ...
b) 38, 38, 38, 38, ...
c) 96, 94, 92, 90, ...
d) 70, 65, 60, 55, ...
e) 41, 46, 51, 56, ...
f) 6, 16, 26, 36, ...

6. **a)** Start at 1. Skip count forward by 2s. Circle the numbers on a 100 chart.
b) Describe the circle pattern on your 100 chart.
c) Describe the number pattern. Write a pattern rule.
d) Look at the ones digits of the circled numbers. Write the part of the pattern that repeats.

1	2	3	4	5	6	7	8	9	10
11	12	13	14	15	16	17	18	19	20
21	22	23	24	25	26	27	28	29	30
31	32	33	34	35	36	37	38	39	40
41	42	43	44	45	46	47	48	49	50
51	52	53	54	55	56	57	58	59	60
61	62	63	64	65	66	67	68	69	70
[illegible]	[illegible]	73	74	75	76	77	78	79	80
[illegible]	[illegible]	83	84	85	86	87	88	89	90
[illegible]	[illegible]	93	94	95	96	97	98	99	100

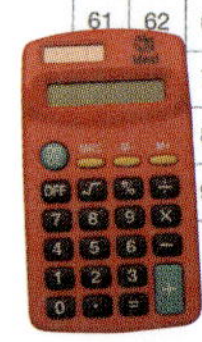

Changing Attributes

You will need

- attribute blocks

- a 6-by-6 grid

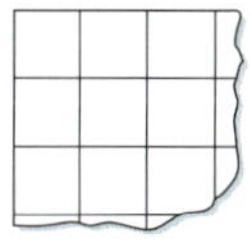

- a paper bag

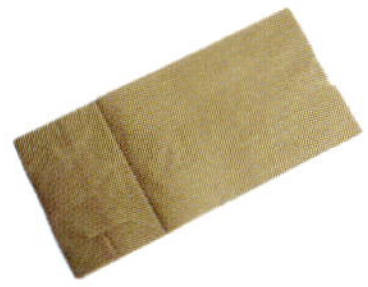

Number of players: 2 to 4

How to play: Place blocks beside other blocks on a grid according to their attributes.

Step 1 Each player takes 8 attribute blocks out of a bag without looking.

Step 2 The player with the most blue triangles goes 1st. The 1st player puts a block anywhere on the 6-by-6 grid.

Step 3 Players take turns placing a block beside, above, or below any block on the board. The new block must have only 1 attribute that is different from a neighbouring block. Players who cannot move lose a turn.

Play until a player runs out of blocks. If no one can move, the player with the fewest blocks left wins.

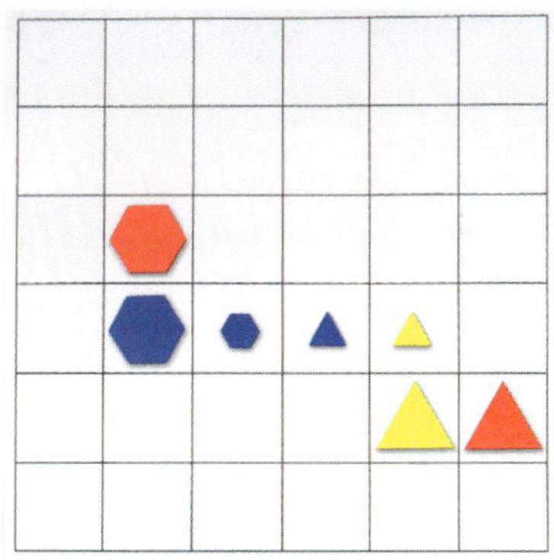

Devon's Turn

I put the large, thin, yellow triangle beside the large, thin, blue triangle.

The size, thickness, and shape are the same. The colour is different.

4 Patterns in T-Charts

Goal **Use a t-chart to represent and extend growing patterns.**

Jack makes square picture frames using craft sticks. He has 30 sticks. He predicts that 7 frames can fit across the bulletin board.

You will need

- craft sticks

- t-charts

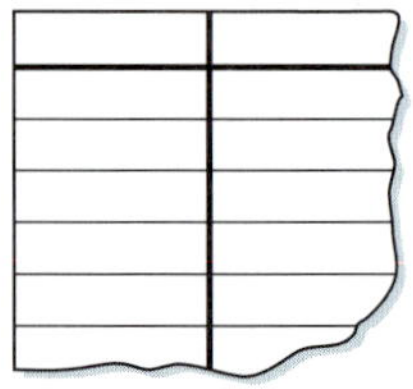

? Does Jack have enough sticks for 7 frames?

Jack's Frames

I made a **t-chart** to solve the problem.

One column shows the number of frames.

The other column shows the number of sticks.

After making 4 frames, I found a pattern in the t-chart:

4, 8, 12, 16, ...

The pattern starts at 4 and adds 4 each time.

I extended the pattern to complete the t-chart.

I need 28 sticks for 7 frames. I have enough.

Number of frames	Number of sticks
1	4
2	8
3	12
4	16
5	20
6	24
7	28

1 frame uses 4 sticks.

2 frames use 8 sticks.

t-chart
A way to organize information in a chart with 2 columns

Reflecting

1. a) How did Jack use the t-chart to solve the problem?
   b) How would you use the t-chart to find the number of sticks needed for 5 frames?
2. What is the pattern rule for the number of sticks?
3. Explain how you would use the pattern rule to predict the number of sticks for 10 frames.

Checking

4. Brady wants to make 10 square frames that share sides. Use a t-chart.
   a) How many sticks does she need?
   b) What is the pattern rule?

Number of frames	Number of sticks
1	4
2	
3	
4	

Practising

5. Jessica wants to make 7 triangle frames.
   a) How many sticks does she need?
   b) What is the pattern rule?

Number of frames	Number of sticks
1	3
2	
3	
4	

6. Rashad's pattern has frames that share sides.
   a) How many sticks are needed for 10 frames?
   b) What is the pattern rule?
   c) Predict how many sticks are needed for 15 frames. Explain how you know.
   d) Extend the pattern to check your prediction.

5 Communicate About Patterns

Goal **Describe a pattern.**

Rachel noticed a pattern on her beach towel.

? How could Rachel describe the pattern?

Rachel's Description

I told some of my classmates about my towel pattern. They wrote comments.

My towel has a pattern.
The pattern makes a rectangle shape.
4 shapes repeat: sun, cloud, sun, rain.
2 colours repeat: yellow, white.

How could you use the word "attribute" in your description?

Is this important?

Why did you say there are 4 shapes? I only see sun, cloud, and rain.

I like how you described the changing attributes separately.

It's good that you told how the 4 shapes and 2 colours are changing.

A. What did Rachel's classmates like about her description?

B. How would you answer their purple questions?

Reflecting

1. What part of the Communication Checklist is each purple question about?

Communication Checklist

- ☑ Did you show the right amount of detail?
- ☑ Did you use math language?

Checking

2. Rose described the pattern on her beach towel.
   a) What are some strengths in Rose's description? Use the Communication Checklist.
   b) Improve Rose's description.

Rose's Description

My towel pattern shows yellow, orange, yellow, orange, ...
I see a counting pattern in the rays of each sun. That pattern is like skip counting by 10s.

Practising

3. Describe the pattern on this beach towel. Use the Communication Checklist to help you.

Skills Bank

LESSON

1 **1.** Sketch the part that repeats to extend the pattern. List the attributes that change. Tell how they change.

a) 

b) 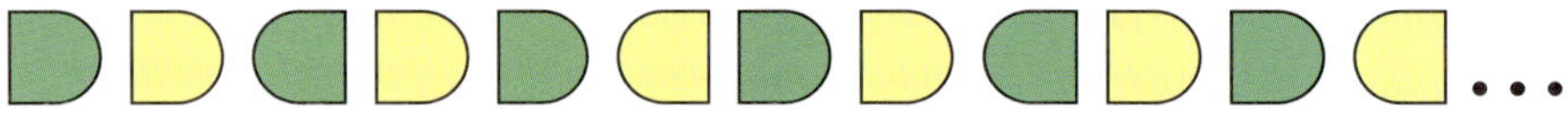

c) 

2. Predict the 14th pattern block in this pattern. Extend the pattern to check your prediction.

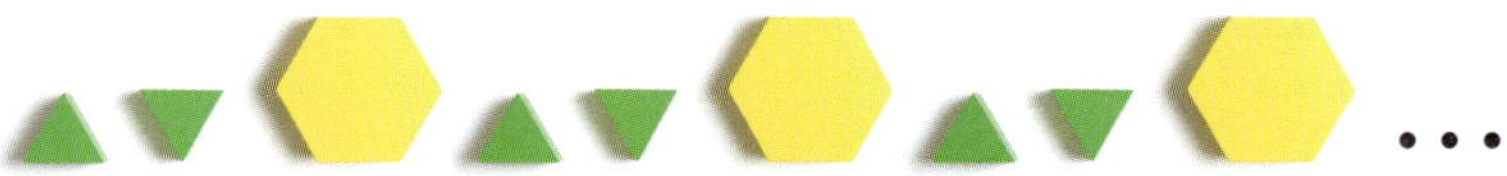

3. a) Create a pattern with 2 changing attributes. Use pattern blocks. Make your pattern repeat 3 times. Trace your pattern.

b) List the attributes that change. Tell how they change.

2 **4.** List the attributes that change in each name pattern. Tell how they change.

a) KeIsHaKeIsHaKeIsHa...

b) CHARLIECHARLIECHARLIE...

3 **5.** Place counters on a 100 chart. Extend each pattern for 5 more numbers. Write each pattern rule.

a) 60, 55, 50, 45, ...

b) 33, 38, 43, 48, ...

c) 17, 19, 21, 23, ...

d) 100, 90, 80, 70, ...

1	2	3	4	5	6	7	8	9	10
11	12	13	14	15	16	17	18	19	20
21	22	23	24	25	26	27	28	29	30
31	32	33	34	35	36	37	38	39	40
41	42	43	44	45	46	47	48	49	50
51	52	53	54	55	56	57	58	59	60
61	62	63	64	65	66	67	68	69	70
71	72	73	74	75	76	77	78	79	80
81	82	83	84	85	86	87	88	89	90
91	92	93	94	95	96	97	98	99	100

3

6. Circle each pattern on a 100 chart.
Describe the pattern the circles make.
Describe the number pattern.
   a) Start at 10 and skip count forward by 2s.
   b) Start at 80 and skip count backward by 5s.

4

7. Gabe eats 1 bowl of cereal every day.
   a) Extend the t-chart for 1 week.
   b) How many bowls of cereal will Gabe eat in 1 week?

Day	Total number of bowls
1	1
2	2

8. Amelia goes to 2 soccer practices every week.
   a) Extend the t-chart for 5 weeks.
   b) What is the pattern rule for the number of practices?

Week	Total number of practices
1	2
2	4

9. Tyler reads 3 books every month.
   a) Extend the t-chart for 6 months.
   b) What is the pattern rule for the number of books?
   c) Use the pattern rule to predict the number of books Tyler will read in 8 months.
   d) Extend the t-chart to check your prediction.

Month	Total number of books read
1	3

10. Maria is making 7 spider costumes for a dance recital.
   a) Extend the t-chart for 7 costumes.
   b) How many legs will 7 spider costumes have altogether?
   c) What is the pattern rule for the number of legs?
   d) Use the pattern rule to predict the number of legs for 9 spider costumes.

Total number of costumes	Total number of legs
1	8

Problem Bank

LESSON

1 **1.** Coral snakes are poisonous and have a yellow, red, yellow, black repeating pattern on their skin.

a) Which snake is the coral snake?

b) Does the rhyme "Red touching yellow, dangerous fellow" describe the coral snake pattern? Explain.

A B

2. What will the 30th shape in this repeating pattern look like? How do you know?

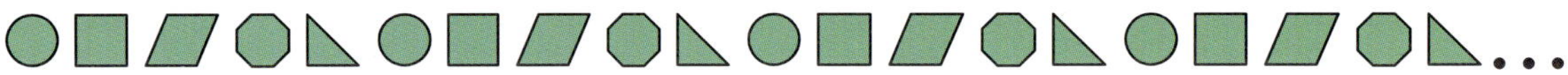

3 **3.** A book has pages numbered from 1 to 100. How many times is the digit 0 used in writing the page numbers? How do you know?

4. How many 3-digit numbers that are less than 300 end in 5? How do you know?

5. The 20th number in this pattern is 100.
5, 10, 15, 20, …
Make a pattern where the 20th number is 140.

4 **6.** Michel made this growing pattern with counters.

a) How many counters will be in the 6th shape? Use a t-chart.

b) What is the pattern rule for the number of counters?

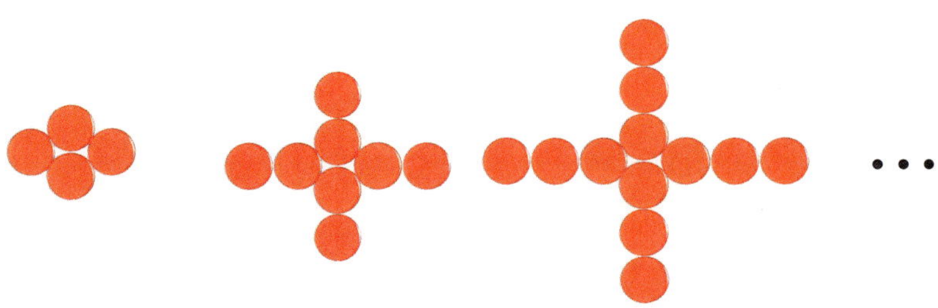

1st shape 2nd shape 3rd shape

LESSON

Chapter Review

2 **1.** List the attributes that change. Tell how they change.

a) 

b) VERNON VERNON VERNON VERNON VERNON VERNON …

3 **2.** Place counters on a 100 chart for each pattern.
Extend and describe each pattern made by the counters.

a) 4, 14, 24, 34, …
b) 86, 84, 82, 80, …
c) 15, 17, 19, 21, …
d) 100, 95, 90, 85, …
e) 22, 27, 32, 37, …
f) 90, 80, 70, 60, …

3. Write a pattern rule for each number pattern in Question 2.

4 **4.** a) Complete a t-chart with 5 rows for the fish pattern.
b) Write the pattern rule for the number of fish.
c) Predict the number of fish in picture 8. How do you know?

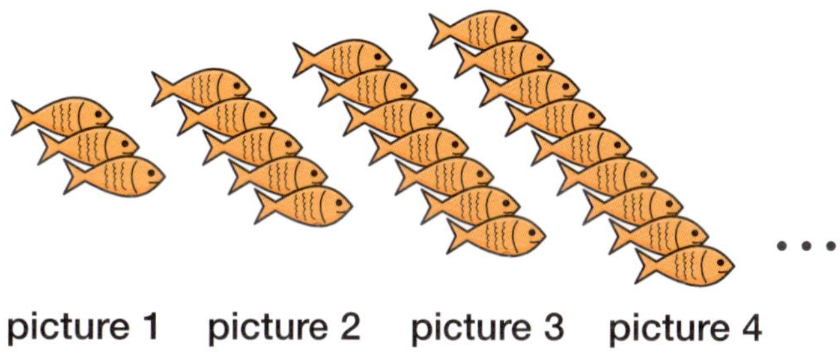

5. a) Make these shapes with counters.
b) Show the pattern in a t-chart.
Extend the t-chart for 8 shapes.
c) How many counters are in the 5th shape?
d) What is the pattern rule for the number of counters?
e) Predict the number of counters in the 10th shape.
Explain how you know.

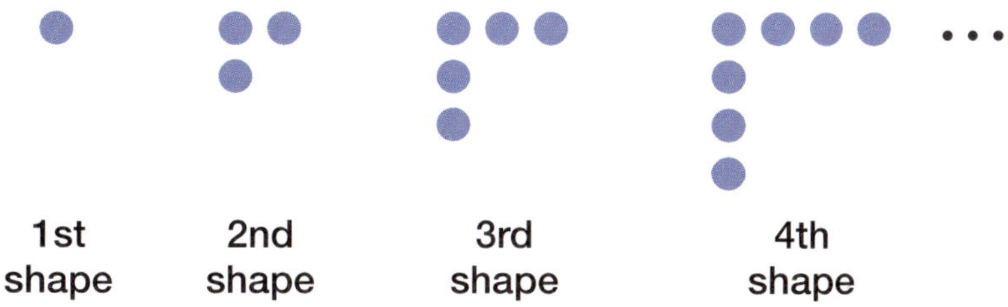

Chapter Task

Shape Patterns and Number Patterns

Kate created this shape pattern using red and white tiles.

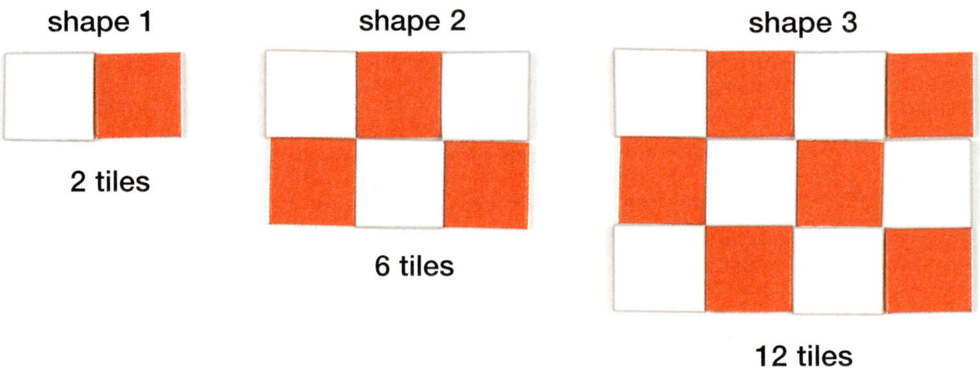

? What number patterns can you see in Kate's shape pattern?

A. Make shape 4. Draw it on grid paper.

B. Describe Kate's shape pattern using words.

C. Complete a t-chart to show the number of tiles in each shape.

D. Extend the t-chart for shape 5. Explain how you completed the chart.

E. Describe other patterns in Kate's shape pattern.

Shape	Number of tiles
1	2
2	6
3	
4	

Task Checklist

- ✓ Did you use a t-chart to show each pattern?
- ✓ Did you describe changes from one shape to the next?

CHAPTER 2

Numeration

Goals

You will be able to

- **represent numbers to 1000 in a variety of ways**
- **round, compare, and order 3-digit numbers**
- **solve problems using organized lists**
- **use ordinal numbers**
- **estimate a number of objects**
- **count and estimate money amounts**

Out to the ball game

Getting Started

You will need

- base ten blocks

- play coins

Numbers

There are 24 pencil crayons in this pack.

Amit shows 3 ways to represent the number 24.

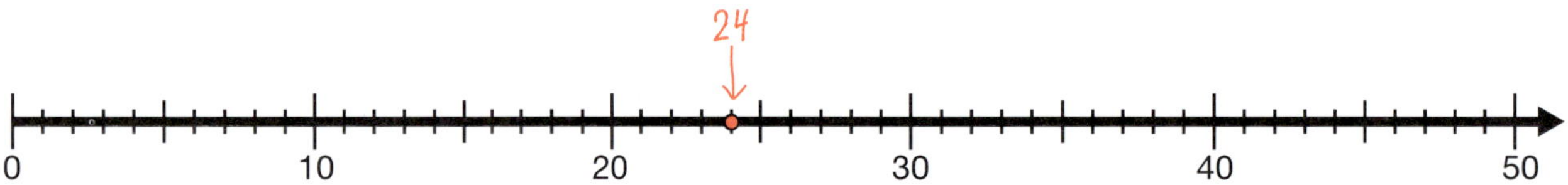

number line

24

numeral

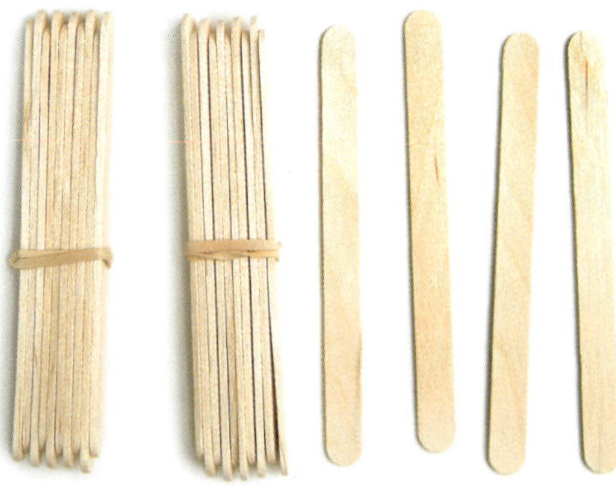

model

? What are some other ways to represent the number 24?

A. The number 24 can be written like this: 2 tens 4 ones.
Which of Amit's ways shows this best? Explain.

B. Use other models to show 24.

C. You are the 24th person in line.
How many people are ahead of you?

D. Which number is greater, 24 or 42?
Explain how you know.

E. What other places have you seen the number 24?

Do You Remember?

1. Write the words for the number before and the number after each number.

a) twelve **b)** eighteen

2. Write the **numeral** for each set of blocks.

a)

b)

3. How do you know 4 tens 3 ones is the same as 3 tens 13 ones?

4. Write the total amount of money shown.

a)

b)

5. Sketch or describe a set of coins that has a total value of 71¢.

1 Representing Numbers

You will need
- base ten blocks

Goal **Represent numbers using numerals, number words, models, and drawings.**

Jessica skipped 97 times in 1 minute.

? How can you represent the number 97?

Jessica's Numbers

As I skip, I count out loud.

I say, 1, 2, 3, 4, 5, 6, 7, 8, 9, **10**.

Then I say, 1, 2, 3, 4, 5, 6, 7, 8, 9, **20**.

Then, 1, 2, 3, 4, 5, 6, 7, 8, 9, **30**.

I call out each ten: ten, twenty, thirty, forty, fifty, sixty, seventy, eighty, ninety.

And I count by ones between tens.

I can show my total, 97, in many ways.

numeral: 97

numeral in **expanded form**: 90 + 7

numerals and words: 9 tens 7 ones

number word: ninety-seven

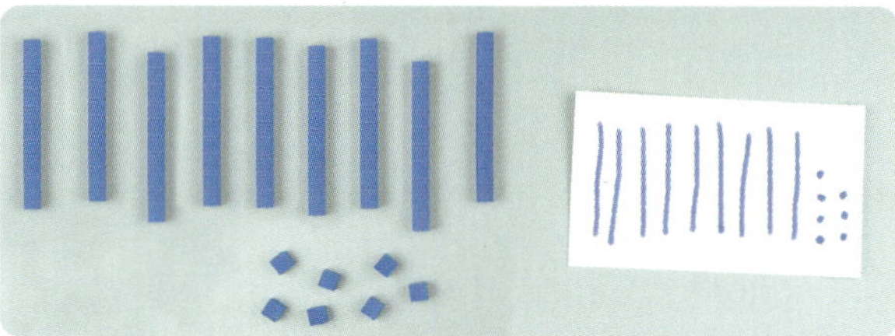

a model a sketch

expanded form
A way to write a number that shows the value of each digit

Reflecting

1. Read these numbers. Describe what happens to the **digits** in the tens place.

   21, 22, 23, 24, 25, 26, 27, 28, 29, 30,
   31, 32, 33, 34, 35, 36, 37, 38, 39, 40,
   41, 42, 43, …

digit

A number symbol

The digits are 0, 1, 2, 3, 4, 5, 6, 7, 8, and 9.

Checking

2. Ineke Kwant, from the Netherlands, set a record for doing 54 double turns in 1 minute of skipping.
   a) Model this number. Sketch the model.
   b) Write 54 as ■ tens ■ ones.
   c) Write 54 in expanded form.
   d) Write 54 using the number word.

Practising

3. a) What numeral does 40 + 6 represent?
   b) Model 40 + 6 with blocks. Sketch the model.
   c) Write 40 + 6 as ■ tens ■ ones.
   d) Write 40 + 6 using number words.

4. Write the numeral and number word for each.

   a) 

   b) 

   c) 

5. Matt skipped sixty-one times in 1 minute.
   a) Model sixty-one with blocks. Sketch the model.
   b) Write sixty-one in expanded form.

6. Sketch the blocks. Then write the expanded form, numeral, and number word for each.
   a) 8 tens 2 ones   b) 9 tens   c) 17 ones

2 Renaming Numbers

Goal **Represent and rename numbers to 1000 with numerals and words, models, and drawings.**

During his National Hockey League career, Wayne Gretzky set a record of 894 goals in regular season games.

You will need

- base ten blocks

- a place value chart

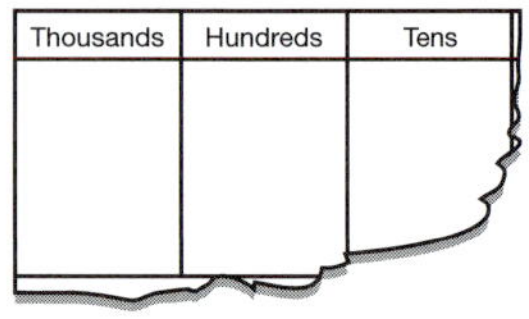

? How can you represent and rename 894 in different ways?

regroup
Show the same number in a different way

10 tens → 1 hundred

Rose's Models

I can **regroup** some blocks to show the number in a different way. Then I can rename the number.

Thousands	Hundreds	Tens	Ones
	8 hundreds	9 tens	4 ones

Thousands	Hundreds	Tens	Ones
	7 hundreds	19 tens	4 ones

A. Which blocks did Rose regroup?

B. Show 3 other ways to model 894.
Sketch each model.
Write the number of hundreds, tens, and ones for each.

C. Which way of modelling 894 uses the fewest blocks?
Why does this make sense?

Reflecting

1. What did you do to show 894 in different ways?
2. Rose modelled 1000 with 1 thousand block.
   Jay modelled 1000 with 9 hundreds 8 tens 20 ones.
   Explain why the values are the same.

Checking

3. Mario Lemieux had a 46-game scoring streak in which he scored 39 goals and 103 points.
   a) Model 103 with blocks. Sketch the model.
   b) Write 103 as ■ hundreds ■ tens ■ ones.
   c) Regroup the blocks for 103 in 2 other ways. Sketch each model. Rename each as ■ hundreds ■ tens ■ ones.

Practising

4. Use blocks to find each missing number.
   a) 386 = ■ hundreds 18 tens 6 ones
   b) 754 = 6 hundreds ■ tens 14 ones

5. Show each with as few blocks as possible. How many of each type of block did you use? Write each numeral.
   a) 
   b) 7 hundreds 27 tens 30 ones
   c) 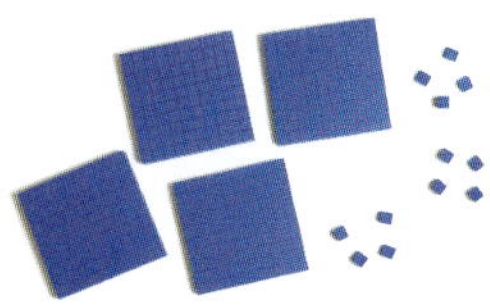
   d) 100 tens

6. Which of these is *not* another name for 607? How do you know?
   A. 5 hundreds 10 tens 17 ones
   B. 5 hundreds 10 tens 7 ones
   C. 5 hundreds 9 tens 17 ones
   D. 4 hundreds 19 tens 17 ones

Thousands	Hundreds	Tens	Ones
			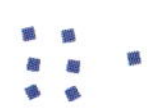

3 Place-Value Patterns

You will need
- a calculator

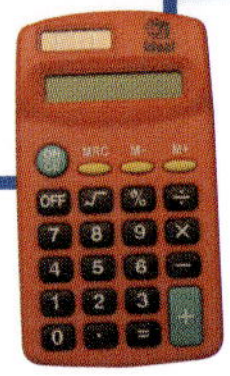

Goal **Describe how the digits of numbers change in place-value patterns.**

Charlie was adding to 231 with his calculator.

He pressed 231 [+] 10 [=] [=] [=] [=] [=].

? How can you predict what will be on the calculator display?

Charlie's Number Pattern

I know 231 + 10 = 241.

When I add 1 ten, the tens digit increases by 1.

Every time I press [=], the calculator adds another 10.

A. Start at 231. Add 10 over and over. What will be on the display after you push the equals sign 3 times?

231 [+] 10 [=] [=] [=]

B. Continue pressing [=] until you pass 291. How does the pattern change after 291?

C. Start the pattern again. This time, record 10 numbers that belong in the pattern.

D. Describe how the digits change in the pattern.

E. Choose a start number that's about 500. Predict the 10th number in the pattern when you add 10 over and over. Then check your prediction.

F. Start at 760. Subtract 10 over and over. Then repeat parts C and D for this pattern.

760 [−] 10 [=] [=] [=]
and so on

G. Choose a start number that has 2 digits.
Add 100 over and over.
Then repeat parts C and D for your pattern.

■■ [+] 100 [=] [=] [=]
and so on

H. Start at 1000. Subtract 100 over and over.
Then repeat parts C and D for this pattern.

1000 [−] 100 [=] [=] [=]
and so on

Reflecting

1. Describe how the digits change when you add or subtract 10 over and over.
2. Describe how the digits change when you add or subtract 100 over and over.

Mental Math

Adding Tens

Nisha's Mental Math

I thought of adding tens when I added 23 and 20.
2 tens plus 2 tens is 4 tens, or 40. 40 plus 3 is 43.

$$\begin{array}{r} 23 \\ +\ 20 \\ \hline 43 \end{array}$$

A. Why does the last digit in Nisha's answer stay the same after adding tens?

Try These

1. Use Nisha's mental math method to add.
   - **a)** 28 + 10 = ■
   - **b)** 20 + 16 = ■
   - **c)** 15 + 30 = ■
   - **d)** 84 + 10 = ■
   - **e)** 66 + 20 = ■
   - **f)** 50 + 46 = ■
2. Use Nisha's mental math method to subtract.
   - **a)** 23 − 10 = ■
   - **b)** 33 − 20 = ■
   - **c)** 54 − 30 = ■
   - **d)** 66 − 30 = ■
   - **e)** 99 − 50 = ■
   - **f)** 82 − 60 = ■

4 Rounding to Estimate Numbers

You will need

- number lines

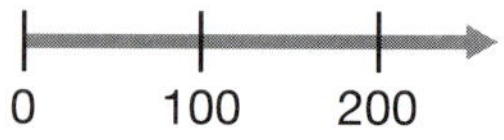

Goal **Round 3-digit numbers.**

237 people came to the concert.

? What rounded number belongs in the headline?

Rashad's Rounding

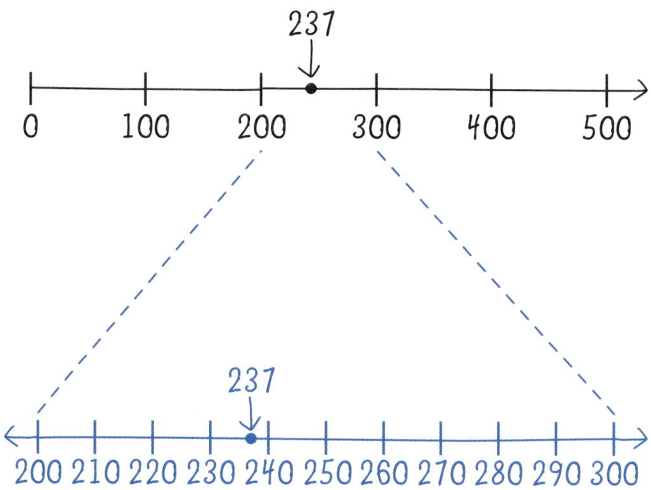

I marked 237 on this number line marked in hundreds.

237 is closer to 200 than to any other hundreds.

237 rounds down to 200.

I think the headline should say "about 200."

Or I could mark 237 on a number line marked in tens.

237 is closer to 240 than to any other tens.

237 rounds up to 240.

So the headline would say "about 240."

Reflecting

1. List some numbers, other than 237, that are about 200 after **rounding to the nearest hundred**. Use a number line.
2. List all the numbers, other than 237, that are about 240 after **rounding to the nearest ten**.
3. 250 people came to a track meet.
   Rashad rounded 250 to 300.
   Sharleen rounded 250 to 200.
   Explain why both estimates are reasonable.

rounding to the nearest hundred
Estimating a number to the closest number of hundreds

83 rounds up to 100.

rounding to the nearest ten
Estimating a number to the closest number of tens

83 rounds down to 80.

Checking

4. Round each number to the nearest hundred.
   a) 318 b) 98 c) 272 d) 655
5. Round each number to the nearest ten.
   a) 69 b) 25 c) 807 d) 795

Practising

6. Round each number to the nearest hundred.
   a) 99 b) 469 c) 551 d) 950
7. Round each number to the nearest ten.
   a) 84 b) 75 c) 885 d) 414
8. Round the number to create a headline:
   $719 was spent on computer equipment.
9. About 350 students are expected to attend a new school. Has the number been rounded to the nearest hundred or to the nearest ten? Explain how you know.
10. A headline says, "Almost 900 people were at the game." Exactly how many people might have been there? Explain.

5 Comparing and Ordering

Goal **Compare and order whole numbers.**

You will need

- number cards (0 to 9)

- base ten blocks

- a place value chart

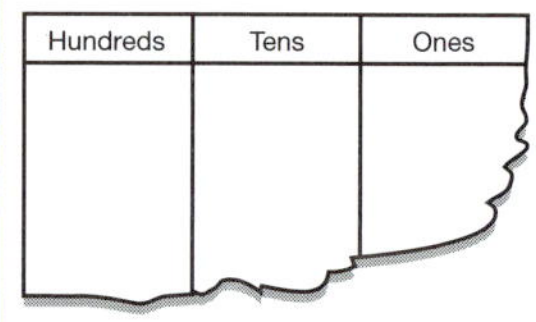

A world high-jump record, in centimetres, is the least number that can be made using each of these digits once.

5 4 2

? What is the high-jump record?

Keisha's Models

First I made the number 542.

Hundreds	Tens	Ones
5	4	2

Then I made the number 524.

Hundreds	Tens	Ones
5	2	4

To see which is less, I compared place values starting at the left.

Both numbers have 5 hundreds.

542 has more tens than 524.

542 is greater than 524.

But I don't think anyone can high jump 524 cm.

A. What other numbers can you make using each digit 5, 4, and 2 once?

B. Order all the numbers with 5, 4, and 2 from least to greatest.

C. Which number is the world high-jump record? Show this with base ten blocks on a place value chart. Explain how you know by looking at the numbers.

Reflecting

1. Why do you look from left to right when comparing numbers to order them?
2. Show that a number with a ones digit of 5 can be less than a number with a ones digit of 2.
3. How do you know that a 2-digit number is always less than a 3-digit number?

Checking

4. Use each of these digits once.

   7 **0** **8**

   a) What is the greatest number possible?
   b) What is the least number possible?

Practising

5. Which number in each pair is greater? Explain how you know.
   a) 100 or 311
   b) $555 or $505
   c) 98 years old or 105 years old
   d) 771 pages or 778 pages

6. 4 schools raised this money in a walk-a-thon: $471, $417, $411, $477. Order the amounts from least to greatest.

7. List all the numbers between 350 and 550 that use each of these digits once.

   5 **8** **3**

Mid-Chapter Review

LESSON

1 **1.** Model each number. Sketch the model. Write the numeral and number word. Write the expanded form.
a) 6 tens 4 ones **b)** 8 tens 9 ones **c)** 4 tens

2 **2.** Write the numeral. Write each as ■ hundreds ■ tens ■ ones.
a)

b)

3. **a)** Model 912 with base ten blocks. Sketch the blocks.
b) Write 912 as ■ hundreds ■ tens ■ ones.

4. Find the missing number.
1000 = 8 hundreds ■ tens 50 ones

3 **5.** Write the next 4 numbers in the pattern when you add 100 over and over.
a) 217, ■, ■, ■, ■ **b)** 505, ■, ■, ■, ■ **c)** 26, ■, ■, ■, ■

6. Write the next 4 numbers in the pattern when you subtract 10 over and over.
a) 620, ■, ■, ■, ■ **b)** 530, ■, ■, ■, ■ **c)** 900, ■, ■, ■, ■

4 **7.** 379 visitors were at the science fair.
Round the number to create a headline.

8. Round each number to the nearest hundred.
a) 878 **b)** 110 **c)** 542 **d)** 650

9. Round each number to the nearest ten.
a) 21 **b)** 98 **c)** 995 **d)** 805

5 **10.** Which number in each pair is greater? Explain.
a) 406 pages or 460 pages **b)** 338 days or 38 days

11. Students raised this money in a skip-a-thon:
\$412, \$342, \$244, \$483.
Order the amounts from least to greatest.

Math Game

Duelling Digits

Number of players: 2 or 3

How to play: Use number cards to make the greatest number.

Step 1 Shuffle the number cards. Place them face down in a pile.

Step 2 Take the top card and place it on your place value chart. Once a card is on a chart, it cannot be moved.

Step 3 Take turns. Continue until all the spaces on the charts are filled.

Step 4 Compare your numbers. The player with the greatest number gets 1 point.

Continue playing until a player has 6 points.

You will need

- 3 sets of number cards (0 to 9)

- a place value chart

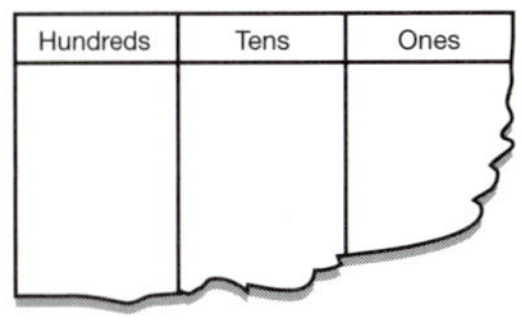

Tiffany's Number

Hundreds	Tens	Ones
3	1	3

Michael's Number

Hundreds	Tens	Ones
	1	0

On my 1st turn, I got 0.
On my 2nd turn, I got 1.
1 is a low number, so I put it in the tens place.
I hope my last digit is greater than 3!

Another way to play: The player with the least number gets 1 point.

6 Ordinal Numbers

You will need

- number lines

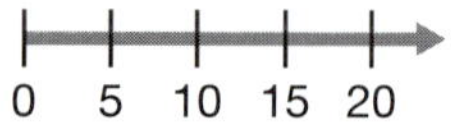

Goal **Use numbers to describe order.**

Everyone in a marathon race won a medal if they finished the race. 4 friends won these medals.

Manuel finished ahead of Josh, Pat, and Diane.

Josh and Pat finished between Manuel and Diane.

Pat was ahead of Josh.

? Which medals did Manuel, Diane, Josh, and Pat win?

Gabe's Ordering

I used a number line to get started.
I drew 4 arrows to show the positions of the 4 runners.

Now I'll try to label the names.

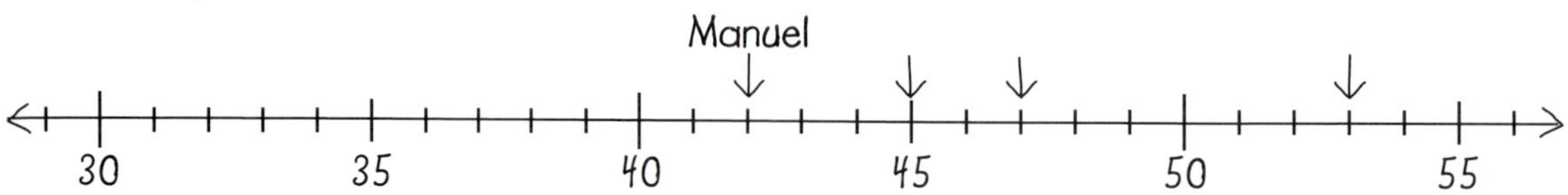

Manuel is ahead of the others, so he is 42nd.

A. Which friend won the medal for 53rd place?

B. Which medals did the other 2 friends win?

Reflecting

1. How did you decide how to label the names on the number line?
2. a) Manuel was in 42nd place. How many runners were ahead of Manuel?
   b) How many runners were in the group starting with Manuel and ending with Diane?
   c) How many places behind Manuel was Diane?
3. Why do you think 42nd, 45th, 47th, and 53rd are called **ordinal numbers**?

Checking

4. a) Kim was 64th in the race. How many runners were ahead of her?
   b) Use a number line. How many places was Manuel ahead of Kim?
5. Matt was 7 places behind the 23rd person in the race. Use the number line to find out what medal Matt won.

Practising

6. Alex was 27th in the race. Use the number line to find out how many places Alex was ahead of Matt.
7. a) Continue this pattern past 800: 607, 617, 627, 637, ...
   b) What is the 15th number in the pattern?
   c) How many numbers are before the 15th number?
8. If the pattern continues, what do you know about the 17th person? Use pictures, numbers, and words.

1st person:
standing
long sleeves
no pompoms

7 Estimating the Number of Objects

Goal **Estimate, then count the number of objects.**

You will need

- large counters such as linking cubes

- small counters such as ones blocks or beads

- a can

? How can you estimate the number of objects?

A. Use large counters. Put 30 counters in a can. Pour some of the counters onto a table.

a) Estimate the number of counters you poured. Explain your thinking. Record your estimate in a chart.

Part	Estimate	Count
A		

b) Count to check your estimate. Record the number in your chart. Is your estimate reasonable? Explain.

B. Put the counters back in the can. Put more of the same type of counters in the can. Continue as in part A but pour more counters.

C. Use small beads or small counters. Put a few hundred counters in the can. Pour some of the counters onto the table.

a) Estimate the number of counters you poured. Explain your thinking. Record your estimate in your chart.

b) Count to check your estimate. Record the number in your chart. Is your estimate reasonable? Explain.

D. Put the counters from part C back in the can.
Put more of the same type of counters in the can.
Continue as in part C but pour more counters.

An inukshuk is built to guide people travelling in the Arctic where there are no trees.

An inukshuk is a pile of stones that looks like a person.

The Nunavut flag shows an inukshuk.

E. Juan's class used beads to make flag pins.
Juan used 66 white beads in his Nunavut flag pin.
Estimate each number of beads in Juan's flag pin.

a) yellow beads

b) red beads

c) all the beads

F. Compare your estimates for part E with other students' estimates.
Are your estimates reasonable? Explain.

Reflecting

1. a) Was it easier to estimate the number of larger counters or smaller counters?
Explain your thinking.

b) Was it easier to estimate when you poured fewer counters or more counters?
Explain your thinking.

2. Was estimating the number of counters on a table different from estimating the number of beads in Juan's flag pin? Explain your thinking.

3. When might you estimate a number of objects outside school?

8 Estimating and Counting Money

You will need

- play money

Goal Estimate, count, and trade money.

Lyn took some money from her piggy bank.

? How can you represent Lyn's money?

Lyn's Money

First I'll estimate.

2 toonies and 4 loonies are $2 + $2 + $1 + $1 + $1 + $1.
That's $8 and some more coins.
I have a little more than $8.

Then I'll count my money.

I have 2 toonies 4 loonies
3 dimes 8 pennies.
That's 8 dollars and 38 cents.

The number before the **decimal point** tells the number of dollars.

The number after the decimal point tells the number of cents.

$8.38
8 dollars
decimal point
38 cents

penny
1¢
$0.01

nickel
5¢
$0.05

dime
10¢
$0.10

quarter
25¢
$0.25

1 dollar coin or loonie
$1.00

2 dollar coin or toonie
$2.00

A. Explain a different way to estimate the value of Lyn's money.

B. How can you show $8.38 with 1 bill and no dimes?
Show 2 ways.

C. Lyn can write the value of her dimes and pennies as 38¢, or as $0.38.
Wei has 2 quarters and 4 nickels.
Write the value of Wei's money in 2 ways: $■.■■ and ■■¢.

D. Fred traded a $100 bill for five $20 bills. What other ways can he trade his $100 bill for bills?

$5.00
$5

Reflecting

1. You can trade bills and coins to show the same amount in different ways. Explain with 2 examples.

$10.00
$10

Checking

2. Estimate the amount. Then write the exact amount.
   a $5 bill, 1 toonie, 1 nickel, 2 pennies

3. Trade bills or coins to show the amount in Question 2 in 2 different ways.

$20.00
$20

Practising

4. Show each amount in 3 different ways.
   a) 67¢ **b)** $3.00 **c)** $5.45 **d)** $10.00

5. Write each amount in 2 ways: $■.■■ and ■■¢.
   a) 3 quarters **b)** 12 nickels **c)** 9 pennies

$50.00
$50

6. Doug traded a $50 bill. Which of these do *not* describe bills he might get? How do you know?
   A. two $20 bills, one $10 bill
   B. three $10 bills, three $5 bills
   C. ten $5 bills
   D. one $20 bill, four $10 bills

$100.00
$100

7. Use play money. Suppose you made a stack of dimes the length of your longest finger.
   a) Predict how many dimes would be in the stack.
   b) Estimate the total value of the dimes.
   c) Build the stack. Count the dimes. Record the value.
   d) Compare your answers for part c) with your estimates.

8. Repeat Question 7 with quarters.

9 Solve Problems Using Organized Lists

You will need

- base ten blocks

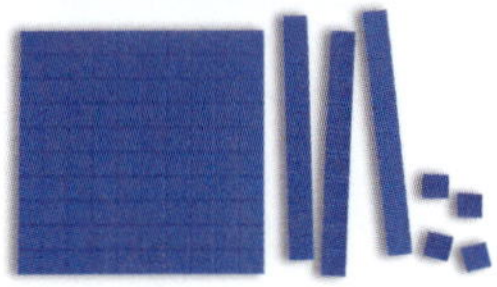

- a place value chart

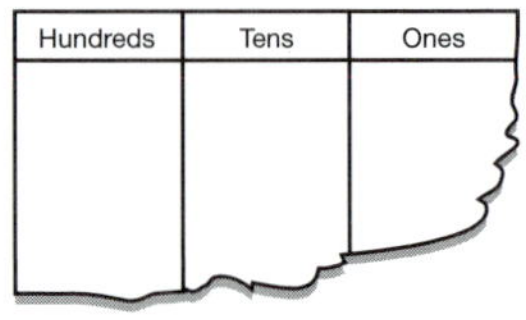

Goal **Solve place-value problems using an organized list.**

Rachel chose 6 base ten blocks.

The value of her blocks is more than 200 and less than 220.

? Which blocks did Rachel choose?

Ben's Solution

Understand the Problem

There are 6 blocks, which can be hundreds, tens, or ones.

The total value is between 200 and 220.

There must be 2 hundreds blocks.

Make a Plan

I need to find 4 blocks with a total value less than 20.

I'll use a chart to list the different combinations for the 4 other blocks.

Carry Out the Plan

I'll start with 4 tens 0 ones and record it in the chart. Then I'll use 1 less ten and 1 more one each time.

Hundreds	Tens	Ones	Value	Does it work?
2	4	0	240	too much
2	3	1	231	too much
2	2	2	222	still too much
2	1	3	213	this works
2	0	4	204	this works too

Rachel could have chosen 2 hundreds 1 ten 3 ones, or 2 hundreds 0 tens 4 ones.

Reflecting

1. a) How did Ben know there were 2 hundreds blocks?
   b) How did he know that the value of the 4 other blocks must be less than 20?
2. How did Ben know that he had found all the possible answers?
3. Why is Ben's chart called an **organized list**?

organized list

The strategy of following an order to solve a problem

Checking

4. Derek has 8 base ten blocks worth between 300 and 400. What blocks could he have?
   Find all the possible answers using an organized list.

Practising

5. Alana has 5 base ten blocks.
   She has at least one of each type of block.
   The value of her blocks is greater than 140.
   What blocks could she have?
6. Saman has at least one of each type of base ten block.
   The value of his blocks is 203.
   What blocks could he have?

1¢

7. You have at least one of each coin shown.
   The value of your coins is $1.73.
   a) What coins might you have?
   b) How do you know that you have found all the answers?

$1

10¢

8. Use the clues to figure out the mystery house number.
   - The house number is a 3-digit odd number.
   - The number is greater than 930.
   - The sum of the digits in the number is 14.

CHAPTER 2

10 Counting Patterns

Goal **Skip count by 2s, 5s, and 25s.**

You will need

- play coins

- a calculator

Sharleen has a toonie and 11 quarters.

? Does Sharleen have enough money to buy this teddy?

Sharleen's Pattern

A toonie is 200¢. Each quarter is 25¢.
I'll start with 200 and skip count by 25s
to figure out how much money I have.

200 225 250 275 ...

A. Complete Sharleen's counting.

B. What is the last number Sharleen should count? How do you know?

C. Does Sharleen have enough money to buy the teddy? How do you know?

D. Sharleen wants to know how many nickels she can get if she trades her toonie for nickels. She counts backward: 200, 195, 190, 185, ….

- **a)** Complete Sharleen's counting.
- **b)** What is the last number Sharleen should count? How do you know?
- **c)** How many nickels can Sharleen get? How do you know?

Reflecting

1. a) Look at parts A to C. Explain Sharleen's method.
   b) What other ways could Sharleen use to find out if she has enough money?
2. Describe how the patterns in the ones digits and in the tens digits change when you add 25 over and over to 200.
3. Look at part D. Why did Sharleen begin counting with 200? Why did she count backward by 5s?

Checking

4. a) Start at 1000. Write the first 5 numbers for skip counting by 2s to 964.
   b) Predict the ones digits in the next 6 numbers.
   c) Use a calculator to check your prediction.

1000 [−] 2 [=] [=] [=]
and so on

Practising

5. Start at 93 and skip count forward by 2s. Count until you reach a number greater than 110.
6. Start at 425 and skip count forward by 25s. Write only the 9th number. Check with a calculator.
7. Jack used a calculator. He skip counted backward from 175 by 5s.
   a) Predict the first 10 numbers on the calculator display.
   b) Do you think the calculator display will show the number zero? Explain why or why not. Check with a calculator.
8. Create a money problem you can solve by skip counting. Show the solution.
9. Takeo skip counted from 400 to 800. He said 705.
   a) Did he skip count by 2s, 5s, 10s, 25s, or 100s? Is there more than one answer? Explain how you know.
   b) Write 3 other numbers in Takeo's counting pattern.

Math Game

Race for 2 Toonies

Number of players: 2 or 3
How to play: Collect and trade coins up to $4.

Step 1 Spin the spinner.
Take the coin that you spin.

Step 2 Take turns.

Step 3 Trade coins when it is possible
to have fewer coins.

Continue playing until a player has 2 toonies.

You will need

- play coins

- a spinner

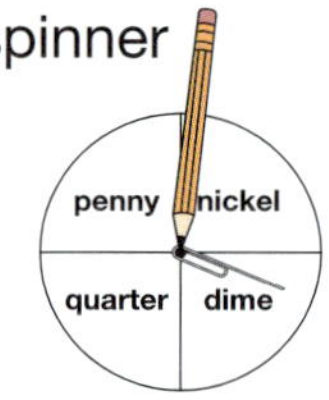

- a paper clip

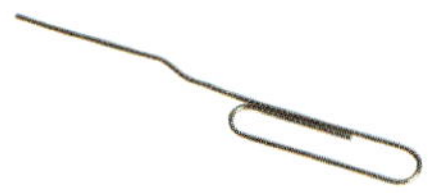

Lee's Trade

I have 3 nickels and 1 dime.
I'll trade my coins for 1 quarter.

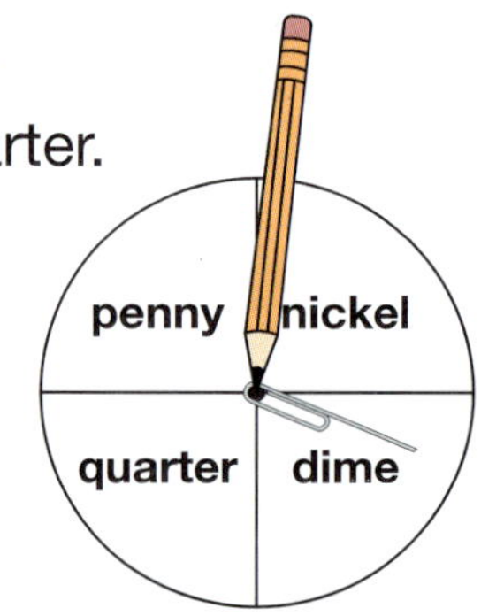

Another way to play:

- Each player starts with 2 toonies.
- Give back the coin that you spin.
- Trade coins when it is necessary to give back a coin.
- Continue playing until a player has no money left.

Skills Bank

LESSON

1 **1.** Model each number. Sketch the model.
a) seventy-one **b)** 2 tens 5 ones **c)** 40 + 6 **d)** 80

2 **2.** Complete ■ hundreds ■ tens ■ ones for each set of blocks. Then write the numeral.

a)

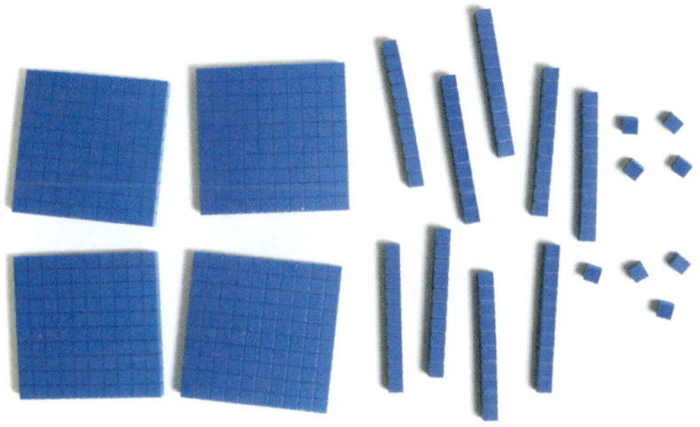

b)

3. Model each number. Sketch the model.
a) 362 **b)** 5 hundreds 6 ones **c)** 186 **d)** 3 hundreds 9 tens

4. Regroup and rename each number in different ways.

a)

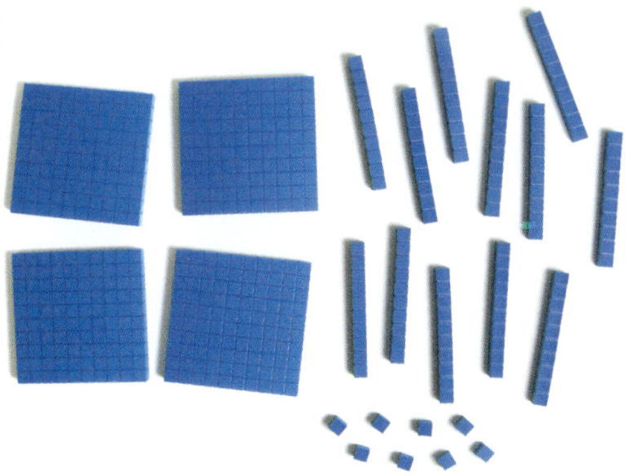

b)

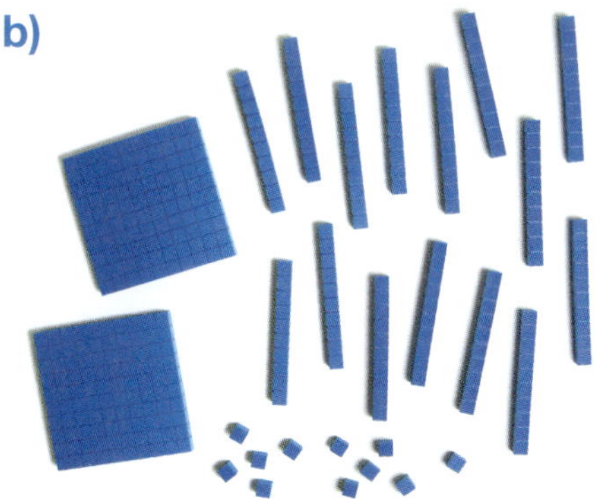

5. Which of these is *not* a name for 706?
A. 6 hundreds 10 tens 16 ones
B. 6 hundreds 10 tens 6 ones
C. 6 hundreds 9 tens 16 ones
D. 7 hundreds 0 tens 6 ones

6. Which are names for 1000?
A. 10 hundreds
B. 9 hundreds 10 tens
C. 9 hundreds 9 tens 9 ones
D. 9 hundreds 9 tens 10 ones

3

7. Predict how each pattern was created.
Check your prediction using a calculator.
Write the next 3 numbers in each pattern.
a) 570, 560, 550, …
b) 260, 270, 280, …
c) 197, 198, 199, …
d) 103, 203, 303, …

8. Suppose you start with 537 and add 10 over and over.
Which numbers are *not* in the pattern? How do you know?
A. 987 B. 877 C. 905 D. 873

4

9. Round each number to the nearest ten and to the nearest hundred.
a) 88 b) 773 c) 229 d) 355 e) 402 f) 808

5

10. Which number in each pair is greater?
a) 98 or 924 b) $385 or $376 c) 506 days or 560 days

11. Order from least to greatest.
a) 605, 472, 230, 198
b) 273, 27, 26, 268
c) 780, 870, 727, 872
d) 912, 91, 219, 19

6

12. a) What is the 19th letter of the alphabet?
b) How many letters come before the 19th letter?
c) What letter is 5 places after the 3rd letter in the alphabet?

7

13. a) Fill a jar with counters. Estimate the number of counters.
b) Count the counters. Is your estimate reasonable? Explain.

8

14. Lyn wants to buy a yo-yo that costs $2.55.
What coins could she use? List 5 different answers.

15. Show 2 ways to make each amount of money.
a) $1.50 b) $4.00 c) $6.75 d) $0.80

10

16. Rashad has 3 toonies and 9 quarters.
Skip count to calculate the value of his money.

17. Ming started at 684 and skip counted by 2s to 708.
Ian started at 708 and skip counted by 2s to 684.
How are the patterns the same?
How are they different?

Problem Bank

LESSON

2 **1. a)** There is a mystery number between 337 and 400.
This number has 2 digits that are the same.
The sum of all the digits is 12.
What is the mystery number?

b) Create and solve a problem about a mystery number.

3 **2.** What happens to the digits when you add 11 over and over to a 2-digit number?

4 **3.** Each student at Juan's school needs a magazine for a project. There are 432 students.
The magazines are sold in boxes of 100.
How many boxes do they need? Explain your thinking.

6 **4.** Which number is greatest? Which is least?
Explain your thinking.

A. the 10th number that ends in 5
B. the 40th odd number
C. the 20th number with at least one 2

5. 100 people are in the friendship dance line.

Josie is 10 places behind the 54th person in the dance line.
Kate is the 23rd person from the end of the dance line.
Pete is 20 places behind Josie.

Who is closest to the end of the dance line?

8 **6.** Adam has more than $1.00 in his pocket.
He has some coins that are worth less than $1.00.
He can't make change for a dollar.
What coins does he have? Find more than one answer.

9 **7.** The digits in 987 add to 24. Make as many 3-digit numbers as you can with digits that add to 24.

8. Show all the ways to make 40¢ without using pennies.

Chapter Review

LESSON

1 **1.** Model each number. Sketch the model. Then write the numeral, expanded form, and number word.
a) 9 tens 3 ones **b)** 3 tens 9 ones

2 **2.** Regroup and rename each number in different ways.
a)
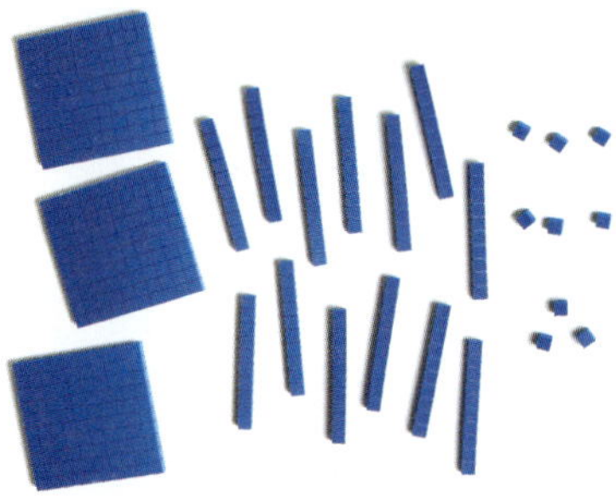
b)
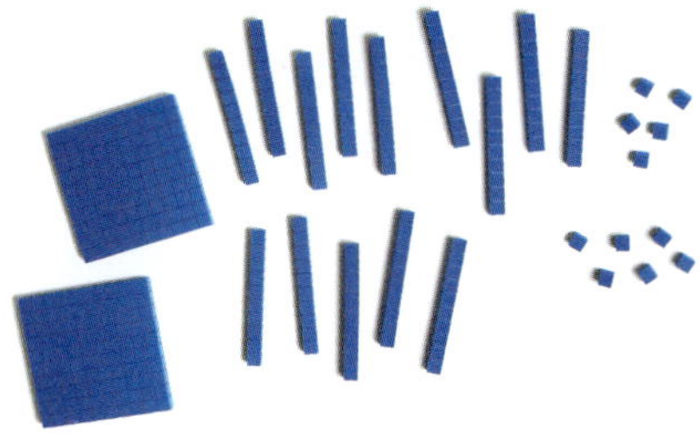

3 **3.** Suppose you start with 420 and subtract 10 over and over. Which numbers are *not* in the pattern? How do you know?
A. 409 **B.** 380 **C.** 70 **D.** 510

5 **4.** **a)** Make 4 different numbers using each digit 3, 1, and 8 once.
b) Order the numbers from least to greatest.
c) Round each number to the nearest hundred.

5. Akilah researched the lengths for some snakes in British Columbia and Alberta.

Snakes	Length (centimetres)
Night snake	thirty-seven
Northern Pacific rattlesnake	eighty-five
Sharp-tailed snake	18
Prairie rattlesnake	ninety-three
Hognose snake	49

a) Write the number words as numerals.
Write the numerals as number words.
b) Which snake is closest to 40 cm long?
c) Which snakes are about 90 cm long?
d) Which snakes are longer than 50 cm?

6 **6.** 100 people are waiting in line for the next show.

a) Suzanne is the 99th person in line.
How many people are in front of Suzanne?

b) There is only 1 person ahead of Tony.
What is Tony's position?

c) There are 17 people ahead of Carla.
What is Carla's position?

7 **7.** **a)** Estimate the number of dots in this picture.
Explain how you estimated.

b) Count the dots. Is your estimate reasonable? Explain.

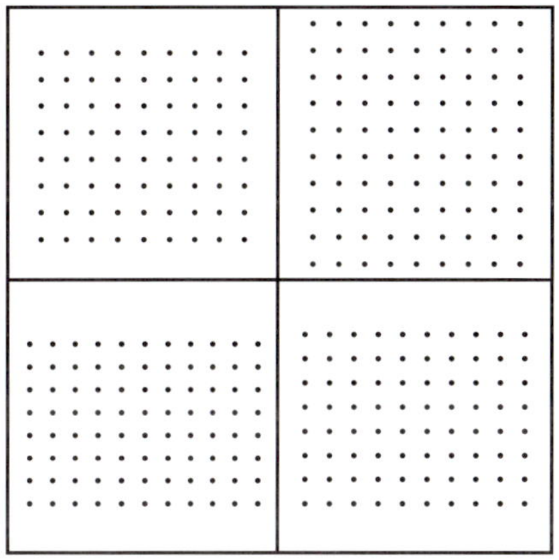

8 **8.** **a)** Find the value.

b) Show a different way to make the amount in part a).

9. Ping traded a $100 bill for $20 bills and $5 bills.
What bills might she get? Give 3 answers.

9 **10.** Tim has 7 base ten blocks. He has hundreds and tens, but no ones. The value is between 100 and 400.

What blocks could he have? Find all the possible answers.

10 **11.** Ian entered 19 on his calculator and skip counted by 5s.

a) Use a calculator. Write the first 5 numbers.

b) Predict the next 5 numbers. Check your prediction.

c) Describe the pattern in the ones digits and the pattern in the tens digits.

d) Which of these numbers are in Ian's pattern?
Explain how you know. Use a calculator to check.
73 100 299 144

Chapter Task

Palindromes

A palindrome reads the same forward and backward. Numbers like 111 and 343 are palindromes.

? What are all the palindromes between 400 and 800?

A. List all the palindromes between 400 and 800. How do you know you found them all?

B. Make sure the palindromes from part A are in order from least to greatest. How do you know that they are in order?

C. Which palindrome is the 25th number in the list? How do you know it's the 25th number?

Task Checklist

- ✓ Did you organize your work so it is easy to follow?
- ✓ Did you explain your thinking?
- ✓ Did you use math language?

Data Management

Goals

You will be able to

- sort and organize data
- collect, describe, and display data
- create and interpret pictographs
- create and interpret bar graphs with scales
- communicate about data in graphs

Reading material

Getting Started

Sorting and Graphing

The principal asked Sukan's class to clean up the gym storage room.

? How can you use a graph to represent the equipment in the storage room?

You will need

- grid paper

- sports equipment cutouts

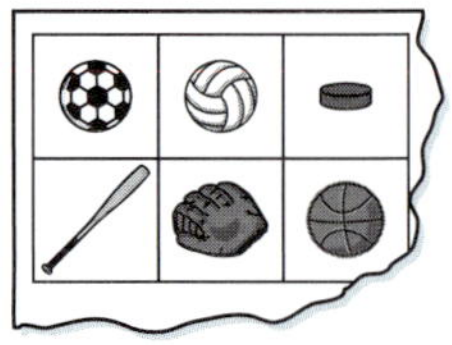

- scissors

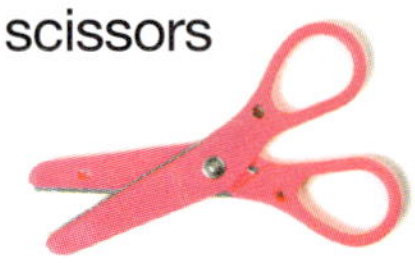

A. Sort the equipment.
Compare your sorting with someone else's.

B. Make a **bar graph** to represent your sorting from part A.

C. What does your graph show about the equipment?

D. Why might it be useful for the class to sort the equipment?

Do You Remember?

1. Describe 2 ways to sort these shapes.

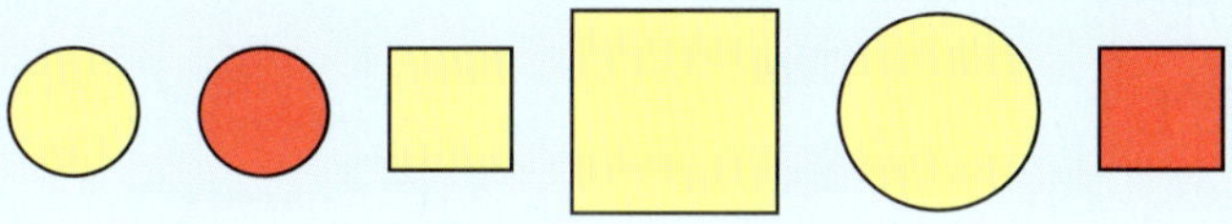

2. a) What does this graph show? List 3 things.
   b) Why is this called a **pictograph**?

3. a) What does this graph show? List 3 things.
   b) Why is there no bar for Franca?
   c) What is the title of the graph?
   d) What are the labels?

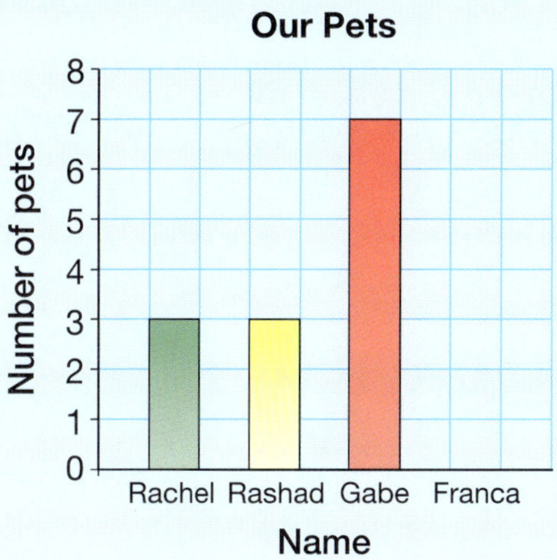

1 Venn Diagrams

Goal **Sort and classify objects using Venn diagrams.**

Rashad's Venn Diagram

I'm sorting foods using a **Venn diagram**.
I'm using 2 **attributes**: colour and type of food.
The beans are green, but beans are not a fruit.
The apple is green and is a fruit.
The potato is not a fruit and is not green.

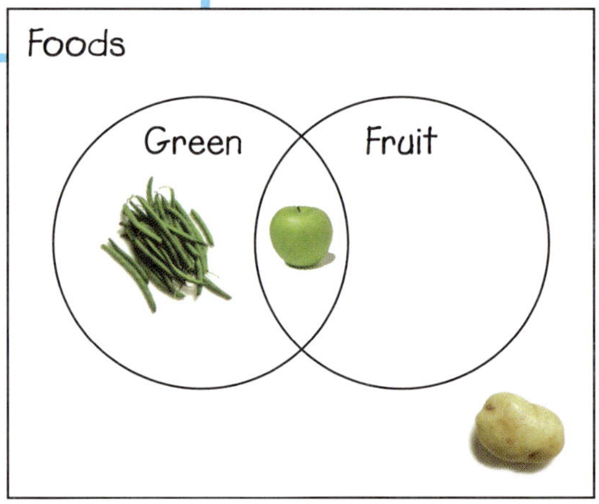

? How can you sort the other foods using the Venn diagram?

A. Where would you put the red apple in the Venn diagram? Why?

B. Where would you put the carrots? Why?

C. Finish sorting the foods using the Venn diagram. Explain your strategy.

D. Make 2 new labels for the circles. Sort the foods in a new way.

You will need

- Venn diagrams

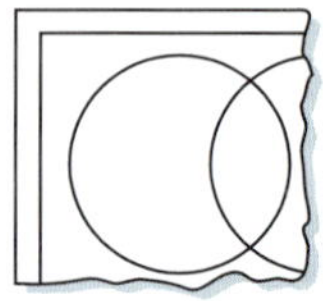

- food cutouts

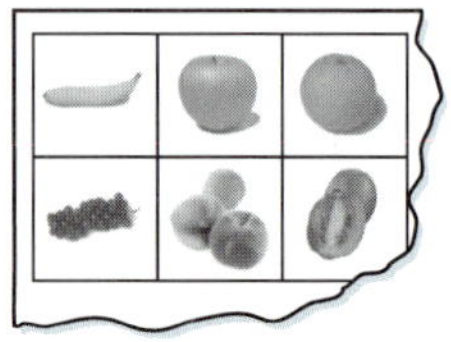

- scissors

- classroom objects

Reflecting

1. a) Describe the parts of Rashad's Venn diagram.
   b) Name at least one other food for each part.
2. When you sorted, did you put objects in the overlap? Why or why not?

Checking

3. a) Sort these fruits using the Venn diagram.
Explain your strategy.

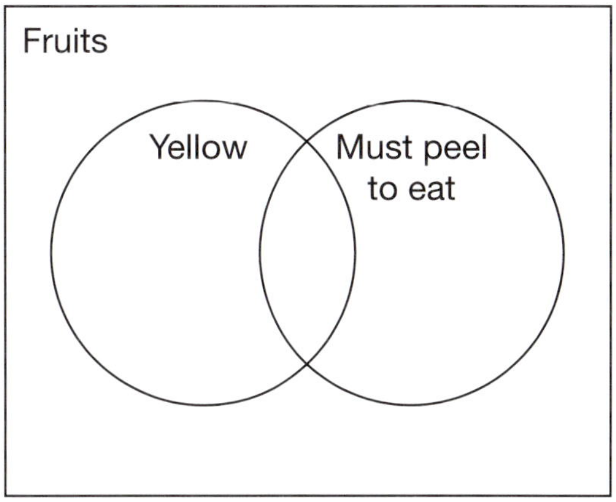

b) Make 2 new labels for the circles.
Sort the foods in a new way.

Practising

4. a) Sort classroom objects using the Venn diagram.
Explain your strategy.

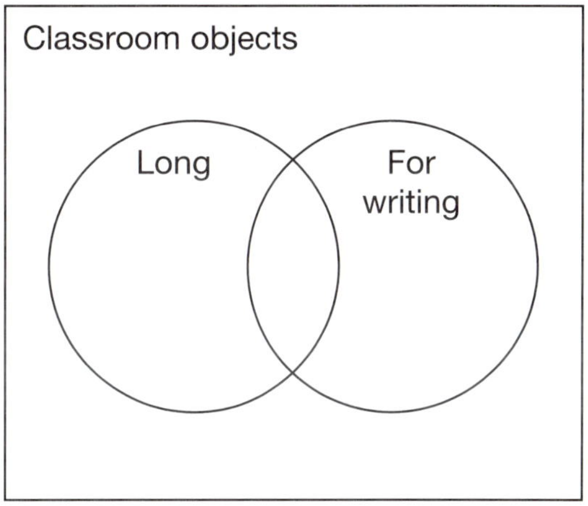

b) Draw or name at least one more item for each part of the Venn diagram.

5. a) Pick 2 attributes you could use to sort shoes.

b) Label a Venn diagram.

c) Sort the shoes using the Venn diagram.
Explain your strategy.

2 Conducting a Survey

Goal **Create a question for a survey, and collect and organize data.**

? How can you use a survey to find out about your classmates?

Understand

You can use one of these topics, or you can create your own topic.

- snacks
- games
- movies
- books
- animals
- sports

Make a Plan

Use a survey to collect **data** about what your classmates like.

data
Collected information

A. Choose a topic.

B. Make up a question for your survey.
Your question should have at least 3 possible answers.

C. Predict the answer you will get most often.

D. Create a **tally chart** to record your data.
Record each answer with a tally: |
Record 5 answers like this: ||||̸

tally chart
A chart that uses tally marks to count data

Carry Out the Plan

E. Ask your survey question.
Record each answer using your tally chart.

Look Back

F. Look at your data.
Compare your results with your prediction.
What did you find out?

Where Do You Read?

Place	Tally
in bed	||||̸	
in a chair	||||̸ ||||̸
outside	||||̸ ||
other	|||

Reflecting

1. Did your classmates find your question easy to answer?
2. If you did this survey again, would you do anything differently? Why or why not?
3. Suppose you asked each group your question. What do you predict about their answers? Why?
   a) another Grade 3 class
   b) a Grade 8 class
   c) a kindergarten class
   d) a group of adults

Curious Math

It Takes All Sorts

Look at these shapes.

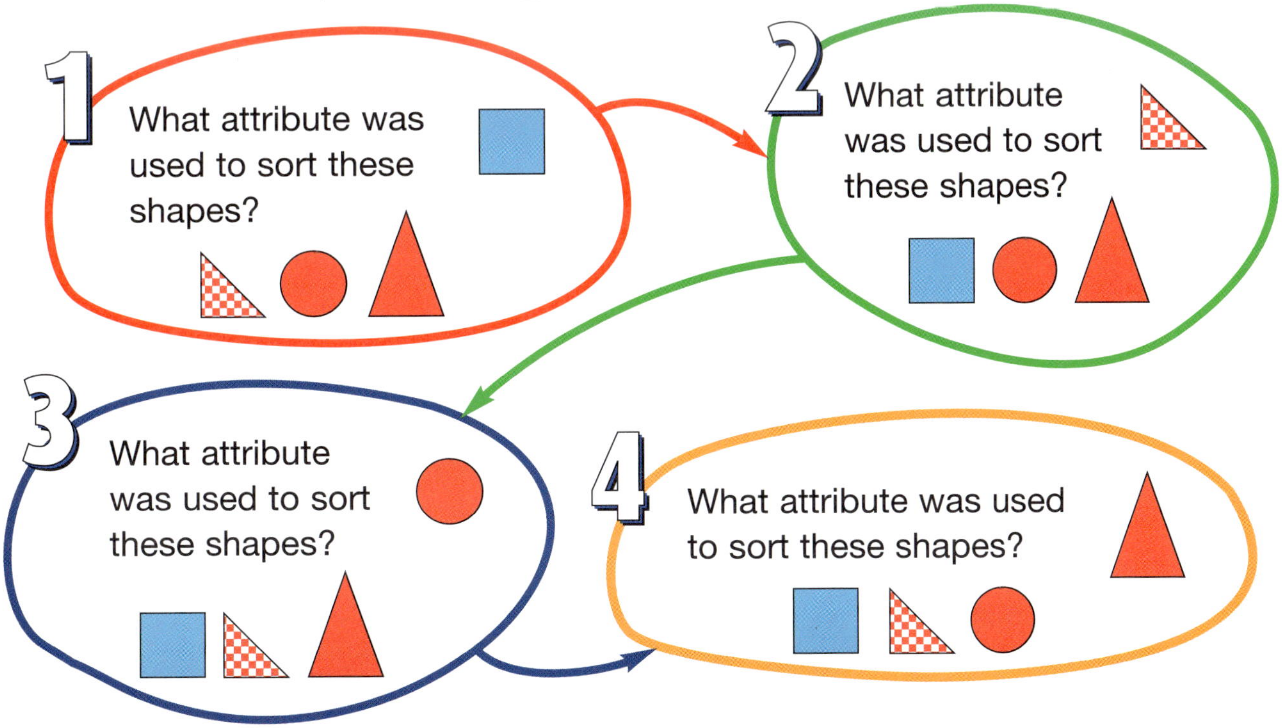

3 Reading and Creating Pictographs

Goal **Interpret and create pictographs.**

Sharleen counted each type of animal in her stuffed animal collection.

? How can Sharleen display her data in a pictograph?

Sharleen's Pictograph

Step 1 I'm going to use stickers for the animals in my **pictograph**.

Step 2 I have 25 stuffed animals. I don't have 25 stickers, so I'll let each sticker **represent** 2 animals. This is a **scale** of 2.

Step 3 I'll skip count to find the number of stickers I need.

10 dogs: 2, 4, 6, 8, 10 — I need 5 stickers.
14 bears: 2, 4, 6, 8, 10, 12, 14 — I need 7 stickers.
1 cat — I need half a sticker.

Step 4 I'll write a label for each type of stuffed animal.

Step 5 I'll stick on the stickers for numbers of animals.

Step 6 I'll give the graph a title and describe the scale.

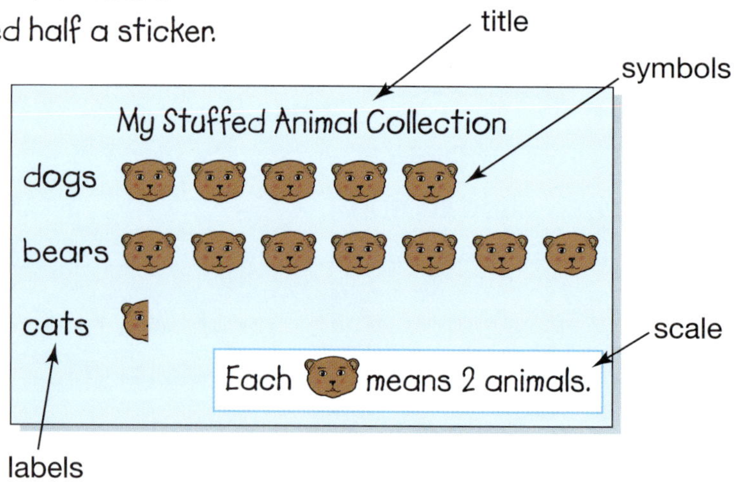

pictograph
A graph that uses pictures or symbols to represent data

scale
The number of items represented by each symbol in a pictograph

Reflecting

1. Why is there half a sticker for cats?
2. What would the graph look like if Sharleen used each scale?
   a) 1 b) 5 c) 10
3. Ben wants to know how many more stuffed dogs than cats Sharleen has. How can he find out?

Checking

4. Ty has 20 picture books, 10 chapter books, 5 board books, and 5 nonfiction books.
   a) Draw a pictograph for Ty's books. Include a scale. Use Sharleen's steps.
   b) Order the types of Ty's books from fewest to most. How do the numbers of books show the order? How does your graph show the order?
   c) How many books does Ty have altogether?
   d) How many fewer board books than picture books does Ty have? How does your graph show this?

Practising

5. Lee has 6 Yukon flags, 10 Manitoba flags, 8 Saskatchewan flags, and 1 Newfoundland flag.
   a) Draw a pictograph for Lee's flags. Use a scale of 2.
   b) How many flags does Lee have altogether? How does your graph show this?
   c) How many more flags does Lee have for Manitoba than for Newfoundland? How does your graph show this?

6. Lyn has 45 adventure movies, 25 comedies, and 10 cartoons in her movie collection. The pictograph shows the adventure movies.
   a) How many movies does each  in the pictograph represent: 2, 5, or 10? Explain how you know.
   b) Draw and complete the pictograph.
   c) Create a problem you can solve with your pictograph.
   d) Show how to solve your problem.

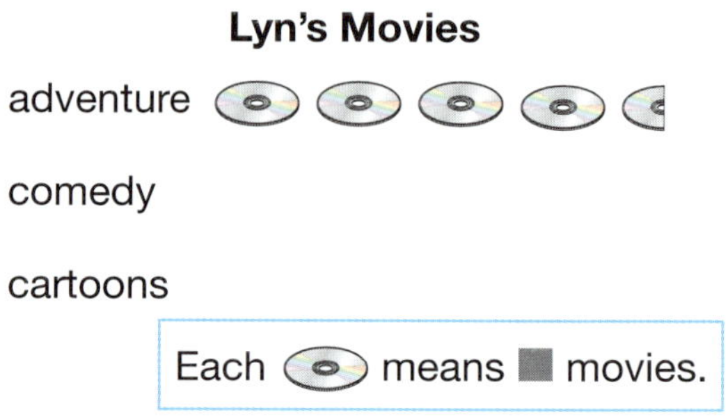

7. Juan and Tiffany collect comics. Tiffany has 2 times as many of each type of comic as Juan.
   a) How many Scooby-Doo comics does Juan have?
   b) How many comics does Juan have altogether?
   c) Order the types of Juan's comics from most to fewest. How does the graph show the order?
   d) What is the order of the types of Tiffany's comics? Use your answer for part c) to explain how you know.

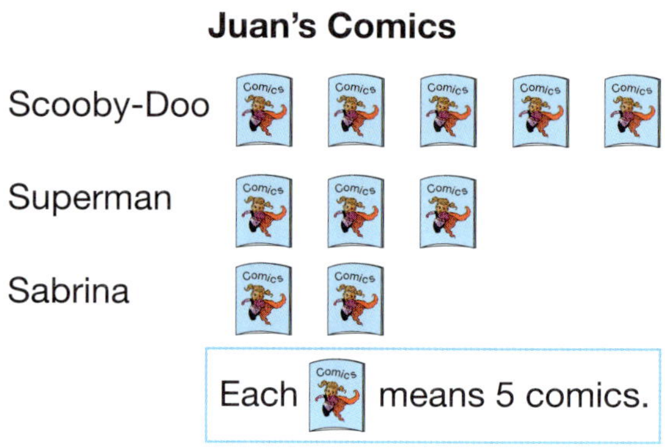

8. Use the graph from Question 7.
   a) Draw a pictograph for Tiffany's comic collection. Use a scale of 10.
   b) How are the graphs for Juan and Tiffany alike? Why does this make sense?
   c) Could you use a scale of 2 or 5 for Tiffany's graph? Explain your thinking.
   d) List 3 things your graph shows about Tiffany's comics.
   e) Suppose Tiffany was given 10 more Sabrina comics. How would your graph change?

Paper Folds

Here is a square sheet of paper with holes punched in it.

This is what the paper looks like when it is folded on the dotted line.

Try These

1. Draw what each sheet of paper looks like when it is folded on the dotted line.

a) 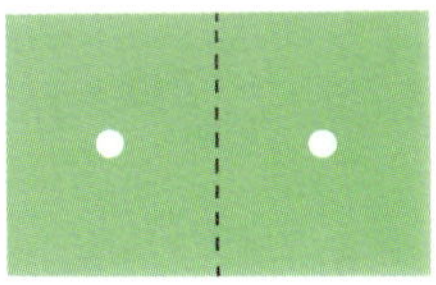

b) 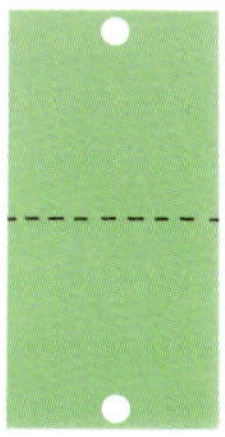

c) 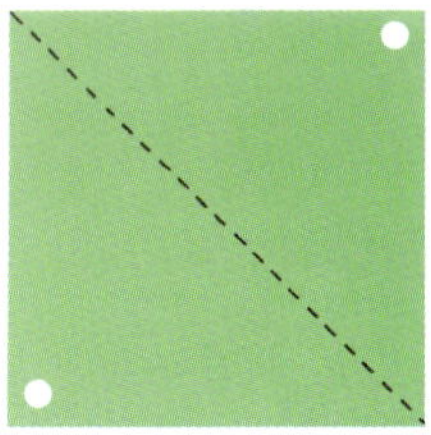

2. These sheets of paper have been folded on a dotted line. Draw what each sheet looks like when it's unfolded.

a) 

b) 

c) 

4 Bar Graphs with Scales

Goal Interpret and create bar graphs using scales of 2, 5, or 10.

You will need

- grid paper

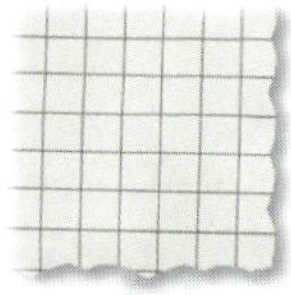

- a calculator

Amit counted visitors to the zoo. He organized his data in a tally chart.

? How can Amit display the data in a bar graph?

Visitors to the Zoo

Age group	Tally	Total
adults	卌 卌 卌	15
children	卌 卌 卌 卌 卌 卌 卌 卌	40
teens	卌 卌 卌 卌 卌 卌	30

Amit's Graph

I tried to graph my data using 1 square for 1 visitor, but the bar for children was too tall to fit on my paper. The same thing happened when I tried 1 square for 2 visitors and 1 square for 5 visitors. I decided to use 1 square for 10 visitors. This is a **scale** of 10.

Step 1 I drew the lines for the **axes**. I put 0 at the bottom and labelled the top of the 1st square as 10.

Step 2 I counted up by 10 for each square. I stopped at 50.

Step 3 I wrote labels for the groups of visitors and for the axes.

Step 4 I drew the bars.

Step 5 I wrote a title for my graph.

scale

The number of items represented by each square in a bar graph

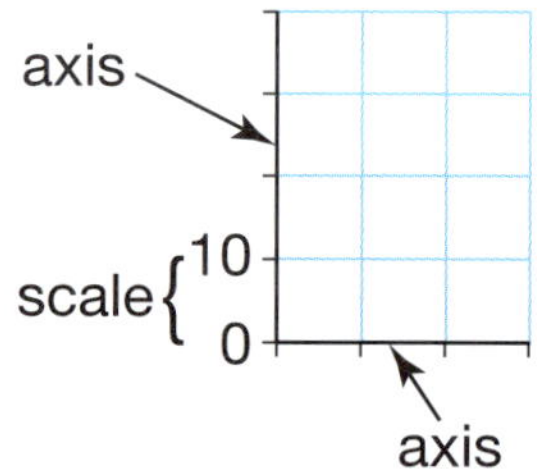

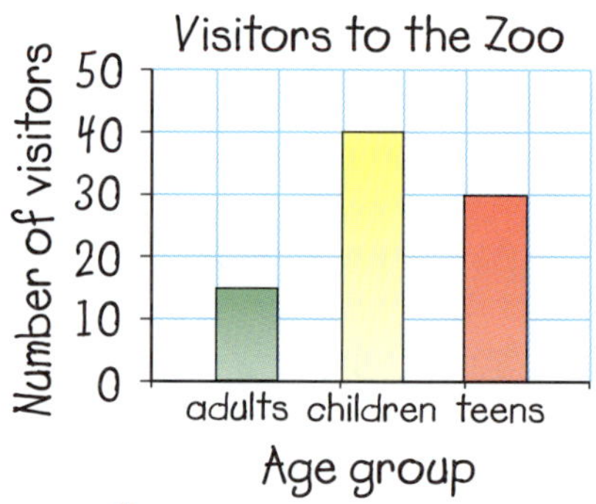

Reflecting

1. a) Why does a scale of 10 make sense for the data?
   b) Why does a scale of 1 or 2 not make sense for the data?
2. Look at the bar graph of visitors to the zoo. Why is the bar for children 1 square higher than the bar for teens?
3. Keisha wants to know how many visitors Amit counted. Explain how to use each of these to calculate the total.
   Then explain which way you prefer.
   a) the totals in Amit's chart
   b) the tallies in Amit's chart
   c) Amit's graph
4. What else does Amit's graph show about visitors to the zoo? List 3 things.

Checking

5. Carlos counted visitors to the monkey exhibit.
   a) Complete Carlos's tally chart.
   b) Draw a bar graph to display the data. Use a scale of 2.
   c) Would a scale of 10 make sense for the data? Explain.
   d) What does the graph show? List 3 things.

Visitors to the Monkey Exhibit

Time	Tally	Total
morning	卌 卌 |	
afternoon	卌 卌 ||	
evening	卌 卌	

6. a) Draw a pictograph to display Carlos's data for Question 5. Use a scale of 2.
   b) Do you think your bar graph or your pictograph shows Carlos's data better? Why do you think this?

Practising

7. Kim asked visitors to the zoo what province they were from.
   a) Complete Kim's tally chart.
   b) Display Kim's data in a bar graph. Use a scale of 2, 5, or 10.
   c) Order the provinces from most visitors to fewest visitors. Explain how the bar graph can help you figure out the order.
   d) How many more visitors were from Manitoba than Saskatchewan? How do you know?

Where Zoo Visitors Are From

Province	Tally	Total
British Columbia	𝍸 𝍸 𝍸 𝍸	
Alberta	𝍸 𝍸 𝍸 𝍸 𝍸	
Saskatchewan	𝍸 𝍸	
Manitoba	𝍸 𝍸 𝍸	
Quebec	𝍸	

8. Use the data in Question 7.
   a) How many visitors did Kim ask altogether?
   b) How many visitors were from Alberta?
   c) How many visitors were not from Alberta?
   d) How are your answers for parts a) to c) related?

9. Nikka surveyed 35 visitors to the zoo.
   a) What question do you think she asked?
   b) Which scale did she use for the graph: 2, 5, or 10? Explain how you know.
   c) Suppose Nikka used a scale of 1. How many squares tall would the graph be? Explain how you know.

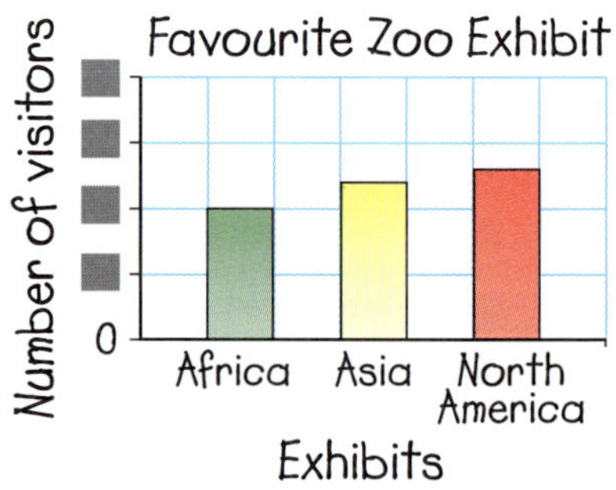

10. a) Create an addition problem about Nikka's graph for Question 9.
    b) Solve your problem.

11. a) Create a subtraction problem about Nikka's graph for Question 9.
    b) Solve your problem.

LESSON

Mid-Chapter Review

1 **1.** Sort these plates. Put the letters for the plates in a Venn diagram. Explain your strategy.

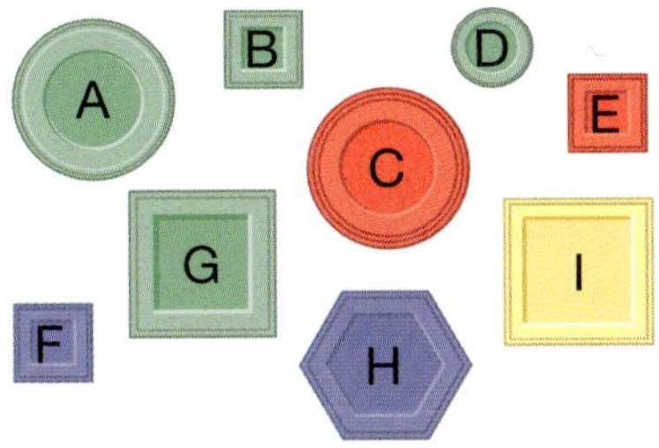

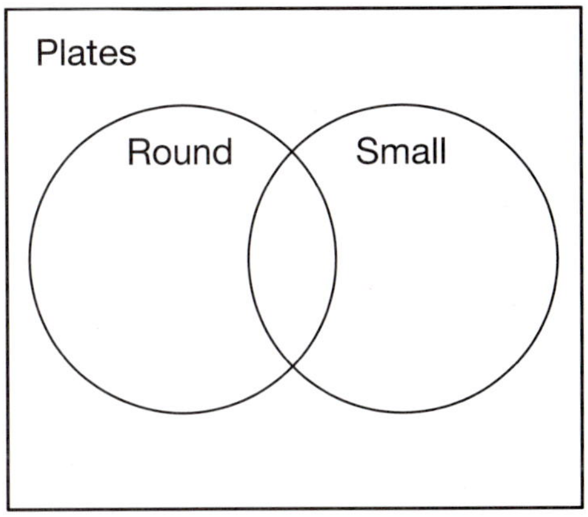

2 **2.** Suppose you want to know what kinds of snacks your classmates eat.

a) What questions can you ask to find out?

b) Write a question that has only 3 possible answers.

c) Draw a tally chart you could use for recording answers to your questions.

3 **3.** This pictograph shows the number of guests who came to dinner.

a) How many guests did Lisa have?

b) How many more guests did Lisa have than Kivi?

c) How many guests did Lisa, Kivi, and Marc have altogether?

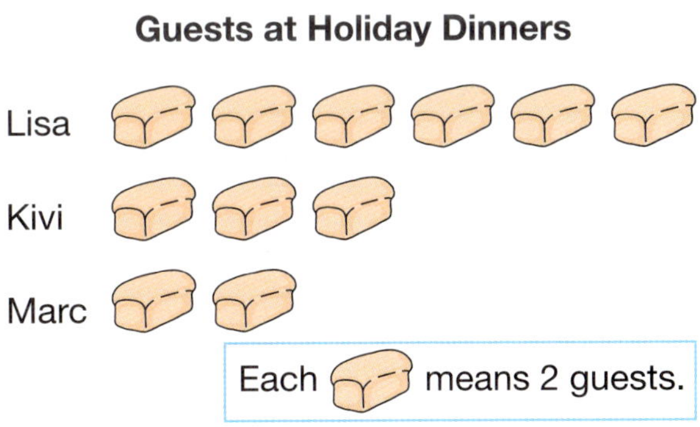

4 **4.** Kanu asked his relatives where they were born.

a) How many relatives did Kanu ask?

b) Make a bar graph to show Kanu's data. Use a scale of 2.

c) Make a pictograph to show Kanu's data. Use a scale of 2.

d) How are your graphs the same? How are they different?

Where Were You Born?

Place	Tally
Canada	𝍸 𝍸 ||
Nigeria	𝍸 |
Australia	|

5 Communicate About Data

Goal **Interpret displays of data, and discuss them using math language.**

Nisha found this graph that shows the number of hours some animals sleep in a day.

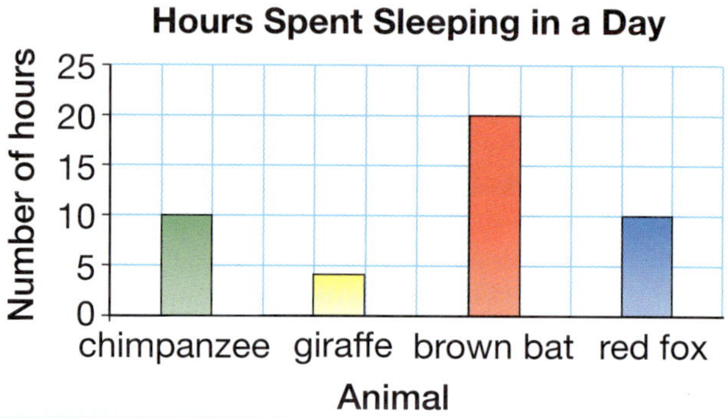

? How can Nisha describe the graph?

Nisha's Description

The graph is a bar graph.
Each square on the graph means 5 hours of sleep.

The brown bat sleeps the most.
The giraffe doesn't sleep for very long.
The chimpanzee and the red fox both sleep for 10 hours.

A. What else can Nisha say about the graph? Use the Communication Checklist.

Communication Checklist

- ✓ Did you use the right amount of detail?
- ✓ Did you use math language?

Reflecting

1. How did the Communication Checklist help you improve Nisha's description of the graph?
2. What parts of a bar graph should you look at when you want to describe what it shows?

Checking

3. Michael described this graph.

Hours Spent Sleeping in a Day

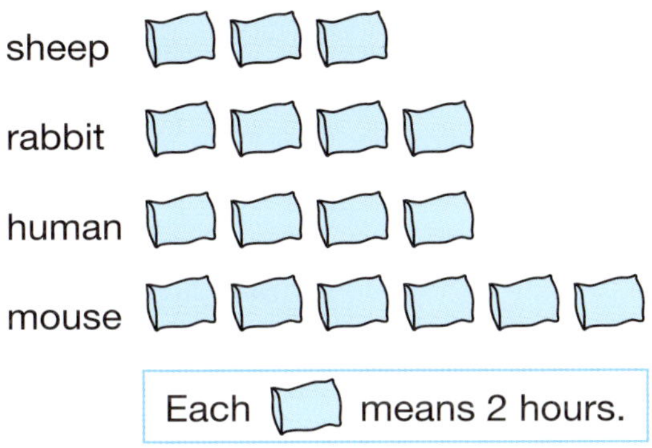

Michael's Description

The graph is a pictograph.

The title is "Hours Spent Sleeping in a Day."

The scale shows that each  means 2 hours.

A sheep sleeps less than a human.

A rabbit sleeps the same number of hours as a human.

a) What math language did Michael use in his description?

b) What else can Michael say about the graph? Use the Communication Checklist.

Practising

4. Describe this graph.
Use the Communication Checklist.

Hours I Slept Last Night

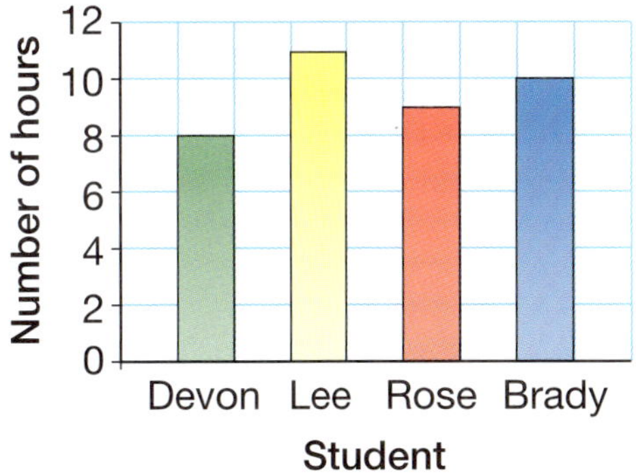

6 Measuring to Collect Data

Goal **Collect data by measuring, and display the data.**

You will need

- centimetre grid paper

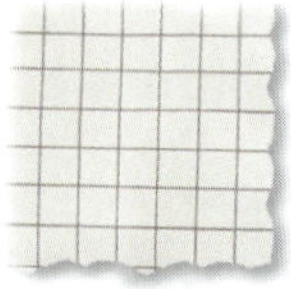

- a calculator

- scissors

- tape

Juan thinks the difference between the length and width of shoes is always about the same.

? How can Juan find out if the differences between shoe lengths and widths are about the same?

Juan's Plan

Each square on centimetre grid paper is 1 cm long.

I can trace a shoe on centimetre grid paper.

Then I can count the squares to measure the length and width.

A. Make a prediction about the differences between shoe lengths and widths. Why do you think this?

B. a) Trace a classmate's shoe on centimetre grid paper so that the squares show the length and the width.

b) Count the squares to measure the length to the nearest centimetre. Record the data in a chart. Count the squares to measure the width to the nearest centimetre. Record the data in your chart.

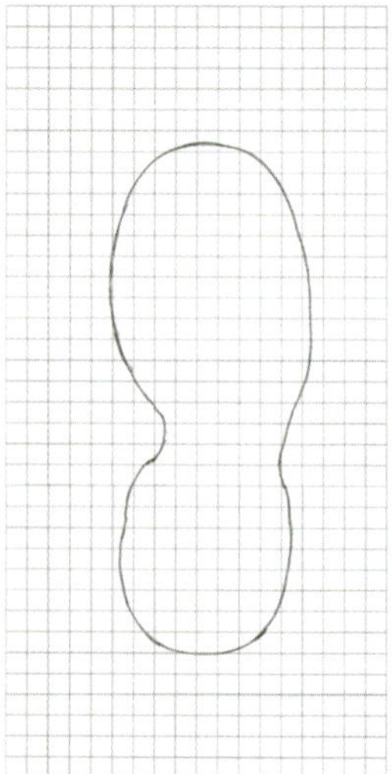

Student	Length (centimetres)	Width (centimetres)	Difference (centimetres)

C. Calculate the difference between the length and width of the shoe. Record the difference in your chart.

D. Repeat parts B and C for at least 5 other classmates.

E. **a)** What is the greatest difference between the length and width of a shoe?

b) What is the least difference?

F. Draw a bar graph to display the data from your chart. Use a scale of 2, 5, or 10.

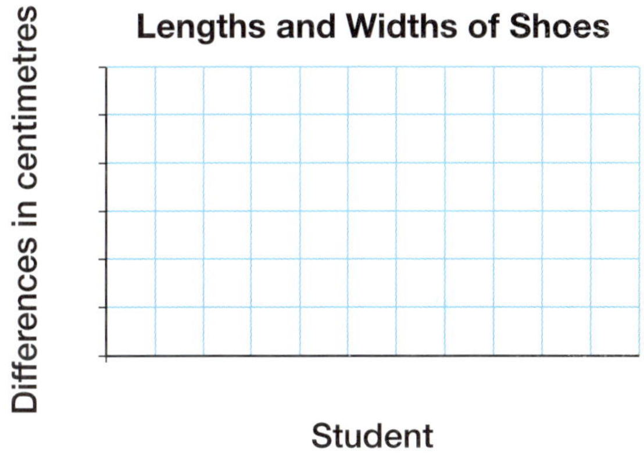

G. Look at your graph. What conclusion can you draw about differences between shoe lengths and widths?

H. Look at graphs your classmates made for other students. Would you change your conclusion from part G? Why or why not?

Reflecting

1. What other ways could you measure the lengths and widths of shoes? Which way do you think is best? Why?
2. Is it easier to compare differences between shoe lengths and widths using a chart or graph? Explain.
3. Could you change the order of the bars in your bar graph to make it easier to compare differences between shoe lengths and widths? Explain why or why not.
4. Do you think anyone might use the data you collected? Explain your thinking.

CHAPTER 3

7 Collecting Data

You will need

- a calculator
- data sources such as books, newspapers, and a computer with Internet access
- grid paper

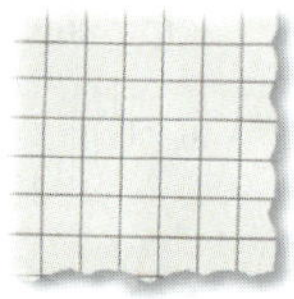

Goal **Collect data from written and technology sources, and display the data.**

Brady is creating a Web site about her province.

Ian is looking for data about bears for a school project.

Lyn is finding outer space data for a trivia game.

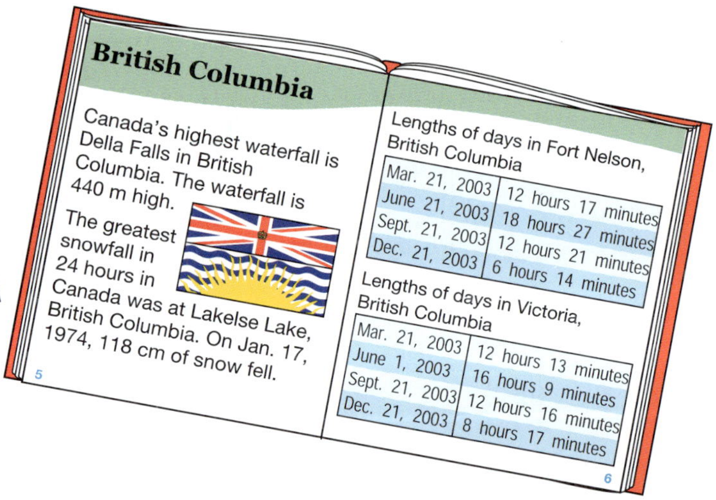

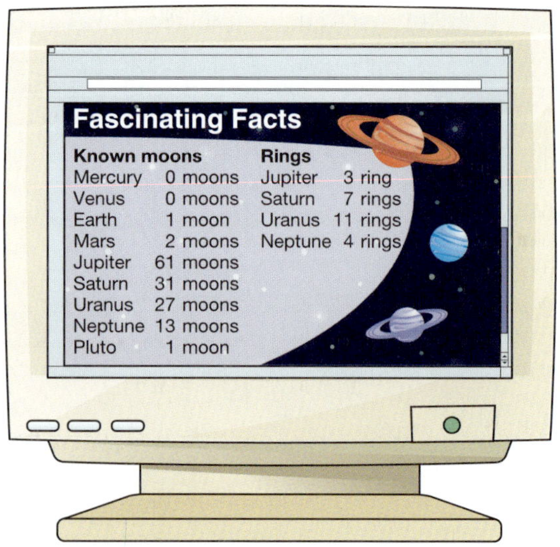

? How can you collect and display data?

A. Describe each student's data.

a) Brady **b)** Ian **c)** Lyn

B. What other sources could each student use for data?

a) Brady **b)** Ian **c)** Lyn

C. Choose the data Brady, Ian, or Lyn is collecting.
Create an addition or subtraction problem.
Solve your problem.

D. Choose any 3 sources for data.
What data could you collect with each?
- a book or magazine
- the Internet
- a CD-ROM or DVD
- a newspaper
- the radio
- the television

E. Where could you find data for each topic?
a) movies **b)** your favourite author **c)** computer games

F. Choose a question for collecting data,
or make up your own question.
- How long are some animals, snakes, or sea creatures?
- How much do your favourite foods cost?

a) What sources can you use for the data?
b) Collect the data. Decide how to record it.
c) Display your data in a graph or another way.
d) What conclusions can you draw about your data?
Explain the reasons for your conclusions.

Reflecting

1. Who do agree with? Explain your reasons.
Ben says, "I keep track of sports by listening to the radio."
Charlie says, "I read sports magazines and the newspaper."
Rachel says, "I like to use the Internet to find out about sports."
2. When do you collect data? How do you collect it?
3. Suppose you conducted a survey of your classmates for the question: What's the best source for data?
a) What choices would you give?
b) Predict the answer you would get most often.
Explain the reason for your prediction.

Skills Bank

LESSON

1 **1. a)** Sort these animals using the Venn diagram. Explain your strategy.

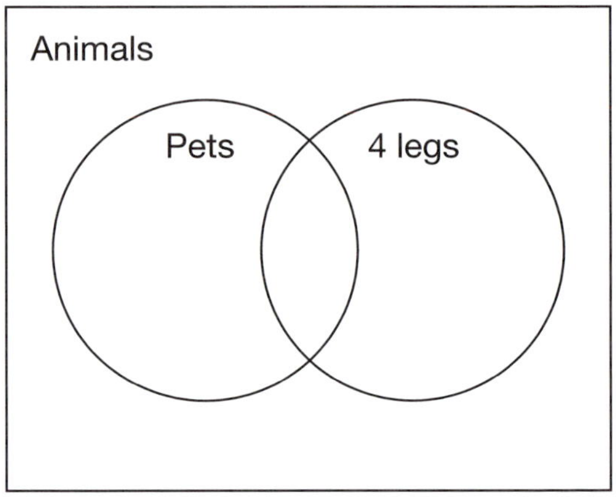

b) Make 2 new labels for the circles. Sort the animals in a new way.

3 **2.** Ryan has 11 adventure movies, 6 comedies, and 15 cartoons in his movie collection.

The pictograph shows the adventure movies.

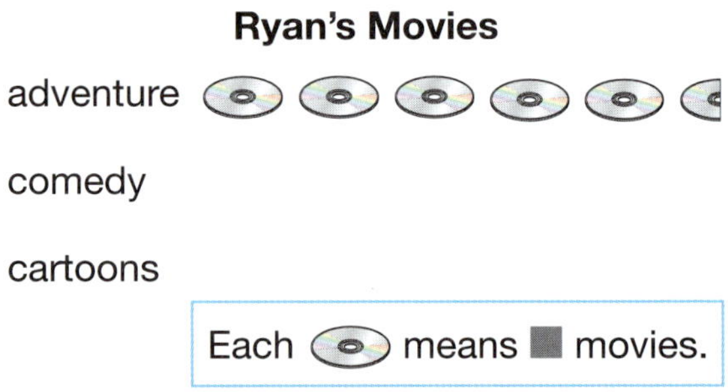

a) How many movies does each (disc) in the pictograph represent: 1, 2, 5, or 10? Explain how you know.

b) Copy and complete the pictograph.

3. Use your pictograph from Question 2.

a) Order the types of Ryan's movies from fewest to most. Explain how the pictograph can help you figure out the order.

b) How many movies does Ryan have altogether? Show your work.

c) How many more cartoons than comedies does Ryan have? How does your graph show this?

4

4. 5 friends are in-line skating.

a) Draw a bar graph to show the number of skates, elbow pads, wrist guards, and helmets they are wearing. Use a scale of 2.

b) What does your graph show? List 3 things.

5. Nikka surveyed 70 visitors to the zoo.

a) What question do you think she asked?

b) Which scale did she use for the graph: 2, 5, or 10? Explain how you know.

c) How many people visited the African exhibit?

d) Why do you think Nikka drew the bars from most to fewest visitors?

e) Suppose Nikka used a scale of 1. How many squares tall would the tallest bar be?

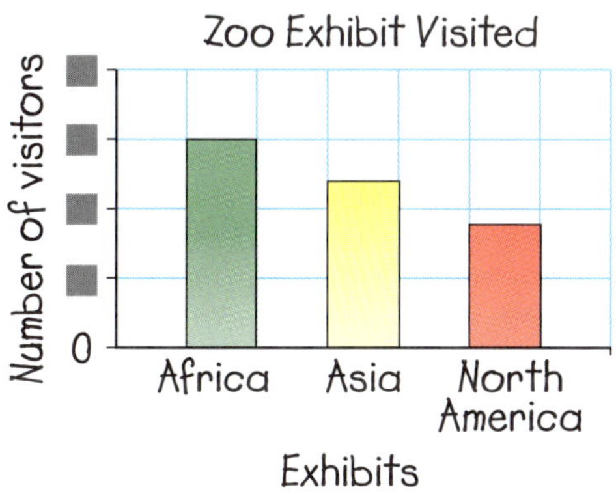

7

6. Choose 2 topics.
Name 3 sources for the data about each topic.

- heights of animals
- times for television programs
- costs of movie tickets
- dates for hockey games

Problem Bank

LESSON

1

1. a) Copy the Venn diagram.
Use it to sort the numbers 4, 5, 10, 20, and 25.

b) How many numbers are in the overlap?

c) Find a different way to sort the numbers.
Make a new Venn diagram.

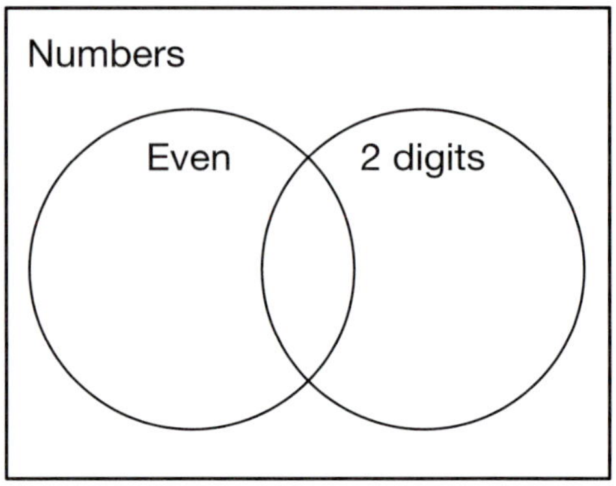

2. Sort the numbers 0 to 10 in this chart.

	Even	Odd
Less than 4		
4 or greater		

3

3. Danny recorded some data in this tally chart.

a) What question could Danny have asked?

b) Make a pictograph of the data.

Number of ■	Tally
0	||
1	||||
2	𝍸 |||
3	
4	𝍸 𝍸 𝍸

4. Nicky's family recycled 30 bottles in 3 weeks.
They recycled 2 more bottles in week 2 than in week 1.
They recycled 4 more bottles in week 3 than in week 1.

a) How many bottles did they recycle each week?

b) Show the number of bottles recycled each week in a pictograph.

c) Create a problem about your graph.

d) Solve your problem.

3

5. This pictograph shows the birthday seasons for a class.
   a) How many students were born in the summer?
   b) How many more students were born in the spring than in the fall? Explain how you know.
   c) Who might use this information? Why?

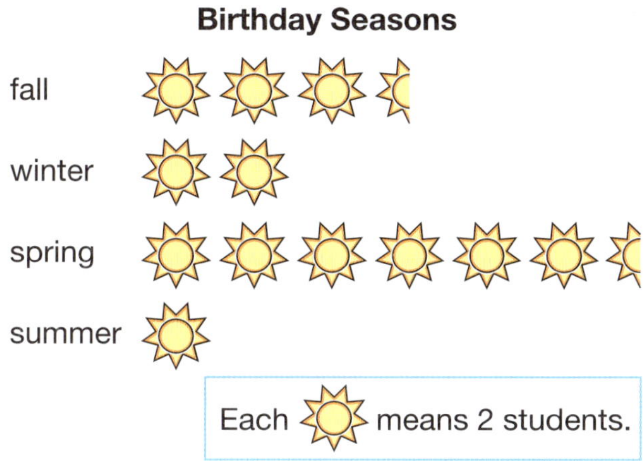

4

6. Adriano surveyed some Grade 3 students. He displayed the data in this bar graph.
   a) How many more students wear digital watches than analog watches?
   b) How many students were surveyed? Explain how you know.
   c) What do you think the survey question was?

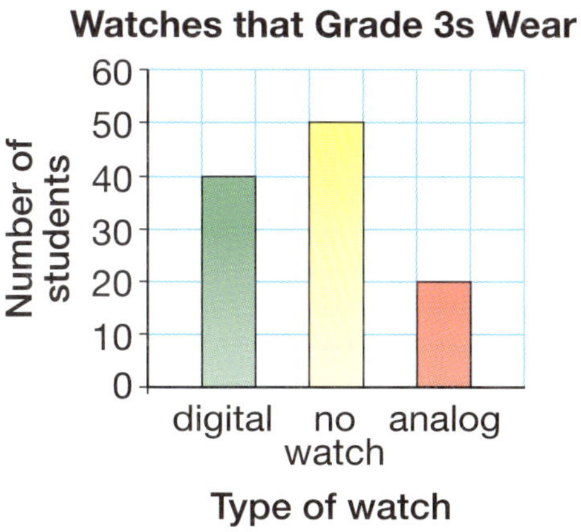

digital analog

LESSON

Chapter Review

1 **1.** Sort these foods in the Venn diagram. Explain your strategy.

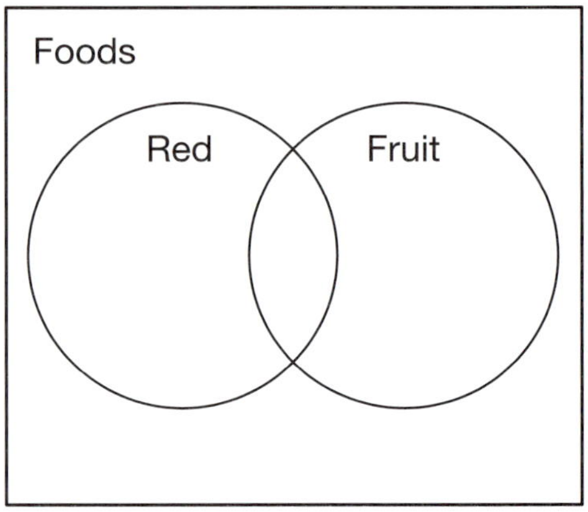

2 **2.** Write a survey question to find out what your classmates like to do on weekends.

3 **3. a)** Tien asked her classmates to choose their favourite type of pet. Draw a pictograph of her data. Use a scale of 2.

b) How many students did Tien survey?

c) How many chose cats?

d) How many did not choose cats?

e) How are the answers for parts b) to d) related?

Favourite Type of Pet

Pet	Tally
cat	𝍸 𝍸
bird	||||
dog	𝍸 𝍸 𝍸 |
other	||

4. Kevin and Gabby graphed the same data for their school. What is the scale of Gabby's pictograph? Explain how you know.

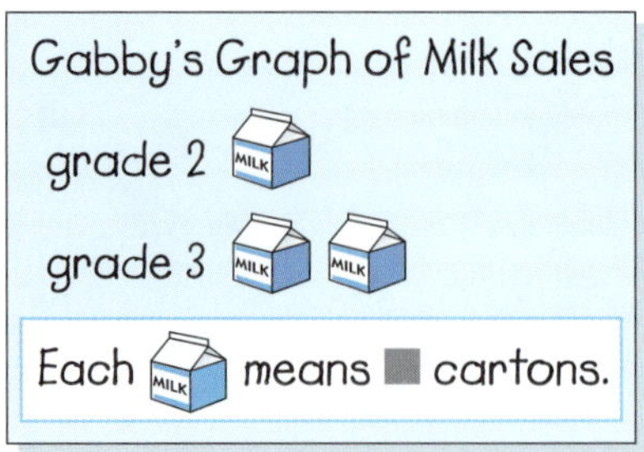

4 **5.** Jessica asked her friends about their favourite sports.

Our Favourite Sports

Sport	Tally
hockey	𝍸
skating	𝍸 𝍸 ||
football	

a) Draw a bar graph to show the information in the chart. Use a scale of 2.

b) Order the sports from the most favourite to the least favourite.

c) How many more friends chose skating than hockey?

d) Suppose Jessica surveyed 3 more friends who chose football. How would your bar graph change?

e) Create and solve a subtraction problem about your graph.

5 **6.** Omar thinks there should be more magazines in the library. He asked his classmates what they like to read. He represented the data in a bar graph.

a) Describe Omar's bar graph. Use the Communication Checklist.

b) How could Omar use this information?

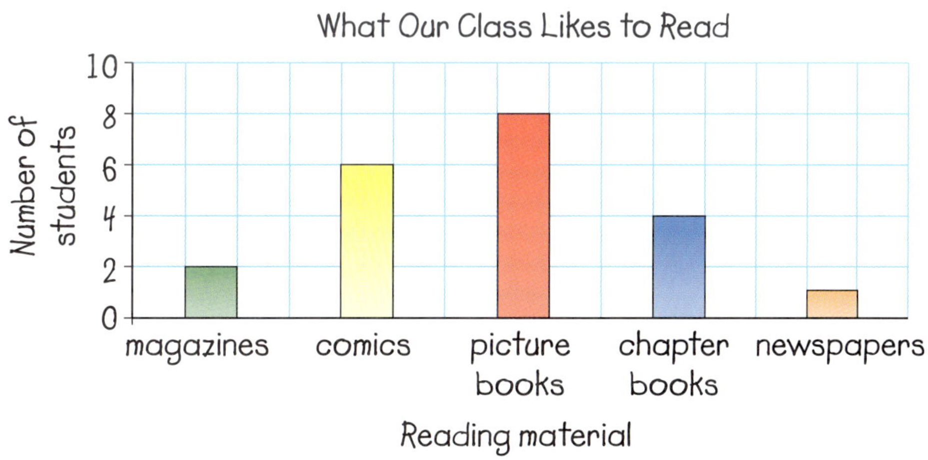

7 **7.** Choose 4 sources for data.
Give an example of data you might collect with each.

- conduct a survey
- measure
- read a book
- read a newspaper
- search the Internet
- use a CD-ROM or DVD

Chapter Task

Graphing Data About Names

? What can a graph show about the names of your classmates?

Understand

A. Record the names of your classmates.

B. Before you make a graph, think about how to sort the names into groups. Will the groups overlap?

Make a Plan

C. Decide what labels to use for the sorted groups.

Carry Out the Plan

D. Sort the names and record your results.

E. Draw a graph of your results.

Look Back

F. Look at your graph and make sure the scale is appropriate.
Explain how you chose the scale.

Communicate

G. Describe what your graph shows about the names of your classmates.

Task Checklist

- ☑ Did you include all the parts of your graph?
- ☑ Did you describe your graph using math language?
- ☑ Did you compare the groups?

Cumulative Review

Cross-Strand Multiple Choice

1. Name 2 attributes that change in this pattern.

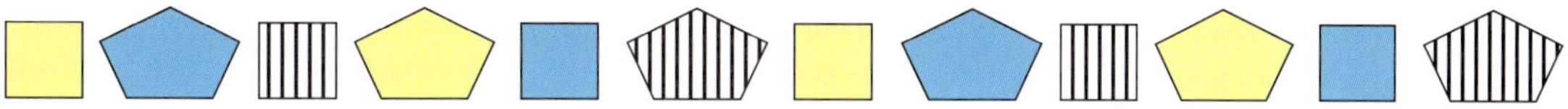

A. shape, colour
B. lines, position
C. shape, yellow
D. blue, square

2. How are these patterns the same?
1, 6, 11, 16, 21, ...   43, 48, 53, 58, ...
E. Both grow by adding 10.
F. Both repeat the same number.
G. Both change by subtracting 5.
H. Both grow by adding 5.

3. Choose the block model that does not show 101.
A. 
B. 
C. 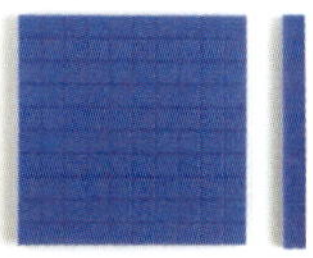
D. 

4. Jon and Kyle are in line behind Rajit.
Lyn is just in front of Jon and just behind Kyle.
Kyle is 30th in line. What is Jon's place in line?
E. 29th **F.** 30th **G.** 31st **H.** 32nd

5. Where should 3 and 8 be sorted?
A. 3 outside the circles and 8 in the Even circle
B. 3 in the Red circle and 8 in the overlap
C. 3 outside the circles and 8 in the overlap
D. 3 in the overlap and 8 in the Red circle

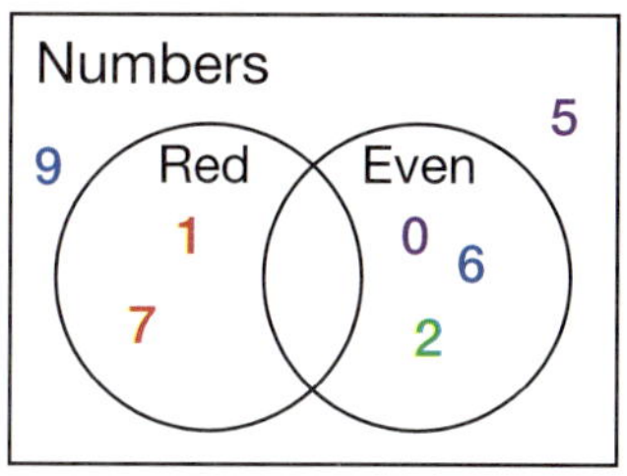

6. Which information about the graph is not true?
E. 15 more students drink juice than pop.
F. 5 fewer students drink milk than juice.
G. 10 more students drink milk than water.
H. 10 fewer students drink pop than milk.

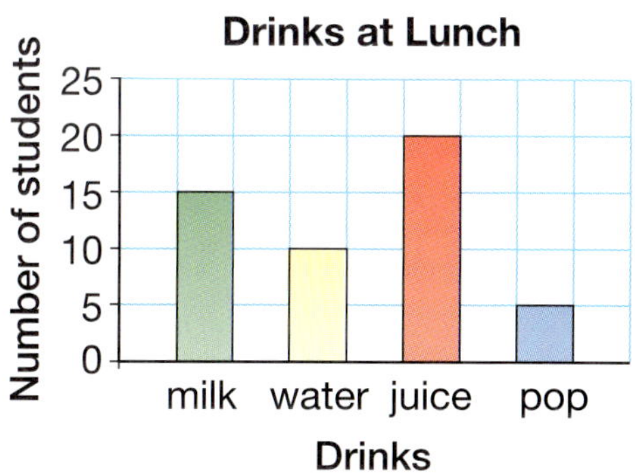

Cross-Strand Investigation

Reduce, Reuse, Recycle

November

S	M	T	W	T	F	S
					1	2
3	4	5	6	7	8	9
10	11	12	13	14	15	16
17	18	19	20	21	22	23
24	25	26	27	28	29	30

7. Garbage is picked up outside Jason's store every second day. It was picked up on November 1.

- **a)** List the dates for the next 5 days the garbage was picked up.
- **b)** What is the date for the 10th day the garbage was picked up?
- **c)** Describe a number pattern in the November calendar.

8. a) The newspapers for recycling are tied in bundles of 50. How many papers are there in all? Show how you know.

50 50 50

b) Erika needs to buy some newspapers for a project. She has this money. How much money does she have?

9. Matthew thinks his family creates too much garbage. Write 3 survey questions that he could ask his family to find out.

10. a) Gina collected data about garbage at her home for 8 weeks. Display her data on a bar graph. Use a scale of 2.

b) What does the graph tell you about Gina's garbage?

Gina's Data

Week	Number of bags
1	4
2	4
3	8
4	4
5	4
6	8
7	4
8	4

CHAPTER 4

Addition and Subtraction

Goals

You will be able to

- **relate subtraction to addition**
- **describe patterns in an addition table**
- **use mental math to add and subtract**
- **solve addition and subtraction problems by acting them out**
- **estimate sums and differences of 2-digit numbers**
- **add and subtract 2-digit numbers**

Numbers in games

Getting Started

You will need

- counters

Adding and Subtracting

Jay's classroom has 4 fish tanks.
There are different numbers of fish in the tanks.

Jay has 14 new fish to add to the tanks.
He wants to add some fish to each tank.
Each tank can hold 12 fish.

? How many new fish can Jay put in each tank?

A. Show one way to add the 14 new fish to the tanks. Use counters.

B. Draw pictures to show the number of fish you add to each tank.

C. Write at least 2 addition sentences to describe what you did with Jay's fish.

D. Write at least 2 subtraction sentences to describe what you did with Jay's fish.

E. Create your own addition and subtraction problems about fish tanks. Show solutions to your problems.

Do You Remember?

1. Complete each number sentence.

a) $5 + 3 = ■$ **c)** $7 + 2 = ■$ **e)** $9 - 6 = ■$ **g)** $7 - 5 = ■$

b) $3 + 4 = ■$ **d)** $4 + 6 = ■$ **f)** $8 - 2 = ■$ **h)** $10 - 8 = ■$

2. Add or subtract.

a) $\begin{array}{r} 6 \\ +\ 2 \\ \hline \end{array}$ **b)** $\begin{array}{r} 7 \\ +\ 3 \\ \hline \end{array}$ **c)** $\begin{array}{r} 6 \\ -\ 4 \\ \hline \end{array}$ **d)** $\begin{array}{r} 9 \\ -\ 7 \\ \hline \end{array}$

3. Copy each number sentence.
Circle the **sum**. Underline the **difference**.

a) $1 + 8 = 9$ **b)** $10 - 5 = 5$

4. Write a number sentence for this picture.

CHAPTER 4

1 Relating Subtraction to Addition

You will need

- counters

Goal **Use fact families to relate addition and subtraction.**

Where My Clothes Are

Dirty clothes should be put in the hamper.
Clean clothes should be put in the drawer.
But it takes too much time
And it takes too much work,
So I throw them all over the floor.

BRUCE LANSKY

Charlie's T-shirts

I have 13 T-shirts altogether.
Some are in a drawer and 5 are on the floor.
I can use counters to represent the T-shirts.

? How many of Charlie's T-shirts are in a drawer?

A. Complete these addition sentences about the T-shirts.
5 + ■ = 13   ■ + 5 = 13

B. What does each number in the addition sentences tell about the T-shirts? Explain your thinking.

C. Complete these subtraction sentences about the T-shirts.
13 − 5 = ■   13 − ■ = 5

D. What does each number in the subtraction sentences tell about the T-shirts? Explain your thinking.

Reflecting

1. You wrote 4 number sentences about the T-shirts. They form a **fact family**. How do you know?
2. Charlie subtracted $12 - 8 = 5$. How can you use facts from a fact family to show this is not correct?

fact family

A set of number facts that use the same numbers

Fact family for 2, 4, and 6:

$4 + 2 = 6$
$2 + 4 = 6$
$6 - 2 = 4$
$6 - 4 = 2$

Checking

3. Charlie has 16 socks.
   Some are in a drawer and 9 are on the floor.
   a) Complete these number sentences about Charlie's socks.
      $16 - 9 = ■$ $9 + ■ = 16$
   b) What does each number sentence tell about Charlie's socks?
   c) Write the other 2 number sentences in this fact family.

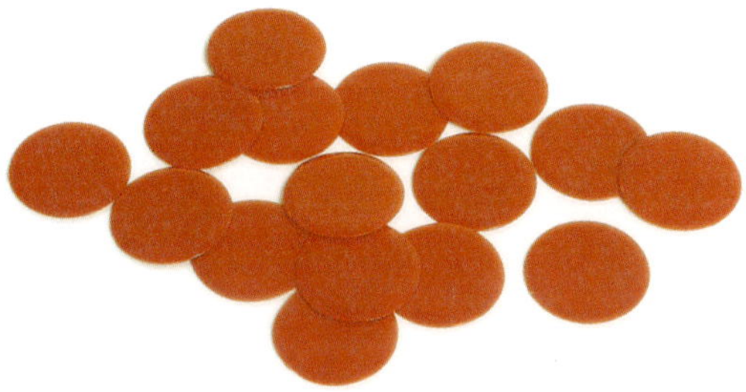

Practising

4. Charlie has 14 hats.
   8 are in a drawer and some are on the floor.
   How many are on the floor?
   Show how you can use a fact from a fact family to check.
5. Charlie has 7 mitts in a drawer and 8 on the floor.
   How many mitts does he have?
   Show how you can use a fact from a fact family to check.
6. Find each missing number. Then write a subtraction sentence that belongs in the same fact family.
   a) $8 + ■ = 16$ b) $■ + 7 = 13$ c) $■ + 5 = 11$
7. Create a problem about clothes on the floor and in a drawer. Write the fact family for your problem.

2 Making an Addition Table

You will need

- an addition table

+	0	1	2	3	4	5
0	0					
1		2				
2			4			
3				6		

- pencil crayons

Goal Describe patterns in an addition table.

Rachel started making an addition table.

? What patterns can you find in the addition table?

A. Colour your addition table to match Rachel's.

a) Describe the pattern for the sums on the yellow diagonal.

b) Write the first 3 sums on a different diagonal going in the same direction.

c) Predict the pattern for the sums on the diagonal.

d) Complete the diagonal to check your prediction.

B. a) Describe the pattern for the sums on the **blue** diagonal.

b) Describe the pattern for the sums in the **red** row.

c) Describe the pattern for the sums in the **green** column.

C. a) How are the patterns for the sums in the **red** row and the **green** column the same? How are they different?

b) How are the patterns for the sums on the **blue** diagonal and the **yellow** diagonal different?

diagonal

column

row →

+	0	1	2	3	4	5	6	7	8	9
0	0								8	9
1		2							9	
2			4					9	10	
3				6			9		11	
4					8	9			12	
5					9	10			13	
6				9			12		14	
7	7	8	9	10	11	12	13	14	15	16
8		9							16	
9	9							16	17	18

You write the sum of 9 + 7 in 2 places: where row 9 and column 7 meet and where row 7 and column 9 meet.

D. Complete the addition table.

E. Use **orange**. Draw a box around any 3 squares in a row.

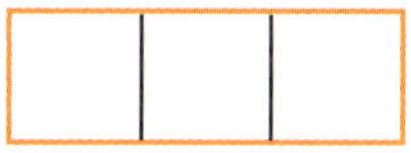

- **a)** What do you notice about the middle sum?
- **b)** Is this the same for any 3 sums in a row? Explain your thinking.
- **c)** Is it the same for any 5 sums in a row? Explain your thinking.

F. Use **brown**. Draw a box around any 2-by-2 square.
What do you notice about the sums?
Repeat this for other 2-by-2 squares.

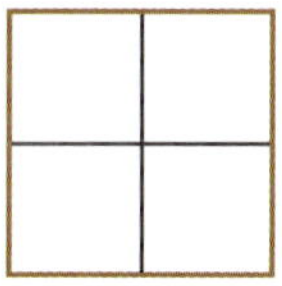

G. Use **purple**. Draw a box around any 3-by-3 square.
What do you notice about the middle sum?
What do you notice about the other sums?
Repeat this for other 3-by-3 squares.

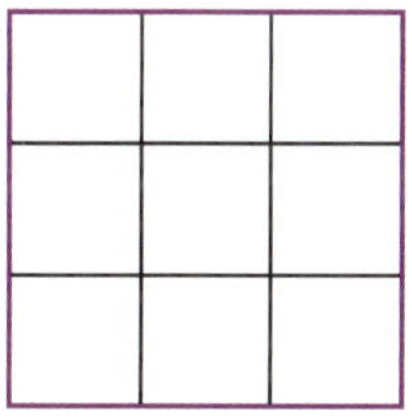

Reflecting

1. **a)** How are the sums on one side of the **yellow** diagonal the same as the sums on the other side of it? How are they different? Explain why.
   b) How are the sums on one side of the **blue** diagonal the same as the sums on the other side of it? How are they different? Explain why.
2. Describe a different pattern in the table. Ask someone to find the pattern.
3. Suppose you had completed the sums in row 4 and column 7 on an addition table. How could you use patterns to complete the table?

CHAPTER 4

3 Adding and Subtracting Tens

Goal **Add and subtract tens.**

Nisha's class wants to send Ontario pins to 110 students in British Columbia. The class already has 3 bags of pins. Nisha found 4 more bags at the store.

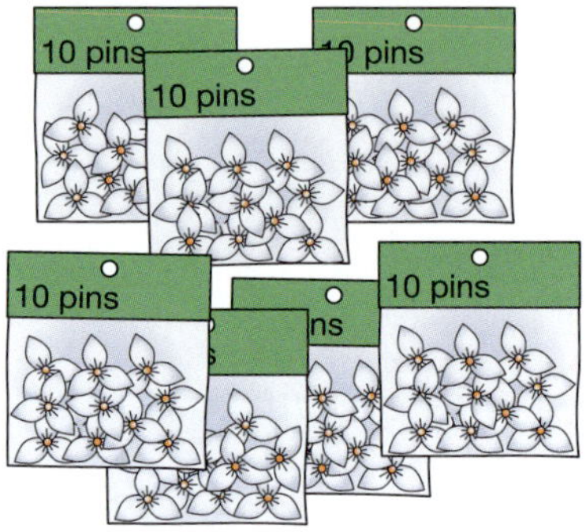

? How many more pins does Nisha's class need?

Nisha's Strategy

Step 1 I added to see how many pins we already have. I used place value. 30 is 3 tens. 40 is 4 tens.

3 tens	30
+ 4 tens	+ 40
7 tens	70

We have 70 pins. We need 110 pins altogether.

Step 2 I subtracted the number of pins we have from the number of pins we need. 110 is 11 tens. 70 is 7 tens.

11 tens	110
− 7 tens	− 70
4 tens	40

We need 40 more pins.

Reflecting

1. How do you know that 110 is the same as 11 tens? Use words or pictures to explain.
2. Describe how Nisha used number facts to add and subtract tens.
3. a) Describe how Nisha can use subtraction to check her addition.
   b) Describe how Nisha can use addition to check her subtraction.

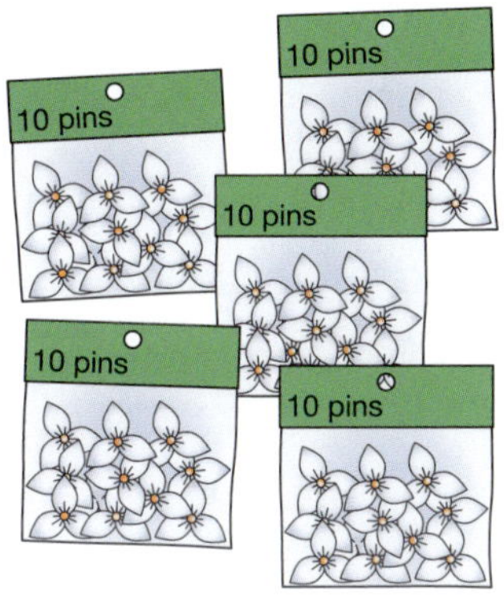

Checking

4. Nisha's class has 50 Ontario pins to send to Nunavut. They want to send 130 pins. How many more pins do they need?

Practising

5. Complete. Add or subtract to check.
   a) $50 + 40 = ■$ b) $140 - 50 = ■$
6. How can the fact $9 + 8 = 17$ help you to add $90 + 80$? Explain your thinking.
7. Todd's class had 70 Alberta pins and 80 Nova Scotia pins. They gave away 50 of each. How many pins do they have left?

8. Write the addition or subtraction fact you will use to calculate each answer. Then add or subtract.
   a) $\begin{array}{r} 70 \\ +\ 30 \\ \hline \end{array}$ b) $\begin{array}{r} 50 \\ +\ 60 \\ \hline \end{array}$ c) $\begin{array}{r} 120 \\ -\ 30 \\ \hline \end{array}$ d) $\begin{array}{r} 160 \\ -\ 80 \\ \hline \end{array}$
9. Alex's class received 90 pins altogether from Nova Scotia and Alberta. They have 50 more Nova Scotia pins than Alberta pins. How many Alberta pins do they have?

4 Mental Addition and Subtraction

You will need

- Treasure Staircase game board, rules, cards, and game markers

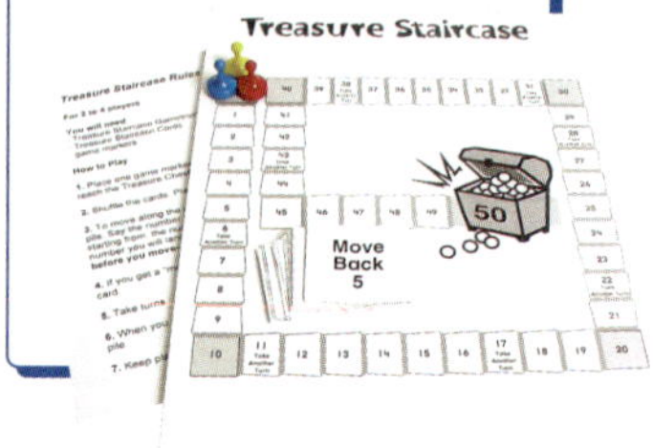

Goal Use mental math strategies to add and subtract 1-digit and 2-digit numbers.

? How can you figure out where to move on a game board without counting every space?

Rashad's Move

My marker is on 27.
My card says,
"Move back 9."

Rose's Move

My marker is on 27, too.
My card says,
"Move forward 8."

Gabe's Move

My marker is on 25.
My card says,
"Move forward 7."

A. How can each player decide where to move without counting every space?

a) Rashad b) Rose c) Gabe

B. Figure out where to move. Explain your thinking.

a)

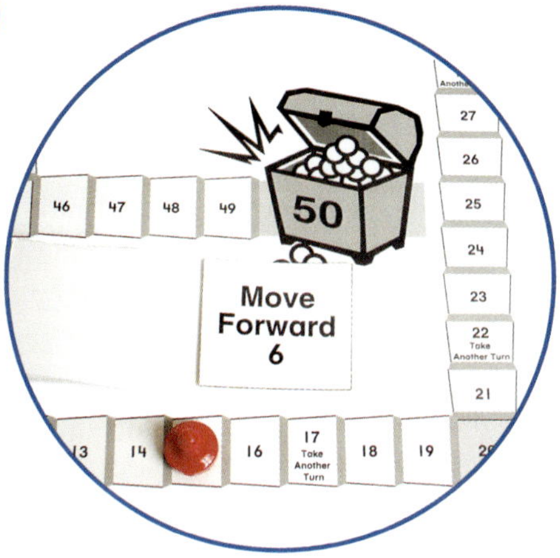

b)

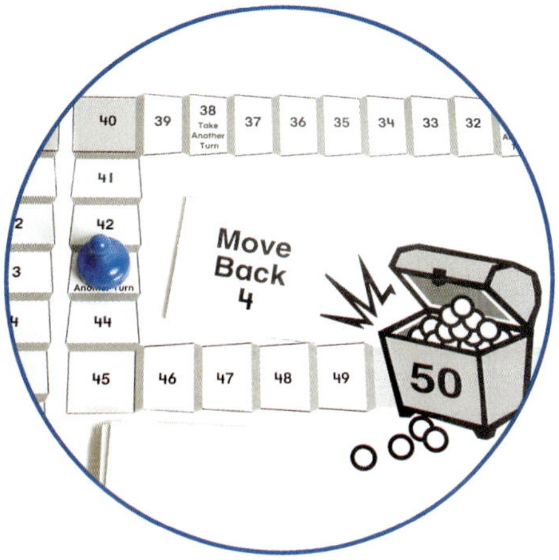

C. Play the game. Use mental math strategies to decide where to move without counting every space.

Reflecting

1. Describe the mental math strategies you used in the game. Give an example to show how each strategy helped you.

2. a) Describe a mental math strategy you can use for adding 9 to a 2-digit number.
   b) Describe a mental math strategy you can use for subtracting 9 from a 2-digit number.

3. a) When might you add or subtract numbers mentally in everyday situations?
   b) Write a problem that you can solve by adding or subtracting mentally. Show how to solve your problem. Explain why you calculated mentally.

LESSON

Mid-Chapter Review

1 **1.** Complete each addition sentence.

a) 7 + ■ = 16 **b)** 2 + ■ = 11 **c)** 7 + ■ = 12 **d)** 8 + ■ = 12

2. Write one subtraction sentence from the same fact family as each addition sentence in Question 1.

3. Complete each subtraction sentence.

a) 13 − ■ = 6 **b)** 14 − ■ = 7 **c)** 17 − ■ = 8 **d)** 15 − ■ = 9

4. Tien has 17 felt markers.
Some are at school and 9 are at home.
How many are at school? Show your work.
Show how you can use a fact from a fact family to check.

5. Mario had \$11.
He spent some and has \$9 left.
How much did he spend?

3 **6.** Add or subtract.

a) $\begin{array}{r} 7 \text{ tens} \\ +\ 5 \text{ tens} \\ \hline \end{array}$ **c)** $\begin{array}{r} 14 \text{ tens} \\ -\ 5 \text{ tens} \\ \hline \end{array}$ **e)** $\begin{array}{r} 70 \\ +\ 40 \\ \hline \end{array}$ **g)** $\begin{array}{r} 120 \\ -\ 40 \\ \hline \end{array}$

b) $\begin{array}{r} 5 \text{ tens} \\ +\ 8 \text{ tens} \\ \hline \end{array}$ **d)** $\begin{array}{r} 15 \text{ tens} \\ -\ 9 \text{ tens} \\ \hline \end{array}$ **f)** $\begin{array}{r} 90 \\ +\ 80 \\ \hline \end{array}$ **h)** $\begin{array}{r} 170 \\ -\ 80 \\ \hline \end{array}$

4 **7.** Use mental math to add or subtract.

a) 46 + 8 = ■ **c)** 54 − 7 = ■ **e)** 25 − 9 = ■ **g)** 71 + 6 = ■

b) 38 + 7 = ■ **d)** 71 − 6 = ■ **f)** 46 − 8 = ■ **h)** 89 + 3 = ■

8. Explain a strategy you used to add or subtract in one part of Question 7.

9. Matt started with \$40 and spent \$9.
Alana started with \$35 and spent \$7.
Who has more money now? How much more?
Show your work.

Operation 25

Number of players: 2
How to play: Make number sentences and score points.

You will need

- number cards (1 to 9)

Step 1 Place the number cards face down. Mix up the cards.

Step 2 On your turn, take 3 cards. Make a 2-digit number out of 2 of the cards. (You can choose which 2 cards to use.)

Step 3 Start with the 2-digit number you made. Add or subtract the 1-digit number on the other card. Write a number sentence to show what you did.

Step 4 Find your answer on the number line. The colour tells your score. Record your score.

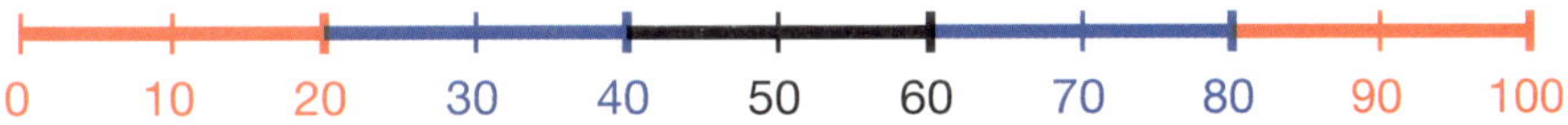

Scoring: 5 points for (orange)
3 points for (blue)
1 point for (black)

Step 5 Return your cards to the pile. Mix up the cards.

Step 6 Take turns playing.

Continue playing until a player has at least 25 points.

Juan's Turn

I picked 3, 7, and 6.

36 − 7 = 29

29 is on a blue part of the line, so I get 3 points.

5 Solve Problems by Acting Them Out

You will need
- counters

- number lines

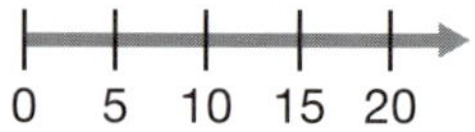

Goal Solve addition and subtraction problems by acting them out.

On Sunday night, Wanda is wearing 42 bandages. Each morning, she pulls off 3 bandages and puts on 1 new one.

? How many bandages will Wanda be wearing next Sunday night?

Sharleen's Solution

Understand
Next Sunday is in 7 days.
I want to know how many bandages Wanda will have on after she takes off 3 and puts on 1 each day for 7 days.

Make a Plan
I'll act it out with 42 counters to represent the bandages.
I'll make a chart to show the number of bandages at the end of each day.

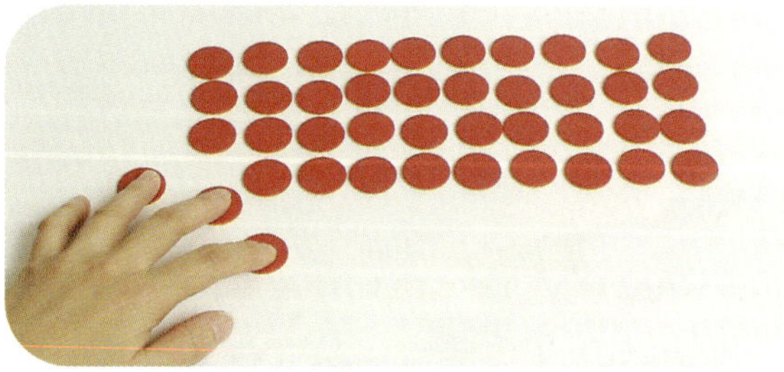

Carry Out the Plan
I'll take away 3, add 1, take away 3, add 1, and so on. I'll do this 7 times.

Start Sun.	Mon.	Tues.	Wed.	Thurs.	Fri.	Sat.	Next Sun.
42	40	38	36	34	32	30	28

Wanda will be wearing 28 bandages next Sunday night.

Reflecting

1. Explain how Sharleen used the counters to act out the problem.
2. How could Sharleen have used the chart to find the answer without counters?

Checking

3. Suppose Wanda continues her pattern. How many bandages will she be wearing the next Sunday night? Act it out using counters or a number line. Show your work.

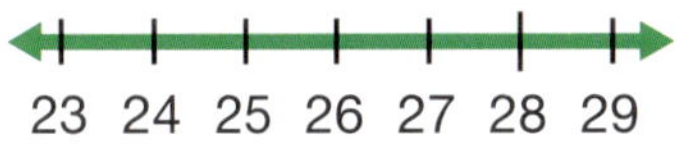

Practising

4. Suppose you are wearing 16 bandages. Each day you take off 7 and put on 10 new ones. How many bandages will you be wearing after 4 days? Show your work.

5. Each birthday, Jasleen gets the same number of birthday charms as her age.
   On her 1st birthday, she got 1 charm.
   On her 2nd birthday, she got 2 charms.
   How many charms will she have altogether on each birthday?
   a) her 4th birthday
   b) her 8th birthday

6. Liam started with 5 skateboard stickers.
   He collected more stickers in 3 equal groups.
   He ended up with between 25 and 30 stickers.
   a) How many stickers could have been in each group Liam collected? Use the counters or the number line to act it out. Explain your choice of method.
   b) Find another possible answer.

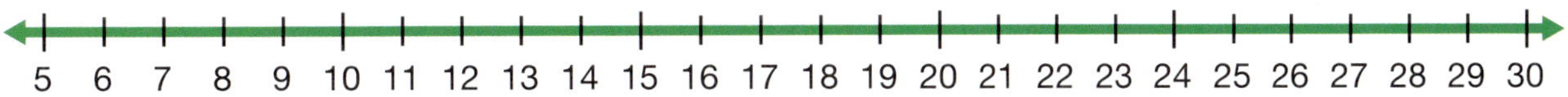

6 Estimating Sums and Differences

Goal **Estimate sums and differences of 2-digit numbers.**

Sukan is lining up 3 stuffed animals on a 100 cm shelf.

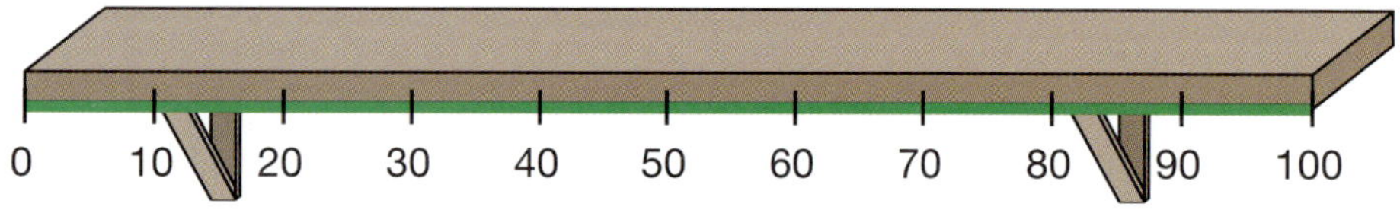

hare: 53 cm

rat: 28 cm

chick: 15 cm

? About how much shelf space will be left over?

Sukan's Animals

I can **round** to **estimate** the length of each animal.
53 cm is about 50 cm.
28 cm is about 30 cm.
Then I can add the rounded numbers to estimate the total length.

A. Estimate the total length of the hare and the rat.

B. Estimate the length of all 3 animals lined up. Explain how you estimated.

C. About how much shelf space will be left over after the 3 animals are lined up?

Reflecting

1. a) Why might someone round to estimate the total length as 50 cm + 30 cm + 10 cm?
   b) What is another way to estimate the total length?
   c) Which way of estimating is better? Explain why.
2. Why do you think Sukan estimated instead of finding an exact answer?

Checking

3. Estimate the total length of an armadillo and a fox. Explain how you estimated.
4. Sukan put the otter at one end of the 100 cm shelf. About how much space is left over? Explain.

armadillo: 39 cm

Practising

5. Estimate the total length of these animals.
   a) a hare (53 cm) and an armadillo
   b) a fox and a rat (28 cm)
6. Sukan put an armadillo on the 100 cm shelf. About how much space is left over? Explain how you estimated.

fox: 56 cm

7. Estimate. Show your work.
   a) 33 + 18
   b) 59 − 37
   c) 24 + 19 + 33
   d) 41 − 18
   e) 18 + 18 + 12
   f) 76 − 57
8. Which animal would leave more space on the shelf: a chick or an armadillo? About how much more space would it leave?
9. a) Show 2 ways to estimate 45 + 39.
   b) Which estimate is closer to the sum? How do you know without adding?

otter: 74 cm

CHAPTER 4

7 Adding 2-Digit Numbers

You will need

- play coins

Goal **Add 2-digit numbers with and without regrouping.**

Penny Sale

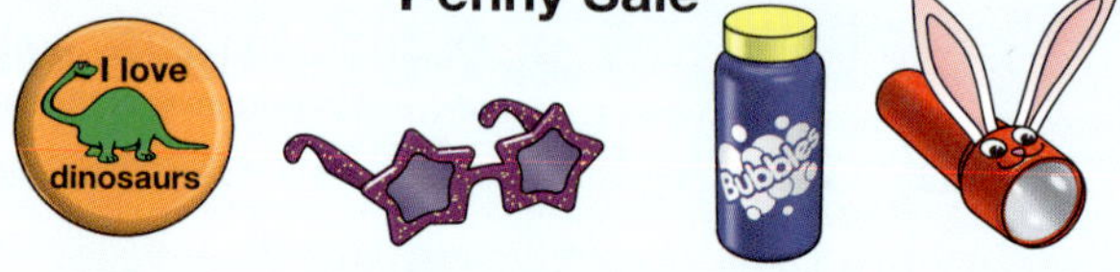

48¢ 56¢ 62¢ 79¢

Lyn has $1.00 to buy 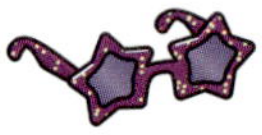

and 

at the Penny Sale.

? Does Lyn have enough money?

Lyn's Addition

Step 1 I showed 56 and 48 using dimes and pennies.

$$\begin{array}{r} 56 \\ +\ 48 \\ \hline \end{array}$$

Step 2 I added the pennies. I regrouped 14 pennies as 1 dime 4 pennies.

$$\begin{array}{r} ^{1}\\ 56 \\ +\ 48 \\ \hline 4 \end{array}$$

Step 3 I added the dimes.

$$\begin{array}{r} ^{1}\\ 56 \\ +\ 48 \\ \hline 104 \end{array}$$

 or 

My 2 items cost 104¢, or $1.04. I have only $1.00, so I don't have enough money.

Amit's Addition

Step 1 I wrote the addition.

$$\begin{array}{r} 56 \\ +\ 48 \\ \hline \end{array}$$

Step 2 I added the tens.

$$\begin{array}{r} 56 \\ +\ 48 \\ \hline 90 \end{array}$$

Step 3 I added the ones and calculated the total.

$$\begin{array}{r} 56 \\ +\ 48 \\ \hline 90 \\ +\ 14 \\ \hline 104 \end{array}$$

Lyn's 2 items cost 104¢, or $1.04. She has only $1.00, so she doesn't have enough money.

Reflecting

1. a) Why did Lyn regroup the 14 pennies as 1 dime 4 pennies in Step 2? Explain.
   b) Explain how Lyn writes the regrouping.
2. How is Amit's way like Lyn's? How is it different?
3. Explain how Amit can estimate to check the sum.

Checking

4. Calculate the total cost. Show your work.

a) 

48¢ and 
62¢

b) 
56¢ and 
79¢

5. Calculate each sum.

a) 37 + 68 = ■ b) 42 + 59 = ■ c) 85 + 65 = ■

Practising

6. Calculate the total cost of  and .

7. Estimate. Then calculate. Use estimates to check.

a) $\begin{array}{r} 27 \\ +\ 42 \\ \hline \end{array}$ b) $\begin{array}{r} 54 \\ +\ 38 \\ \hline \end{array}$ c) $\begin{array}{r} 46 \\ +\ 49 \\ \hline \end{array}$ d) $\begin{array}{r} 73 \\ +\ 78 \\ \hline \end{array}$

8. Which sums are between 150 and 170? Explain how you know.

A. $\begin{array}{r} 49 \\ +\ 99 \\ \hline \end{array}$ B. $\begin{array}{r} 68 \\ +\ 86 \\ \hline \end{array}$ C. $\begin{array}{r} 94 \\ +\ 67 \\ \hline \end{array}$ D. $\begin{array}{r} 81 \\ +\ 93 \\ \hline \end{array}$

9. Amit bought 2 different items at the Penny Sale. Did he spend 72¢, 125¢, or 141¢? How do you know?

10. Create an addition problem about a Penny Sale. Solve your problem.

8 Subtracting 2-Digit Numbers

You will need

- base ten blocks

Goal **Subtract 2-digit numbers with and without regrouping.**

Ben and Brady are comparing basketball scores for the Sharks and the Jets.

Basketball Scores

Game	Sharks	Jets
1	82	64
2	68	46
3	72	56

? How many more points did the Sharks have than the Jets in game 1?

Ben's Block Model

I can match 64 with 82.
The leftover will represent the Sharks' extra points in game 1.

Step 1

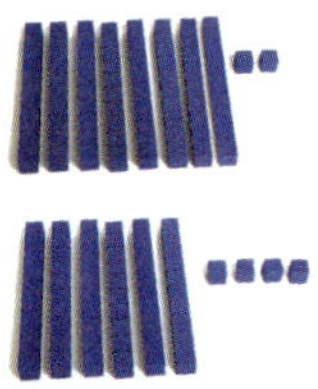

Step 2 I can't match 4 ones with 2 ones, so I regroup 1 ten as 10 ones.

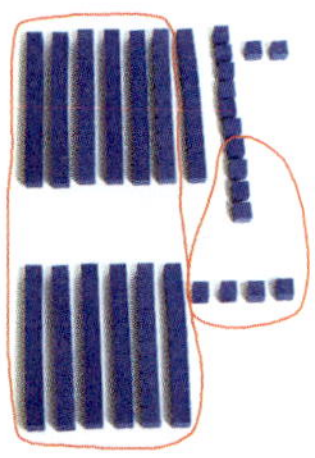

1 ten 8 ones are left over.

The Sharks scored 18 more points than the Jets in game 1.

Brady's Subtraction

I can figure out the difference by subtracting.

Step 1 I can't subtract 4 ones from 2 ones, so I regroup 82 as 7 tens 12 ones.
I subtract 4 ones from 12 ones.

$$\begin{array}{r} 82 \\ -\,64 \\ \hline \end{array} \qquad \begin{array}{r} {\scriptstyle 7\ 12} \\ \not{8}\not{2} \\ -\,64 \\ \hline 8 \end{array}$$

Step 2 I subtract 6 tens from 7 tens.

$$\begin{array}{r} {\scriptstyle 7\ 12} \\ \not{8}\not{2} \\ -\,64 \\ \hline 18 \end{array}$$

The Sharks scored 18 more points than the Jets in game 1.

Reflecting

1. Look back at the numbers Ben and Brady compared: 64 and 82. Are their answers reasonable? Explain how you know.
2. Why is the 82 crossed out in Brady's work?
3. In game 2, the Sharks scored 68 points and the Jets scored 46 points. Would you need to regroup to find the difference? Why or why not?

Checking

4. Subtract to compare the scores in game 2.
5. Calculate each difference. Add to check.
   a) 76 − 49 = ■ b) 87 − 34 = ■ c) 40 − 28 = ■

Practising

6. In game 3, the Sharks scored 72 points and the Jets scored 56 points. Subtract to compare the scores.
7. Estimate. Then calculate. Use estimates to check.
   a) $\begin{array}{r} 27 \\ -\ 16 \\ \hline \end{array}$ b) $\begin{array}{r} 90 \\ -\ 65 \\ \hline \end{array}$ c) $\begin{array}{r} 51 \\ -\ 22 \\ \hline \end{array}$ d) $\begin{array}{r} 63 \\ -\ 34 \\ \hline \end{array}$
8. One team has 48 points and another has 92 points. How many more points does the winning team have?
9. In games 4 and 5, the Sharks scored 36 points and 42 points. The Jets scored 85 points altogether.
   a) Which team scored more points in the 2 games? How do you know?
   b) Could the Jets have won both games? Show your work.
10. Create a subtraction problem about 47 points and 71 points. Solve your problem.

Finding 10s

When adding or subtracting, you can look for pairs or groups of numbers that are easy to add or subtract.

8 + 7 + 2 + 6 + 3 − 8 − 2 = ■

10 (7 + 3)

8 + 7 + 2 + 6 + 3 − 8 − 2 = ■

10 (8 + 2)   10 (8 + 2)

A. What is the total?

B. How was finding 10s helpful?

Try These

1. Complete each calculation. Look for pairs or groups of numbers that are easy to add or subtract.
   - **a)** 5 + 7 + 5 = ■
   - **b)** 9 + 4 + 6 + 1 = ■
   - **c)** 1 + 2 + 9 + 8 + 5 = ■
   - **d)** 7 + 8 + 2 + 3 + 6 + 4 = ■
   - **e)** 5 + 1 + 9 + 8 + 2 + 6 + 4 + 5 = ■
   - **f)** 14 + 8 + 2 − 4 = ■
   - **g)** 13 + 12 + 7 + 8 + 1 = ■
   - **h)** 4 + 6 + 8 + 2 + 4 − 7 − 3 − 4 = ■

2. What is the sum of the numbers on the dial? Look for 10s.

Skills Bank

LESSON

1 **1.** Complete each addition sentence.

a) 8 + ■ = 15 c) ■ + 7 = 16 e) 7 + ■ = 11 g) ■ + 9 = 15

b) 6 + ■ = 13 d) ■ + 6 = 12 f) 8 + ■ = 14 h) ■ + 8 = 17

2. Write a subtraction sentence in the same fact family.

a) 5 + 7 = 12 c) ■ + 7 = 14 e) 9 + 4 = 13 g) 4 + ■ = 12

b) 8 + 9 = 17 d) 6 + ■ = 15 f) 8 + 8 = 16 h) ■ + 3 = 11

2 **3.** Add or subtract.

a) 9 + 6 = ■ b) 6 + 8 = ■ c) 14 − 5 = ■ d) 18 − 9 = ■

3 **4.** Calculate each sum.

a) $\begin{array}{r} 40 \\ +\ 60 \\ \hline \end{array}$ c) $\begin{array}{r} 90 \\ +\ 60 \\ \hline \end{array}$ e) $\begin{array}{r} 80 \\ +\ 30 \\ \hline \end{array}$ g) $\begin{array}{r} 20 \\ +\ 90 \\ \hline \end{array}$

b) $\begin{array}{r} 80 \\ +\ 40 \\ \hline \end{array}$ d) $\begin{array}{r} 80 \\ +\ 50 \\ \hline \end{array}$ f) $\begin{array}{r} 60 \\ +\ 70 \\ \hline \end{array}$ h) $\begin{array}{r} 70 \\ +\ 80 \\ \hline \end{array}$

5. Calculate each difference.

a) $\begin{array}{r} 110 \\ -\ 30 \\ \hline \end{array}$ c) $\begin{array}{r} 90 \\ -\ 50 \\ \hline \end{array}$ e) $\begin{array}{r} 170 \\ -\ 90 \\ \hline \end{array}$ g) $\begin{array}{r} 130 \\ -\ 40 \\ \hline \end{array}$

b) $\begin{array}{r} 160 \\ -\ 70 \\ \hline \end{array}$ d) $\begin{array}{r} 130 \\ -\ 70 \\ \hline \end{array}$ f) $\begin{array}{r} 150 \\ -\ 60 \\ \hline \end{array}$

6. Gabe has 120 coins in his collection.
Lyn has 70 coins in her collection.
How many more coins does Gabe have than Lyn?

4 **7.** Add or subtract. Use mental math.

a) 32 + 7 = ■ c) 43 + 9 = ■ e) 46 − 7 = ■ g) 92 − 8 = ■

b) 72 + 8 = ■ d) 82 + 8 = ■ f) 61 − 9 = ■ h) 81 − 7 = ■

6 **8.** Estimate each sum or difference. Show your work.

a) 37 + 48 b) 56 + 32 c) 87 − 39 d) 95 − 73

6 **9.** Solve each problem. Show your work.

a) Estimate the total length of an otter and a rat lined up on a shelf.

b) Suppose you put the rat by itself at one end of a 75 cm long shelf. About how much space is left over?

otter: 74 cm

rat: 28 cm

7 **10.** Calculate each sum.

a) 43 + 21	c) 68 + 77	e) 75 + 68	g) 85 + 76
b) 67 + 33	d) 38 + 89	f) 54 + 57	h) 92 + 99

11. Solve each problem. Show your work.

a) Stuffed animals cost 85¢ at the Penny Sale. How much does it cost to buy 2 stuffed animals?

b) Surprise bags cost 98¢ at the Penny Sale. How much does it cost to buy 1 surprise bag and 1 stuffed animal?

8 **12.** Calculate each difference.

a) 79 − 25	c) 82 − 21	e) 63 − 49	g) 80 − 26
b) 39 − 18	d) 48 − 27	f) 95 − 37	h) 61 − 57

13. Solve each problem. Add to check. Show your work.

a) Team A had 89 points. Team B had 71 points. How many more points did Team A have than Team B?

b) Team C had 93 points. Team D had 79 points. How many more points did Team C have than Team D?

LESSON

Problem Bank

2 **1.** Andrea made 1 yellow, 2 purple, 3 black, 4 silver, 5 blue, 6 pink, 7 gold, 8 red, 9 orange, and 10 green bows.

a) Describe the pattern for the number of bows.

b) How can you calculate the number of bows Andrea made?

c) How many bows did Andrea make?

3 **2.** Andrea has 10 yellow, 20 purple, 30 black, 40 silver, 50 blue, 60 pink, 70 gold, 80 red, 90 orange, and 100 green rolls of ribbon.

a) Describe the pattern.

b) How can you calculate the number of rolls of ribbon Andrea has?

c) How many rolls of ribbon does Andrea have?

6 **3. a)** Complete the sentence.
■5 + ■4 − ■6 is about 60.

b) Find 2 other ways to complete the sentence.
Explain one of your answers.

8 **4.** The sum of the 3 shaded numbers is 87.

a) Find 3 numbers in an L shape with a sum between 40 and 60.

b) Find at least one more answer for part a).

c) Create your own addition or subtraction problem using the numbers in the chart.

1	2	3	4	5	6	7	8	9	10
11	12	13	14	15	16	17	18	19	20
21	22	23	24	25	26	27	28	29	30
31	32	33	34	35	36	37	38	39	40
41	42	43	44	45	46	47	48	49	50
51	52	53	54	55	56	57	58	59	60
61	62	63	64	65	66	67	68	69	70
71	72	73	74	75	76	77	78	79	80
81	82	83	84	85	86	87	88	89	90
91	92	93	94	95	96	97	98	99	100

5. Complete the calculations.
Use each digit from 0 to 7 only once.

16	■2	■5	81	6■
+ 16	− 36	+ 29	− ■■	+ 17
3■	16	9■	64	8■

LESSON

Chapter Review

1 **1.** Bryn has 17 pencil crayons altogether.
Some are on the floor and 8 are on her desk.
   a) How many are on the floor?
   b) Write the fact family for Bryn's pencils.

2. Complete each number sentence.
   a) 9 + ■ = 16   **b)** 16 − 9 = ■   **c)** 7 + ■ = 14   **d)** 14 − 7 = ■

2 **3.** Why is it easy to add 0? Give 2 examples.

4. Why is it easy to add or subtract 1?
Give an addition and a subtraction example.

3 **5.** Add or subtract.

a)	b)	c)	d)
60	70	130	180
+ 60	+ 50	− 70	− 90

4 **6.** Use mental math to calculate 73 − 8. Describe 2 ways.

7. Use mental math.
   a) Ian's marker is on 28.
   His card says "Move back 8."
   What number will Ian land on?
   b) Mary's marker is on 37.
   Her card says "Move forward 9."
   What number will Mary land on?
   c) Kyle's marker is on 36.
   He moved back 8.
   Lee moved forward 9 and landed
   on the same spot as Kyle.
   Where did Lee start?

5 **8.** Kara takes 1 step forward, then 2 steps backward.
She repeats this again and again. She takes 20 steps altogether.
How many steps is she from where she started?
Show your work.

6 **9.** Which 2 answers are closest to 40?
Estimate, then check. Show your work.

A. 37 + 19 **B.** 52 − 9 **C.** 65 − 26 **D.** 28 + 18

10. Estimate each sum or difference. Show your work.

a) 57 + 35 **c)** 42 + 29 **e)** 68 − 29 **g)** 41 − 29
b) 23 + 65 **d)** 94 + 36 **f)** 92 − 68 **h)** 54 − 25

7 **11.** Use the digits 2, 5, and 7 to complete this addition.

$$\begin{array}{r} 5\blacksquare \\ +\ \blacksquare 5 \\ \hline 11\blacksquare \end{array}$$

12. Create an addition problem with 83 and 49.
Solve your problem.

8 **13.** Calculate. Then add or subtract to check.

a) 80 + 40 = ■ **c)** 54 + 98 = ■ **e)** 150 − 60 = ■ **g)** 90 − 18 = ■
b) 63 + 26 = ■ **d)** 23 + 47 = ■ **f)** 76 − 46 = ■ **h)** 94 − 25 = ■

14. When Lia's dog was a puppy, it was 27 cm tall.
Lia's dog is 60 cm tall.
How many centimetres did her dog grow?

15. Halley sold 45 cartons of milk on Tuesday and 37 cartons of milk on Wednesday.

a) How many cartons of milk did he sell altogether?
b) How many more cartons did he sell on Tuesday than on Wednesday?

16. Complete this subtraction in 4 ways.

$$\begin{array}{r} 5\blacksquare \\ -\ 3\blacksquare \\ \hline \end{array}$$

17. Create a subtraction problem with 58 and 92.
Solve your problem.

18. You can get 70 by adding 35 + 35.
Show 70 in 4 other ways.
Use addition and subtraction.

Chapter Task

Swimming Schedules

Sonia and Malcolm signed up for a swim-a-thon.
Each person must swim some lengths each day for 7 days.
Sonia says she will swim 70 lengths altogether.
Malcolm says he will swim 50 lengths altogether.

? How many lengths could Sonia and Malcolm swim each day?

A. Find one way to complete Sonia's schedule. Check that the total is correct.

Sonia's Lengths Each Day

Sun.	Mon.	Tues.	Wed.	Thurs.	Fri.	Sat.
5	7		9			

B. Create a schedule for Malcolm. Explain how you chose the numbers.

C. Who swam more lengths by the end of Wednesday: Sonia or Malcolm? How many more lengths? Show your steps.

Task Checklist

- ✓ Do your numbers give the correct total?
- ✓ Did you explain your thinking?
- ✓ Did you use math language?

CHAPTER 5

Measuring Length, Time, and Temperature

Goals

You will be able to

- estimate, measure, and compare lengths in centimetres, metres, and decimetres
- explain how long a kilometre is
- choose the best unit to measure length
- estimate, measure, and compare perimeters
- tell time, and estimate and measure lengths of time
- solve problems using charts
- estimate and read temperature

Landing the long jump

Getting Started

Measuring Optical Illusions

Drawings that play tricks with our eyes are called optical illusions.

? Which is greater: the height of the hat or the length of its brim?

A. Compare the hat height and the brim length just by looking. Which looks greater?

B. Choose a small object that you can use to measure the hat. What unit did you choose? Why?

C. Measure the hat height and the brim length with your unit. Which measure is greater? Is this what you predicted?

You will need

- small objects such as linking cubes or paper clips

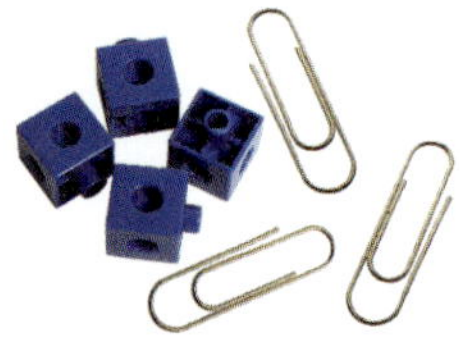

- a 30 cm ruler

D. Compare the red and blue lines in each drawing.
Which line do you think is longer: red or blue?
Check by measuring the lines with a ruler.

a)

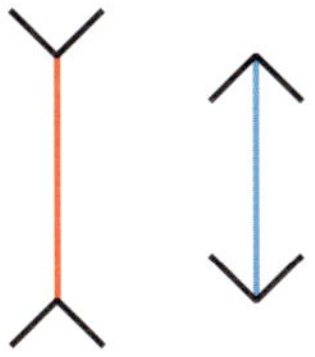

b)

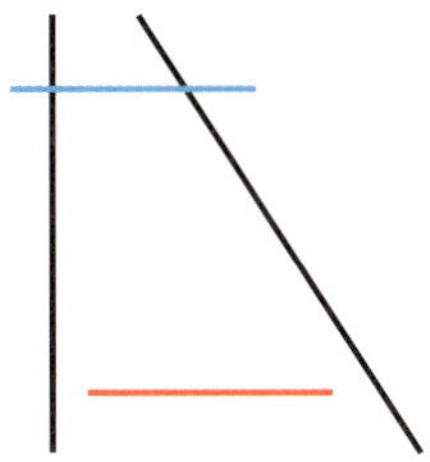

c)

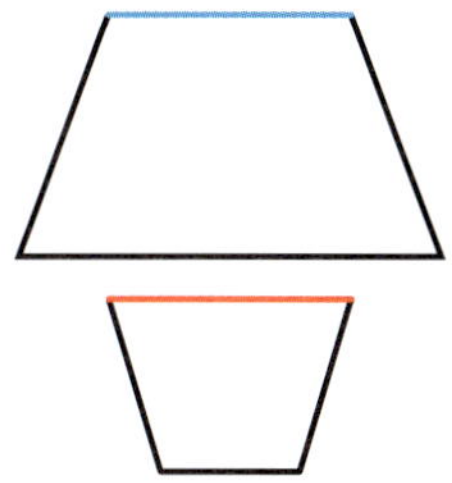

Do You Remember?

1. Which would you use to measure each object: centimetres or metres?

- **a)** the length of an eraser
- **b)** the length of a snowmobile
- **c)** the height of a building
- **d)** the width of your classroom

2. Sukan read the temperature outside on Monday.
She read the temperature again 3 days later.

- **a)** What day did she read the 2nd temperature?
- **b)** Did the temperature outside rise or fall? How do you know?

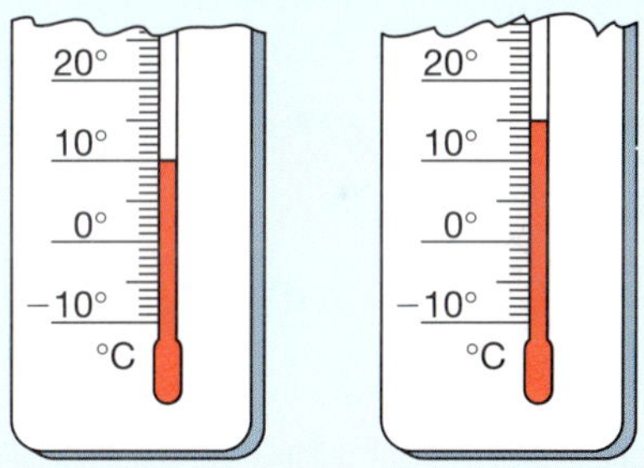

Monday **3 days later**

3. Name each month.

- **a)** the month after January
- **b)** the month before May
- **c)** the month between August and October

4. Measure the distance around the outside of each shape.
Use your fingertip.
Which shape has a greater distance around it?

CHAPTER 5

1 Measuring in Centimetres

Goal **Estimate, measure, and compare lengths in centimetres.**

You will need

- a ruler

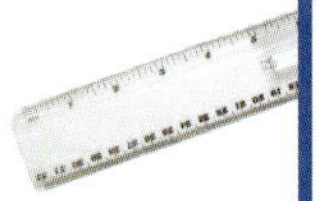

- objects (about 30 cm long) to measure

Rachel has found a poster that she wants to buy.
It is 30 **cm (centimetres)** wide.
She needs to know if the poster will fit in a space on her wall, but she doesn't have a ruler.

? What could Rachel use to find out if the poster will fit on her wall?

Rachel's Estimation Plan

I think my fingertip is about 1 cm wide.

I think my hand is about 10 cm wide.

I can use my hand and fingers to find an object that is about 30 cm long.

centimetre (cm)
A unit of measurement for length

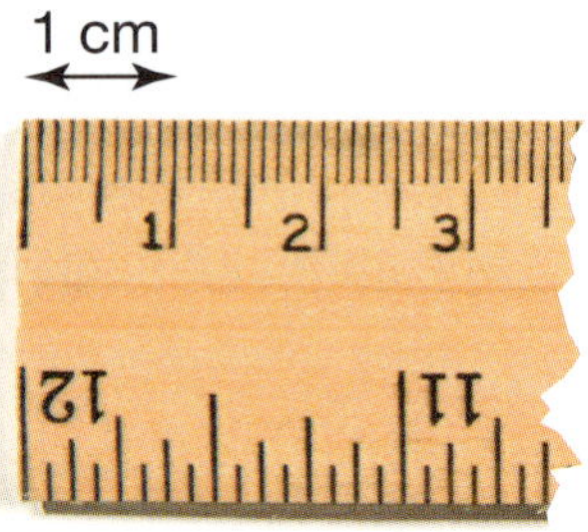

A. Look for 5 objects that you think are about 30 cm. Use your fingers or hands to estimate each length or height. Record each estimate in a chart.

Object	Estimated length or height	Measured length or height (to nearest centimetre)
stuffed rabbit	30 cm	

B. Use a ruler to measure each length you estimated. Remember to line up 0 cm on the ruler with one end of an object.
Record the measurements in your chart.

C. Order the objects from least to greatest length or height.

D. Which of the objects that you measured could be used to find out if the poster will fit? Explain.

Reflecting

1. Is using your finger or hand a good way to estimate lengths in centimetres? Explain.
2. When you were looking for 30 cm lengths, did you use your finger or your hand? Why?
3. Some of the lengths you measured were between 2 of the centimetre marks on your ruler.
   How did you decide what the measurement was?

4. Sometimes you need an estimate.
   Sometimes you need an exact measurement.
   Describe a situation where you might estimate a length instead of measuring it exactly.

2 Measuring in Metres and Centimetres

Goal **Estimate, measure, and compare lengths in metres and centimetres.**

Lee told his friends about a new playground.

He says that the bridge between the climber and the slide is about 2 giant steps long.

You will need

- objects from Lesson 1
- yarn

- scissors

- a metre stick

? About how long is your giant step?

A. Take 2 giant steps. Cut a piece of yarn that goes from where you started to where you stopped.

B. Choose an object you measured in centimetres. Estimate how many of this object it will take to match the length of your yarn. Record your estimate.

C. Measure the length of the yarn using the object. Record your measurement.

D. Is the yarn longer or shorter than a **metre (m)**? Compare with a metre stick.

E. Is the length of your yarn closest to 1 m, 2 m, or 3 m? Explain your answer.

F. Would 1 giant step be a good way to estimate 1 m? Explain your answer.

G. Measure the yarn again, but this time use metres and centimetres. Measure the whole metres first.

H. Find 3 distances in your classroom that are longer than your giant step. Estimate and measure each distance. Record your work in a chart.

Distance	Estimated distance	Measured distance (to nearest metre)	Measured distance (metres and centimetres)
my desk to the door	3 m	4 m	3 m 63 cm

metre (m)

A unit of measurement for length

1 m = 100 cm

Reflecting

1. Are all giant steps about the same length? Explain why your answer makes sense.
2. Which of the distances that you measured in part H was longest? Explain how you know.
3. Would a metre stick be good for measuring if it didn't have centimetre marks on it? Explain.
4. Would it be easy or difficult to measure your yarn in metres and centimetres using a 30 cm ruler? Why?

3 Measuring in Decimetres

Goal **Estimate, measure, and compare lengths in decimetres.**

You will need

- base ten blocks

- yarn

- scissors

- a measuring tape

Devon's class made papier mâché spiders. The students will hang their spiders from the ceiling with yarn.

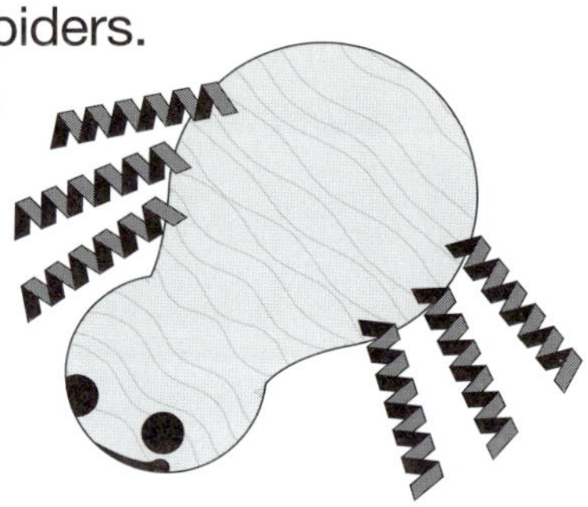

Devon will use **decimetres** and centimetres to measure. He wants his yarn to be 8 **dm** 5 cm long.

decimetre (dm)

A unit of measurement for length

1 dm = 10 cm

1 m = 10 dm

? How can Devon measure his yarn?

Devon's Measurement Plan

I can line up base ten blocks to measure.

I know that a rod is 1 dm long, and a cube is 1 cm long.

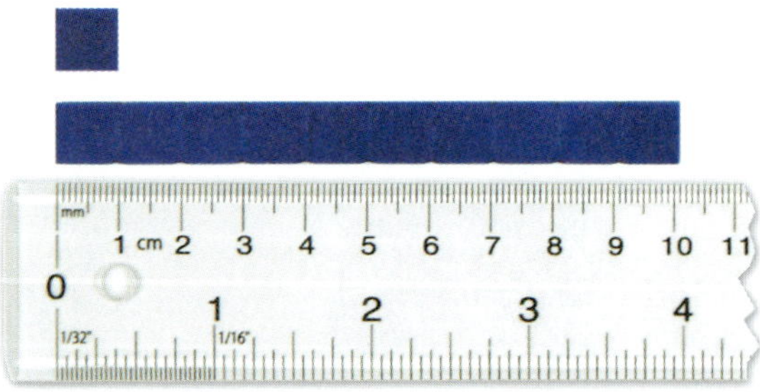

A. Use Devon's method to cut a piece of yarn 8 dm 5 cm long.

B. Devon could use 4 rods and 45 cubes to show 8 dm 5 cm. Show 3 different ways to use rods and cubes to show the length of Devon's yarn. Record each way in a chart as rods and cubes and also as decimetres and centimetres.

Devon's yarn 8 dm 5 cm long

Base ten blocks (rods and cubes)	Length (decimetres and centimetres)
8 rods 5 cubes	8 dm 5 cm

C. Nisha wants a piece of yarn 1 m long for her spider. Repeat parts A and B for Nisha's yarn.

D. Who has a shorter piece of yarn: Devon or Nisha? How do you know?

E. Without measuring, cut a piece of yarn the length you would use to hang a spider. Estimate its length to the nearest decimetre. Measure with a measuring tape.

Reflecting

1. Explain how to use the ruler to measure the length of each piece of yarn to the nearest decimetre.
   a) purple **b)** yellow **c)** red

2. **a)** When could you measure in decimetres? Why?
   b) When would it make sense to measure in centimetres? Why?

Checking

3. **a)** Estimate a height to the nearest decimetre.
   b) Measure the height in decimetres and centimetres.

4. Which is closer to 5 dm? How do you know?
   A. 5 dm 9 cm **B.** 4 dm 5 cm

Practising

5. **a)** Draw a line that you estimate is close to 2 dm long.
   b) Measure the line. Is it close to 2 dm? Explain.

6. Which lengths are longer than 1 dm? How do you know?
   A. 14 cm **B.** 6 cm **C.** 10 cm **D.** 25 cm

7. Which lengths are between 8 dm and 1 m? How do you know?
   A. 103 cm **B.** 8 dm 1 cm **C.** 98 cm **D.** 1 m 2 cm

8. **a)** Find 3 distances in your classroom that you estimate are between 5 dm and 10 dm.
   b) Predict the order of the distances from longest to shortest.
   c) Measure to check.

4 Comparing Lengths to a Kilometre

You will need

- a metre stick

- a calculator

Goal Explain how long a kilometre is.

Rose will raise $1.00 for each **kilometre (km)** she walks in a charity event. She's not sure how long a kilometre is.

? About how long is 1 km?

Rose's Solution

I know that my giant step is about 1 m.

1 km is 1000 m. That's about 1000 giant steps.

I will use a school bus to help me imagine 1 km.

I can go from the front of my school bus to the back in 10 giant steps.

I can skip count with a calculator to find out how many buses I could walk past with 1000 giant steps.

0 [+] 10 [=] [=] [=] [=]

I had to press [=] 100 times to get to 1000.

I would walk past 100 school buses to go 1 km!

kilometre (km)
A unit of measurement for length
1 km = 1000 m

A. Check to make sure your giant step is 1 m. Use a metre stick.

B. Measure the length of your classroom in giant steps. Skip count with a calculator to figure out the number of times you could cross your classroom if you took 1000 giant steps.

C. Choose another distance to measure with giant steps. How many times would you need to walk this distance to go 1 km? Skip count with a calculator.

Reflecting

1. If you lined up 100 bicycles, would the distance be greater than 1 km, less than 1 km, or about 1 km? Explain your thinking.
2. How many kilometres do you think you could walk in the charity event? Explain your thinking.
3. Kilometres are used to measure the distance between cities. Explain why this makes sense.

Checking

4. If you lined up each item, would the distance be greater than 1 km, less than 1 km, or about 1 km? Explain.
   a) 1000 schools
   b) 1000 metre sticks
   c) 1000 cars
   d) 10 school buses
   e) 100 shoes
   f) 1000 hockey sticks

5. Look at the distances in Question 4. Which is longest? Which is shortest? Explain how you decided.

Practising

6. If you lined up each item, would the distance be greater than 1 km, less than 1 km, or about 1 km? Explain.
   a) 100 chairs
   b) 100 metre sticks
   c) 1000 elephants
   d) 1000 bicycles
   e) 100 paper clips
   f) 1000 children holding hands

7. Look at the distances in Question 6. Which is longest? Which is shortest? Explain how you decided.

8. Name a place that you estimate is about 1 km from your school. Explain how you estimated.

5 Choosing an Appropriate Unit

Goal **Choose centimetres, metres, or kilometres to measure lengths, and order lengths with different units.**

Gabe is looking up world records for a class trivia game.

When he wrote these records, he forgot to write the units.

? What are the missing units?

	Measurement
longest beetle	18 ■
distance the fastest insect can fly in 1 hour	32 ■
tallest flagpole	160 ■
longest swimming pool	480 ■
tallest living tree	112 ■

Gabe's Measurements

The measurements are all lengths, so they could be in centimetres, metres, or kilometres.

Beetles are small. They would be measured in centimetres. I think the world's longest beetle must be 18 cm long.

I'll write the symbol for centimetres, cm, next to 18 in the chart.

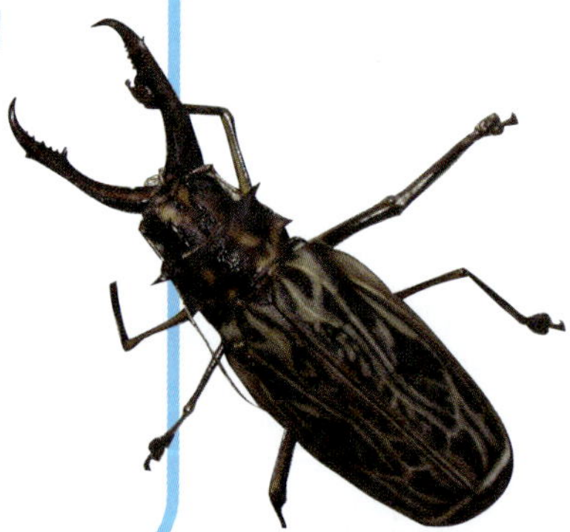

Amazonian giant beetle

A. Complete Gabe's table with the most appropriate unit for each length.

B. Explain how you chose each unit.

C. Order the lengths from least to greatest. Which measurement will you start with? Why?

D. Explain your steps for ordering the measurements.

Reflecting

1. Which row on Gabe's table was the most difficult for you to complete? Why?
2. How do you know whether to use metres or kilometres for long lengths?
3. How do you know whether to use centimetres or metres for short lengths?

Checking

4. Sophie has more measurements to add to the trivia game.
   a) Complete Sophie's table with the most appropriate unit for each length.
   b) Order the lengths from least to greatest.

	Measurement
longest snake	10 ■
longest butterfly wingspan	30 ■
height of Niagara Falls	48 ■
largest wingspan of a bird	4 ■
length of Lake Ontario	311 ■

Practising

5. Complete each statement using centimetres, metres, or kilometres. Explain your choice.
   a) Kieran's dog is about 55 ■ long.
   b) Kieran and his dog walk about 2 ■ each day.
   c) The leash is about 1 ■ long.

6. Which would you use to measure each distance: centimetres, metres, or kilometres? Explain your choice.
   a) the length of a truck
   b) the height of a bicycle
   c) the distance across an ocean
   d) the length of a hamster
7. Name an object that might have each length.
   a) 2 km
   b) 2 cm
   c) 2 m
8. Name 2 things you would measure using each unit. Choose things that are not in this lesson.
   a) centimetres
   b) metres
   c) kilometres

6 Measuring Perimeter

Goal **Estimate, measure, and compare perimeters.**

You will need

- square tiles

- a ruler

Keisha will sew 16 squares together to make a rectangular quilt. She will add a trim that costs a lot.

Keisha wants the quilt to have the least **perimeter** possible. She needs to arrange the quilt squares to use the shortest length of ruffle.

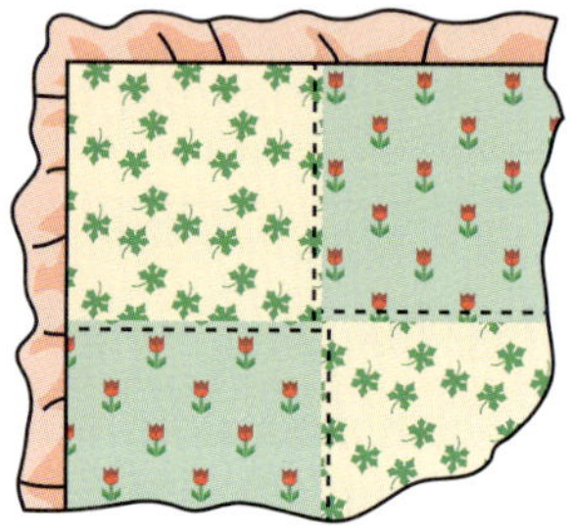

perimeter
The distance around the outside of a shape

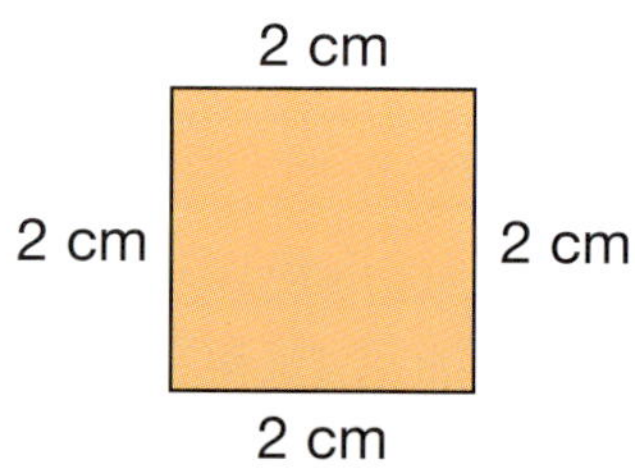

This square has a perimeter of 8 cm.
$2 + 2 + 2 + 2 = 8$

? What rectangle of quilt squares will have the least perimeter?

Keisha's Rectangles

I need to find the rectangle with the least perimeter.

I'll use tiles to model the quilt.

A. Arrange 16 tiles to make a rectangle. Trace the outside of your rectangle on paper.

B. Use your 10 cm hand measure to estimate the perimeter of your rectangle. Measure the perimeter with a ruler and record the length.

C. Rearrange the 16 tiles to make 2 more rectangles. Trace each rectangle. Estimate, measure, and record the perimeter of each rectangle.

D. Order the perimeters from least to greatest.

Reflecting

1. Explain how you measured the perimeter of one of your rectangles.
2. What are the side lengths of the rectangle with the least perimeter? What shape should the quilt be?

Checking

3. Calculate the perimeter of this frame.

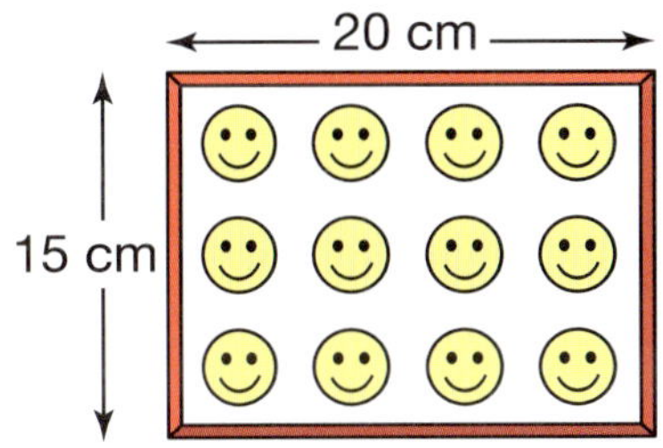

4. a) Make a rectangle with 8 square tiles. Trace the rectangle. Measure the perimeter.
   b) Make a different rectangle with 8 square tiles. Trace the rectangle. Estimate the perimeter. Measure to check.

Practising

5. Calculate each perimeter. Show your work.
   a) a tennis court

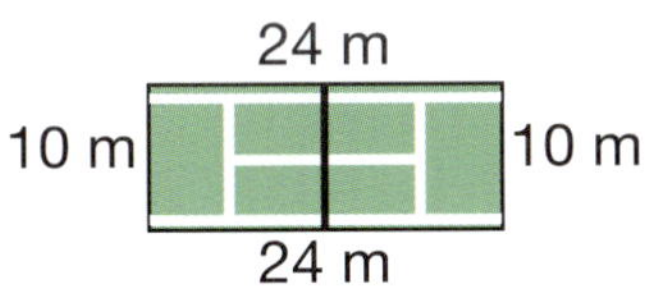

   b) the head of a drum

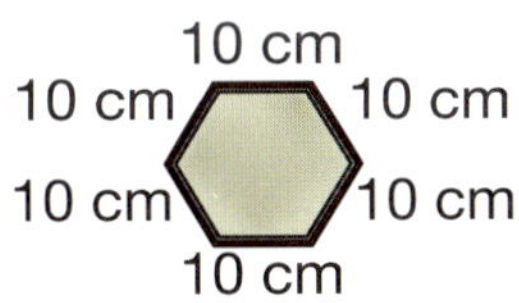

6. What is the perimeter of the park?

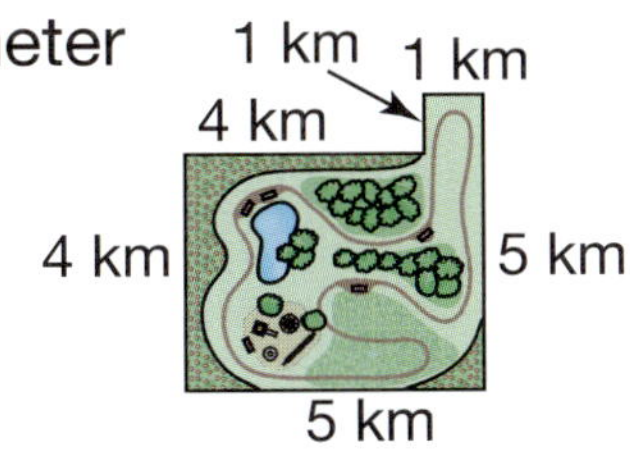

7. Choose 3 objects with perimeters you can measure.
   a) Predict the order of the objects from greatest to least perimeter.
   b) Choose one object. Estimate the perimeter. Measure the side lengths. Calculate the perimeter.
   c) Repeat part b) for the other objects.
   d) Check your prediction from part a).

LESSON

Mid-Chapter Review

1 **1.** Estimate the length of each picture in centimetres. Measure the length of each picture to the nearest centimetre.

a) a paper clip **b)** an eraser **c)** a pencil sharpener

2 **2.** Estimate each length. Is it less than 1 m, about 1 m, or greater than 1 m?

a) the length of a paper airplane
b) the distance a paper airplane flies
c) your height
d) the height of your desk

3 **3.** Choose 2 objects. Estimate each length in decimetres. Measure each length to the nearest decimetre. Which is longer?

4 **4.** Name 3 objects or distances for each measurement.

a) about 1 cm **b)** about 1 m **c)** about 1 km

5 **5.** What would you use to measure each distance: centimetres, metres, or kilometres?

a) the height of a house
b) the width of your finger
c) the length of a skipping rope
d) the length of a river

6 **6.** Emilie built toy fences around her animal figures.

a) Find the perimeter of each animal pen.
b) Order the perimeters from least to greatest.

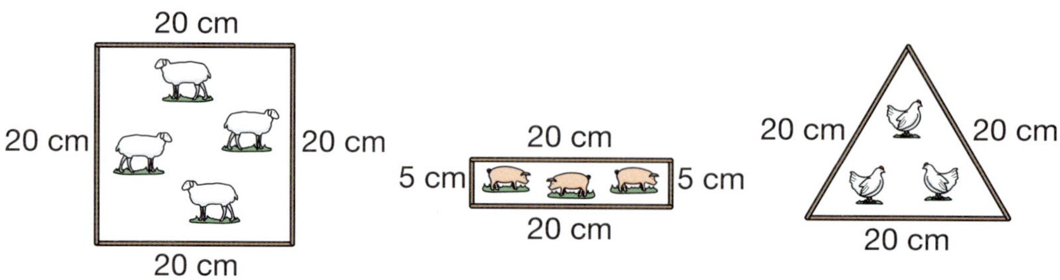

Comparing Body Lengths

You will need

- a ruler

- a metre stick

- a measuring tape

Which statements are true for you?
Check each distance by measuring.
Record your measurements on a labelled drawing.

1 My elbow is about halfway between my shoulder and my wrist.

5 My height is about the same as my arm span.

4 The distance from my wrist to my elbow is about the same as the length of my foot.

2 My knee is about halfway between my hip and my ankle.

3 My walking step is about the same length as my leg.

7 Telling Time

You will need

- a time line

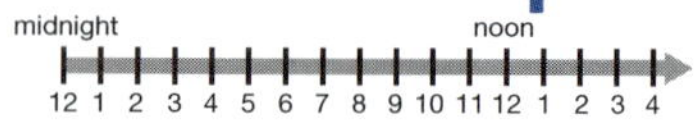

Goal Tell and write time.

Jack's alarm is set for 7:00 in the morning.
When he wakes up, the clock shows 6:53.

? Is it time for Jack to get up?

Jack's Clock

My clock shows the time with numbers.

The hour is on the left side.

The minutes after the hour are on the right side.

My clock shows 6:53, so it's 53 minutes after 6:00.

I can say six fifty-three.

There are 60 minutes in 1 hour.

The clock will read 6:54, 6:55, 6:56, 6:57, 6:58, and 6:59 before it reads 7:00.

I don't have to get up yet. I think I'll stay in bed!

Reflecting

1. Would a clock ever say 6:63? Explain.
2. a) A clock shows 6:53 twice between midnight on May 1 and midnight on May 2. Explain why.
   b) What might you be doing at each of these times?

Checking

3. Sharleen starts hockey practice at 9:00.
   a) Look at her watch. How can you say the time?
   b) What other times will the clock show before her practice starts?

Practising

4. Write each time the way it would look on Jack's clock.
   a) ten thirty-five
   b) twenty minutes after nine
   c) thirteen minutes after three
   d) six fifteen
   e) eight fifty-five
   f) twenty-two minutes past twelve

5. How would you say each time?

   a) 

   b) 

   c) 

6. Can you tell if the time on Sharleen's watch in Question 3 is in the morning or evening? Explain your thinking.

7. Write a time for each.
   a) wake-up time
   b) when school begins
   c) when lunch begins
   d) when lunch ends
   e) when school ends
   f) bedtime

8. Place each time from Question 7 on a time line.

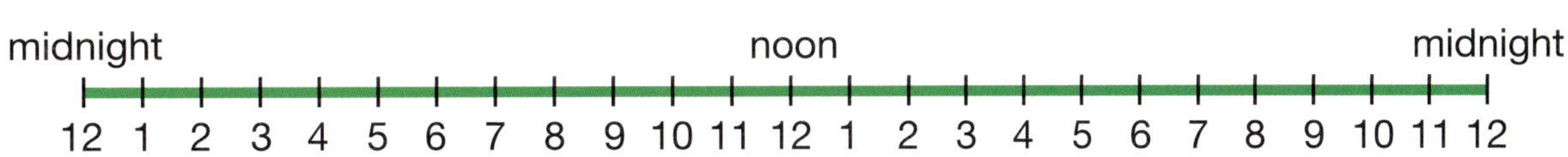

8 Measuring How Time Passes

Goal **Estimate and measure the passage of time in minutes.**

You will need

- schedules

Activity	Start time
drive to park	9:30
Elephant Roundup	10:45

Michael's family took a trip to the African Lion Safari. The trip schedule shows what they did at the park.

Our Trip Schedule

Activity	Start time	Finish time
drive to park	9:30	10:45
Elephant Roundup	10:45	11:15
Parrot Paradise	11:15	12:00
lunch	12:00	1:00
boat tour	1:00	
Misumu Bay		
drive home		

? How long did the trip take?

Michael's Schedule

To figure out how long something takes, I count the hours, then the minutes.

Yesterday morning, we left home at 9:30, and got to the park at 10:45.

9:30 to 10:30 is 1 hour.
10:30 to 10:45 is 15 more minutes.
So our drive took 1 hour 15 minutes.

A. How long did Michael's family spend doing each activity before lunch?

B. The boat tour was 40 minutes long. What time did it finish? Write this time on your schedule.

C. At the end of the boat tour, they went to Misumu Bay. Write the start time on your schedule. They left the park 1 hour 20 minutes later. Write the finish time for Misumu Bay on your schedule.

D. The drive home took the same length of time as the drive to the park. Write the start and finish times for the drive.

E. How much time did Michael's family spend on their trip?

Reflecting

1. If you know the start time is 2:45 and the activity will last 20 minutes, how can you figure out the finish time?
2. There are 60 seconds in 1 minute. You used hours and minutes to talk about Michael's schedule. Why didn't you use seconds?

Checking

3. Mandy works at the African Lion Safari.
   a) Mandy sold boat tickets for 1 hour 45 minutes. What time did she finish?
   b) How long did each of Mandy's first 3 activities take?
   c) How long did Mandy work that morning?

Mandy's Morning Schedule

Activity	Start	Finish
help feed animals	7:00	7:30
work at gate	7:30	10:00
break	10:00	10:15
sell boat tickets	10:15	

Practising

4. Amit is planning his Saturday morning.
   a) Complete his schedule with times that make sense.
   b) Figure out how long Amit's activities will take altogether.

Amit's Schedule

Activity	Start	Finish
eat breakfast	7:00	
play outside		
help with chores		
visit Rachel	11:00	

5. Decide which you would use for each: seconds, minutes, hours, or days. Then estimate the length of time for each.
   a) count to 10
   b) drink a glass of water
   c) watch a movie
   d) watch a television commercial

9 Solve Problems Using Charts

You will need

- a calculator

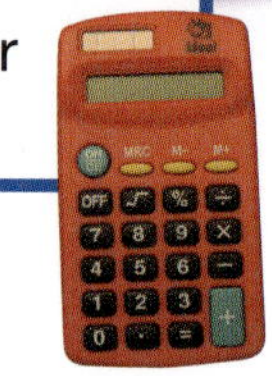

Goal Use a chart to solve problems.

? **How many days and weeks are there in a year?**

The Month Poem

Thirty days has September,
April, June, and November.
All the rest have thirty-one,
Saving February alone,
Having twenty-eight, rain or shine,
And in leap years, twenty-nine.

Lyn's Solution

Understand

This poem tells how many days are in each month.
I know that 7 days make 1 week.

Make a Plan

I can use a chart to list the number of days and weeks in each month.

Month	Days	Weeks + Days
January	31	4 weeks + 3 days
February	28	4 weeks
March	31	4 weeks + 3 days
April	30	4 weeks + 2 days
May	31	4 weeks + 3 days
June	30	4 weeks + 2 days
July	31	4 weeks + 3 days
August	31	4 weeks + 3 days
September	30	4 weeks + 2 days
October	31	4 weeks + 3 days
November	30	4 weeks + 2 days
December	31	4 weeks + 3 days
total	365	48 weeks + 29 days

Carry Out the Plan

Step 1 I took the number of days from the poem and put it in the Days column.

Step 2 I calculated the number of weeks in each month. I put the answer in my Weeks + Days column.

$$31 = \underbrace{7 + 7 + 7 + 7}_{4 \text{ weeks}} + 3$$

January has 4 weeks and 3 days.

Step 3 I used a calculator to find the total number of weeks and days. There are 365 days, or 48 weeks and 29 days, in a year.

29 days is the same as 4 weeks and 1 day.

$$29 = \underbrace{7 + 7 + 7 + 7}_{4\text{ weeks}} + 1$$

I'll add that to 48 weeks. $48 + 4 = 52$

There are 365 days, or 52 weeks and 1 day, in a year.

Reflecting

1. Explain how Lyn's chart helped her calculate the number of weeks in a year.
2. If the year is a leap year, how does Lyn's answer change?

Checking

3. Lyn turned 9 on Jan. 1. Use her chart to write her age on the next June 5 in 3 ways. Show your work.
   a) years + days
   b) years + weeks + days
   c) years + months + days

Practising

4. Ben turned 9 on Aug. 1. Use Lyn's chart to write Ben's age on the next Dec. 16 in 3 ways. Show your work.
   a) years + days
   b) years + weeks + days
   c) years + months + days
5. What is Ben's age on the next Jan. 8 to the nearest month?
6. a) In 2003, July 1 was a Tuesday. What day of the week was Sept. 2, 2003?
   b) Explain how to use Lyn's chart to solve this problem.

10 Measuring Temperature

Goal **Estimate, read, and record temperature.**

Rashad wants to go swimming after school.

He wonders if the water in the pool will feel cool or warm.

? How warm does 25°C feel?

Rashad's Experiment

I'll use a thermometer to measure the temperature of some hot water, some warm water, and some cool water.

My thermometer measures temperatures in **degrees Celsius (°C)**.

I'll start with some water from the tap that is mostly hot.

I know water boils at 100°C.

I estimate that the hot water will be about 70°C.

The line inside my thermometer shows 55°C.

That's still a lot hotter than the pool!

You will need

- a thermometer

- tap water

- cups or mugs

- thermometer outlines

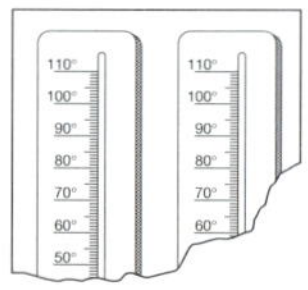

degree Celsius (°C)

A unit of measurement for temperature

boiling water	100°C
body temperature	37°C
fridge temperature	7°C
ice water	0°C
freezer temperature	−18°C, or 18 degrees below zero

A. Complete Rashad's experiment. Record the results in a chart.

B. How do you think the pool water will feel when Rashad jumps in? Explain.

Water	Temperature	
	Estimate	Measure
hot	70°C	55°C
warm		
cool		

Reflecting

1. Explain how you estimated the water temperatures.
2. Explain how you measured the temperatures.
3. Sukan read the temperature −5°C as 5 degrees below zero. Explain what this means.

Checking

4. Estimate and then measure the temperature in your classroom. Use a thermometer outline. Mark each temperature.
   a) the temperature you measured
   b) 10°C warmer
   c) 10°C cooler

Practising

5. Estimate and then measure the temperature in the hall.
6. Write the temperature from the themometer that matches each.
   a) swimming outside
   b) a fever
   c) skating outside in a backyard rink
   d) a hot drink
   e) watching a movie inside

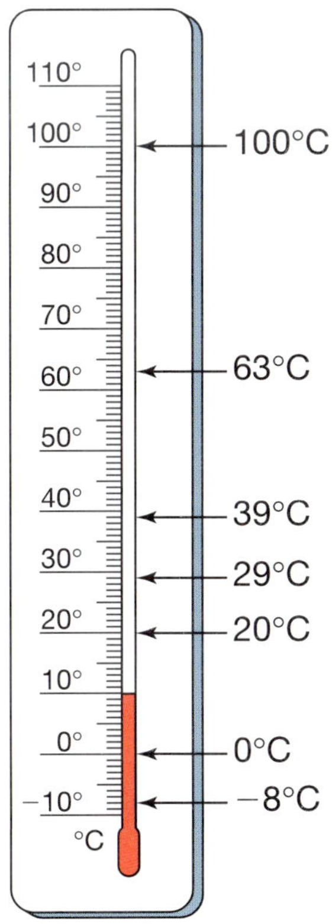

7. Research the high and low temperatures in your area last year. Use a thermometer outline. Mark the temperatures.

Graphing Your Day

You can represent your day on a bar graph.

1 Make your own graph for a weekday.
Choose your activities.
Estimate the number of hours you usually spend doing each activity.
Colour a square for each whole hour and part of a square for part of an hour.
Explain how you estimated.

You will need

- grid paper

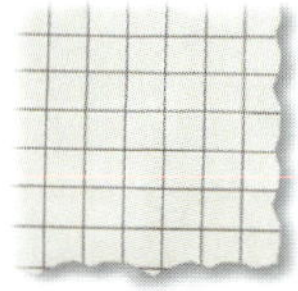

- pencil crayons

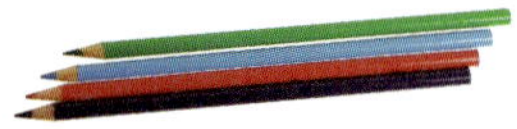

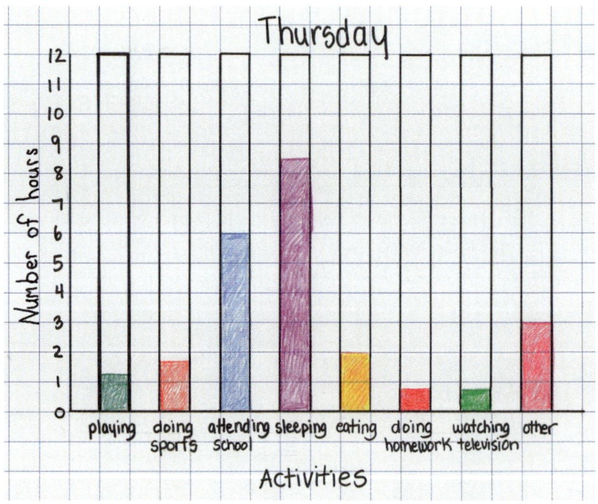

2 Describe the shape of your graph.
Suppose you ordered the activities from the longest to the shortest time.
Would this change the shape of your graph? Explain.

3 Make your own graph for a weekend day.

4 How are your graphs different?
Why does this make sense?
What do your graphs show about how you spend your time?

Adding and Subtracting Hundreds

Brady lives 1 km from school.
Some of her friends live between her and the school.

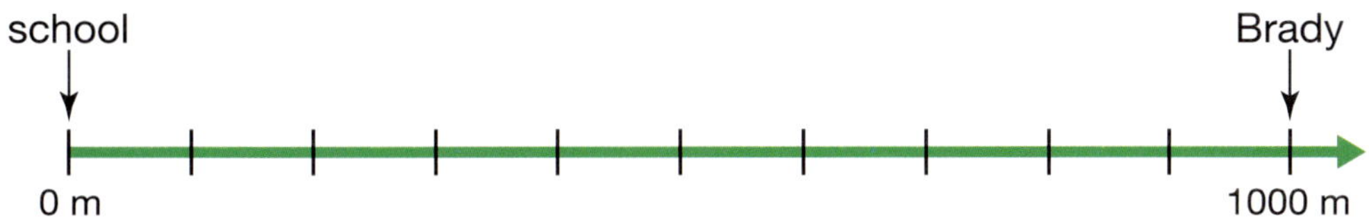

Distance from School

Student	Distance
Juan	300 m
Jack	500 m
Gabe	800 m
Rose	200 m
Sharleen	600 m

A. Copy the number line.
Use arrows to show where each person lives.

B. Why can you calculate 1000 − 300 to figure out how much farther Brady walks to school than Juan?

C. How does knowing 10 − 3 help you solve part B?

Try These

1. How can you use mental addition to add 300 + 200?
2. How can you use mental subtraction to subtract 800 − 300?
3. Which student walks 400 m farther than Sharleen on the way to school?
4. Which student walks 200 m less than Jack on the way to school?
5. How far does Juan walk if he walks all the way home with Jack and then walks back to his own home?
6. Each student walks to school in the morning and home in the afternoon.
Which students walk more than 1 km altogether?

LESSON

Skills Bank

1 **1.** Estimate the length of each line.
Then measure each line to the nearest centimetre.

a) 

b) 

c) 

d) 

e) 

2. Use a ruler to draw a line of each length.
a) 3 cm **b)** 8 cm **c)** 12 cm

3 **3.** **a)** Find an object that you estimate is about 3 dm long.
Measure to check.
b) Repeat part a) for 4 dm and for 40 dm.

5 **4.** Name 2 objects you could measure using each unit.
a) centimetres **b)** metres **c)** kilometres

5. Complete each statement using centimetres, metres, or kilometres.
a) Jessica is about 120 ■ tall.
b) Jessica got a puppy from her uncle who lives 6 ■ away.
c) The puppy is about 40 ■ long.
d) Jessica can throw the puppy's ball about 6 ■.

6 **6.** Estimate each perimeter. Then measure the sides and calculate each perimeter.

a) 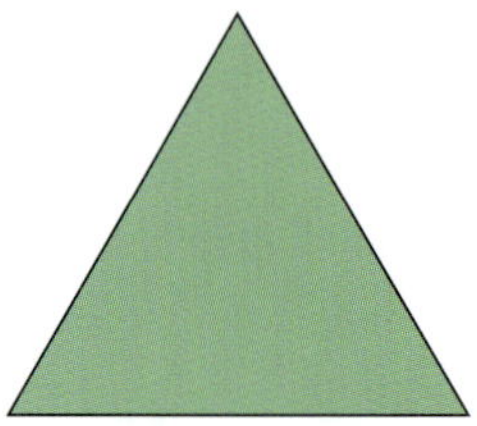

b) 

6 **7.** **a)** Which 2 shapes have the same perimeter?
b) What is the perimeter of the other shape?

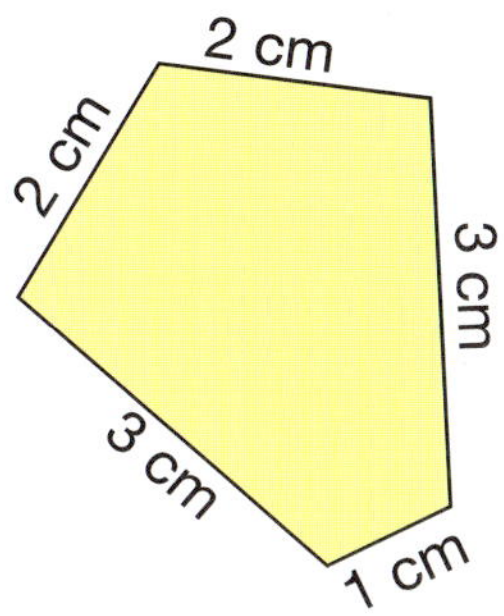

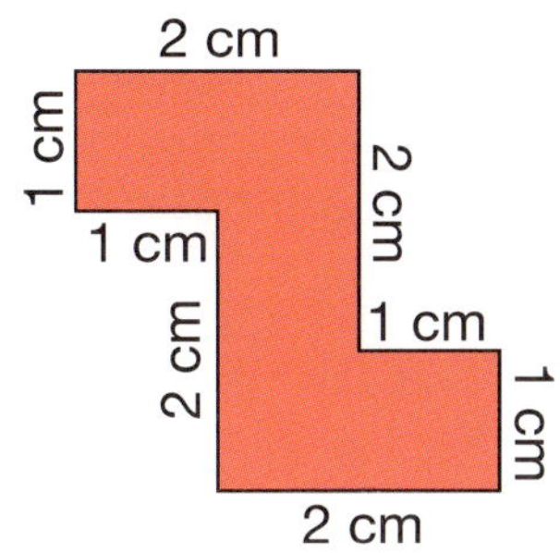

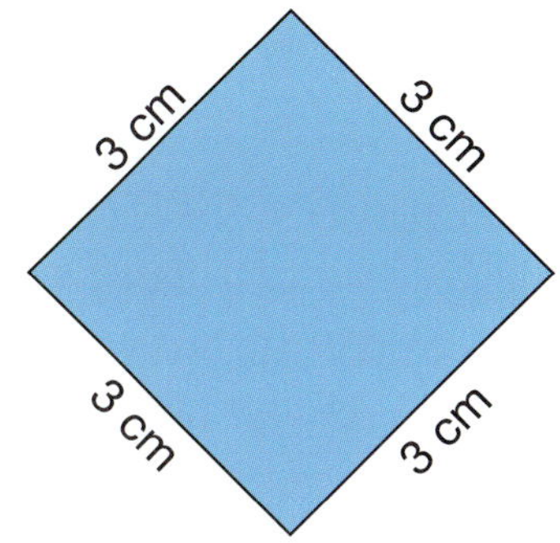

7 **8.** Write each time.

a) three thirty
b) six forty
c) ten fifteen
d) nine ten
e) twelve past eleven
f) six minutes after four

9. How would you say each time?

a)

b)

8 **10.** Saturday morning, Mila rode her bike from 10:30 to 11:45.
How long did she ride her bike?

10 **11.** Read and record the temperature on each thermometer.

a)

b)
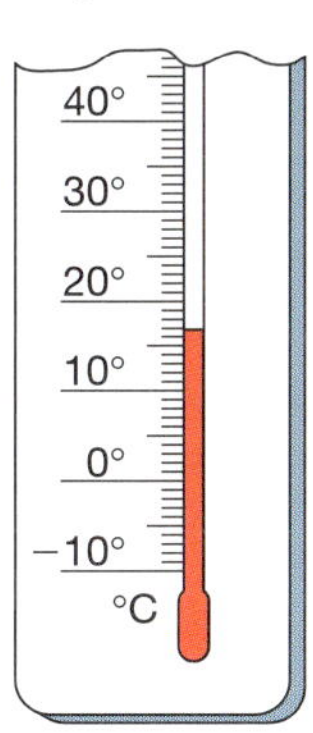

c)
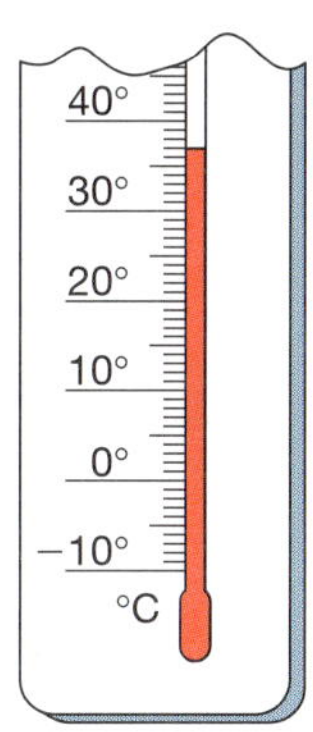

d)
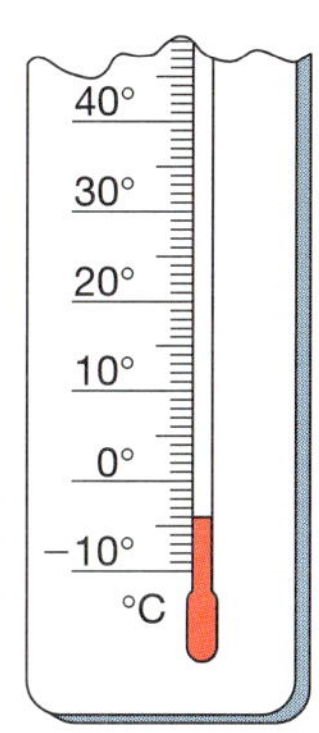

12. Estimate a temperature that would make sense for each.

a) juice from the fridge
b) hot chocolate
c) a warm spring day
d) a cold winter day

LESSON

Problem Bank

1

1. A nickel is 2 cm wide.

a) How many nickels would it take to match your height from head to toe?

b) What is the total value of that many nickels? Show your work.

2

2. A grasshopper jumps in this pattern. How many jumps would it need to get past the end of a metre stick if it started at 0 cm and continued in this pattern? Show your work.

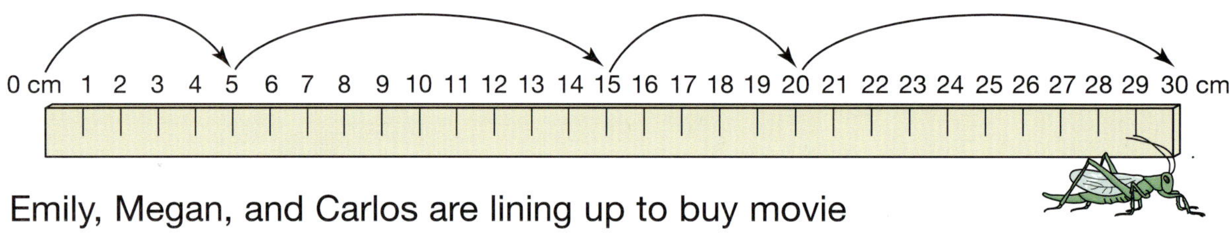

3. Emily, Megan, and Carlos are lining up to buy movie tickets. The picture shows where each person is in the line. How far is Carlos from the ticket seller?

4

4. Tina is on the way to Walkerville. She is 30 km from Walkerville and 60 km from Runnerville.

a) How far apart are the towns if Tina is between them? Explain your thinking.

b) How far apart are the towns if Walkerville is between Tina and Runnerville? Explain your thinking.

6 **5.** How many students could stand shoulder to shoulder around the perimeter of your classroom? Show your work.

7 **6.** How many 0s does a digital clock show between noon and the end of a school day?
Show your work.

7. **a)** Use all of the digits 2, 4, and 6 to write 4 times on a clock. Make 2 of the times in the morning. Make the other 2 times in the afternoon.

b) Put the clock times in order from earliest to latest for the same day.

c) Choose 2 of your clock times.
Write a sentence to describe what you might be doing at each time.

8 **8.** Your class is going to the museum.
The bus leaves at 9:00 in the morning.
It returns at 3:10 in the afternoon.
The bus trip is 40 minutes each way.

a) Will you spend more or less than 1 hour in total on the bus? Explain your thinking.

b) How long will you spend at the museum?
Show your work.

9 **9.** Fatima's birthday is the 8th day of the 8th month.
Jason's birthday is the 10th day of the 10th month.

a) What date is each person's birthday?

b) How many days apart are their birthdays?

10 **10.** The high temperature on Monday was 8°C.
On Tuesday, it went up 4°C to 12°C.
On Thursday, it went down 2°C to 5°C.
What happened on Wednesday?

LESSON

Chapter Review

1

1. Measure each picture to the nearest centimetre.

a) 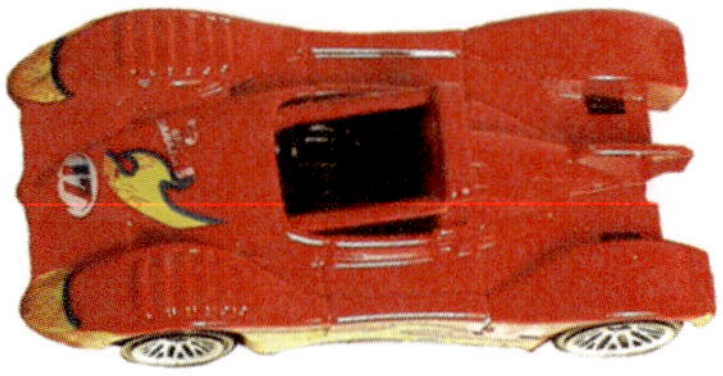

b) 

2

2. A matching bracelet and necklace are joined to make a longer necklace. Is the new necklace longer than 1 m? How do you know?

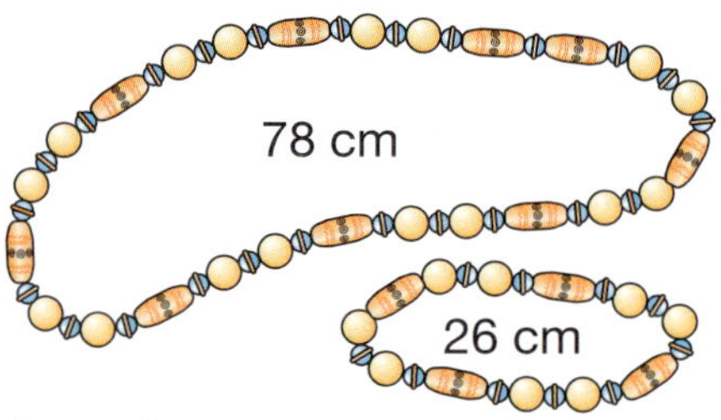

3

3. Kumiko wants to measure the length of her classroom.

a) She has a metre stick marked in centimetres, decimetres, and metres. Which unit should she use? Explain your thinking.

b) Use the unit you chose. Measure the length of your classroom.

4

4. Paul, Amy, and Ming are hiking.

a) How far apart are Paul and Ming?

b) If Paul has walked 2 km, how far has Ming walked?

Paul is behind Amy.

Amy is 2 km ahead of Paul and 4 km behind Ming.

Ming is ahead of Amy.

5 **5.** Complete each statement. Use centimetres, metres, or kilometres. Explain.

a) My pen is about 1 ■ wide.
b) The building is 25 ■ tall.
c) The height of a flagpole is 7 ■.
d) We drove 80 ■ in 1 hour.

6 **6. a)** Predict which is longest in your classroom: the distance around the garbage pail, the perimeter of the largest book, or the height of the door.
b) Estimate each measurement. Measure to check.

7 **7.** Write each time.

a) nine twenty-six
b) 42 minutes after 8

8 **8.** Here are the feeding times at the zoo.

a) How long is the feeding time at each exhibit?
b) What 2 types of animals cannot be fed by the same person? Explain your thinking.

Feeding time	Exhibit
9:00–9:25	polar bears
9:30–9:45	giraffes
9:25–10:00	camels
9:50–10:30	seals

9. Some students measured how long they spend going to and from school in a week. About how many hours does each student spend going to and from school in a week?

Student	Length of time to and from school (minutes)
Devon	100
Lois	70
Alison	200
Deb	90
Alex	440

9 **10.** Which would you use to measure each: days, weeks, months, or years? Explain why.

a) your age
b) the summer holidays
c) the winter

11. Groundhog Day is February 2. Spring begins on March 21. How many days are there from Groundhog Day to the first day of spring if it is not a leap year? Show your work.

10 **12.** Describe what you might wear on a day with each outdoor temperature.

a) 15°C
b) 38°C
c) 0°C
d) −10°C

Chapter Task

Funny Olympics

You are planning the Funny Olympics.
Here are some ideas.

- penny thumb toss
- tissue-paper kick
- cotton-ball puff
- paper-clip flick
- create your own activity

? What activities could you do in 1 hour?

Part 1: Trying Out Activities

A. Make a team of 3. Choose 3 activities.

B. Do your 3 activities. Each person takes 2 turns. Measure and record the distances. Use metres and centimetres.

C. Who won each activity? Show your work.

D. Estimate how long each activity should take: 5 minutes, 10 minutes, or 15 minutes.

Part 2: Creating a Schedule

E. Make a schedule of activities for the 1-hour Funny Olympics. You can spend 5 minutes, 10 minutes, or 15 minutes on an activity.

Time	Activity	Amount of time
1:00 to ■		

F. Is it possible to do 7 activities in 1 hour? Explain.

Task Checklist

- ✓ Did you record the distances in a chart?
- ✓ Is your schedule clear?
- ✓ Did you explain your thinking?

CHAPTER 6

Adding and Subtracting with Greater Numbers

Goals

You will be able to

- estimate sums and differences
- add and subtract 2-digit and 3-digit numbers
- create and solve addition and subtraction problems
- communicate about solutions for addition problems
- estimate with money
- calculate the change

The town fair

You will need

- base ten blocks

Getting Started

Adding and Subtracting

If you catch a big fish at the Fish Pond, you win a big prize.
If you catch a small fish, you win a small prize.

? How many small fish could be in the pond?

A. What do you think "up to 40 big fish" means?

B. What 2 numbers could make this sentence true?

■  + ■  = 70 fish

C. Model your 2 numbers. Use the models to show that the numbers make the sentence true.

D. Show 2 ways to make this sentence true.

There are ■  and ■ .

Write an addition sentence for each.

E. What is the least possible number of small fish? How do you know?

F. What is the greatest possible number of small fish? How do you know?

G. Create a subtraction problem about the pond. Show how to solve your problem.

Do You Remember?

1. Add or subtract.
   a) 42 + 10 = ■ b) 62 − 10 = ■ c) 78 − 8 = ■ d) 50 + 70 = ■

2. Estimate.
   a) 45 + 27 is about ■. b) 73 − 42 is about ■.

3. Add.
   a) 34 + 52 b) 48 + 27 c) 56 + 75 d) 89 + 91

4. Subtract.
   a) 89 − 27 b) 45 − 19 c) 63 − 36 d) 80 − 47

5. Write each amount in 2 ways: with $ and with ¢.
   a) 5 quarters and 3 dimes b) 4 nickels and 6 pennies

CHAPTER 6

1 Estimating Sums

You will need

- number lines

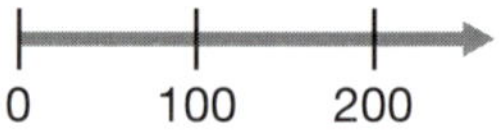

Goal **Estimate in addition situations.**

? About how many people rode the roller coaster on both days?

Day	Number of riders
Thursday	183
Friday	421

A. What easy-to-add numbers are close to 183 and 421?

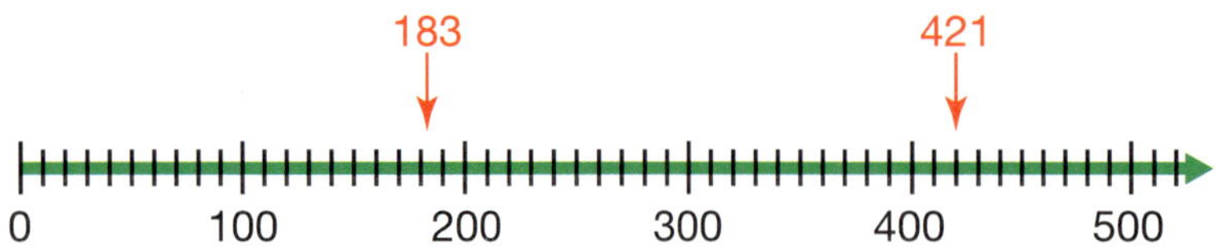

B. Estimate the total number of riders.
Use the easy-to-add numbers from part A.
Write the addition sentence you used.

C. Estimate the total number of riders in a different way.

Reflecting

1. Rounding to the nearest hundred is a way to get easy-to-add numbers. Why?
2. What other easy-to-add numbers might you use to estimate 183 + 421? Explain your answer.
3. a) When might you use an estimate of the number of riders?
   b) When might you use an exact sum?

Checking

4. a) Round the number of people who rode the Ferris wheel each day.
   b) Estimate: About how many people rode the Ferris wheel altogether? Write the addition sentence you used.

Number of Riders

Day	Ferris wheel	Meteorite
Monday	276	397
Tuesday	418	387

Practising

5. About how many riders were there on Monday? Use the chart in Question 4.

6. Estimate each sum.
   Write the addition sentence you used.
   a) 289 + 97 b) 412 + 518 c) 326 + 560

7. a) Show 2 ways to estimate 252 + 354.
   b) Suppose the numbers represent the number of Meteorite riders in 2 days. When would you use each method of estimating? Why?

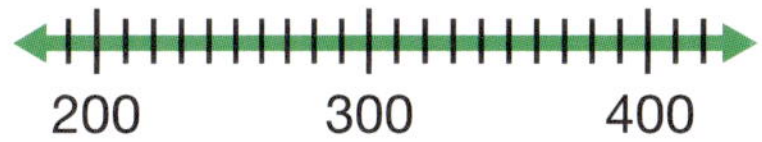

8. Jessica estimated \$249 + \$349 by rounding each number to the nearest hundred. Is that a good strategy? Explain.

9. Create an addition problem that has an answer of about 800.

10. Choose 2 or more of these numbers to give a sum between 300 and 400. How many different combinations can you make? Write the addition sentences you used.

204	99	172
195	358	10
149	6	122

2 Adding with Base Ten Blocks

You will need

- base ten blocks

Goal **Add 2-digit and 3-digit numbers using concrete materials.**

Lee's class is counting the number of cars that pass the school each hour.

They want to show the town council that there should be a traffic light near the school.

? How many cars passed the school between 9:00 in the morning and noon?

Time	Number of cars
9:00 – 10:00	58
10:00 – 11:00	47
11:00 – noon	38

Lee's Addition

This is an addition problem.
I can model the numbers with base ten blocks.

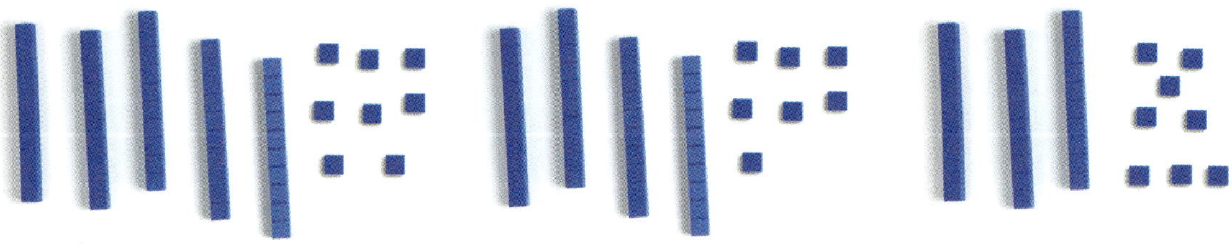

A. What does each set of blocks show?

B. How many tens are there altogether?

C. How many ones are there altogether?

D. How many cars passed the school between 9:00 in the morning and noon?

Reflecting

1. a) How did you calculate the sum for part D?
   b) How can you represent your calculation in writing?
2. How can Lee estimate to check his addition?
3. Does it matter if you start adding with the ones or the tens? Explain.

Royal Canadian Mint

Checking

4. Suppose Lee's class counted 227 cars in the afternoon. How many cars passed the school during the whole day? Show your answer in 2 ways. Use base ten blocks.

Practising

5. The Royal Canadian Mint in Ottawa allows tourists to visit. Buses from 2 schools arrived at the same time.

   How many students came from these schools?

School	Number of students
Victoria Street	118
Bailey Street	156

6. Estimate. Then add. Use estimates to check.

   a) $\begin{array}{r} 79 \\ +\ 64 \\ \hline \end{array}$ b) $\begin{array}{r} 265 \\ +\ 124 \\ \hline \end{array}$ c) $\begin{array}{r} 302 \\ +\ 578 \\ \hline \end{array}$ d) $\begin{array}{r} 437 \\ +\ 298 \\ \hline \end{array}$

7. One night, 67 parents came to prepare for the family gathering at Brady's school. 147 other parents came the next morning. How many parents came altogether?
8. Some people think there is one *right* way to add numbers like 89 + 98. Explain how you would show them that there is more than one right way.
9. Create a problem for 89 + 98. Solve your problem.

3 Adding 2-Digit and 3-Digit Numbers

Goal **Add 2-digit and 3-digit numbers using pencil and paper.**

You will need

- base ten blocks

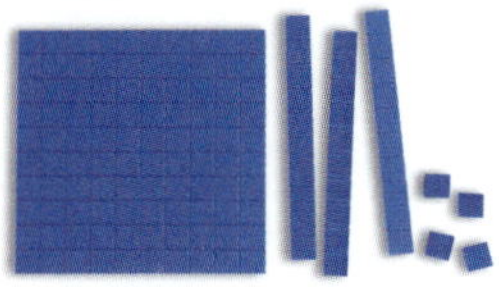

- a place value chart

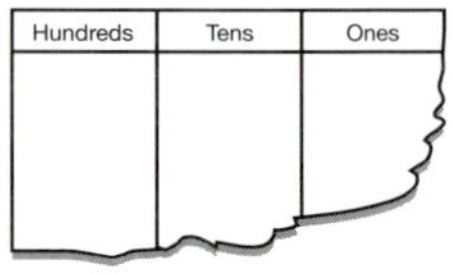

- a calculator

Keisha has 247 stamps from North America and 65 stamps from Africa.

? How many stamps does Keisha have?

Keisha's Addition

First I estimated.
247 + 65 is about 250 + 50, or about 300.
I have about 300 stamps.
Next I used base ten blocks to calculate.

Step 1 I modelled the numbers.

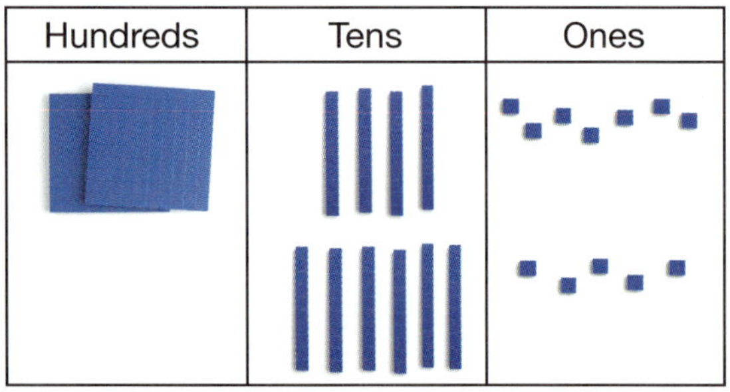

I used pencil and paper to record.

```
  247
+  65
-----
```

Step 2 I added the ones. 7 ones and 5 ones are 12 ones.
I **regrouped** 12 ones as 1 ten 2 ones.

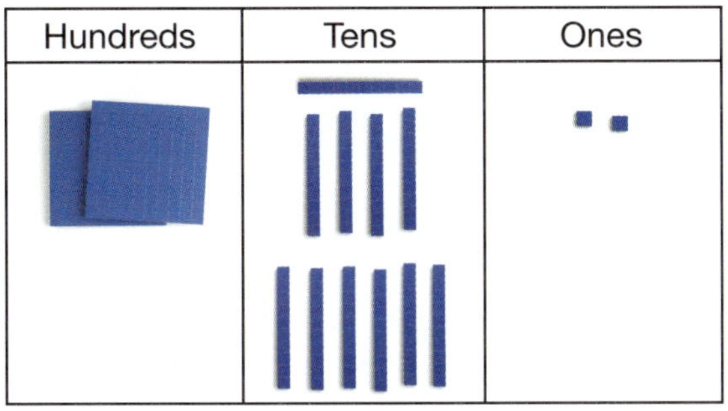

$$\begin{array}{r} {}^{1} \\ 247 \\ +\ 65 \\ \hline 2 \end{array}$$

Step 3 I added the tens. 1 ten and 4 tens and 6 tens are 11 tens.
I regrouped 11 tens as 1 hundred 1 ten.

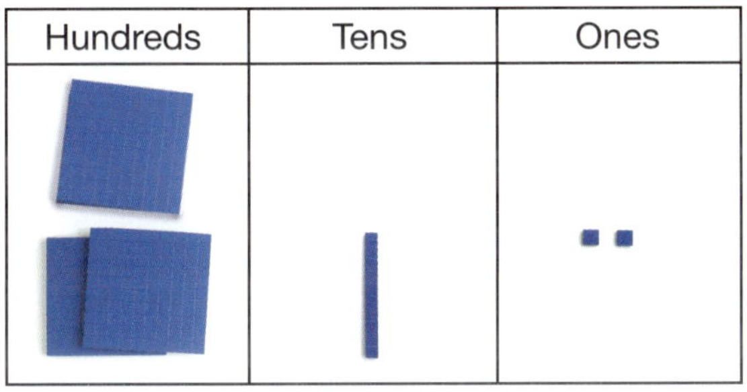

$$\begin{array}{r} {}^{1\,1} \\ 247 \\ +\ 65 \\ \hline 12 \end{array}$$

Step 4 I added the hundreds.
1 hundred and 2 hundreds are 3 hundreds.

I have 312 stamps altogether.

$$\begin{array}{r} {}^{1\,1} \\ 247 \\ +\ 65 \\ \hline 312 \end{array}$$

Reflecting

1. a) In Step 2, why did Keisha regroup 12 ones as 1 ten 2 ones? How did she record this regrouping?
   b) In Step 3, why did Keisha add 1, 4, and 6?
2. Keisha can use her method to add 247 + 52 without regrouping. Explain why.
3. Compare Keisha's estimate with the sum. Does her calculated answer make sense? Explain.

Checking

4. Juan has 318 stamps from Canada and 74 stamps from Europe. How many stamps does he have altogether? Use a calculator to check.

Practising

5. Calculate the total number of stamps in each collection. How do you know each calculated answer makes sense?
   a) 278 stamps from Canada and 42 other stamps
   b) 164 stamps from Canada and 285 other stamps

6. Estimate. Then calculate. Use estimates to check.
   a) 358 + 17 = ■ b) 741 + 168 = ■

7. Add. Use a calculator to check.
   a) 472 + 235 = ■ b) 455 + 377 = ■

8. Diane has 126 stickers in one album and 93 stickers in another album. How many stickers does she have?

9. Describe the errors. Then correct the errors.

   a) $\begin{array}{r} {\scriptstyle 2\,6} \\ 359 \\ +\ 17 \\ \hline 511 \end{array}$ b) $\begin{array}{r} 389 \\ +\ 264 \\ \hline 543 \end{array}$

10. What is the missing digit in this addition sentence? The same digit goes in every place.
    1■■ + 62■ = ■16

11. Michael's coin album holds 500 coins. Will he be able to put all of his coins in 1 album? Explain.

Michael's Coins

Type of coin	Number of coins
Canadian	218
Asian	118
other	145

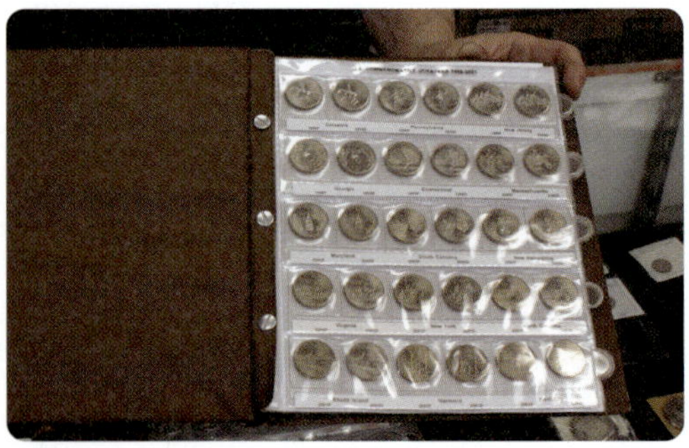

Checking Addition

You will need

- a calculator

Here's a curious method for checking addition.
Add the digits across until you get 1-digit sums.
If they match, your addition is probably correct.

Add	Check		
738 →	7 + 3 + 8 = 18 →	1 + 8 = 9	→ 9 + 4 = 13 → 1 + 3 = 4
+ 256 →	2 + 5 + 6 = 13 →	1 + 3 = 4	
994 →	9 + 9 + 4 = 22 →	2 + 2 = 4	

Compare

1 Add using a calculator.
Check your work using the method above.

a)	b)	c)	d)
207	345	623	562
322	374	238	227
+ 105	+ 198	+ 47	+ 91

Here's a way to estimate to check calculator addition.

Add	Estimate
467	about 500
78 →	about 100
232	about 200
+ 25 ↗	+
802	about 800

Compare

2 Add using a calculator. Estimate to see if your answer makes sense.

a)	b)	c)	d)
314	131	334	446
12	97	255	196
260	412	51	215
+ 37	+ 83	+ 76	+ 55

4 Communicate a Solution to a Problem

Goal **Explain a solution to a problem.**

Glynis built 2 identical cars.
She used 110 pieces altogether.
How many pieces are in each car?

? How can Amit explain how he solved the car problem?

Amit's Rough Copy

I wrote a rough copy to explain how I solved the car problem.

I'll use the Communication Checklist to help me think of what to change when I write my good copy.

Communication Checklist

- ✓ Did you show all the steps?
- ✓ Did you explain your thinking?

Understand the Problem

The number of pieces is the same for each car.

When you add that number to itself, you get 110.

Make a Plan

I will try guessing and testing different numbers.

Carry Out the Plan

100 + 100 = 200

50 + 50 = 100

53 + 53 = 106

55 + 55 = 110

There are 55 pieces in each car.

I like how I showed my problem-solving steps.

I should tell why I chose these numbers to add.

I should tell how I checked my answer.

A. Explain how Amit could check his answer.

Reflecting

1. How did Amit use the Communication Checklist to make comments about his rough copy?

Checking

2. Ben used 100 pieces to build 2 cars.

   One car has 4 more pieces than the other car.

   How many pieces are in each car?

   a) Tiffany explained how she solved the problem. List some strengths of Tiffany's explanation.

   b) What could Tiffany change to improve her explanation?

Tiffany's Explanation

Understand the Problem

I need to find 2 numbers that add to 100.

One number is 4 more than the other.

Make a Plan

I will try adding different numbers.

Carry Out the Plan

20 + 24 = 44 ⟵ too small

50 + 54 = 104 ⟵ too big

46 + 50 = 96 ⟵ a bit too small

48 + 52 = 100 ⟵ right answer

One car has 48 and the other has 52.

Practising

3. Glynis and Ben used 328 pieces to build a town. Glynis used 10 more pieces than Ben. How many pieces did each person use?

   a) Solve the problem.

   b) Explain how you solved the problem. Use the Communication Checklist.

Mid-Chapter Review

LESSON

1

1. Estimate. Write the addition sentence you used.

a) 437 + 472   b) 362 + 289   c) 453 + 258   d) 684 + 199

2. Look at part c) in Question 1.
Charlie estimated 450 + 250 = 700.

a) Explain Charlie's estimate.

b) Which estimate is closer to the sum, yours or Charlie's?

c) Is Charlie's method useful for other parts in Question 1? Explain your thinking.

3. Look at part d) in Question 1.
Why would 884 be a good estimate?

2

4. Calculate 318 + 149 = ■.
Show your work with pictures and numbers.

3

5. Estimate. Then calculate. Use estimates to check.

a) 376 + 216   b) 266 + 485   c) 772 + 184   d) 687 + 214

6. Add. Use a calculator to check.

a) 538 + 171   b) 419 + 381   c) 325 + 387   d) 562 + 279

7. Jason caught 512 herring. Alissa caught 328 herring. How many herring did they catch altogether?

8. Marie has 147 blue beads and 289 red beads to make bracelets. How many beads does she have?

4

9. a) What numbers might go in the blanks?
36■ + 4■■ = 800

b) Find another possible solution. Explain what you did.

Adding and Subtracting Using Tens

Rachel and Juan subtracted 7 from 23 in parts.

Rachel's Subtraction

$23 - 7 = \blacksquare$

7 is 3 + 4.

First I'll subtract 3 from 23.

Then I'll subtract 4 from what's left.

$23 - 3 = 20$

$20 - 4 = 16$

Juan's Subtraction

$23 - 7 = \blacksquare$

7 is 10 − 3.

First I'll subtract 10 from 23.

Then I'll add 3 to what's left.

$23 - 10 = 13$

$13 + 3 = 16$

A. Why did Rachel subtract 3 first?

B. Why did Juan subtract 10 first?

Try These

1. Subtract using Rachel's mental math method.

a) $25 - 7 = \blacksquare$ **b)** $28 - 9 = \blacksquare$ **c)** $36 - 8 = \blacksquare$

2. Subtract using Juan's mental math method.

a) $25 - 6 = \blacksquare$ **b)** $44 - 7 = \blacksquare$ **c)** $63 - 8 = \blacksquare$

3. Add using tens.

a) $25 + 7 = \blacksquare$ **c)** $28 + 3 = \blacksquare$ **e)** $25 + 8 = \blacksquare$

b) $35 + 6 = \blacksquare$ **d)** $44 + 7 = \blacksquare$ **f)** $63 + 9 = \blacksquare$

5 Estimating Differences

You will need
- number lines

Goal **Estimate in subtraction situations.**

Devon wants to collect 500 bottles to win a computer game.

He has collected 156 bottles so far.

? About how many more bottles must Devon collect to win a game?

Devon's Estimate

First I found 156 on a number line.

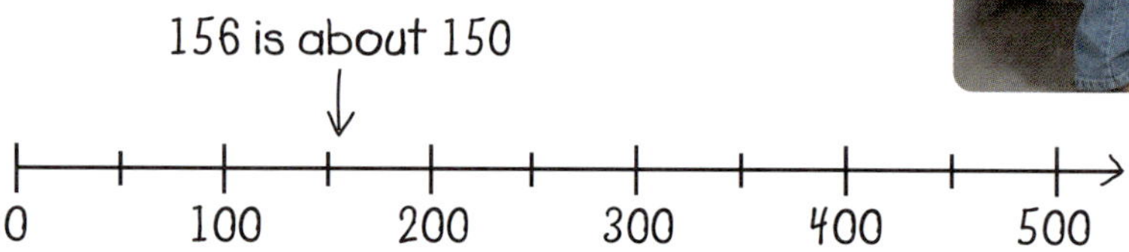

A. Use the number line to estimate how many more bottles Devon must collect to win a game. Explain how you estimated.

B. Is your estimate higher or lower than the exact answer? Explain how you know.

C. Explain a different way to estimate to solve the problem.

Reflecting

1. Why do you think Devon estimated 156 as 150 instead of rounding 156 to 160?
2. Why do you think Devon estimated instead of calculating an exact answer?

Checking

3. Mona and Rebecca would like to win computer games by collecting 500 bottles. About how many more bottles does each girl need? Explain how you estimated.
   a) Mona has 383 bottles.
   b) Rebecca has 217 bottles.

4. Look at your estimates from Question 3. Are your estimates high or low? Explain how you know.

Practising

5. Estimate each difference. Write the subtraction sentence you used.
   a) 400 − 285
   b) 617 − 99
   c) 158 − 43
   d) 873 − 213

6. Look at Question 3. About how many more bottles does Mona have than Rebecca? Explain how you estimated.

7. a) Estimates for 317 − 148 and 318 − 153 might be the same. Explain why.
   b) Create another subtraction with the same estimate.
   c) Create a problem for your subtraction from part b). Solve your problem.

8. How would you estimate each subtraction to get as close as possible to the difference? Why?
   a) 349 − 251
   b) 712 − 223

6 Adding and Subtracting to Compare

You will need

- base ten blocks

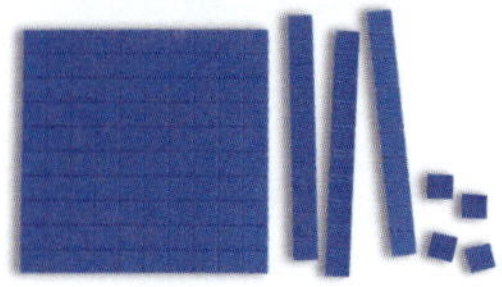

- number lines

Goal **Compare numbers using addition and subtraction.**

Ralf Laue set a record by holding 326 playing cards at once.

Jessica's cousin can hold 114 cards.

? How many more cards can Ralf hold than Jessica's cousin?

A. How do you know that the answer is greater than 200?

B. Show how to use a number line to solve the problem.

C. Show 2 ways to add on to 114 to solve the problem. Use base ten blocks. Sketch pictures to record your work.

D. Show 2 ways to subtract from 326 to solve the problem. Use base ten blocks. Sketch pictures to record your work.

Reflecting

1. How were your 2 ways of adding to solve $114 + \blacksquare = 326$ the same? How were they different?
2. How were your 2 ways of subtracting to solve $326 - 114 = \blacksquare$ the same? How were they different?
3. Would you add or subtract to find how much greater 250 is than 175? Give a reason.

Spill the Beans

You will need

- Spill the Beans game board

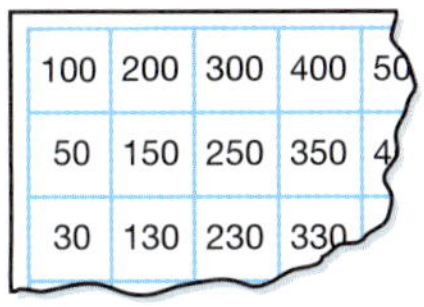

- 2 beans or counters

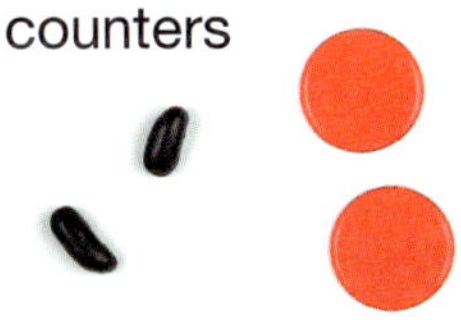

Number of players: 2 to 4
How to play: Add pairs of numbers on a game board. Then subtract to find your score.

Step 1 Spill 2 beans or counters onto the game board. Add the numbers where the beans land. Record the sum.

Step 2 Repeat Step 1.

Step 3 Now you have 2 sums. Subtract. Score 5 points if the difference ends in 00. Score 3 points if it does not.

Step 4 Take turns.

Play until a player reaches 25 points.

100	200	300	400	500
50	150	250	350	450
30	130	230	330	430
70	170	270	370	470
80	180	280	380	480
100	200	300	400	500

Ian's Turn

My beans landed on 130 and 50.

$130 + 50 = 180$

I spilled the beans again.
My beans landed on 380 and 400.

$380 + 400 = 780$

I subtracted.

$780 - 180 = 600$

The difference ends in 00. I get 5 points!

7 Subtracting from 3-Digit Numbers

Goal **Subtract from 3-digit numbers using pencil and paper.**

You will need

- base ten blocks

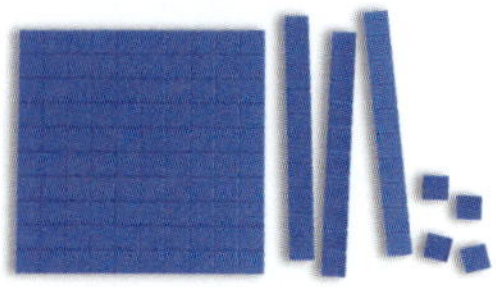

- a place value chart

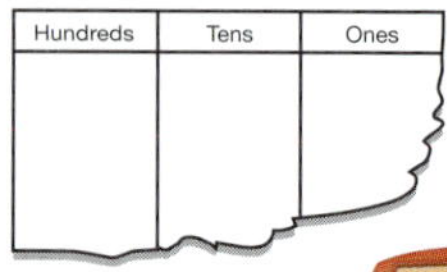

- a calculator

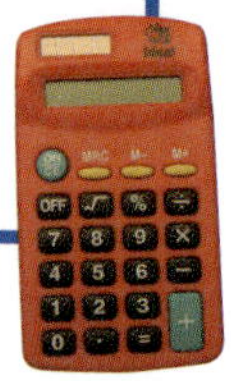

There are 217 novels in the library.
24 novels are checked out.

? How many novels are left in the library?

Michael's Subtraction

Step 1 I modelled 217 with base ten blocks.
I needed to take away 24 novels.
First I took away 4 ones.

Hundreds	Tens	Ones
		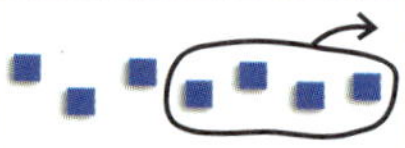

I also used pencil and paper.

$$\begin{array}{r} 217 \\ -\ 24 \\ \hline 3 \end{array}$$

Step 2 I needed to take away 2 tens.
There weren't enough tens, so I regrouped 1 hundred as 10 tens.
Then I had 1 hundred 11 tens.

Hundreds	Tens	Ones

$$\begin{array}{r} {\scriptstyle 1\ 11} \\ \not{2}\not{1}7 \\ -\ 24 \\ \hline 3 \end{array}$$

Step 3 Then I took away 2 tens.

Hundreds	Tens	Ones
	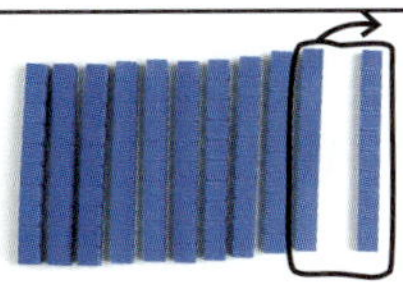	

```
 1 11
 2̶1̶7
- 24
 193
```

There are 193 novels left in the library.

Reflecting

1. a) Why did Michael regroup 1 hundred as 10 tens?
   b) How did Michael record the regrouping?
2. When would you use regrouping while subtracting?
3. a) How can Michael estimate to check his subtraction?
   b) How can Michael use addition to check his subtraction?

Checking

4. There are 405 children's books in the library.
   117 of the books are checked out.
   How many books are left?
   Use a calculator to check.

Practising

5. There are 850 books in the library.
   472 of the books are still in the library.
   How many books are checked out?
   Use a calculator to check.

6. Subtract. Show your work. Check by adding.

a)		b)		c)		d)	
	844		243		652		602
	− 34		− 27		− 289		− 425

7. Estimate. Then calculate. Use estimates to check.

a) $\begin{array}{r} 387 \\ -\ 92 \\ \hline \end{array}$ b) $\begin{array}{r} 467 \\ -\ 285 \\ \hline \end{array}$ c) $\begin{array}{r} 570 \\ -\ 157 \\ \hline \end{array}$ d) $\begin{array}{r} 708 \\ -\ 519 \\ \hline \end{array}$

8. Subtract to check these additions. Correct any errors.

a) $373 + 439 = 712$ b) $546 + 354 = 800$

9. You check the answer to a subtraction question by adding $235 + 147$.

a) What was the subtraction question? How do you know?

b) Why is there more than one answer?

10. 2 numbers between 200 and 300 have a difference of 84. What could the numbers be? Explain your steps.

11. a) To make subtracting 369 from 782 easier, Kayo added 1 to each number. Show how to use base ten blocks for Kayo's subtraction.

I'll think of 782 - 369 as 783 - 370.

b) Do you think Kayo's method makes the subtraction easier? Explain your thinking.

c) For $455 - 127$, Kayo added 3 to each number. Show Kayo's subtraction.

d) Show how to use Kayo's method for $341 - 96$.

12. Complete this subtraction. Explain your thinking.

$\begin{array}{r} 565 \\ -\ \blacksquare\blacksquare\blacksquare \\ \hline 278 \end{array}$

13. Henri's family drove 226 km on Monday. On Tuesday, they drove 37 km farther than on Monday.

a) How far did they drive in these 2 days?

b) By Wednesday evening, they had driven 715 km. How far did they drive on Wednesday?

c) They took a shortcut home and drove 684 km. How much shorter was the trip home?

Digit Difference

You will need

- 3 sets of number cards (1 to 9)

Number of players: 2 or 3
How to play: Choose 3-digit numbers to make the greatest difference.

Step 1 Shuffle the cards.
Place them face down in a pile.

Step 2 Each player takes 6 cards. Arrange them to make two 3-digit numbers to subtract.
Put the greater number on top.

Step 3 Calculate the difference.
Check each other's subtraction.
The player with the greatest difference gets 1 point.

Play until a player reaches 5 points.

Rose's Subtraction

$$\begin{array}{r} 665 \\ -\ 123 \\ \hline 542 \end{array}$$

CHAPTER 6

8 Choosing a Calculation Method

Goal Choose the best way to add or subtract.

To win a computer game, you need 900 points.
Ian had 727 points and then earned 178 more.
Did he win a game?

You will need

- base ten blocks

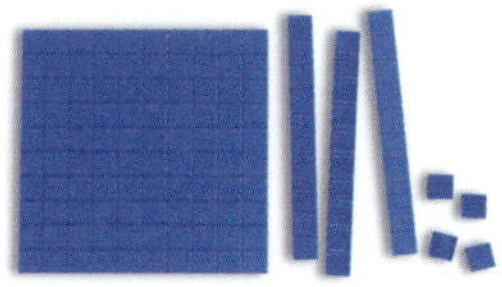

- a place value chart

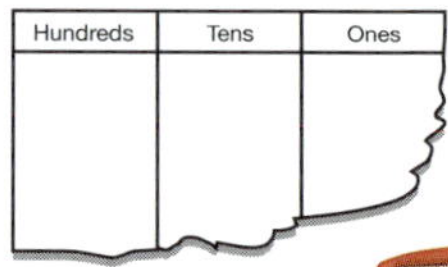

- a calculator

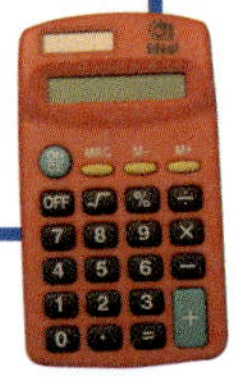

? Which method would you use?

A. Would you estimate to find the answer? Explain your thinking.

B. Choose 3 people's methods to use. Show what you did.

C. Which method do you think works best? Explain why.

D. Lyn has 315 points. How many more points does she need to win?

a) Would you estimate to find the answer? Explain your thinking.

b) Choose 3 people's methods to find out how many more points Lyn needs.

c) Which method do you think works best? Explain why.

E. Create an addition or subtraction problem that you would solve in each way.

Solve each problem.

a) with paper and pencil

b) with a calculator

c) with base ten blocks

d) in your head

Charlie's Way

I'd calculate in my head.

Sharleen's Way

I'd use a calculator.

Ben's Way

I'd use pencil and paper.

Rose's Way

I'd use base ten blocks.

Reflecting

1. Look at the problems you wrote for part E. Explain why your choice of method makes sense.
2. a) What method would you use to add 623 and 199? Why?
   b) What method would you use to subtract 347 from 386? Why?
3. What do you ask yourself to decide whether you can add or subtract in your head?

Curious Math

Count to 1000

You will need

- base ten blocks

Here's a way to subtract 769 from 1000 by counting.

Count from 769 to 770. 1 one

Count from 770 to 800. 3 tens 

Count from 800 to 1000. 2 hundreds 

That's 2 hundreds 3 tens 1 one, so 1000 − 769 = 231.

You can check by adding 231 and 769.

2 hundreds 3 tens 1 one + 7 hundreds 6 tens 9 ones
That's 9 hundreds 9 tens 10 ones, or 1 thousand, so 231 + 769 = 1000.

1. Count to subtract. Check by adding. Show your work.
   a) 1000 − 923 = ■
   b) 1000 − 457 = ■
   c) 1000 − 105 = ■
   d) 1000 − 34 = ■

9 Estimating with Money

You will need

- play coins

- a calculator

Goal **Estimate sums and differences for amounts of money.**

Brady ordered a sandwich and soup.
Kim ordered a piece of pie.

? About how much more did Brady spend than Kim?

Brady's Estimation

I can estimate the cost by thinking of each amount as cents.

A sandwich costs $2.75.
$2.75 is $2 and $0.75.
That's 200¢ and 75¢, or 275¢.
275¢ rounds up to 300¢,
so $2.75 rounds to $3.

Soup costs $1.39.

A. Use Brady's method to round the cost of the soup.

B. Estimate the total cost of Brady's order.
Record the estimate with $.

C. Estimate how much more Brady paid than Kim.
Explain how you estimated.

D. Use a calculator. Find the exact cost of Brady's order.
2 [.] 75 [+] 1 [.] 39 [=]

E. Use a calculator. Find how much more Brady paid than Kim.

Reflecting

1. How is estimating a sum or difference with dollars and cents the same as with whole numbers? How is it different?
2. Show how you can use coins to calculate how much more Brady spent than Kim.
3. a) When might you estimate the cost in a restaurant?
   b) When might you use an exact cost?

Checking

4. Eduardo ordered a sandwich and juice. Nina ordered soup. About how much more did Eduardo spend than Nina?

Practising

5. Choose 2 items from the Smalltown Diner menu.
   a) Estimate the difference in cost. Then use a calculator to subtract. Use your estimate to check.
   b) Estimate the total cost. Then use a calculator to add. Use your estimate to check.
6. Estimate each sum or difference.
   a) $\$2.14 + \$3.69$
   b) $\$3.10 + \$1.97$
   c) $\$1.47 - \$0.79$
   d) $\$4.27 - \$2.39$
7. Create your own estimation problem about the Smalltown Diner menu. Solve your problem.
8. Daniel has $5.00. He wants to buy soup, milk, and a sandwich at Smalltown Diner. Should he estimate, use a calculator, or use money to find out if he has enough money?

   Explain your choice. Use your choice of method to solve the problem.

10 Calculating Change

You will need

- play money

- a calculator

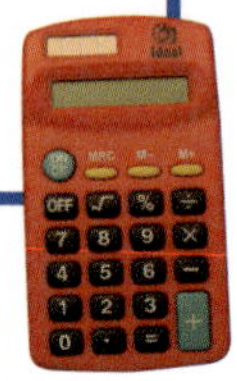

Goal Make purchases and change for amounts up to $10.00.

Jack has a $10.00 bill.

? How much change should Jack get if he buys a soccer ball?

Lyn's Calculation

A soccer ball costs $6.75.

I'll add on to $6.75 to reach $10.00.

I'll add on 1 quarter, or 25¢, to reach $7.00.

I'll add on 3 loonies, or $3.00 more, to reach $10.00.

Jack's change is $3.00 + 25¢, or $3.25.

Jack's Calculation

I'll use a calculator to subtract.

10 [.] 00 [−] 6 [.] 75 [=] 3.25

My change is $3.25.

Reflecting

1. Jack's change could be 1 quarter and 3 loonies. What different coins might Jack get for his change?
2. Why can you use addition or subtraction to calculate change?
3. Add Jack's change to the cost of the soccer ball. Why does this answer make sense?

Checking

4. Tracy has $10.00 to buy 3 tennis balls.
   a) How much change should she get?
   b) What change might Tracy get?

5. How much change should Tracy get if she uses a $10.00 bill to buy goggles?

Practising

6. Calculate the change.
   What bills or coins might the change be?
   a) You have $5.00.
      A water bottle costs $3.75.
      Your change will be ■.
   b) You have $4.00.
      It costs $2.50 to swim.
      Your change will be ■.
   c) You have $5.00.
      Skate laces cost $3.60.
      Your change will be ■.
   d) You have $10.00.
      A lacrosse ball costs $7.91.
      Your change will be ■.

7. Louie has a $10.00 bill. He wants to buy 2 items at the Smalltown Sports summer sale.
   a) What can he buy? Find as many different answers as you can. Show your work.
   b) What is the most change he can get? Show your work.
   c) What is the least change he can get? Show your work.

8. a) What is the greatest number of different items Tracy can buy at the summer sale with $10.00? How do you know?
   b) How much will Tracy's change be? Show your work. What bills or coins might Tracy get for change?

Skills Bank

LESSON

1

1. Estimate each sum.
Write the addition sentence you used.
a) 278 + 393
b) 250 + 489
c) 421 + 517
d) 350 + 521
e) 528 + 78
f) 345 + 246
g) 788 + 81
h) 132 + 674

2. Estimate each sum.
Write the addition sentence you used.
a) 376 + 23
b) 528 + 56
c) 662 + 275
d) 387 + 238

2

3. The Iroquoian Kanata Village in Brantford welcomes tourists.
The number of tourists last Wednesday morning is shown.
How many tourists visited altogether that morning?

Time	Number of tourists
9:00–10:30	176
10:30–noon	145

4. Add. Use base ten blocks.
a) 84 + 77 = ■
b) 736 + 25 = ■
c) 492 + 247 = ■

3

5. 187 parents came to meet teachers in Sukan's school one night and 34 other parents came the next morning.
How many parents came altogether?

6. Add. Show your work.
a) 56 + 12
b) 621 + 56
c) 626 + 269
d) 401 + 332

7. Estimate the total number of stamps. Then calculate.
a) 365 stamps from Canada and 24 other stamps
b) 419 stamps from Canada and 49 other stamps
c) 324 stamps from Canada and 134 other stamps
d) 181 stamps from Canada and 274 other stamps

5 **8.** Estimate each difference.
Write the subtraction sentence you used.

a) 393 − 215 **c)** 603 − 189 **e)** 708 − 419
b) 523 − 329 **d)** 828 − 354 **f)** 226 − 179

9. Estimate each difference.
Write the subtraction sentence you used.

a) $\begin{array}{r} 507 \\ -\ 39 \\ \hline \end{array}$ **b)** $\begin{array}{r} 752 \\ -\ 316 \\ \hline \end{array}$ **c)** $\begin{array}{r} 518 \\ -\ 423 \\ \hline \end{array}$ **d)** $\begin{array}{r} 418 \\ -\ 269 \\ \hline \end{array}$

7 **10.** There are 725 children's books in the library.
276 of the books are checked out.
How many books are left?

11. Subtract. Check by adding.

a) $\begin{array}{r} 734 \\ -\ 44 \\ \hline \end{array}$ **b)** $\begin{array}{r} 620 \\ -\ 177 \\ \hline \end{array}$ **c)** $\begin{array}{r} 501 \\ -\ 425 \\ \hline \end{array}$ **d)** $\begin{array}{r} 555 \\ -\ 236 \\ \hline \end{array}$

12. There were 647 beads in a jar.
After Andi made a bracelet, there were 368 left.
How many beads did Andi use?
Use a calculator to check.

8 **13.** Add or subtract. Explain why you used mental math, a calculator, base ten blocks, or pencil and paper.

a) 375 + 125 = ■ **c)** 396 + 438 = ■ **e)** 345 + 243 = ■
b) 850 − 350 = ■ **d)** 524 − 285 = ■ **f)** 565 + 199 = ■

9 **14.** Estimate each sum or difference.

a) $\begin{array}{r} \$4.76 \\ +\ \$1.05 \\ \hline \end{array}$ **b)** $\begin{array}{r} \$2.95 \\ +\ \$0.99 \\ \hline \end{array}$ **c)** $\begin{array}{r} \$3.84 \\ -\ \$1.48 \\ \hline \end{array}$ **d)** $\begin{array}{r} \$4.05 \\ -\ \$2.73 \\ \hline \end{array}$

10 **15.** Martin had a loonie. He bought a stamp for 21¢.
Write the change in each way: $■.■ ■ and ■ ■¢.

16. Calculate the change from a $10.00 bill.
What bills or coins might the change be?

a) $6.50 item **b)** $5.68 item **c)** $8.99 item

LESSON

Problem Bank

1 **1.** Paco and Jacob estimate that they have about 600 marbles altogether.

Find at least 2 ways to fill in the missing digits to make this true.

Marble Count

Paco	3■■
Jacob	2■■
	about 600

3 **2.** 2 numbers are missing.
■■■ + ■■■ = 433
The 1st number is 1 greater than the 2nd number.
What are the missing numbers?
Show your work. Explain your steps.

3. How many children can travel on any 2 buses?
Find as many answers as you can.

4. The perimeter of a square is between 500 cm and 520 cm.

a) How long could each side be? Explain your steps.

b) Find at least one more answer.

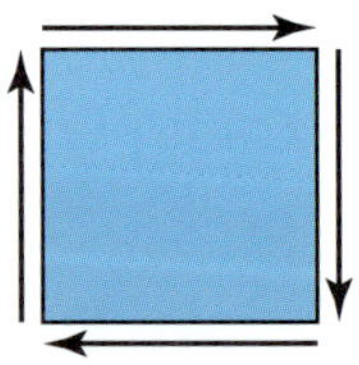

All sides of a square are the same length.

4 **5. a)** Complete this addition using all of the digits 1, 2, 3, 4, 5, and 6. Explain your steps.

b) Find a different way to fill in the blanks using the digits 1 to 6.

```
  ■■■
+ ■■■
-----
  777
```

6. a) Complete this addition using all of the digits 1, 2, 3, 4, 5, 6, 7, 8, and 9. Explain your steps.

b) Is there more than one answer? Explain how you know.

```
  ■■■
+ ■■■
-----
  ■■■
```

5 7. Complete each subtraction in 3 ways.

a) 500 − 2■■ is about 200. b) 500 − 2■■ is about 300.

8. Simone's family is driving from Vancouver to Winnipeg. They have travelled 367 km.

a) Estimate how far they are from Calgary.

b) Use your estimate from part a). About how far are they from Regina? About how far are they from Winnipeg?

7 9. Ink was spilled on part of the librarian's records.

What numbers are covered by the ink?

Type	Number of books		
	In	Out	Total
fiction		55	825
sports	155	38	
animal stories	144		686
science	238	49	
social studies		65	427

10. Find several ways to show 333 on a calculator without using the [3] key. Describe the steps for any 2 of the ways.

10 11. Bronwyn bought 2 items at the Best Restaurant In The West. She got more than $4.00 change from a $10.00 bill.

a) Which items did she buy? Explain your steps.

b) Find more than one answer.

12. Create and solve another menu problem for calculating change. Explain your thinking.

LESSON

Chapter Review

1

1. Estimate each sum. Write the addition sentence you used.

a) 415 + 562 **b)** 348 + 256 **c)** 190 + 96 **d)** 616 + 217

2. Show 2 ways to estimate the sum for 352 + 153.

3. Which 2 sums are closest to 500? Show your work.

A. 479 + 42 **B.** 229 + 314 **C.** 321 + 275 **D.** 199 + 275

3

4. Tien's coin album holds 600 coins. Can Tien put all of the coins in 1 album? Show your work.

Tien's Coins

Type of coin	Number of coins
Canadian	197
Asian	235
European	162

5

5. Estimate each difference. Show your work.

a) 400 − 285 **b)** 158 − 43 **c)** 617 − 99 **d)** 873 − 213

6. Which 2 differences are closest to 200? Show your work.

A. 479 − 342 **B.** 643 − 445 **C.** 371 − 88 **D.** 387 − 201

7

7. Subtract. Check by adding.

a) 213 − 37 **b)** 676 − 253 **c)** 512 − 435 **d)** 568 − 298

8. Estimate. Write the addition or subtraction sentence you used to estimate. Is each answer reasonable? Correct any answer that is not reasonable.

a) 565 + 283 = 748 **b)** 804 − 365 = 561

9. Use the number sentences in the box.

a) Which number sentence has the greatest answer?

b) Which has an answer with 1 in the ones place?

c) Create a problem for one of the number sentences.

A. 165 + 206 = ■
B. 318 + 187 = ■
C. 800 − 288 = ■
D. 512 − 128 = ■

8 **10.** Jessica and Gabe used mental math to add 36 + 47.

Jessica's Addition

Jessica added this way.

36 + 47

76 + 7

83

Gabe's Addition

Gabe added this way.

36 + 47

70 + 13

83

Explain Jessica's method and Gabe's method.
Then choose a method for each addition.
Show your work.

a) 52 + 19 = ■

b) 24 + 68 = ■

c) 349 + 45 = ■

d) 63 + 239 = ■

9 **11.** Estimate the total cost.

a) the bear and the dart game

b) the bear and a book

12. About how much more does the dart game cost than the bear?

10 **13.** How much change would you get?
What bills or coins might the change be?

a) You buy the bear with a $5.00 bill.

b) You buy the dart game with a $10.00 bill.

14. Calculate the change.
What bills or coins might the change be?

a) You have $5.00.
A magazine costs $3.95.
Your change will be ■.

b) You have $4.00.
It costs $2.25 to skate.
Your change will be ■.

c) You have $5.00.
Skate sharpening costs $2.70.
Your change will be ■.

d) You have $10.00.
Lunch costs $6.82.
Your change will be ■.

Chapter Task

Marble Mania

Tian will run a marble game at the school's fun fair.
His game needs 144 marbles.
He finds a store that sells marbles for these prices.

? What do you think is the best way for Tian to buy the marbles?

A. How many marbles do you think are in the large bag? Show your work. Give a reason for your answer.

B. How many small bags would Tian need? Show your work.

C. Which would cost less: only small bags of marbles or a medium bag?

D. What do you think Tian should buy? Explain your answer.

Task Checklist

- ✓ Did you organize your work so it's easy to follow?
- ✓ Did you show all your steps?
- ✓ Did you explain your thinking?

CHAPTER 7

2-D Geometry

Goals

You will be able to

- **describe, identify, and sort 2-dimensional (2-D) shapes**
- **describe and identify congruent shapes**
- **communicate about geometry patterns**
- **identify, extend, and create geometry patterns**

Designing border patterns

Getting Started

Exploring Shapes

This flag quilt is made of 18 shapes.

? How can you name and describe shapes in the flag quilt?

A. Which shapes in the flag quilt are **rectangles**?

B. Which shapes are **triangles**?

C. Which shapes are not rectangles and not triangles?

D. Which shapes look the same?
Describe the ways they look the same.

Do You Remember?

1. Name each shape.

a) b) c)

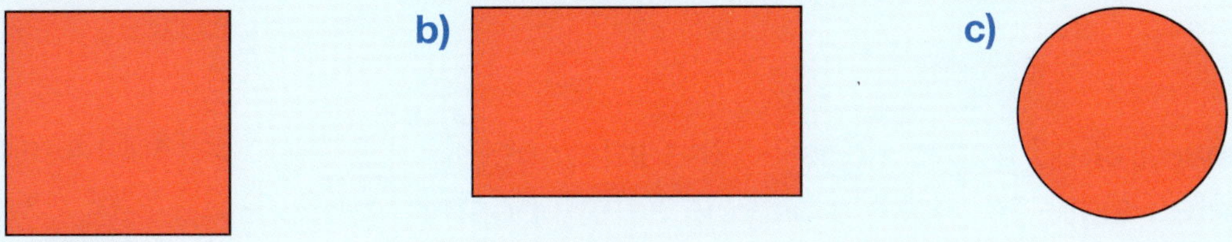

2. Which shapes are not triangles?

A. B. C. D.

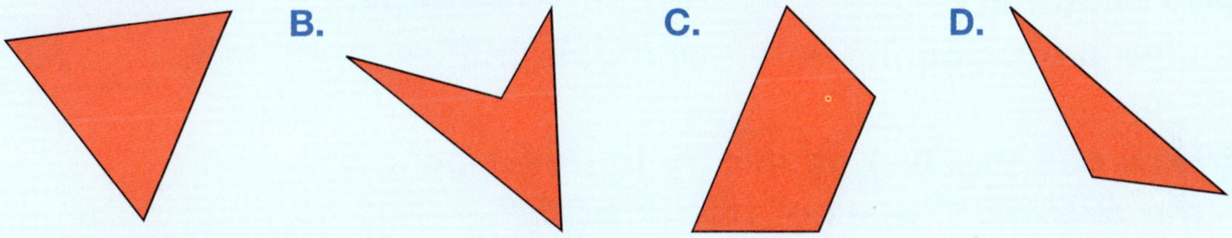

3. How many sides does each shape have?

a) b) c) d)

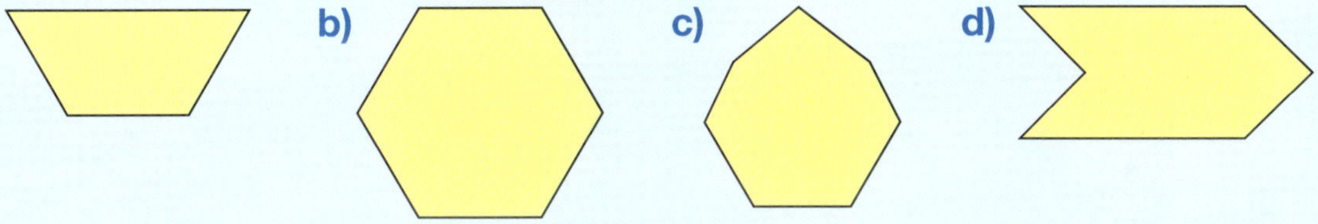

4. a) Sketch the next 3 shapes in this pattern.
b) Describe the pattern.

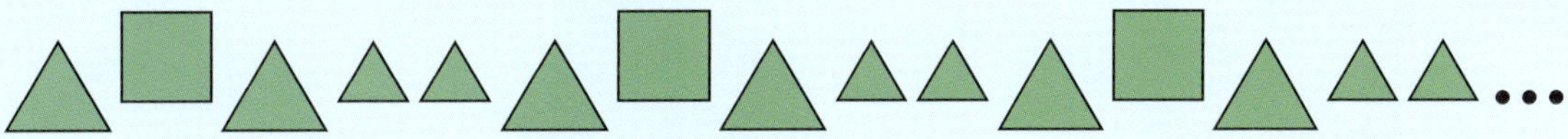

5. Fold a paper square in half.
Then unfold the paper.
Name the shapes you see.
Then describe the shapes.

6. Repeat Question 5 by folding the same square in half to make different shapes.

1 Describing Shapes

You will need

- a ruler

- a square corner

- pattern blocks

Goal Describe and identify 2-D shapes.

Juan researched traffic signs on the Internet. He printed signs to make a bicycle safety poster. All the signs are 2-D shapes that are **polygons**.

Some names of polygons are **triangle**, **rectangle**, **square**, **pentagon**, **hexagon**, and **octagon**.

? How can you use geometry to describe the outside shapes of traffic signs?

polygon
A 2-D shape with sides that are straight lines

triangle
A polygon with 3 sides

rectangle
A polygon with 4 sides and 4 square corners

square
A polygon with 4 equal sides and 4 square corners

A. Describe the shapes of these signs. Use **vertices**, **square corners**, and side lengths. Name the polygons.
  a) *School Zone* **b)** *Yield* **c)** *Railway Crossing*

B. Is any sign on Juan's poster a hexagon? How do you know?

C. Rose made a shape group with some of Juan's signs. She put the *School Crosswalk*, *No Bicycles Allowed*, and *One Way* signs in the group.
   a) What **attributes** do you think Rose used for the group?
   b) Which other signs belong in Rose's group? Explain why they belong.
   c) Which signs do not belong in Rose's group? Explain why they do not belong.

D. a) Make your own shape group with some of Juan's signs. Describe the attributes for your group.
   b) Choose a sign in your group. Explain why it belongs.
   c) Choose a sign that does not belong in your group. Explain why it does not belong.

E. Count the number of sides and the number of vertices for each sign. What do you notice? Explain why this makes sense.

F. Use 2 or more pattern blocks to create your own sign. Use geometry words. Describe your sign for a classmate to copy with pattern blocks.

Reflecting

1. This shape and one of the signs on Juan's poster are both pentagons.
   a) Which sign is it?
   b) How are the pentagons different?

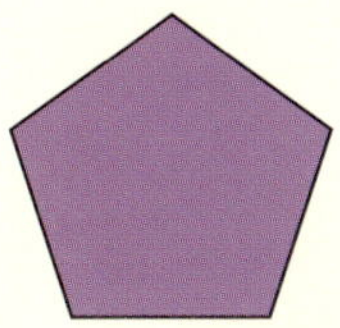

2. Keisha made her sign with **trapezoid** and **square** pattern blocks. Keisha's sign and a *Stop* sign are the same polygon. What is the polygon? Explain why.

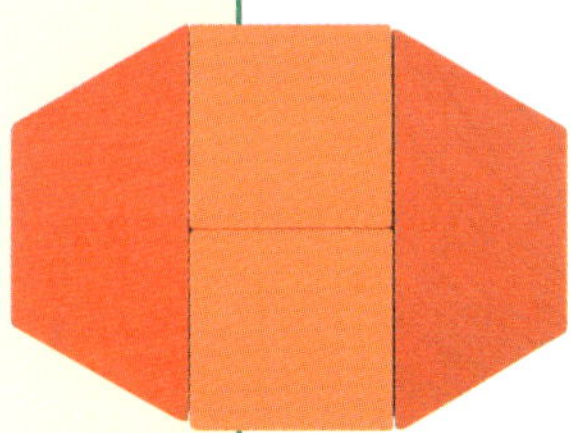

3. Explain how the shape of a sign helps with bicycle safety.

pentagon
A polygon with 5 sides

hexagon
A polygon with 6 sides

octagon
A polygon with 8 sides

vertex (vertices)
The point at the corner of a shape

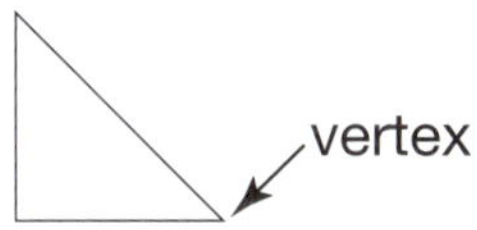

square corner
A vertex that makes a square

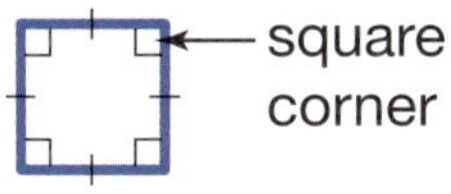

CHAPTER 7

2 Describing Congruent Shapes

You will need

- a tangram

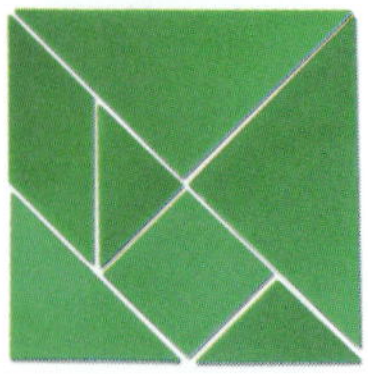

Goal **Match and describe congruent shapes.**

A tangram has 7 shapes called tans.

There are 3 sizes of triangles, 1 square, and 1 **parallelogram**.

? How do you know which shapes are congruent?

Rashad's Discovery

The 2 small triangles are congruent.
I can see that they are the same size and shape when I place one on top of the other.

I can join the 2 small triangles to make a square.
The new square is congruent to the square tan.

A. Are there other congruent tans? Explain.

B. Make a shape that is congruent to the largest triangle tan. Use 2 or 3 tans. Show your work.

C. What tans can go together to make a shape that is congruent to another tan?

parallelogram
A 4-sided shape with opposite sides that are **parallel**

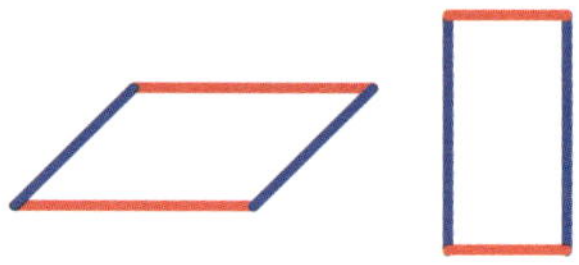

parallel
Always the same distance apart, never crossing or meeting

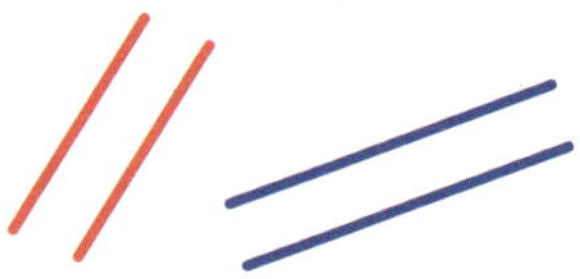

congruent
The same size and shape

Reflecting

1. How can you test whether shapes are congruent? Explain why this works.
2. Are these shapes congruent? Explain.

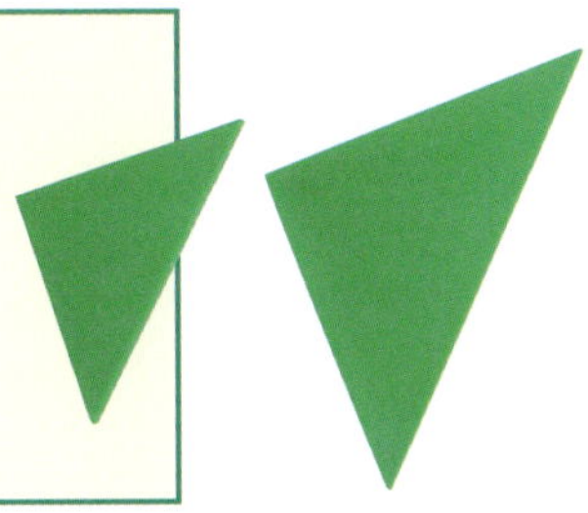

Checking

3. Brodie wants to show his mother that he did not track mud into the house.
   a) How can he prove the tracks are not his?
   b) Will his mother agree? Why or why not?

Practising

4. Which shapes are congruent? How can you check?

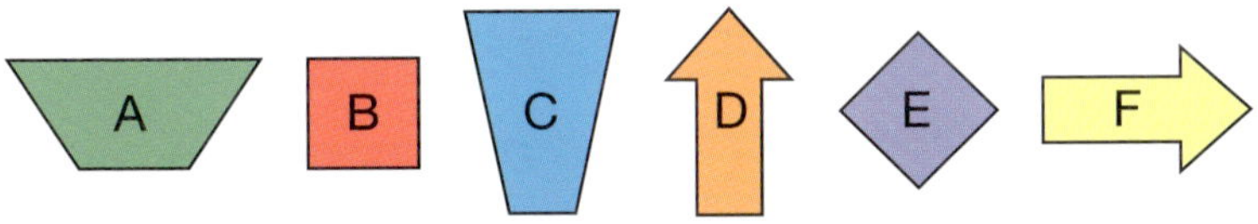

5. Sort the shapes into those that are congruent and those that are not.

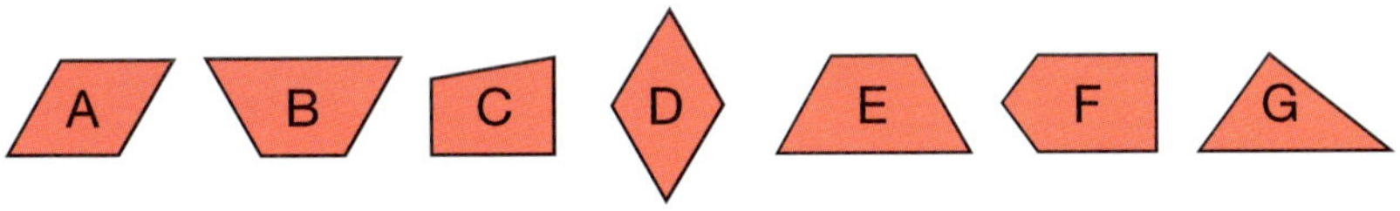

6. Trevor cut cookie dough. How can he check that he made 3 different sizes of cookies?

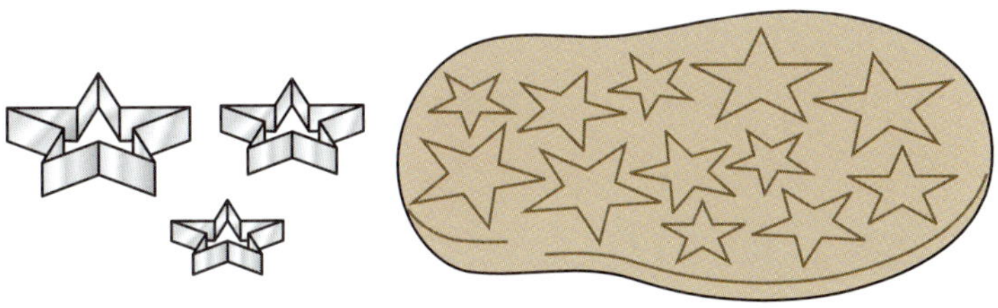

7. Find 2 congruent shapes in your classroom. Name or sketch the shapes. Explain your thinking.
8. a) Find 2 shapes that are the same polygon, but are not congruent. Sketch the shapes. Explain your thinking.
   b) Find 2 shapes that have the same length, but are not congruent. Sketch the shapes. Explain your thinking.

CHAPTER 7

3 Exploring Tangrams

You will need

- 2 tangrams

Goal Create congruent shapes.

? How can you use the 7 tans to make tangram shapes?

Jessica's Tans

I can use the 7 tans to create a swan.

A. Copy Jessica's swan.
Use the tans from 1 tangram.

B. Explain how you used the tans to copy the swan.
Use the names of the polygons.

C. Create your own tangram shape.
Use all or some of the 7 tans from 1 tangram.

D. Copy a classmate's tangram shape.
Use the tans from your other tangram.

Reflecting

1. Look at your tangram shape for part C and the one your classmate made by copying it. How do you know they are congruent?
2. What attributes of tans do you think about when you create or copy a tangram shape?

Making Shapes

Points A and B are 2 vertices of a square.

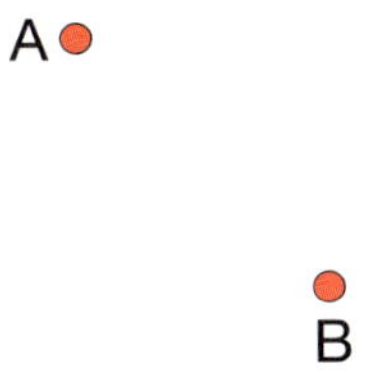

You can make 2 different squares with vertices A and B.

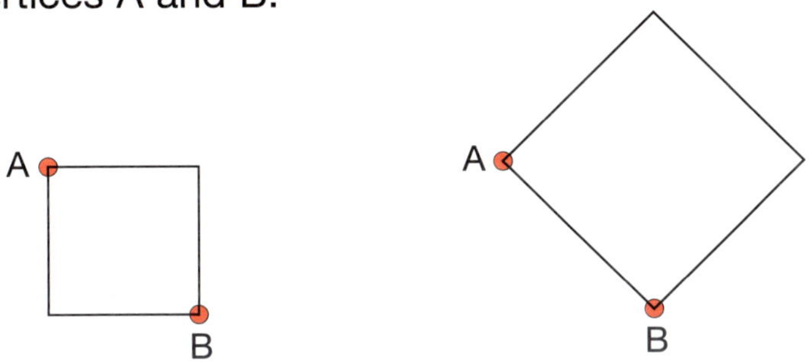

A. Find a 3rd square that has points A and B as vertices.

B. Suppose you have 3 points that are vertices. How many different squares can you draw?

Try These

1. Draw and label 2 points. Draw 3 different triangles with these points as vertices.
2. Draw and label 2 points. Draw 3 different parallelograms with these points as vertices.

4 Communicate About Geometry Patterns

Goal **Use math language to describe geometry patterns.**

You will need

- pattern blocks

- pencil crayons

Devon created this geometry pattern for the border of a bulletin board.
He noticed that 4 or 5 shapes are missing.

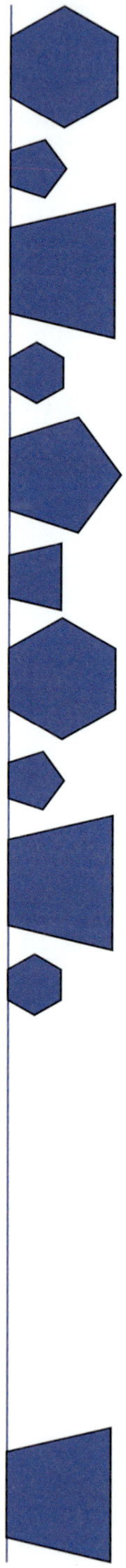

? How can Tiffany explain how to figure out the missing shapes?

Tiffany's Explanation

First I'll describe the pattern.

Then I'll extend it.

I'll use the trapezoid at the bottom to check.

The pattern starts at the top with a large hexagon.
The attributes that change are size and number of sides.
Size: large, small, large, small, large, small, ...
Number of sides: 6, 5, 4, 6, 5, 4, 6, 5, 4, ...

A. What are the strengths of Tiffany's explanation?
Use the Communication Checklist.

B. What would you change to make Tiffany's explanation better?

C. Sketch and describe the missing shapes.

Communication Checklist

- ✓ Did you show the right amount of detail?
- ✓ Did you use math language?

Reflecting

1. How did the Communication Checklist help you improve Tiffany's explanation of Devon's pattern?

Checking

2. Ben described his border pattern.

Ben's Description

The pattern has triangles, pentagons, and squares.

The shapes repeat over and over.

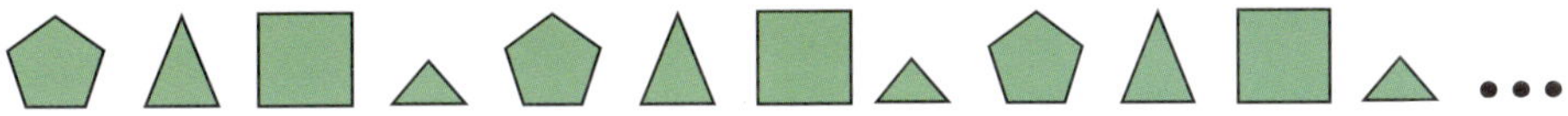

a) What are the strengths of Ben's description? Use the Communication Checklist.

b) Rewrite his description to make it better.

c) Extend the pattern. Sketch and describe the next 3 shapes in the pattern.

Practising

3. Use the Communication Checklist.

a) Describe this bead pattern.

b) What are the strengths of your description?

c) How can you improve your description?

4. a) Use geometry shapes to make your own border pattern.

b) Describe your border pattern.

c) Explain how to extend it.

LESSON

Mid-Chapter Review

1 **1. a)** How many sides does this polygon have?
b) How many vertices does it have?
c) Explain how to use your answer for part a) or part b) to name the shape.

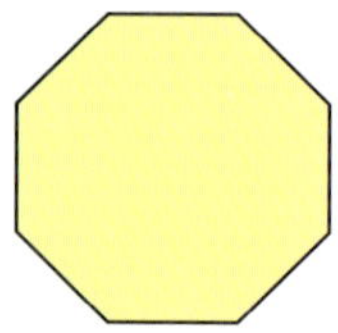

2 **2.** Is the square tan in a tangram congruent to a square pattern block?
Explain your thinking.

3. Which shapes are congruent?

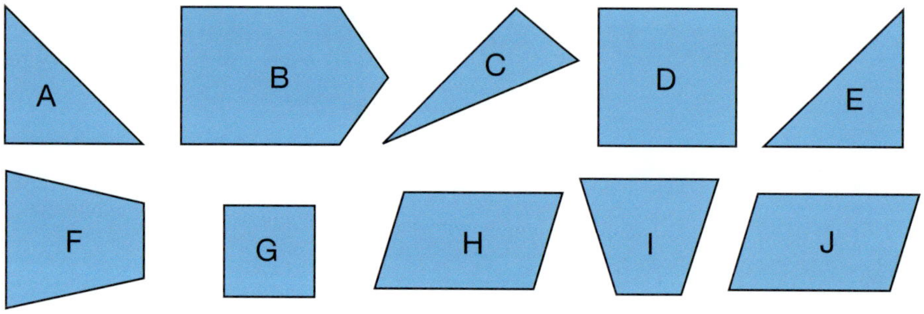

3 **4.** Which tans are congruent?

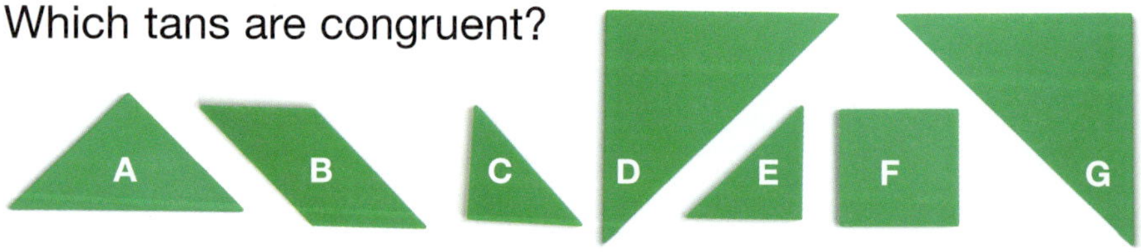

4 **5. a)** Describe the pattern.

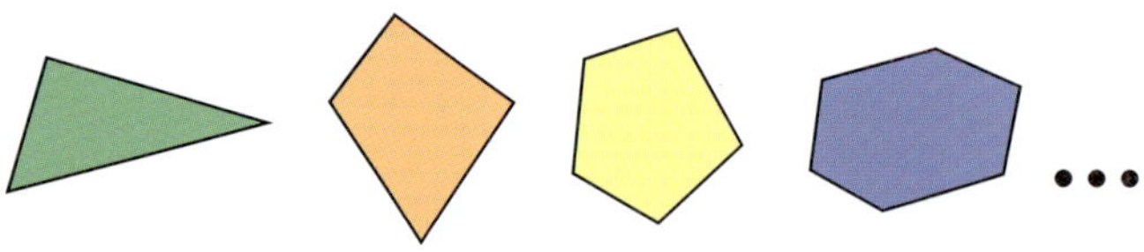

b) What are the strengths of your description?
c) How can you improve your description?
d) Extend the pattern to sketch and describe the 6th shape.

CHAPTER 7

5 Extending Patterns

You will need

- a computer
- computer drawing software

Goal **Extend patterns that have at least 2 changing attributes.**

You can make patterns on a computer.
A computer might give choices like these.

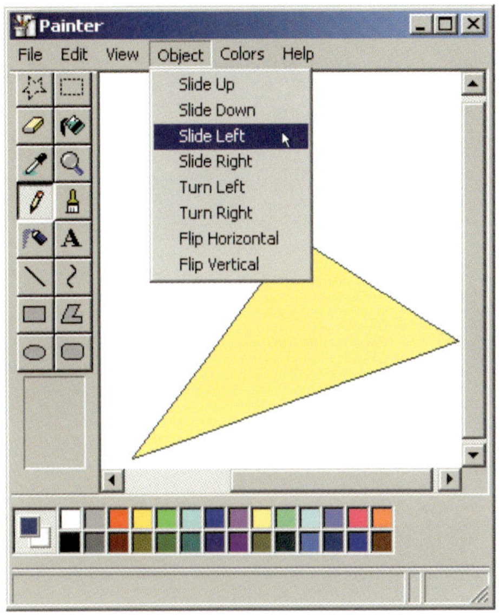

? How can you create your own pattern rules and then try them?

A. Decide how your pattern will start. Draw the starting shape.

B. Choose the changing attributes of your pattern:
- shape
- colour
- size
- position

C. Create your pattern.

D. Write the pattern rule.

E. Trade pattern rules with a partner. Use your partner's rule at least 4 times.

F. Compare your pattern with your partner's pattern. How are the patterns different? How are they the same?

Reflecting

1. Why do you need to identify the starting shape to describe a pattern?

2. Why do you need to identify the changing attributes to extend a pattern?

6 Sorting 2-D Shapes

Goal Compare and sort 2-D shapes.

? In what ways can these 2-D shapes be sorted?

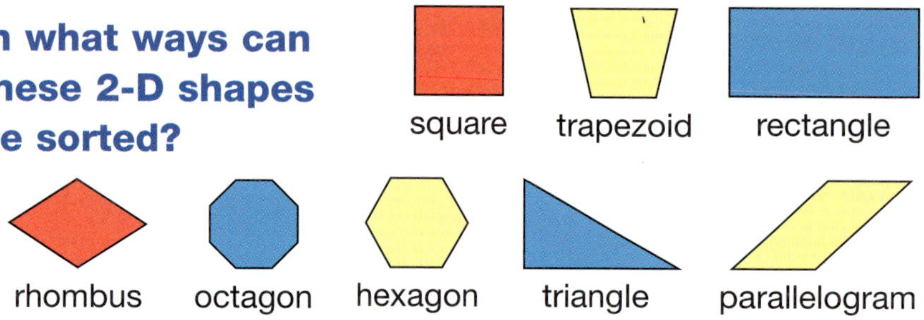

You will need

- shapes

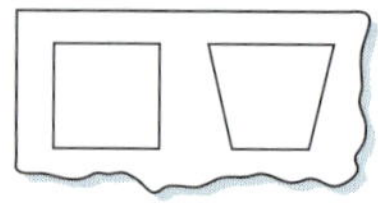

- Venn diagrams

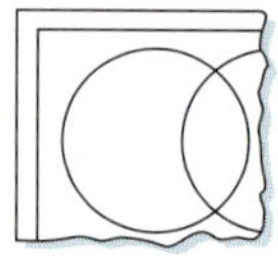

- a tangram

- a ruler

- a square corner

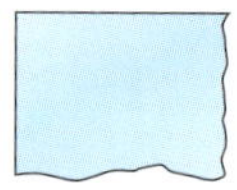

Sukan's Sorting

I sorted with 2 attributes: number of sides and number of square corners.

Shape	4 sides or more	1 square corner or more
hexagon	✓	✗
octagon		
parallelogram		
rectangle		
rhombus		
square		
trapezoid		
triangle		

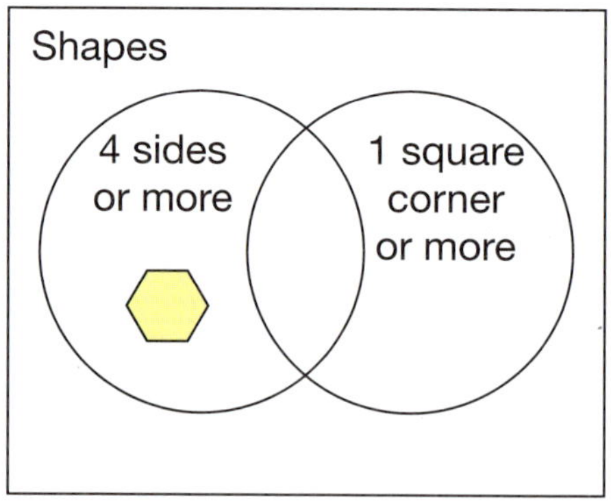

A. Where in the **Venn diagram** should Sukan put the square? Where should she put the triangle?

B. Finish sorting the shapes using the chart and the Venn diagram.

Reflecting

1. Describe the shapes for each of the 4 parts of the Venn diagram.

Checking

2. a) What attributes can you use to sort these shapes?

   b) Sort these shapes using a chart and a Venn diagram.

Practising

3. Brodie is sorting 7 tans using 2 attributes: congruency and number of vertices. Draw a Venn diagram to show Brodie's sorting.

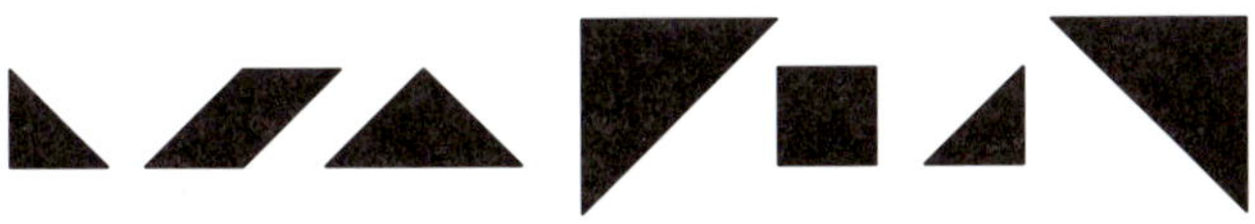

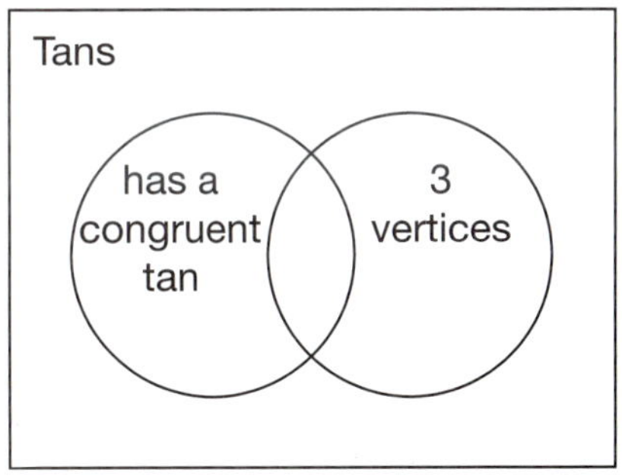

4. Sort these parallelograms using 2 attributes: number of equal sides and number of square corners.

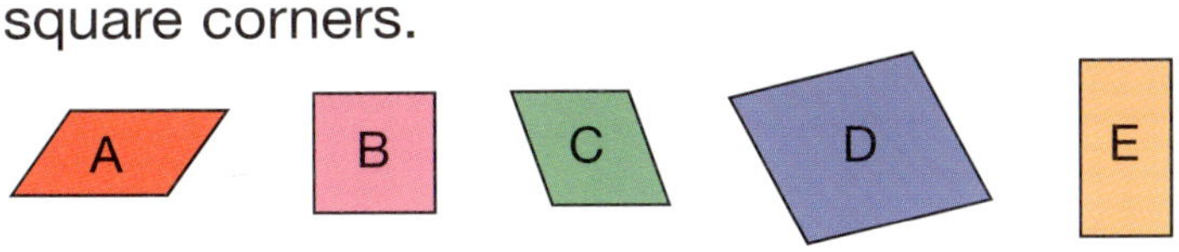

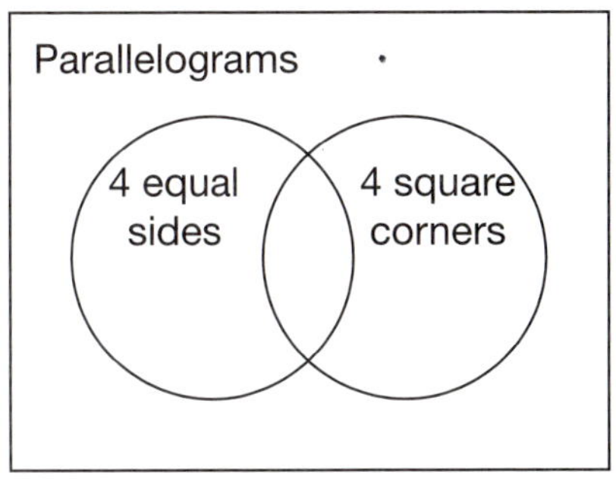

5. Compare these shapes. Describe how the shapes are the same and how they are different.

Skills Bank

LESSON

1 **1.** Name each polygon.

a) A ■ has 5 straight sides.
b) A ■ has straight sides and 6 vertices.
c) A ■ has 4 equal straight sides and 4 square corners.
d) An ■ has straight sides and 8 vertices.

2 **2.** There are 4 cookie cutter shapes.
Identify which cookies were cut from the red, blue, purple, and green cutters.

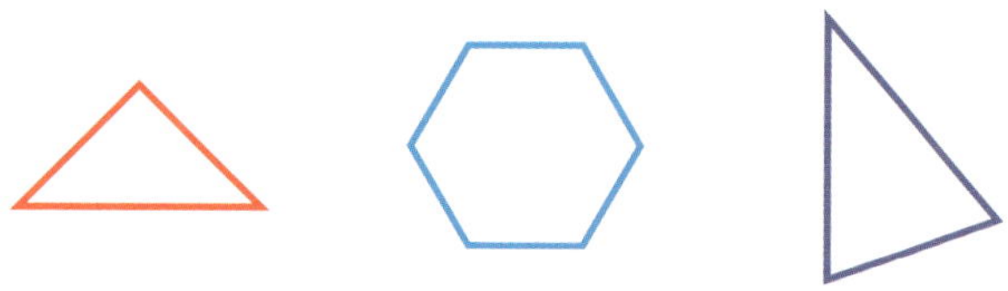

cookie cutters

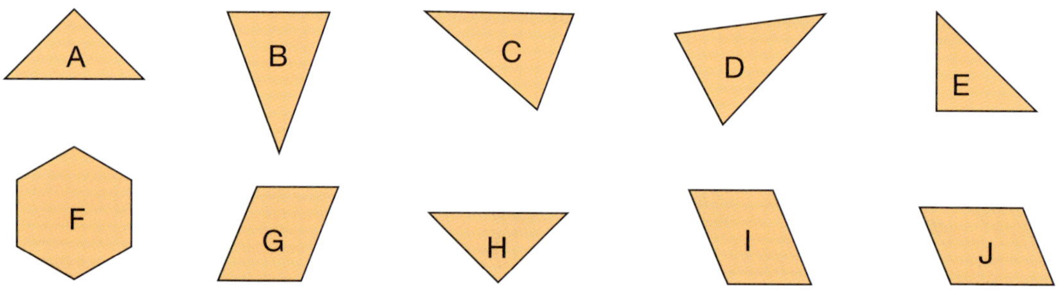

5 **3.** Describe how the attributes change in each pattern.
Sketch the next 3 shapes.
Write a pattern rule for each.

a) 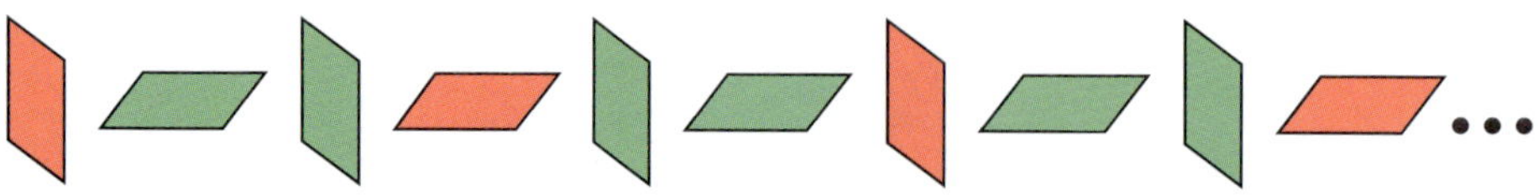

b) 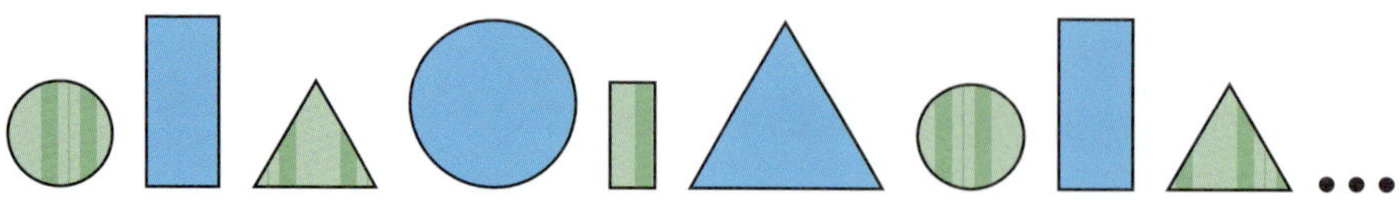

4. a) Find one way to sort the tans.
Tell how you sorted.

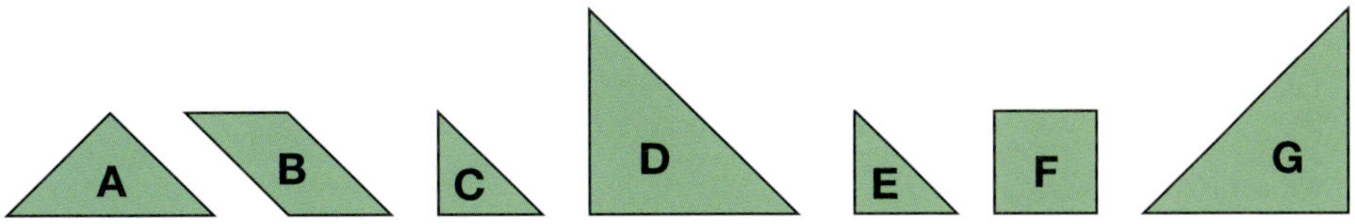

b) Sort the tans another way.
Tell how you sorted.

5. One shape in each group is different from the others.
Which shape is different? Explain.

a)

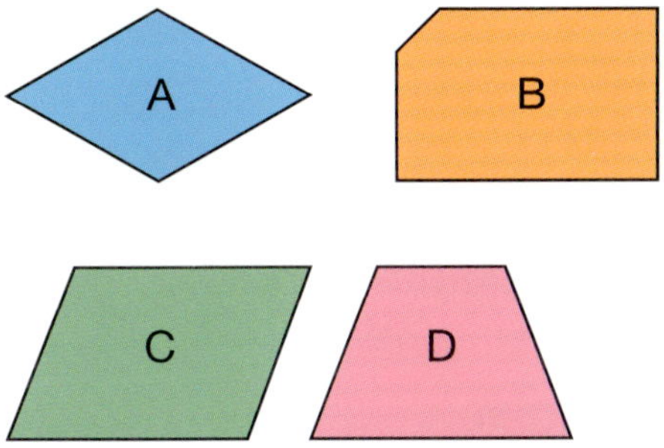

b)

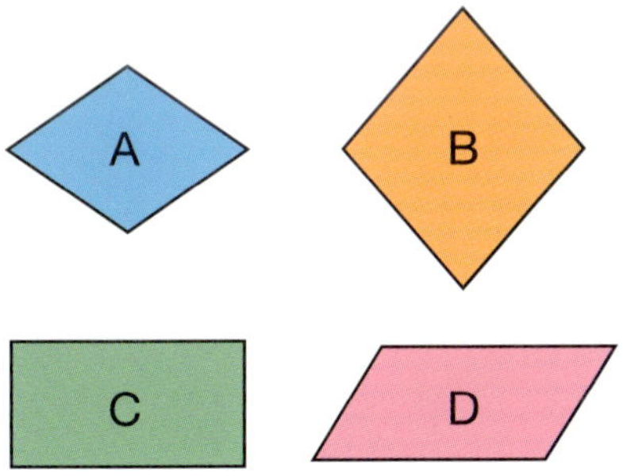

c)

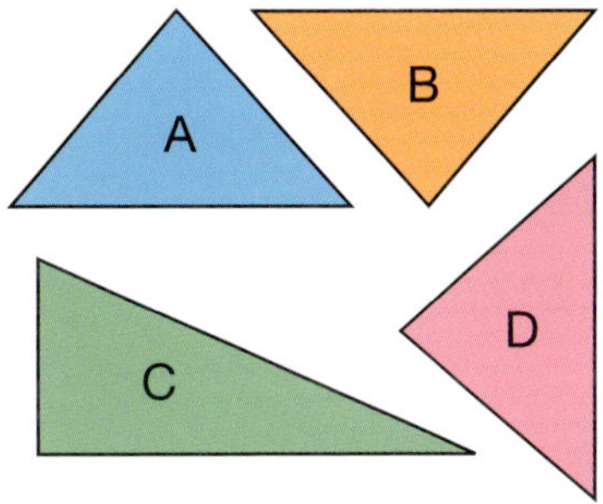

d)

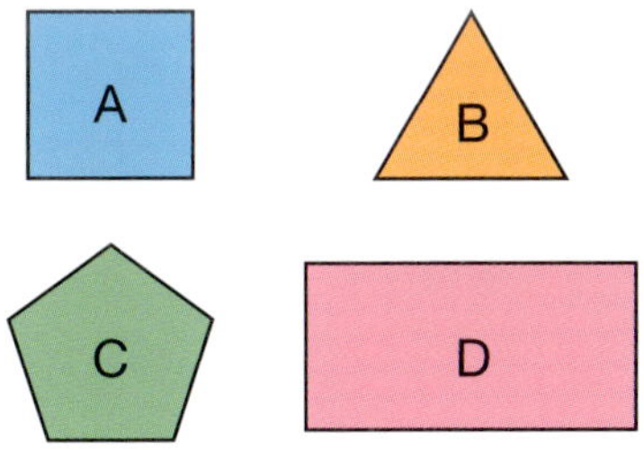

6. Compare the shapes in each pair.
How are they the same?
How are they different?

a)

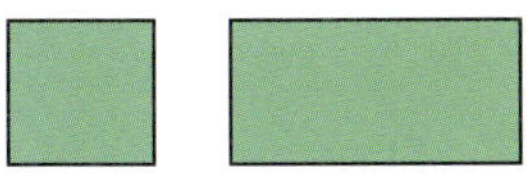

b)

c)

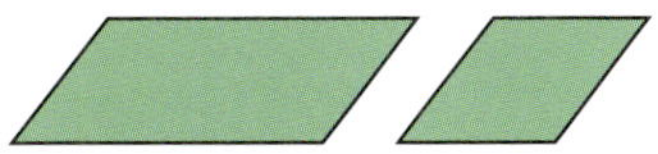

d)

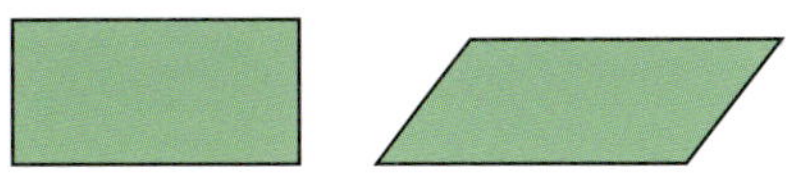

LESSON

Problem Bank

2 **1.** Are the **blue** and **yellow** triangles congruent? Explain how you know.

2. Rachel used 27 pattern blocks to make a turtle.

a) What is the least number of blocks that Rachel could use to make a congruent turtle? List the number of each type of block.

b) What is the greatest number of blocks she could use? List the number of each type of block.

3. A **purple** triangle is not congruent to a **red** triangle. The **red** triangle is not congruent to a **green** triangle. Is it possible for the **purple** and **green** triangles to be congruent? Show how you know.

5 **4.** Which piece is missing from the pattern?

A. 

B. 

C. 

D. 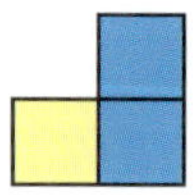

6 **5.** Describe the sorting rule.

a) 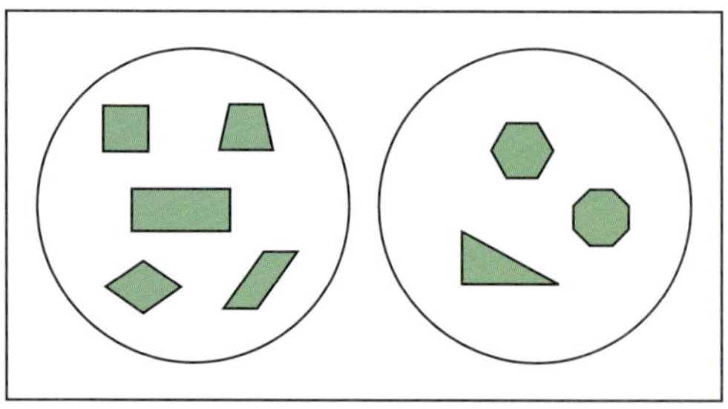

b) 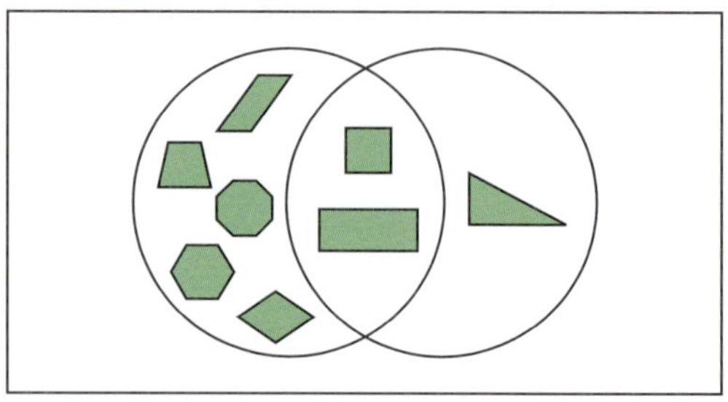

Chapter Review

LESSON

1 **1.** What do you know about the sides and vertices of each polygon?
Sketch each polygon to show your thinking.
a) octagon **b)** pentagon **c)** hexagon

2. You can name this shape a square or a rectangle.
Which name tells more about the shape?
Explain how it tells more.

2 **3.** Which sentences are true?
Explain each answer with an example.
a) Congruent shapes must be the same size.
b) Congruent shapes must be the same colour.
c) Congruent shapes must be the same shape.

3 **4.** Suppose you and a classmate each use the same tans to create tangram shapes.
Will the shapes always be congruent?
Explain with an example.

4 **5.** **a)** Describe this bead pattern.
Use the Communication Checklist.
b) What are the strengths of your description?
c) How can you improve your description?

5 **6.** Create a geometry pattern. Write the pattern rule.

6 **7.** Create a sorting rule to sort the pattern blocks.
Use a Venn diagram. Write your sorting rule.

Chapter Task

Creating a Mosaic

Shirley created this mosaic for the front cover of her work folder.
Create your own mosaic by cutting pieces of coloured paper and gluing them onto a black sheet of construction paper.

- Most of the shapes should have straight sides.
- At least one shape should have more than 4 sides.
- Some shapes should be congruent to each other.
- Most of the black rectangle should be covered with shapes. Try to make a pattern.

? How can you describe your design?

Task Checklist

- ✓ Did you try different arrangements before gluing the shapes?
- ✓ Did you identify the congruent shapes?
- ✓ Did you describe any patterns in your design?
- ✓ Did you use math language?

Cumulative Review

Cross-Strand Multiple Choice

1. Which unit of measurement is not reasonable?
   A. The length of a table is 1 m.
   B. The height of a door is 1 km.
   C. The length of a worm is 1 dm.
   D. The length of an insect is 1 cm.

2. Which might be the temperature when you swim outside?
   E. 0°C **F.** 8°C **G.** 15°C **H.** 29°C

3. Kadin collected 387 juice boxes one week and 418 boxes the next week. How many juice boxes did he collect in total?
   A. 805 **B.** 800 **C.** 795 **D.** 790

4. How many people visited the Web site on the 2nd day?
   E. 517 **F.** 608 **G.** 507 **H.** 618

Web Site Visitors

1st day	2nd day	1st and 2nd day total
297		804

5. Which pairs of shapes look congruent?
   A. shapes A and B
   B. shapes B and D
   C. shapes C and D
   D. shapes A and C

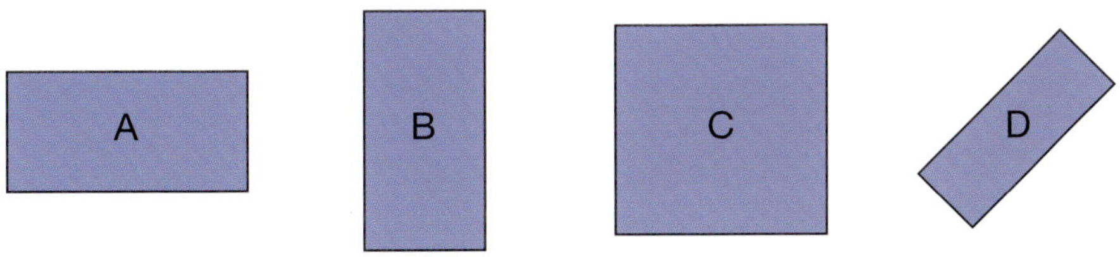

6. Which shape is a pentagon?

E.
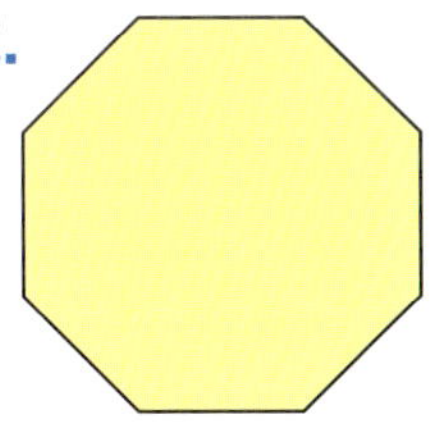

F.
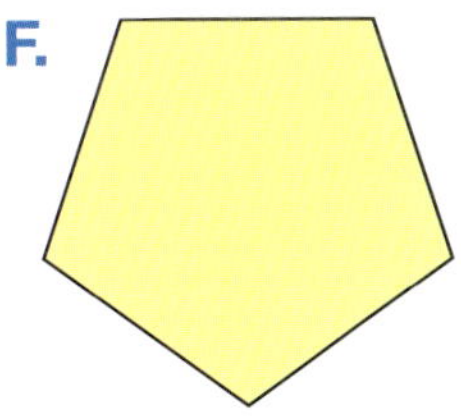

G.
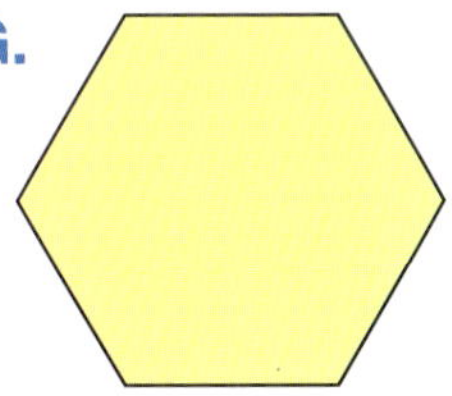

H.
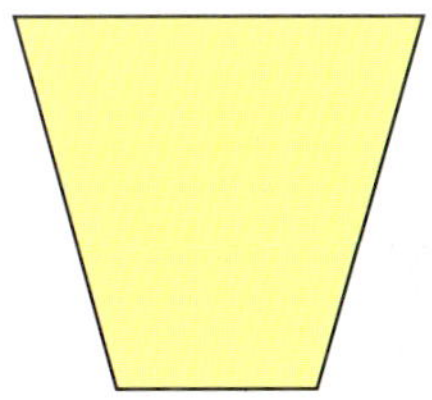

Cross-Strand Investigation

Making and Flying Paper Airplanes

7. You can make airplanes that are different sizes.

A.
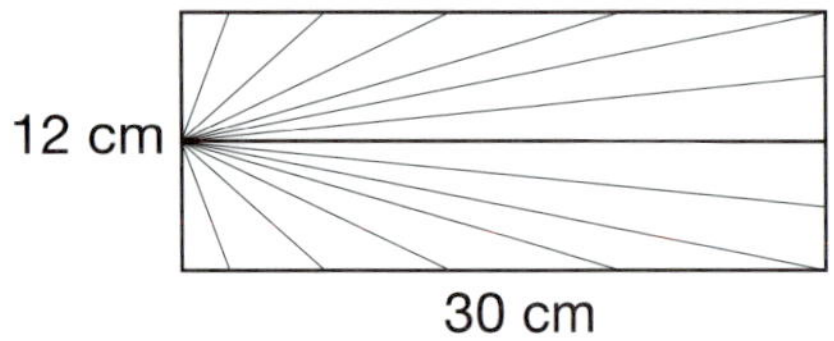

B.
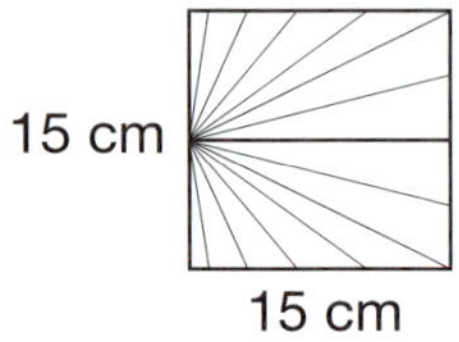

C.
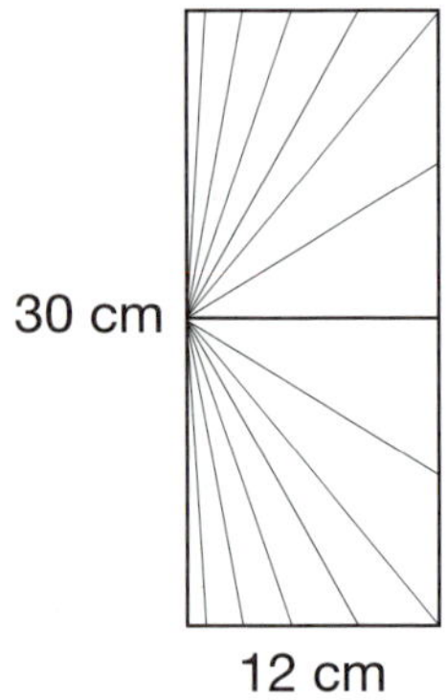

a) Order the airplanes from shortest to longest.

b) Which airplane has the greatest perimeter? Show your work.

8. These are the distances Ben, Kim, and Jakob flew their paper airplanes.

a) What is the difference between the longest and the shortest distances? Show your work.

b) Which distances are between 2 m and 4 m? Explain your thinking.

Distances for Paper Airplane Flights

Student	Distance (centimetres)
Ben	231
Kim	454
Jakob	320

9. a) Sketch any 10 shapes you see in this design. Shapes of different colours can be joined to make different shapes. Number your shapes from 1 to 10.

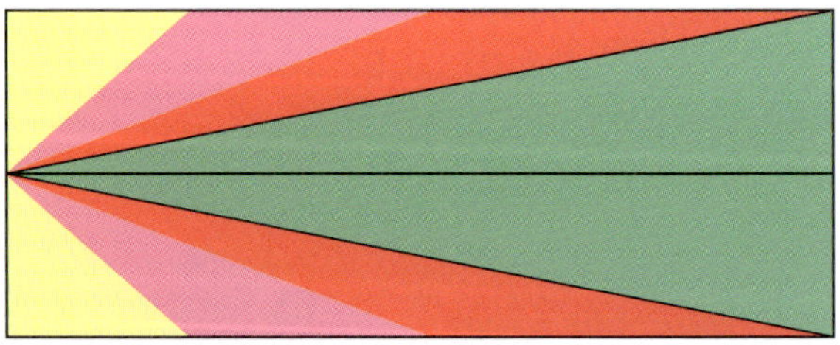

b) Name the polygons for 2 of your shapes. How do you know?

c) Choose any 2 shapes. How are they the same? How are they different?

d) Sort the shapes using 2 attributes: number of sides and number of square corners.

e) Which shapes are congruent? How do you know?

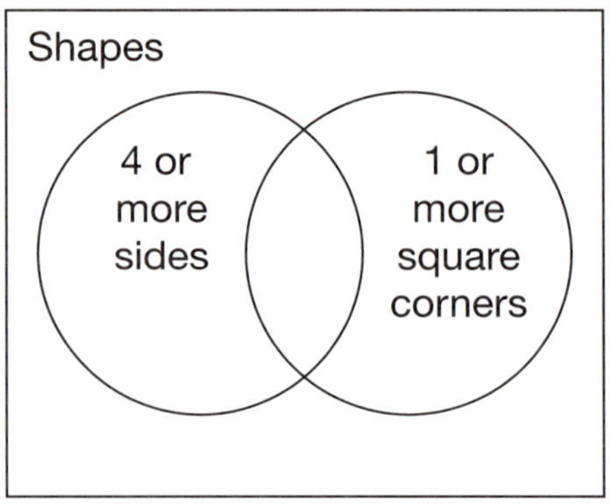

CHAPTER 8

Area and Grids

Goals

You will be able to

- estimate and measure the area of shapes using nonstandard units
- compare and order shapes by area
- solve area problems using models
- describe moving on a map

Bird's-eye view of a neighbourhood

Getting Started

You will need

- letter-sized paper
- scissors

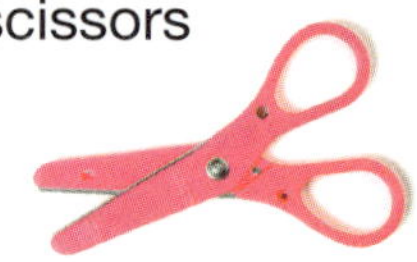

- pattern block triangles

Classroom Areas

Derek's class is making a display of its work over the term.

They decided *not* to use the floor for their display.

? How big are the display areas in your classroom?

A. Choose 3 surfaces that you could use for a display, such as a bulletin board, chalkboard, or table.

B. Estimate the number of sheets of paper needed to cover each surface.

C. Measure the **area** of each surface with the paper. Explain how you measured.

D. Fold the paper. Cut it to make smaller pieces of equal sizes.

E. Estimate the area of each surface using the smaller piece of paper.
Measure the area of each surface using the smaller piece of paper.

F. Was it easier to measure with the larger paper or the smaller paper? Why?

Do You Remember?

1. Estimate the number of each object needed to cover the front of your math book.
   a) your hand **b)** a pencil case **c)** an eraser

2. Measure the area of each shape.
   Use pattern block triangles.
   a)

   b)
   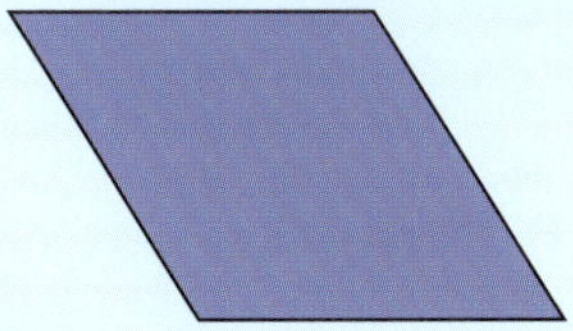
   c)
   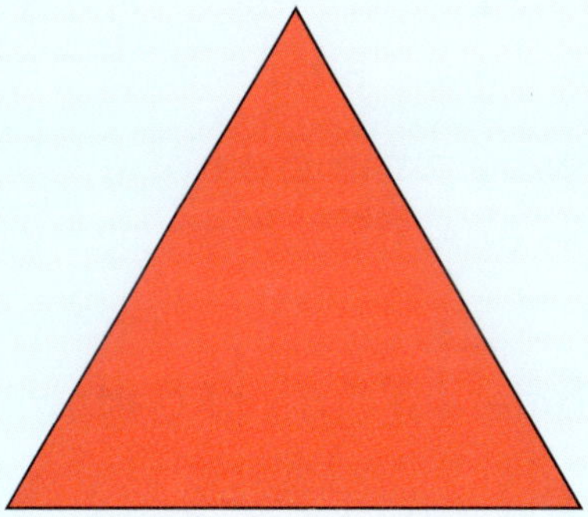

3. Where is each shape compared to the star?
   For example, the circle is above the star.
   a) green **rhombus**
   b) orange triangle
   c) grey square

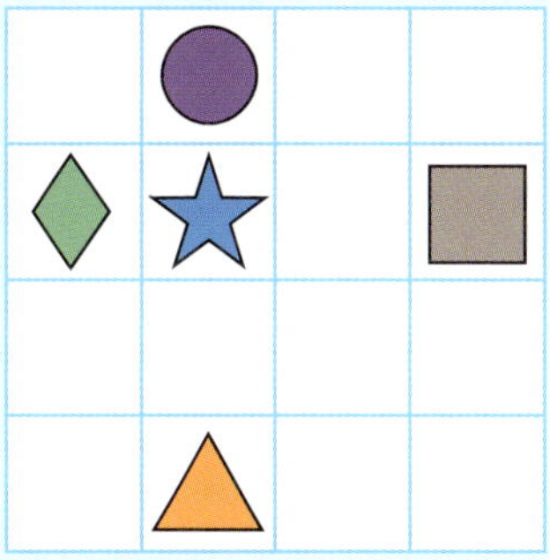

1 Exploring Area

Goal **Compare and order areas using nonstandard units.**

Jack is making a sign to tell everyone about his party. He has lights to go around it.

He wants the sign to have a big area for the words.

You will need

- 4 equal lengths of string

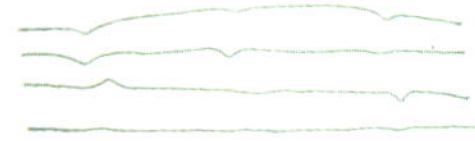

- tape

- pattern blocks

? What shape should Jack use for the sign?

A. Use each piece of string to model a shape for Jack's sign. Make 4 different shapes. Tape each shape to paper.

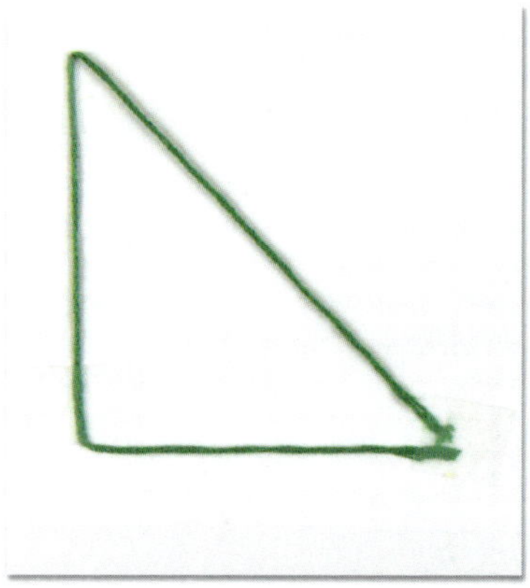

B. Measure the area of each shape using one type of pattern block.

C. Measure the area of each shape using a different type of pattern block.

D. Order your shapes from least to greatest area.

E. Which shape do you think Jack should use for the sign?

Reflecting

1. Explain how you measured the area of each shape.
2. Explain how you ordered the areas of the 4 shapes.
3. Sonya said a hexagon pattern block was best to measure the greatest area. She said a triangle pattern block was best to measure the least area. Why do you think she said this?

2 Measuring Area with Square Units

Goal **Estimate, measure, and compare areas using square units.**

You will need

- scrapbook pages

- large and small square pictures

- scissors

Rose wants to make a scrapbook of her vacation. She has 2 different sizes of scrapbooks.

? Which scrapbook should Rose use?

Rose's Area Measurement

I want to use the page with the greater area. I'll find the area in **square units**.

A. Estimate the number of large squares that will cover a page in scrapbook 1.

B. Test your estimate. Record the area in large square units.

C. Estimate the number of small squares that will cover the page.

D. Record the area of the page in small square units.

E. Repeat parts A to D for scrapbook 2.

F. Which scrapbook has pages with the greater area?

Reflecting

1. Explain the strategy you used for estimating area.
2. Why is the number of square units greater when you use small squares instead of large squares?

square unit
A **nonstandard** unit shaped like a square for measuring area

CHAPTER 8

3 Counting Square Units

Goal **Compare and order areas by counting square units.**

You will need

- grid paper

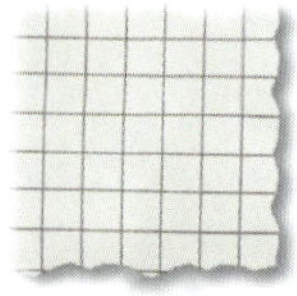

- pencil crayons

Brady designed a beaded hair clip on grid paper.
Each square in the grid represents 1 bead.

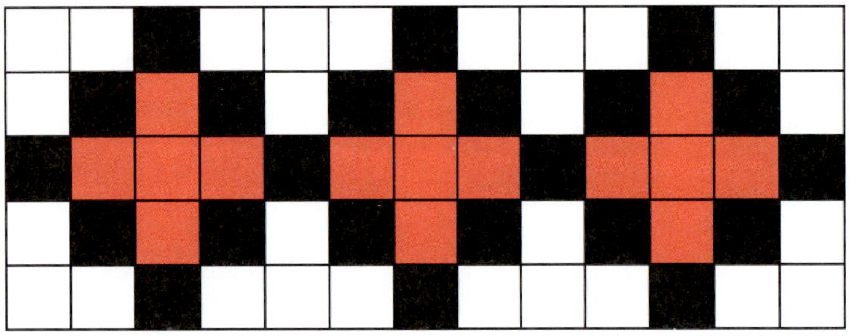

? Which colour of bead does Brady use most?

Brady's Bead Design

I can count the squares to find the area of each colour.
Then I can compare the areas.

A. Estimate which colour of bead covers the greatest area.

B. What is the area of the black part?

C. What is the area of the red part?

D. What is the area of the white part?

E. Order the coloured areas from least to greatest.
Which colour covers the greatest area?

F. Use grid paper. Copy 1 of the **red** parts of Brady's design.
Make 2 other shapes with the same area.

Reflecting

1. Describe the counting strategy you used to count the coloured parts of the bead design.
2. Brady changed her design to look like this. What area is each colour? Explain how you know.

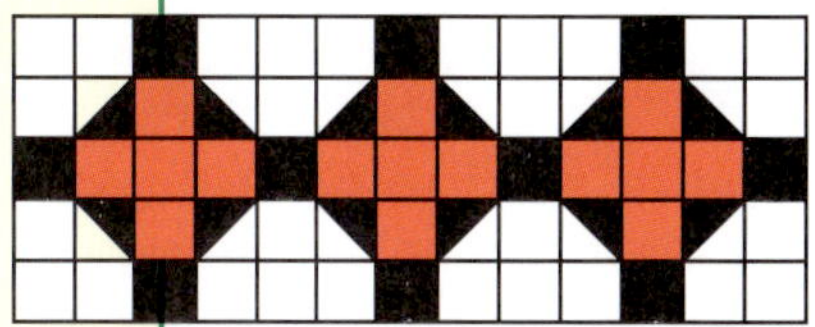

3. Different shapes can have the same area. Explain how you know.

Checking

4. Brady made this bead design.
   a) Estimate which colour covers the greatest area.
   b) What is the area of each colour?
   c) Order the coloured areas from least to greatest.

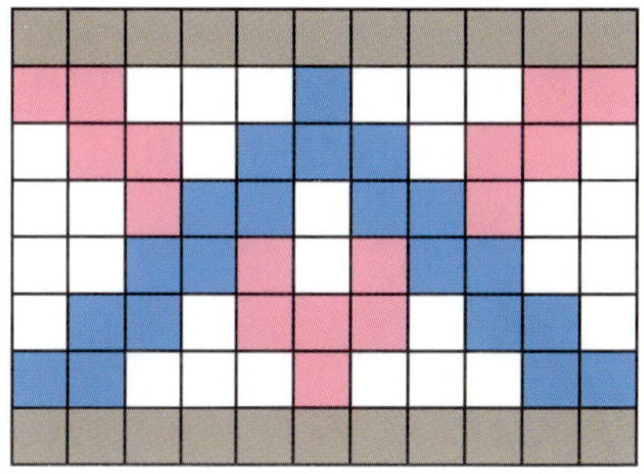

Practising

5. What is the area of each shape in square units?

a) 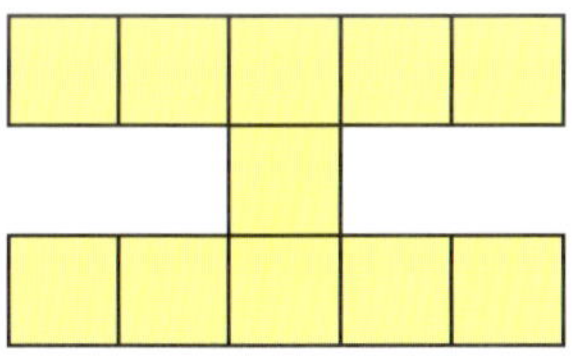

b) 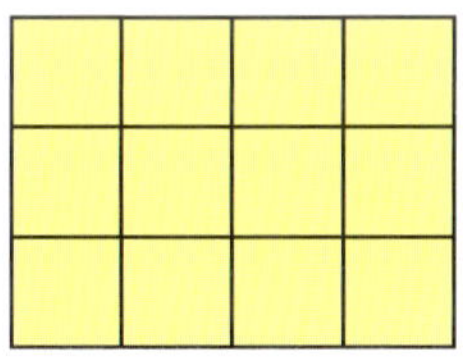

c) 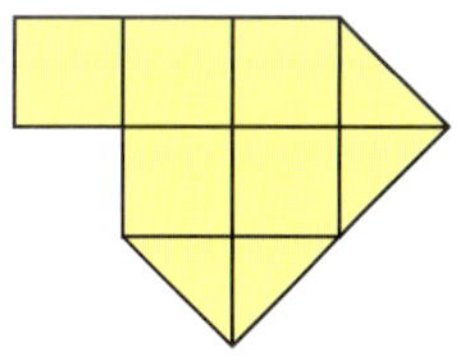

6. Order the shapes in Question 5 from least area to greatest area.
7. Felix made a name tag for his pet. Each square has an area of 1 square unit.
   a) What is the area of each letter?
   b) Order the letters from least area to greatest area.
   c) What is the area of the white part of the tag?

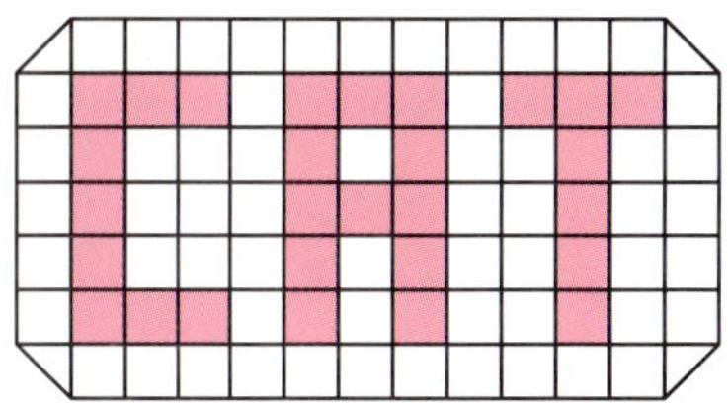

8. Colour 4 different shapes on grid paper. Make each shape with an area of 16 square units.

4 Solve Problems Using a Model

Goal **Use models to solve area problems.**

Amit is designing a pond for the yard. The pond will have an area of 4 square tiles.

A patio will be built with square tiles all around the pond.

You will need

- grid paper

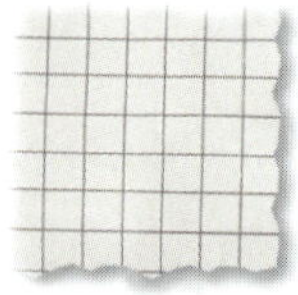

- square tiles

? What shape should Amit make the pond and patio if he wants to use the fewest tiles?

Amit's Pond and Patio Tiles

I used blue tiles to represent the pond tiles.

I used red tiles to represent the patio tiles.

I arranged the 4 tiles for the pond in as many ways as I could.

Then I placed red tiles around each group of blue tiles.

To find the area of each pond and patio, I counted the tiles.

design 1

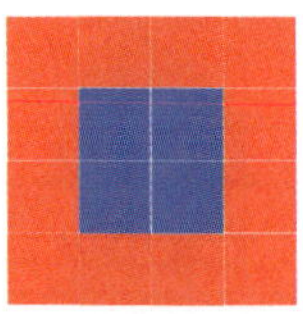

16 square units

design 2

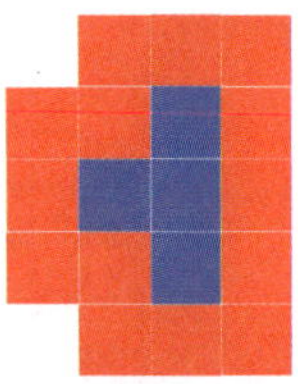

18 square units

design 3

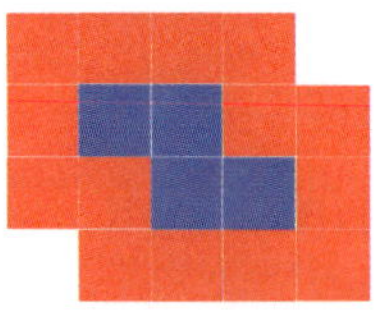

18 square units

design 4

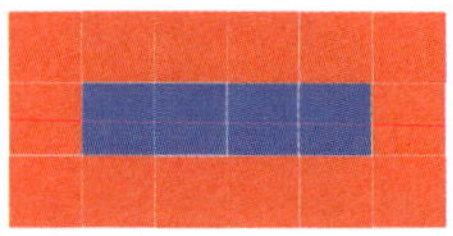

18 square units

design 5

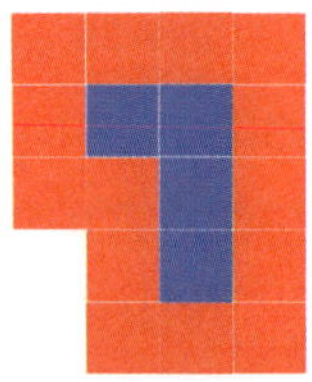

18 square units

I should use design 1 because it uses the fewest tiles.

Reflecting

1. How did making a model help Amit solve the problem?
2. Explain how you could model Amit's problem using square grid paper.

Checking

3. Jake uses 8 tiles to design a T-shaped pond. He wants to use the fewest tiles for a patio all around the pond.
   a) Model all the possible designs for Jake's pond and patio. Use tiles. Sketch your models.
   b) What is the area of each design?
   c) Which design uses the fewest patio tiles?

Practising

4. Kiera has a patio made of 4 green and 4 white square tiles. Her family wants to make a new patio that has double the area.

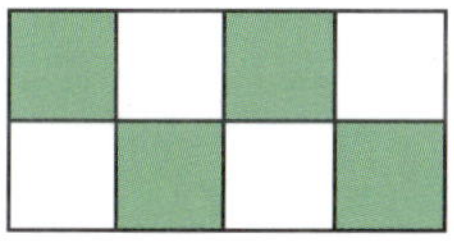

   a) What will the area of the new patio be?
   b) Sketch 3 shapes for the new patio.
   c) Kiera has 8 green tiles and 6 white tiles for the new patio. Does she have enough of each colour? Show your work.

5. a) Design 4 different patios with 8 tiles. Sketch your shapes.
   b) What is the area of each shape?

6. I'm thinking of a shape with 20 square units. What might the shape be? Sketch 2 possibilities.

5 Moving on a Map

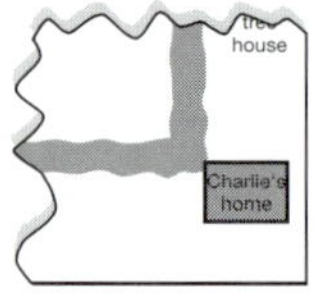

You will need

- Charlie's map
- pencil crayons

Goal **Describe routes on a map.**

Charlie's cousin, Alex, is visiting him. Charlie drew this map and wants to describe routes on the map.

? How can Charlie describe routes on his map?

Charlie's Map

I want to tell Alex how to go from my home to the pond.

I'll use the directions north, south, east, or west.

We must stay on the paths.

Go north from my home past the tree house to the store.

Then go west to the pond.

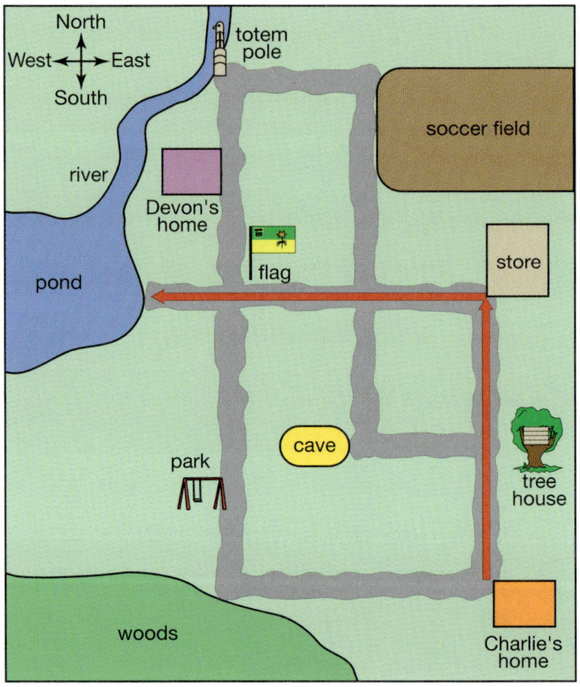

Use the directions north, south, east, or west to describe routes along the paths.

A. Describe how Alex can go back from the pond to Charlie's home along the same route.

B. Draw a route from Charlie's home to the woods, to the park, and then to the totem pole. Use **blue**.

C. Describe the **blue** route.

D. Draw a different route from Charlie's home to the totem pole. Use **orange**.

E. Describe the **orange** route.

Reflecting

1. Charlie described how to go from his home to the pond. You described how to go from the pond to his home. Compare the descriptions.
2. Suppose Charlie is going from the totem pole to the park.
   a) What direction is he going? Explain how you know.
   b) If he turned right, what direction would he be going? Explain how you know.

Checking

3. Draw a yellow route from Devon's home to the tree house. Describe the yellow route. Use the directions north, south, east, or west.

Practising

Use the directions north, south, east, or west.

4. a) Draw a **purple** route from the cave to the store, and then to Devon's home. Describe the **purple** route.
   b) Repeat part a) for a different route from the cave to Devon's home. Use **brown**.
5. a) Draw a new route between 2 places on Charlie's map. Use **green**. Describe the **green** route.
   b) Read your description for someone to draw the path in **red** on their own map.
6. a) Look around. Name an object that is north of you.
   b) Name an object that is east of you.
   c) Describe a route from the object in part a) to the object in part b).
7. Make up your own route problem for Charlie's map or for your classroom. Solve your problem.

Areas of Unusual Shapes

You will need

- grid paper

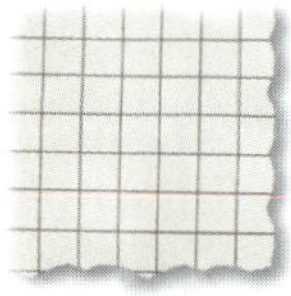

You can estimate areas of shapes by combining parts.

What is the estimated area of this rabbit picture?

Juan's Estimate

The rabbit covers 2 squares completely (12 and 13).

The rabbit covers most of another 5 squares (7, 14, 17, 18, and 19).

There are also 5 squares that have little bits covered (2, 3, 8, 9, and 11).

I'll imagine the squares with little bits combining with the squares that are mostly covered.

The combination makes about 5 full squares.

The area of the rabbit picture is about $2 + 5 = 7$ square units.

Try These

1. Estimate the area of this drum picture in square units.
2. Trace your hand on grid paper. Estimate the area of your hand in square units.

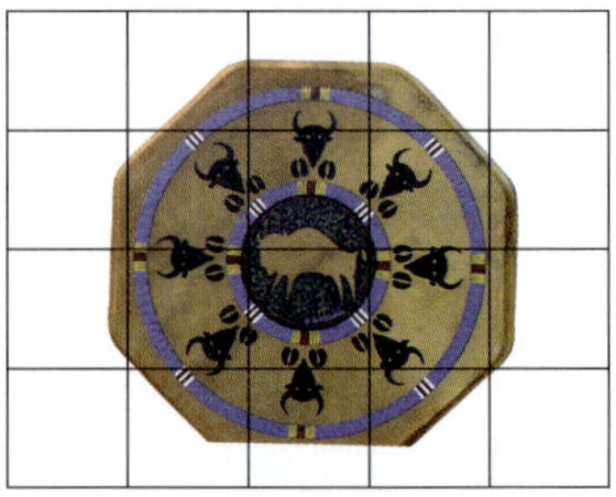

Math Game

Roll to the Star

Number of players: 2
How to play: Roll dice to move toward a star on a grid.

Step 1 Use grid paper. Draw a star in any square.
Label the lower left corner as START.
Mark north, south, east, and west on your grid.

Step 2 Each player places a playing piece on START.

Step 3 Take turns rolling 2 dice. First move east or west using the number on one die.
Then move north or south using the number on the other die.

Each player takes 4 turns.
The player closest to the star wins.

You will need

- large grid paper

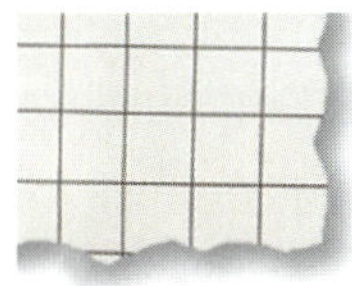

- dice

- 2 tiles

Lyn's Turn

I'm using the blue tile.
I rolled 3 and 4.
I'll move 4 spaces east and 3 spaces north.
I'll be close to the star!

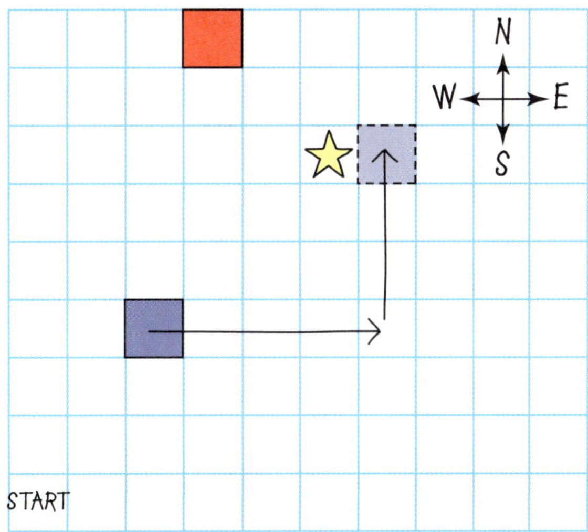

Skills Bank

LESSON

1 **1.** Measure the area of each shape. Use one type of pattern block.

a)

b)

2 **2.** Measure the area of each shape. Use the square pattern block.

a)

b)

3 **3.** What is the coloured area of each shape in square units?

a)

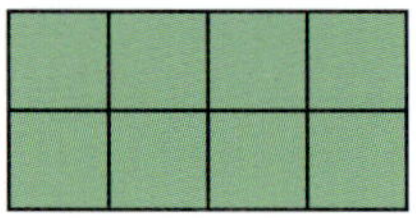

b)

c)

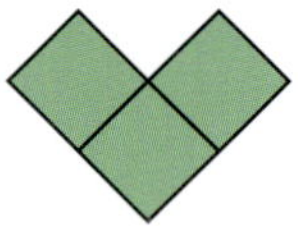

d)

3 **4.** **a)** What is the area of each letter?

b) Order the areas from least to greatest.

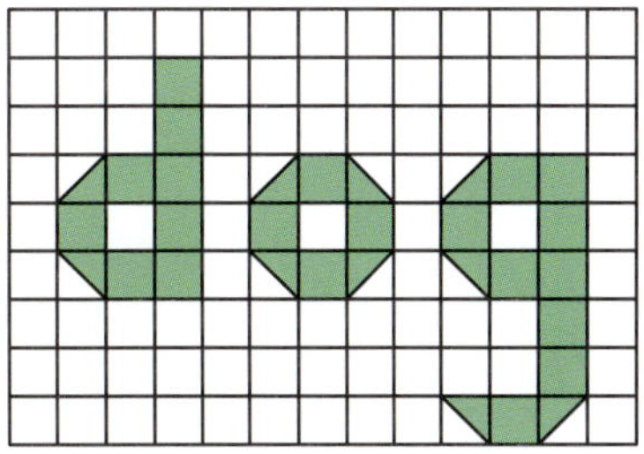

4 **5.** What shapes can you make with an area of 10 square units? Make as many shapes as you can on grid paper. Use only whole squares.

5 **6.** Eva and Karl are on a canoe trip. Use only the directions north, south, east, and west to describe each route.

a) How can Eva and Karl go to the beaver, then to the trout, and then to the otter?

b) How can Eva and Karl go to the sea gull without going over the rocks?

c) How can Eva and Karl go to the moose without going over the rocks? Describe 2 different routes.

Problem Bank

LESSON

1 **1.** Make a design using 2 yellow and 2 blue pattern blocks. Trace the outside of your design.

Estimate the area of your design in green pattern blocks. Explain your estimate. Measure the area in green pattern blocks.

2 **2.** Eli had a square piece of cardboard with an area of 9 square units. It wasn't the right shape for his project, so he cut it up and taped it back together.

What shape might it be? What is its area? Sketch 2 possibilities.

3. Cut out 2 congruent squares. The area of each square is 1 square unit.

a) Fold 1 square along the diagonal. Cut along the fold. Describe the 2 new pieces.

b) Use all 3 shapes to make different shapes. What is the area of each shape? Explain how you know.

c) If only edges of the same length are placed together, how many different shapes with the 3 pieces are possible?

3 **4. a)** Shade in the letters of your name on square grid paper using square units.

b) Estimate the area of your name.

c) Measure the area of your name.

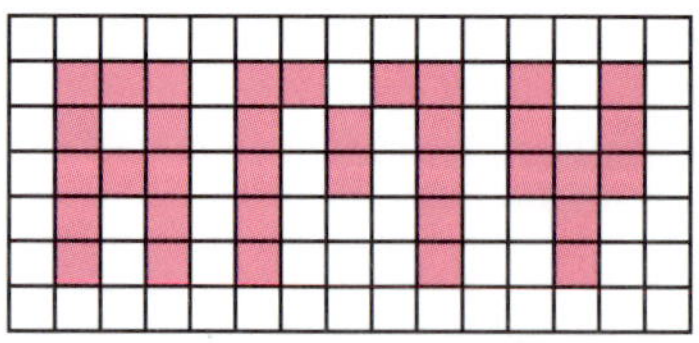

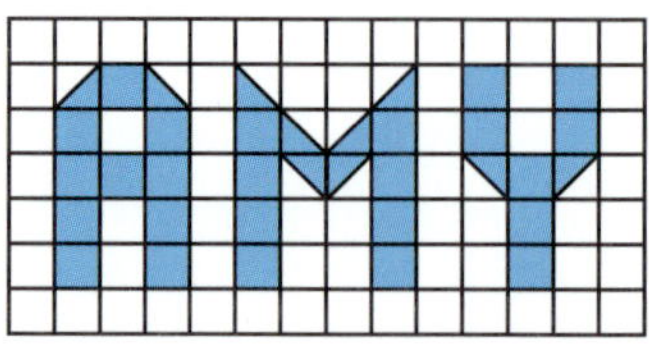

4 **5.** Design a bead bracelet that uses 3 different colours of beads. Use square grid paper.

Each square represents 1 bead. What area is covered by each colour?

4

6. Julia thinks that this picture has the same area as the frame.
Is she right?
How do you know?

7. a) About how much of this grid is green: greater than half or less than half?
Tell how you know.
b) Sketch a 4-by-4 grid and shade half of the squares.
Show other ways to shade half of the grid.
Explain your shading.

8. Shape A is worth 10¢.
a) How much is shape B worth?
b) How many rectangular shapes can you make worth 80¢?
c) How did you use area to solve the problem?

A

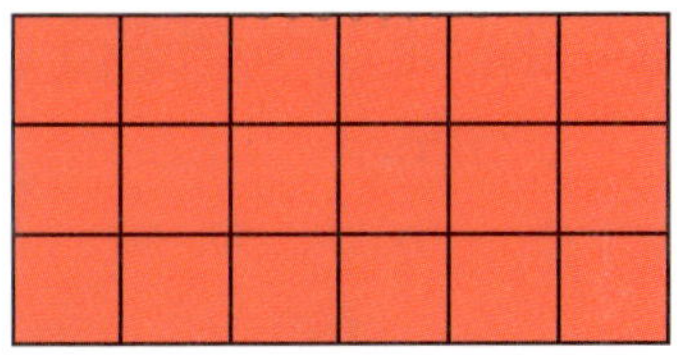

B

9. This blue square has squares of different areas inside it.

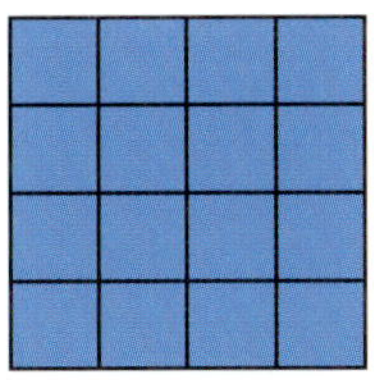

a) Some squares are 1-by-1 squares.
What is the area of each of these?

b) Some squares are 2-by-2 squares.
What is the area of each of these?

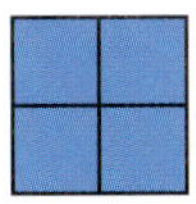

c) What other sizes of squares are there?
What is the area of each size?
d) What is the area of the largest square?

Chapter Review

LESSON

1 **1.** Use blue pattern blocks.

a) Measure the area of each shape.

b) Which shape has a greater area? How do you know?

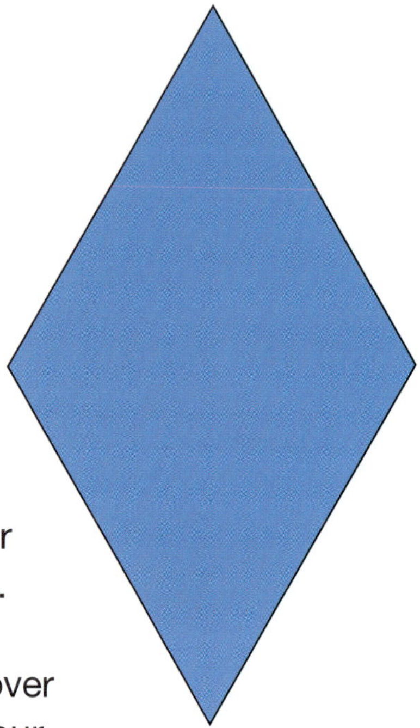

2 **2.** Suppose you are covering your classroom floor before an art class.

a) Which size of paper is better: newspaper or notebook paper? Explain your choice.

b) Estimate using the paper you chose for part a). About how many sheets would cover the floor without overlapping? Explain your estimation strategy.

c) Explain how you could use only 1 sheet of the paper you chose in part a) to measure the floor area.

d) Use your method from part c) to measure the area of the floor of your classroom.

3 **3.** Each square has an area of 1 square unit.

a) Which letter has the least area?

b) What is the area of the grid that does not have letters on it?

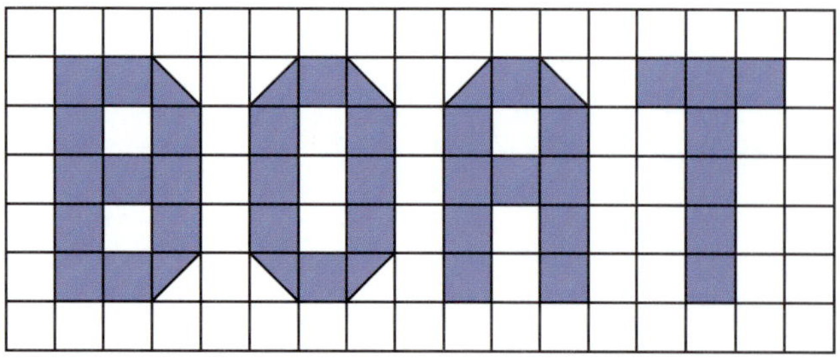

4 **4.** Jenny made this tablecloth from squares of fabric. She wants to make a new tablecloth with twice the area.

a) Could the new tablecloth be a square? Explain.

b) Could the new tablecloth be a rectangle? If so, make models of the possible rectangles. Sketch each model.

c) What will be the area of the red squares in the new tablecloth?

5 **5.** The sun rises in the east and sets in the west.

a) When you face a sunrise, what direction is at your back? Explain how you know.

b) When you face a sunset, what direction is to your left? Explain how you know.

c) Explain how knowing the direction the sun rises can help you find north and south. Sketch a picture to show your answer.

6. Write START in the centre of a number line.

a) Place a marker on START. Roll a die.
If you roll an even number, move right using the number on the die.
If you roll an odd number, move left using the number on the die.
Repeat this 5 more times, or until you go off the left side or the right side.

b) Repeat part a) 10 times.

c) What do you notice? Why do you think this happens?

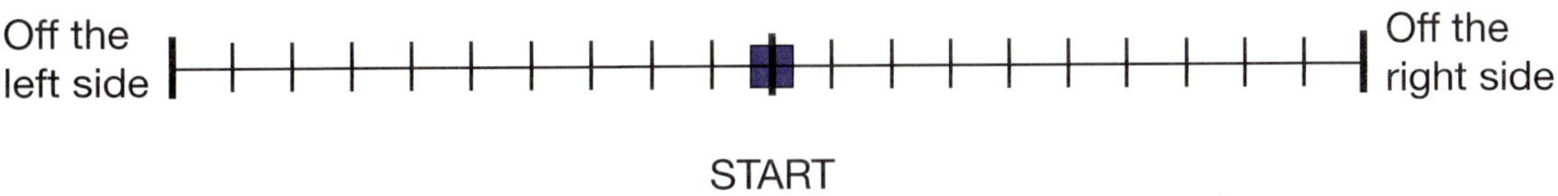

Chapter Task

Placing Furniture

? What is a good plan for placing furniture in a large room?

Part 1

A. Draw the shape of the room you want on large grid paper.

B. Make a model of each piece of furniture you want. Choose from the furniture below or design your own.

C. Arrange your model furniture on the grid paper. Label each piece of furniture and find its area.

D. Decide if you will have carpets. Colour any carpets on the grid paper.

E. How much floor space is not covered by furniture? Explain how you figured this out.

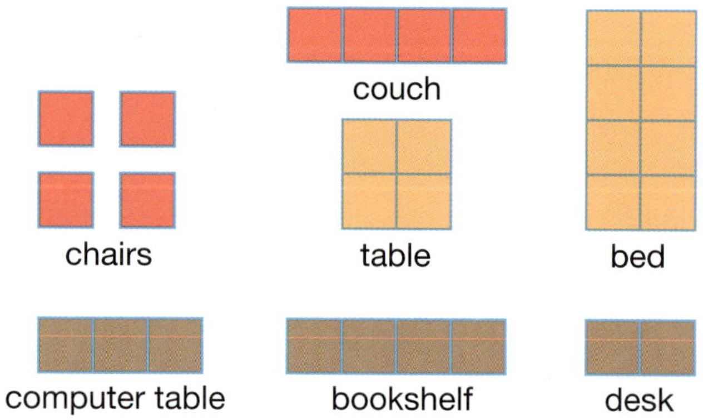

Part 2

Mark north, south, east, and west on your plan. Describe a route you could take from one place to another in the room. Use only the directions north, south, east, and west.

Task Checklist

- ✓ Is there enough room to move around?
- ✓ Is your description clear?
- ✓ Did you use words like 2 squares north and 1 square west?

CHAPTER 9

Multiplication

Goals

You will be able to

- relate multiplication to repeated addition and skip counting
- solve multiplication problems by guessing and testing
- use strategies to multiply
- estimate products

Groups of food

Getting Started

Equal Groups and Repeated Addition

? How many of each kind of food are there?

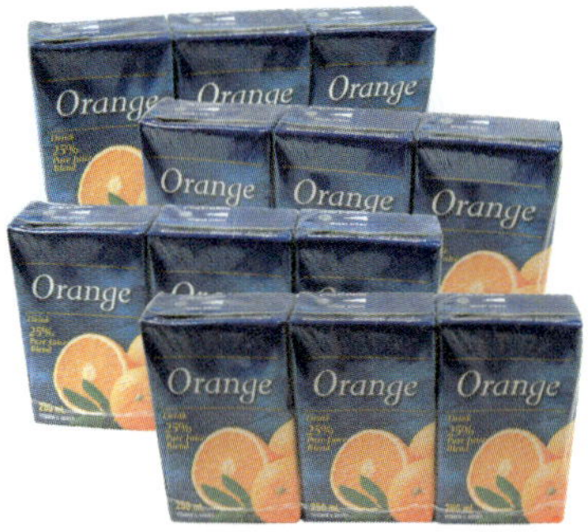

juice boxes

muffins

cobs of corn

chocolates

eggs

cherries

loaves of bread

egg rolls

A. How many packages of muffins are there?
How many muffins are in each package?
How many muffins are there altogether? Use addition.

B. Write an addition sentence for each kind of food.

C. Which is easier to calculate: the number of cobs of corn or the number of chocolates? Explain.

D. Choose an item that usually comes in equal groups of 2, 3, 4, or 5.
Sketch the group.
Make more copies of the group.
How many items are there in all?
Write an addition sentence.

Do You Remember?

1. Calculate the total number. Use repeated addition.
   a) 
   b) 

2. Write the next 3 numbers in each skip-counting pattern.
   a) 5, 10, 15, 20, ■, ■, ■
   b) 10, 20, 30, 40, ■, ■, ■

3. Add.
   a) 2 + 2 + 2 + 2
   b) 6 + 6 + 6
   c) 4 + 4 + 4 + 4 + 4 + 4
   d) 0 + 0
   e) 3 + 3 + 3 + 3 + 3
   f) 5 + 5 + 5

4. a) Skip count by 2s to 10.
   b) What is the sum for 2 + 2 + 2 + 2 + 2?

CHAPTER 9

1

Using Adding to Multiply

You will need

- counters

- number lines

Goal **Multiply using skip counting and repeated addition.**

Lyn repairs bicycles.
It takes her 1 minute to fill each tire on a bicycle.

? How many minutes does it take Lyn to fill the tires on 7 bicycles?

Lyn's Multiplication

There are 7 groups of 2 tires. I can model the tires.

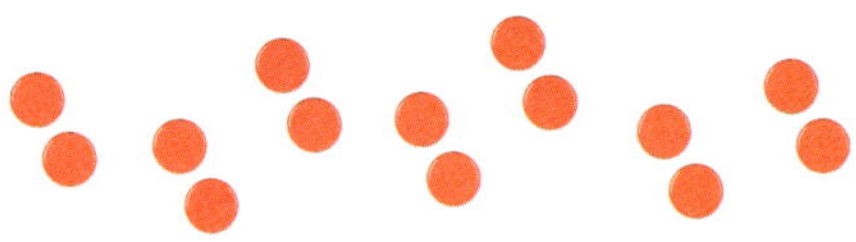

2 + 2 + 2 + 2 + 2 + 2 + 2 = 14

7 groups of 2 = 14

I can skip count by 2s on a number line.

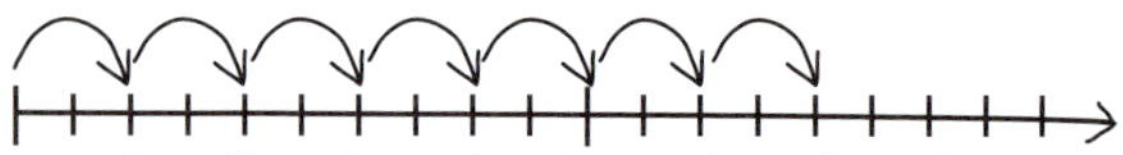

7 skips of 2 = 14

I can write this **multiplication** sentence or fact.

7 x 2 = 14

factors **product**

It says 7 times 2 equals 14.
It takes Lyn 14 minutes to fill the tires on 7 bicycles.

multiplication
Repeated addition

factors
Numbers you multiply

product
The result when you multiply

Reflecting

1. How are Lyn's multiplication sentence and addition sentence alike? How are they different?
2. a) Show 1 group of 7 on a number line.
   b) Write the multiplication sentence.
   c) Explain why it's easy to multiply by 1.
3. a) How long would it take Lyn to fill 0 tires on 6 bicycles? Write the multiplication sentence.
   b) Explain why the products for 7×0 and 0×2 are the same.

Checking

4. There are 7 bicycles. Each bicycle has 5 streamers.
   a) How many streamers are on 7 bicycles? Model with counters and on a number line.
   b) Write an addition and a multiplication sentence.

Practising

5. Show 2 ways to find the total. Write an addition sentence and a multiplication sentence for each.

a) 

bicycle pedals

b) 

bicycle lights

6. Write each multiplication sentence. Use a number line.
   a) 6 groups of 6 hand grips
   b) 5 groups of 8 brake pads
7. Write an addition sentence for each. Calculate each product.
   a) $7 \times 6 =$ ■
   b) $6 \times 7 =$ ■
   c) $5 \times 3 =$ ■
   d) $3 \times 5 =$ ■
   e) $6 \times 5 =$ ■
   f) $5 \times 6 =$ ■
   g) $4 \times 0 =$ ■
   h) $0 \times 4 =$ ■
8. a) Write a story and draw a picture for $4 \times 2 =$ ■.
   b) Repeat part a) for $5 \times 0 =$ ■.

2 Solve Problems by Guessing and Testing

Goal **Use guessing and testing to solve problems.**

20 students in Devon's class picked a favourite sport. This pictograph shows the information.

? How many students does each represent?

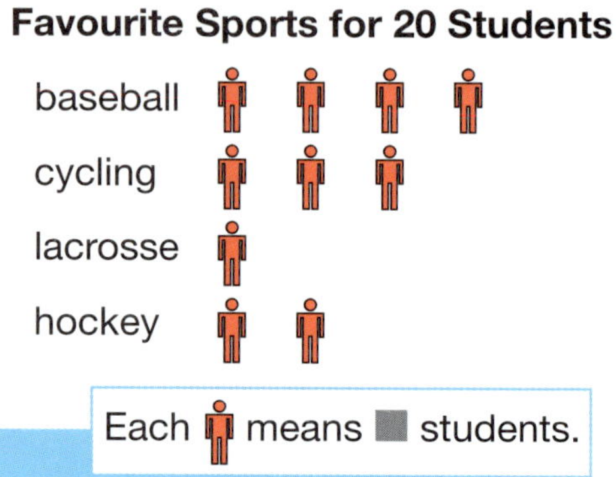

Devon's Solution

Understand

20 students each picked 1 sport, but the graph doesn't have 20 . I have to figure out the **scale** for .

Make a Plan

I can guess a number for and then test it by skip counting or multiplying.

Carry Out the Plan

First I'll guess 5 for .

I'll check by skip counting.

That's going to be more than 20 people.

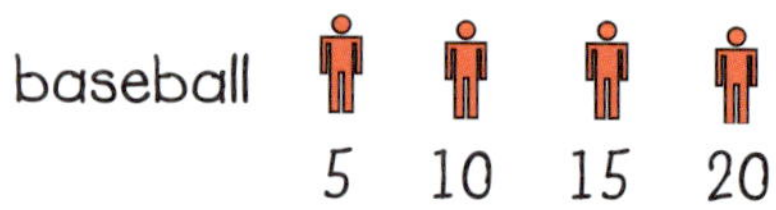

Next I'll try 2 for .

There are 10 . 10 groups of 2 is 20.

$10 \times 2 = 20$

The total number of students is 20.

That's correct, so means 2 students.

Reflecting

1. Why is Devon's strategy called "guessing and testing"?
2. Why do you think Devon's 2nd guess for is a number less than 5?

Checking

3. a) Guess the number of students each represents.
   b) Test your guess. How many students chose each game? Show your work.

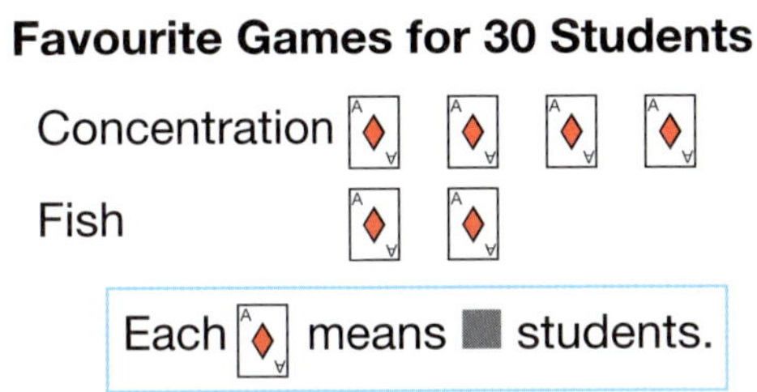

Practising

4. 50 students were surveyed about their favourite ice cream.
   a) Guess the number of students each represents.
   b) Test your guess. How many students chose each flavour? Show your work.

5. Mia has less than $1.00. 2 coins are pennies.
   She has more nickels than pennies.
   She has more dimes than nickels.
   What is the greatest number of dimes she could have?

6. Jordie and Mei-Ling forgot to show what and mean on their graphs.
   a) Who seems to have read more books? Explain.
   b) Create a different scale for each graph so that Jordie has read fewer books than Mei-Ling.
   c) Create a different scale for each graph so that Jordie and Mei-Ling have read the same number of books.

CHAPTER 9

3 Arrays and Multiplication

You will need

- square tiles

Goal **Use arrays to represent and solve multiplication problems.**

12 clowns are marching in a parade.

? How can you arrange the clowns in equal rows?

Nisha's Solution

I can use 12 tiles to model the clowns.
I can arrange them in 2 equal rows.

They could march in 2 rows of 6. $2 \times 6 = 12$

If I look at my model sideways, I see 6 rows of 2. $6 \times 2 = 12$

A. Nisha's model is called an **array**.
Make other arrays for the 12 clowns.
Sketch your arrays and write multiplication sentences.

B. Compare your multiplication sentences.
What do you notice about the products and factors?

array
A rectangular arrangement of objects or pictures

Reflecting

1. Why do you think $2 \times 6 = 12$ and $6 \times 2 = 12$ are called related multiplication sentences?
2. **a)** How is an array with 2 rows of 6 like $6 + 6$?
   b) How is it like skip counting by 6s?
3. Can you draw an array for 6×0 or 0×6? Explain.

Checking

4. Make as many arrays as you can for 14 clowns. Sketch your arrays and write related multiplication sentences.

5. How many stickers are in each array?
Write 2 related multiplication facts for each array.

a) 

b) 

Practising

6. Write 2 related multiplication facts for this array of boxes.

7. Write 2 related multiplication facts for this array of tomatoes.

8. Model 1 array for each. Sketch each array.
Complete 2 related multiplication facts.
a) $7 \times 4 = \blacksquare$ b) $4 \times 8 = \blacksquare$ c) $5 \times 7 = \blacksquare$ d) $8 \times 6 = \blacksquare$

9. Sketch 1 array for each.
Complete 2 related multiplication facts.
a) $9 \times 1 = \blacksquare$ b) $3 \times 10 = \blacksquare$ c) $7 \times 6 = \blacksquare$ d) $5 \times 9 = \blacksquare$

10. Create and solve a problem about any array in Question 9.

11. Model an array for 1×6. Write 2 related multiplication facts.

12. a) Sketch an array for 3×3. Write 1 multiplication fact.
b) Turn your page sideways and look at the array.
How many different multiplication facts fit the array?
c) Show another array like the 3×3 array.

13. a) Sketch all possible arrays for 13 clowns and for 24 clowns.
b) Which number has more arrays? Explain.

LESSON

Mid-Chapter Review

1 **1.** Model each group. Write an addition sentence and a multiplication sentence.

a) 

b) 

2. a) What is the value of 7 nickels? Show your work.

b) What is the value of 0 nickels? Explain.

2 **3.** Guess the number of students each  represents. Test your guess. Show your work.

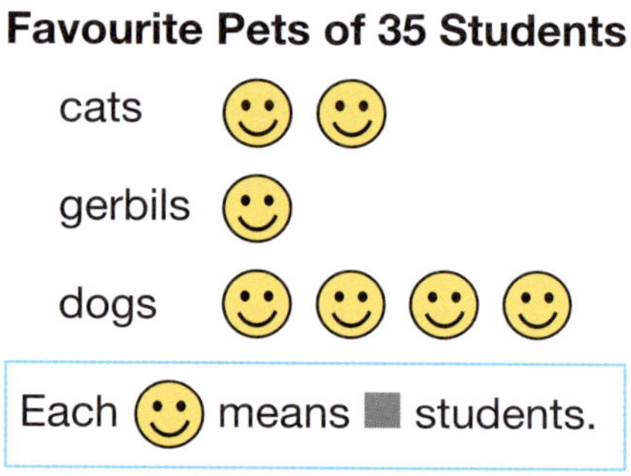

3 **4.** Write 2 related multiplication facts to match each array.

a) 

b) 

5. Sketch an array. Complete each multiplication fact.

a) $7 \times 7 = ■$ **b)** $5 \times 8 = ■$ **c)** $6 \times 1 = ■$ **d)** $4 \times 10 = ■$

6. Find the total number of objects. Use any method.
6 stacks of pennies with 5 pennies in each stack

7. Which multiplication facts are incorrect? Explain.

A. $2 \times 5 = 7$ **B.** $3 \times 4 = 12$ **C.** $1 \times 3 = 13$ **D.** $4 \times 0 = 4$

8. Amit's younger brother is learning about calculating. How would you explain what 4×6 represents?

Math Game

Tap It Out

You will need

- tap cards

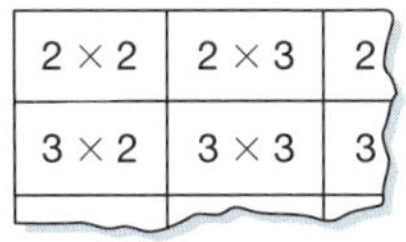

Number of players: 2 to 4
How to play: Tap out multiplication facts on a drum or table.

Step 1 One player takes a multiplication card, making sure that the other players cannot see it. Then the player makes a rhythm pattern for the multiplication.

Step 2 The other players say the multiplication fact for the rhythm pattern. Take turns.

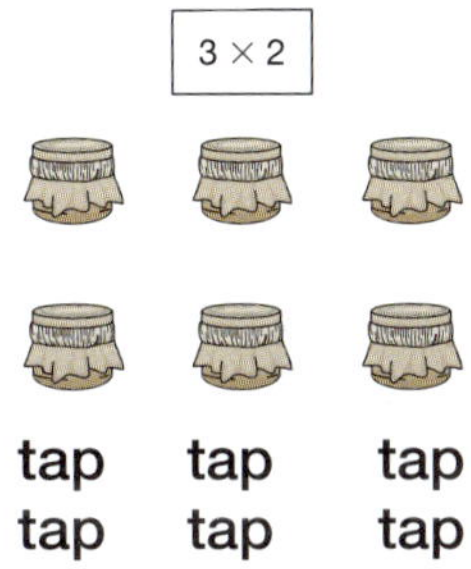

Curious Math

Odd Arrays

This 3-by-3 array shows the sum of 3 odd numbers.

$1 + 3 + 5 = 9$

1. Does a 4-by-4 array show the sum of 4 odd numbers? Explain your answer.

2. Does a 5-by-5 array show the sum of 5 odd numbers? Explain your answer.

CHAPTER 9

4 Doubling

You will need

- counters

Goal **Relate multiplication facts using a doubling strategy.**

Lee is a member of a Cub pack.
There are 4 groups of 6, called sixes, in the pack.

? How can Lee calculate the total number of members in his Cub pack?

Lee's Cub Pack

In 1 group of 6, there are 6 members.

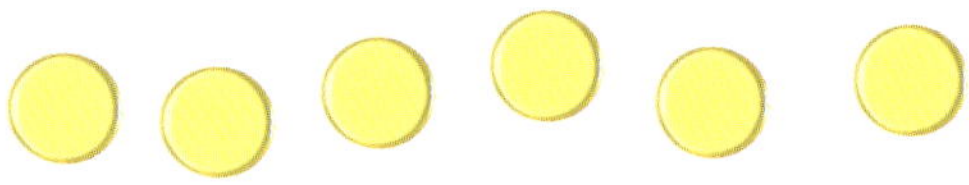

$1 \times 6 = 6$

I'll **double** the number of groups.

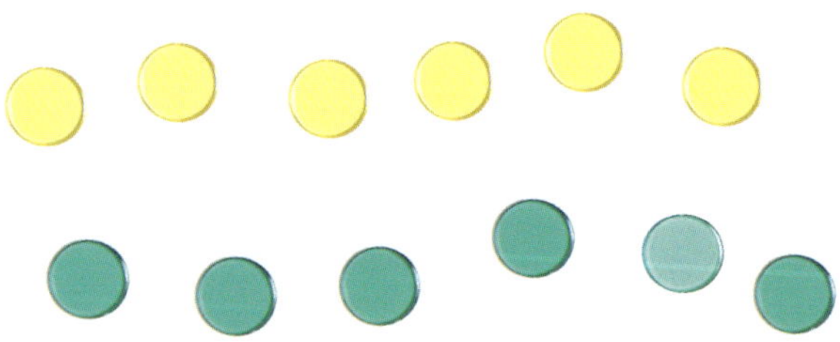

$2 \times 6 = 12$

In 2 groups of 6, there are 12 members.
Now I'll double the groups again.

double
Multiply a number by 2

A. Finish Lee's solution. Double the number of groups again. Write the multiplication fact.

B. How many members are in Lee's Cub pack?

Reflecting

1. a) If you double one factor in a multiplication sentence, what happens to the product?
   b) Does it matter which factor you double? Explain with examples.
   c) What happens when you double one factor if the other factor is 0?

2. To multiply a number by 4, you can double it, then double the product. Explain.

Checking

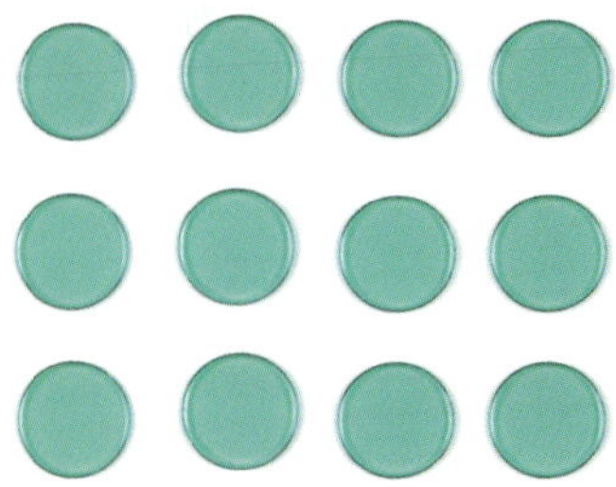

3. a) This array represents 3 rows of 4 badges. Sketch an array for 6 rows of 4 badges.
   b) How does your array show that 6×4 is double 3×4?

4. Use $4 \times 3 = 12$ to calculate $4 \times 6 = ■$.

Practising

5. a) Sketch an array to show 5×5. Write the multiplication fact.
   b) Double the array in part a). Write the multiplication fact.

6. Complete each doubled fact.
   a) $7 \times 3 = 21$, so $7 \times 6 = ■$.
   b) $4 \times 5 = 20$, so $8 \times 5 = ■$.
   c) $1 \times 9 = 9$, so $2 \times 9 = ■$.
   d) $3 \times 0 = 0$, so $6 \times 0 = ■$.

7. How might you use doubling to find each product?
   a) $6 \times 6 = ■$
   b) $8 \times 3 = ■$
   c) $8 \times 6 = ■$
   d) $4 \times 9 = ■$

8. Triplets are 3 children born at the same time. How many children are in 3 sets of triplets? How many children are in 6 sets of triplets?

9. How many socks are needed for each?
   a) 8 sets of twins
   b) 8 sets of quadruplets

CHAPTER 9

5 Relating Multiplication Facts

You will need

- counters

Goal **Show different ways to multiply.**

For her 9th birthday, Keisha got a kitten named Lucky. Cats age more quickly than humans. For every year a cat lives, it ages about 5 human years.

A year from now, I'll be 10 and Lucky will be about 5 in human years!

? When Keisha is 16, how old will Lucky be in human years?

Keisha's Solution

I will be 16 human years old in 7 years.

Lucky will be 7 cat years old in 7 years.

1 cat year = 5 human years

Lucky will be 7×5 years old in human years.

I can use facts I know to calculate 7×5.

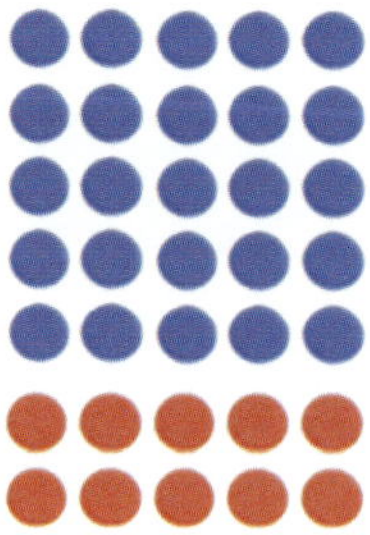

5 groups of 5 is 25.

2 groups of 5 is 10.

25 + 10 = 35

So 7 groups of 5 is 35.

When I turn 16, Lucky will be about 35 in human years!

Reflecting

1. How did Keisha use her answers to 5×5 and 2×5 to find 7×5?
2. What is another way to calculate 7×5 using facts you know?

Checking

3. Complete the multiplication facts.

   a) $4 \times 4 = 16$
   $2 \times 4 = 8$
   So $6 \times 4 =$ ■.

   b) 3 groups of 9 is 27.
   2 groups of 9 is 18.
   So ■ groups of 9 is ■.

4. How does knowing $6 \times 5 = 30$ help you find 6×6?

Practising

5. Model arrays as Keisha did. Show how to calculate each product by using 2 arrays.

   a) $4 \times 9 =$ ■ b) $8 \times 3 =$ ■

6. Jodi delivered flyers every day for 4 weeks in March and 3 weeks in April. How many days did she work altogether? Complete the multiplication sentences.

March

S	M	T	W	T	F	S
				1	2	3
4	5	6	7	8	9	10
11	12	13	14	15	16	17
18	19	20	21	22	23	24
25	26	27	28	29	30	31

April

S	M	T	W	T	F	S
1	2	3	4	5	6	7
8	9	10	11	12	13	14
15	16	17	18	19	20	21
22	23	24	25	26	27	28
29	30					

■ × 7 = ■
■ × 7 = ■
So ■ × 7 = ■.

7. $4 \times 3 = 12$

   a) How does that help you find 4×6?
   b) How does that help you find 4×7?

8. For every year a dog lives, it ages about 7 human years. Marty's dog is 6 years old. How old is Marty's dog in human years?

9. Create and solve a multiplication problem about human years and animal years.

CHAPTER 9

6 Making a Multiplication Table

Goal **Use strategies to complete a multiplication table.**

You will need

- a multiplication table

×	1	2	3
1			
2			
3			

- counters

- a number line

? What are the missing numbers in the multiplication table?

Ben's Multiplication Table

I'll show multiplication facts in a table.

I know 3 groups of 2 is 6.

(column → 2; row → 3)

×	1	2	3	4	5	6	7
1							
2							
3		6					
4							
5							
6							
7							

A. Which numbers in the multiplication table are factors?

B. What are the factors for the product, 6, that Ben showed?

C. Complete a row. How does a row show skip counting?

D. Complete a column. How does a column show skip counting?

E. Complete the table.

F. Talk about the strategies and patterns you used.

Reflecting

1. Look at the products for 2s and 1s. How can they help you figure out the products for 3s?
2. How can the products for 3s help you figure out the products for 6s?
3. a) Draw a box around any 3-by-3 square in your table. Describe 2 patterns.
   b) Predict patterns for other 3-by-3 squares. Check your predictions.

Mental Math

Mental Subtraction

Rachel calculated 70 − 7 by thinking of 10 subtract 7.

Rachel's Method

I think of 70 as 60 + 10.

10 subtract 7 is 3.

$$70 - 7 = 60 + 10 - 7$$
$$= 60 + 3$$
$$= 63$$

A. How can you use Rachel's method to subtract 7 from 60?

Try These

1. Use Rachel's mental math method to subtract.

a) 50 − 7 = ■	c) 60 − 6 = ■	e) 80 − 8 = ■	g) 30 − 3 = ■
b) 30 − 7 = ■	d) 50 − 5 = ■	f) 40 − 4 = ■	h) 100 − 2 = ■

7 Estimating Products

You will need

- a calculator

- play coins

Goal **Solve multiplication problems using estimation.**

Brady's class is making bracelets to give away at the end of an aboriginal day celebration.

They are buying 3 bags of **red** beads and 2 bags of **yellow** beads.

Rashad's Strategy

I know that $1.87 is 187¢.

187¢ rounds up to 200¢ so $1.87 rounds up to $2.

I can estimate the cost of 3 bags of **red** beads by multiplying.

$3 \times \$2 = \$6$

The **red** beads cost about $6.

Brady's Strategy

I'll think of $1.87 as $1.

I can estimate the cost of 3 bags of **red** beads by adding.

$\$1 + \$1 + \$1 = \$3$

The **red** beads cost about $3.

? About how much do the red and yellow beads cost?

A. Use Rashad's strategy. Estimate the cost of the **yellow** beads.

B. What is the estimated cost of the **red** and **yellow** beads with Rashad's strategy?

C. Use Brady's strategy. Estimate the cost of the **yellow** beads.

D. What is the estimated cost of the **red** and **yellow** beads with Brady's strategy?

E. Use a calculator. What is the exact cost of the **red** and **yellow** beads together?

Reflecting

1. a) Explain Rashad's estimation strategy.
   b) Explain Brady's estimation strategy.
   c) The total estimate is closer to the exact cost with Rashad's strategy than with Brady's. Explain why.
2. How would you estimate the cost of the red and yellow beads? Explain your choice.
3. When might you use an estimated cost?

Checking

4. The class is buying 3 bags of **black** beads.

   a) Estimate the cost of the **black** beads. Explain your estimation strategy.
   b) Use a calculator or coins. What is the exact cost?

Practising

5. The class is decorating the classroom with feathers. They are buying 4 bags of **red** feathers.

   a) Estimate the cost of the **red** feathers. Explain your estimation strategy.
   b) Use a calculator. What is the exact cost?
6. The class is buying 2 bags of **black** feathers and 1 bag of **yellow** feathers.

   a) Estimate the cost of the **black** and **yellow** feathers.
   b) Use a calculator or coins. What is the exact cost?
7. Create and solve a multiplication problem for estimating the cost of feathers or beads.
8. A different store has the **red** beads on sale for $1.50 a bag. Li says the total sale price of 3 bags of **red** beads is about 75¢ less than the regular price. Ira says it is about $1.50 less.
   a) How do you think each estimated?
   b) About how much do you think they would save? Why do you think this?

Skills Bank

LESSON

1 **1.** Write an addition sentence and a multiplication fact for each.

a)

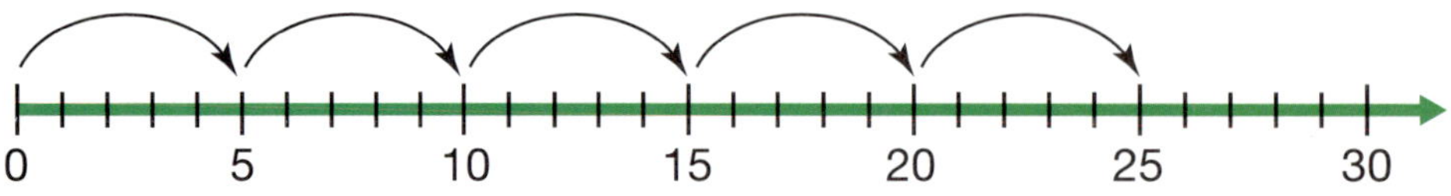

b) 7 groups of 0

c) 9 groups of 3

3 **2.** Write 2 related multiplication facts to match each array.

a) 

b) 

c) 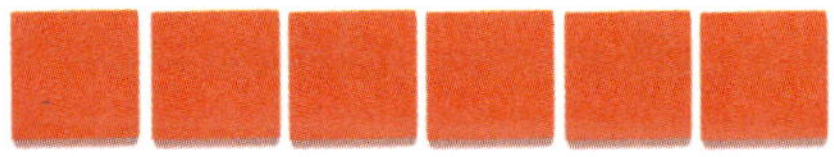

3. Complete each sentence.

a) If I know that $7 \times 5 = 35$, then I know $5 \times ■ = 35$.

b) If I know that $6 \times 7 = 42$, then I know $■ \times 6 = 42$.

4. Multiply. Then write a related fact.

a) $6 \times 3 = ■$ **c)** $1 \times 5 = ■$ **e)** $5 \times 6 = ■$ **g)** $3 \times 7 = ■$

b) $3 \times 0 = ■$ **d)** $7 \times 4 = ■$ **f)** $5 \times 7 = ■$ **h)** $6 \times 4 = ■$

5. Multiply.

a) $4 \times 4 = ■$ **b)** $6 \times 6 = ■$ **c)** $0 \times 0 = ■$ **d)** $1 \times 1 = ■$

4 **6.** Complete each multiplication fact.

a) $2 \times 9 = 18$
$4 \times 9 = ■$

c) $3 \times 3 = 9$
$3 \times 6 = ■$

e) $7 \times 3 = 21$
$7 \times 6 = ■$

g) $3 \times 8 = 24$
$6 \times 8 = ■$

b) $3 \times 5 = 15$
$6 \times 5 = ■$

d) $6 \times 2 = 12$
$6 \times 4 = ■$

f) $5 \times 2 = 10$
$5 \times 4 = ■$

h) $2 \times 8 = 16$
$4 \times 8 = ■$

4 **7.** Kayla has a storybook about 5 sets of quadruplets. There are 2 girls and 2 boys in each set.

a) Write a multiplication sentence for the number of girls.

b) Write a multiplication sentence for the number of children.

5 **8.** Complete each multiplication fact.

a) $4 \times 4 = 16$
$5 \times 4 = 20$
So $9 \times 4 = ■$.

b) $1 \times 9 = 9$
$4 \times 9 = 36$
So $5 \times 9 = ■$.

c) $2 \times 6 = 12$
$6 \times 6 = 36$
So $8 \times 6 = ■$.

d) $4 \times 7 = 28$
$3 \times 7 = ■$
So $7 \times 7 = ■$.

e) $2 \times 8 = 16$
$3 \times 8 = ■$
So $5 \times 8 = ■$.

f) $5 \times 5 = 25$
$4 \times 5 = ■$
So $9 \times 5 = ■$.

6 **9.** How many are there altogether?

a) 3 rows of 6 stamps

b) 4 canoes with 4 paddles in each

c) 5 bags with 5 pennies in each

d) 9 jars with 3 marbles in each

e) number of days in 0 weeks

f) 7 pairs of snowshoes

g) 8 sets of triplets

h) 2 sets of twins

7 **10.** Jessica is buying 4 packages of caribou meat for a barbeque at an aboriginal celebration. Each package costs $2.35.

a) Estimate the total cost.

b) Use a calculator or coins. What is the exact cost?

LESSON

Problem Bank

1 **1.** Which would have more medallions:
4 of Lee's pouches or
3 of Robin's pouches?
How many more?
Show your work.

Lee's pouches Robin's pouches

2. Paul's class has 26 students.
He needs 1 muffin for each student.
Paul buys 7 packages of 4 muffins.
Does he have enough muffins?
Show your work.

3. Write and solve a problem about 6×5.

4 **4.** **a)** Use toothpicks to make 4 triangles.
b) How many toothpicks did you use?
c) Could you have used fewer toothpicks? Explain.

5 **5.** The product of 2 numbers is 12. The difference between the numbers is 4. What are the numbers?

6. A bookstore gives away a bookmark with each book sold.
How many bookmarks has the store given away?

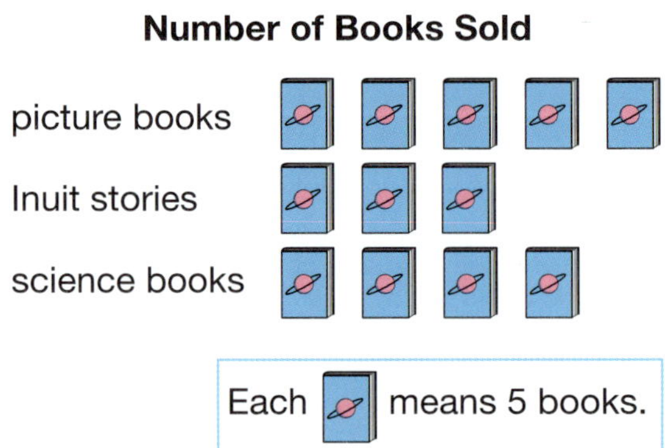

6 **7.** Ananda is thinking of 2 numbers.
She says the sum of the numbers is 7.
What is their product?
Find all the possibilities.

LESSON

Chapter Review

1 **1.** Write a multiplication fact for each picture.

a)

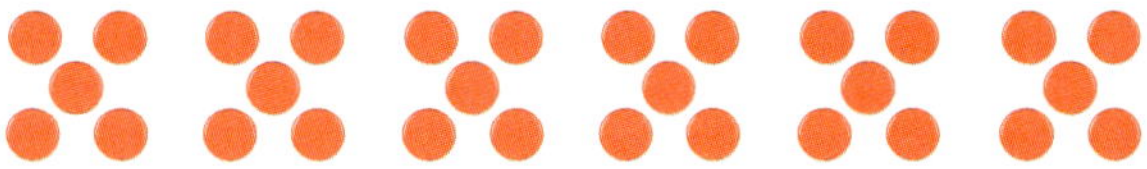

b)

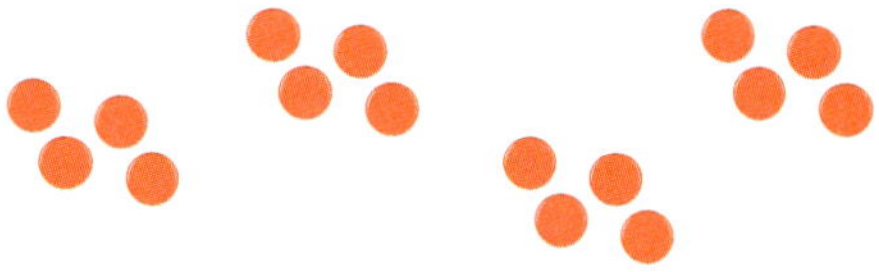

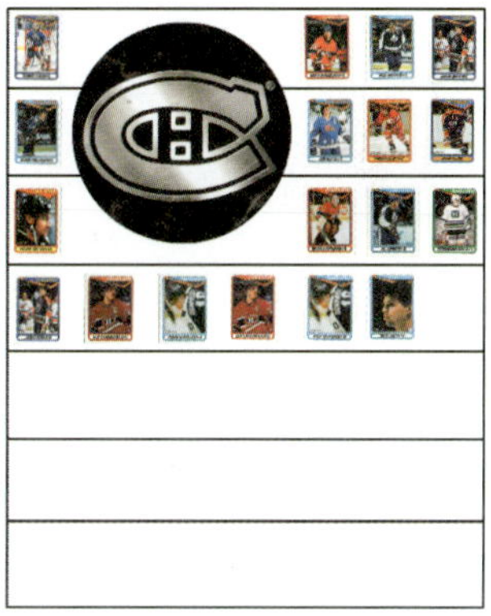

2. What do you notice about the product when 0 is a factor? Explain why this happens.

2 **3.** Fardad has room for 22 more hockey cards on his wall display.
He can buy them in packs of 2 or 5.
How many packs of each could he buy?

3 **4.** Write 2 related multiplication facts to match this array of stars.
How many stars are there?

5 **5.** Complete each number sentence.

a) $9 \times 4 = 4 \times ■$

b) $7 \times 1 = ■$
$7 \times 5 = ■$
$7 \times 6 = ■$

c) $8 \times 3 = 24$
$8 \times 6 = ■$

6 **6.** Calculate each product.

a) $4 \times 2 = ■$
b) $6 \times 6 = ■$
c) $0 \times 4 = ■$
d) $4 \times 5 = ■$
e) $6 \times 2 = ■$
f) $6 \times 4 = ■$
g) $7 \times 7 = ■$
h) $6 \times 7 = ■$

7 **7.** Each package of tennis balls costs $4.59.

a) Estimate the cost of 2 packages.
b) Use a calculator. What is the exact cost?

Chapter Task

Products and Sums

? What happens when you multiply 2 numbers instead of adding them?

This is what George says.

A. Do you agree with George? Give a reason for your answer.

B. What would you say about adding and multiplying the same numbers?

Task Checklist

- ✓ Did you use examples to help you explain?
- ✓ Did you try lots of different pairs of numbers?
- ✓ Did you change George's sentence?

CHAPTER 10

Division

Goals

You will be able to

- **explain division in a variety of ways**
- **use strategies to solve division problems**
- **relate division to multiplication**
- **estimate quotients**

Sharing punch

Getting Started

You will need

- counters

Sharing Tickets

? What are some ways that Keenan and his friends can share tickets at the zoo?

Use counters to show how to solve each problem.

A. 3 friends want to share 12 tickets equally. How many tickets will each person get?

B. Keenan joins the group of 3 before they use any tickets. How many tickets will each person get now?

C. Karla can get 3 cones of animal feed for 1 ticket. How many tickets would she need for 15 cones? Show your thinking.

D. Krista buys 9 tickets. A zoomobile ride costs 3 tickets for each rider. How many friends can Krista take with her? How do you know?

Do You Remember?

1. Write the next 3 numbers in each skip-counting pattern.

a) 0, 2, 4, 6, 8, ■, ■, ■

b) 0, 5, 10, 15, 20, ■, ■, ■

2. Multiply.

a) $2 \times 7 =$ ■ **c)** $4 \times 5 =$ ■ **e)** $2 \times 6 =$ ■ **g)** $5 \times 6 =$ ■

b) $6 \times 3 =$ ■ **d)** $5 \times 3 =$ ■ **f)** $1 \times 7 =$ ■ **h)** $7 \times 7 =$ ■

3. Write the next 3 numbers in each skip-counting pattern.

a) 35, 30, 25, 20, 15, ■, ■, ■

b) 14, 12, 10, 8, 6, ■, ■, ■

4. The pattern rule is "Start at 24 and subtract 4."

a) Write the numbers in the pattern. Continue to 0.

b) How many times did you subtract 4?

1 Sharing to Divide

You will need

- counters

Goal Use words and symbols to describe division by sharing equally.

Charlie enters a contest for free tickets to a powwow. 3 winners will share 18 tickets equally.

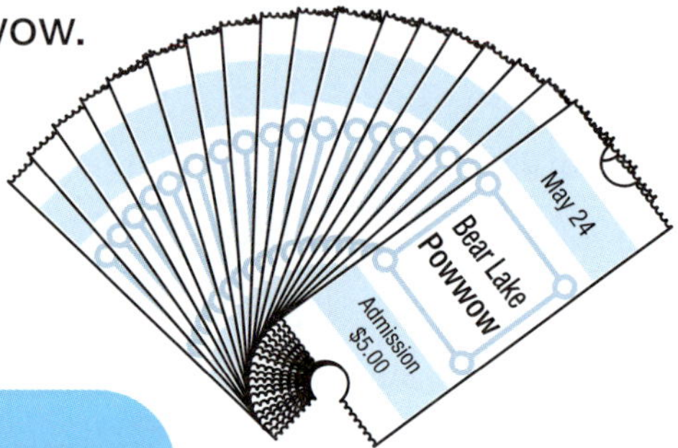

? If Charlie is one of the contest winners, how many tickets will he get?

Charlie's Sharing

I'll model the tickets and winners with 18 counters and 3 groups.

I'd share the 18 counters equally, so 18 is divided into 3 equal groups.

I'll write a **division** sentence: 18 ÷ 3 = ■.

It says 18 divided by 3 is ■.

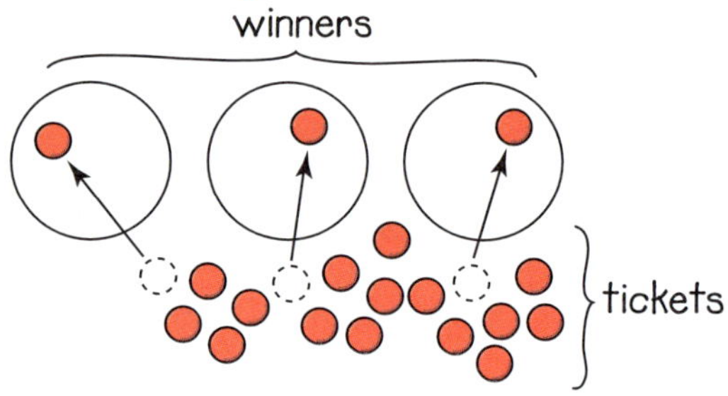

division
Equal sharing or grouping

A. Complete Charlie's sharing with counters. Draw a picture of the finished model.

B. How many tickets will Charlie get if he wins? Complete the division sentence to show the **quotient**.

quotient
The result when you divide
15 ÷ 3 = 5
quotient

Reflecting

1. How did you know when the sharing was done?
2. How do you know that the sharing was equal?
3. How does your picture show multiplication?

Checking

4. 8 tickets are shared equally by 2 winners.

   a) How many tickets does each winner get? Model the problem with counters. Draw a picture of your finished model.
   b) Write a division sentence for the model.
   c) Explain what the division sentence means.

Practising

5. Model each situation for sharing equally. Show your work using pictures, words, and number sentences.

   a) 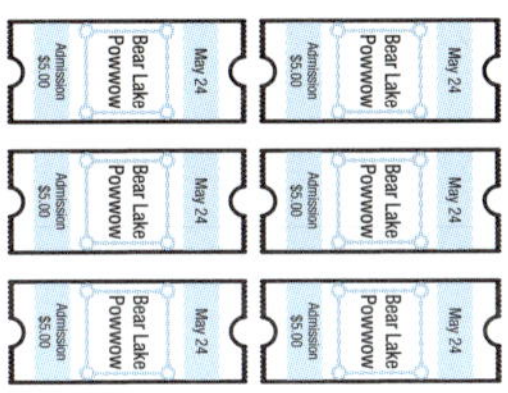 shared by 

   b) 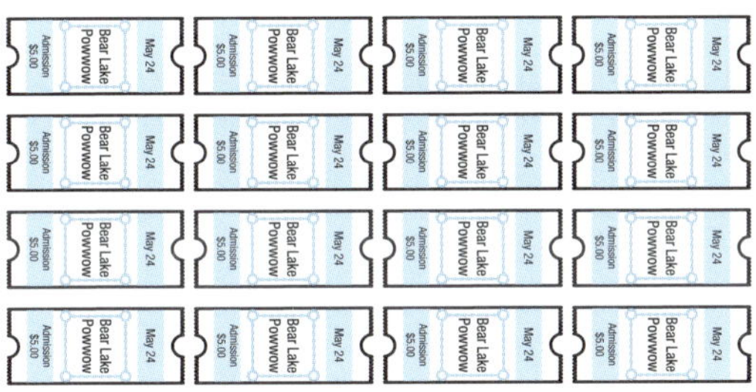 shared by 

   c) 42 cookies shared by 7 people
   d) 6 mangoes shared by 6 people
   e) 18 divided by 9
   f) 7 divided by 1

6. Make up a division problem about sharing 24 tickets equally. Show how to solve your problem.

7. Calculate each quotient. Show your work using pictures and numbers.

   a) $30 \div 6 = ■$
   b) $9 \div 3 = ■$
   c) $25 \div 5 = ■$
   d) $32 \div 8 = ■$
   e) $20 \div 4 = ■$
   f) $28 \div 7 = ■$
   g) $50 \div 5 = ■$
   h) $48 \div 8 = ■$

8. Choose one of your pictures from Question 7. How does your picture show multiplication?

2 Grouping to Divide

You will need

- counters

- a number line

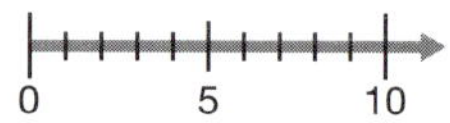

Goal **Divide by counting equal groups.**

14 students work in pairs to read the morning announcements.

? How many pairs of students will there be?

Sharleen's Plan

I'll solve the problem using pairs of counters.
I need 14 counters.

I can count the pairs.

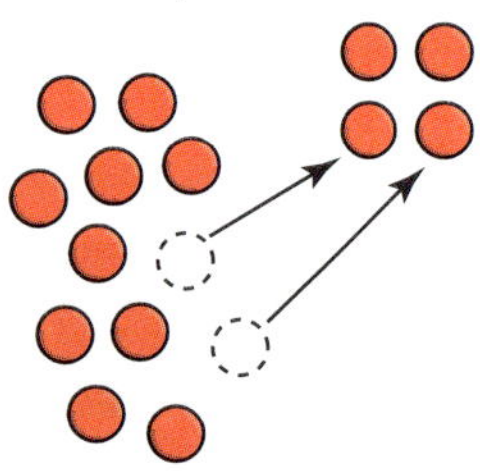

$14 \div 2 = ■$

Amit's Plan

I'll solve the problem using a number line.

I'll skip count backward from 14 by 2s to 0.

I can count the skips.

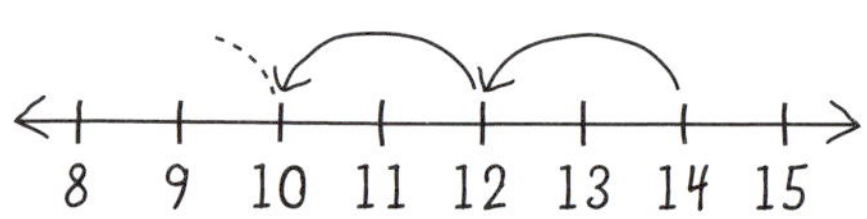

$14 \div 2 = ■$

A. Explain why Sharleen's plan makes sense. Carry out her plan.

B. Explain why Amit's plan makes sense. Carry out his plan.

C. How many pairs of students will read the announcements?

D. Amit says his model shows subtracting over and over. Complete the subtraction sentence for his model.
$14 - 2 - ■ - ■ - ■ - ■ - ■ - ■ = ■$

E. How are Sharleen's and Amit's methods the same?

Reflecting

1. How does Sharleen's model show multiplication as well as division?
2. How is your repeated subtraction sentence like the division sentence?
3. If 15 students read the announcements, how many pairs would there be?
   How is this different from finding pairs for 14?

Checking

4. 24 students run in relay teams of 4.
   a) How many teams are there? Model your solution with counters and with skip counting on a number line.
   b) Write a division sentence to represent the students in teams. What is the quotient?

Practising

5. How many groups of 7 line dancers could you make? Model the groups with counters or number lines. Write a division sentence.
   a) 21 dancers b) 35 dancers
6. Divide. Model the groups with counters.
   a) $20 \div 5 = $ ■
   b) $36 \div 6 = $ ■
   c) $36 \div 3 = $ ■
   d) $49 \div 7 = $ ■
   e) $45 \div 5 = $ ■
   f) $4 \div 1 = $ ■
   g) $40 \div 8 = $ ■
   h) $36 \div 9 = $ ■
7. Li has 10 tickets. Draw the groups of tickets.
   a) How many people can have 5 tickets each?
   b) How many people can have 3 tickets each?

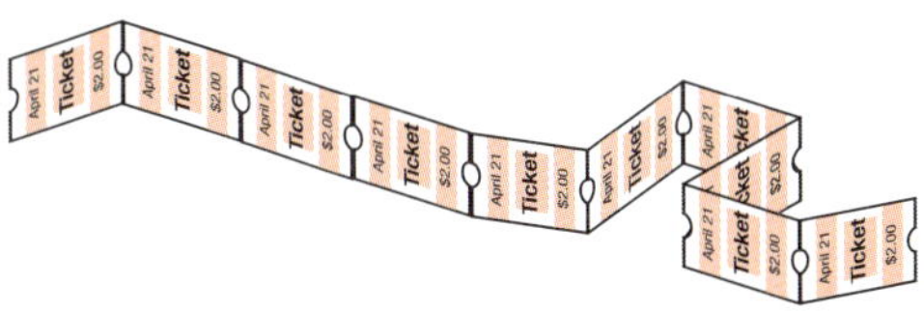

8. This is a division sentence about dancers.
   $24 \div 6 = $ ■
   Create a problem about the dancers.
   Model and solve the problem.

3 Communicate About Division

You will need

- counters

Goal Use a model to explain how to divide.

Ian has 50 apples and 4 baskets.
He puts an equal number of apples in each basket.

? How can you explain how Ian shared the apples?

Michael's Explanation

There are 50 apples and 4 baskets.
Ian wants to put the same number of apples in each basket.
I will use 50 counters to model the problem.
I'll fold a piece of paper into 4 parts to show 4 baskets.
First I'll put 1 apple in each basket.

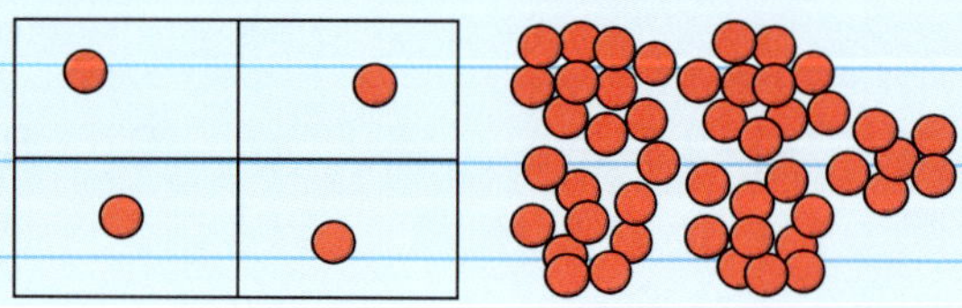

Communication Checklist

- ✓ Did you show enough detail?
- ✓ Did you explain your thinking?
- ✓ Did you include a diagram?

A. Read the Communication Checklist.
How can you tell whether Michael thought of each question when writing his explanation?

B. Complete Michael's explanation.

Reflecting

1. How does Michael's picture make his words easier to understand?
2. Use the Communication Checklist.
   a) What are the strengths of your explanation?
   b) How can you improve your explanation?

Checking

3. a) Jessica explains how to solve this problem.

> **Mila has 36 plums.**
> **She wants to put 3 in each basket.**
> **How many baskets does she need?**

How can you improve Jessica's explanation? Use the Communication Checklist.

b) Complete Jessica's explanation. Use the Communication Checklist.

Jessica's Explanation

There are 36 plums.
I need 3 plums in each basket.
I'll divide to figure out how many groups of 3 I can make from 36.
I'll start with 36 counters.
I'll put 3 counters in each group.

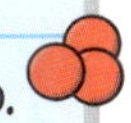

Practising

4. Solve this problem and explain your solution. Use the Communication Checklist.

> **River has 50 pieces of bannock and 6 plates.**
> **He puts an equal number of bannock pieces on each plate.**
> **How many pieces of bannock go on each plate?**

LESSON

Mid-Chapter Review

1

1. 10 tickets are shared equally by 2 winners. How many tickets does each winner get?

   Model the problem with counters. Show your work using pictures, words, and numbers.

2

2. 15 students skip rope in groups of 3.
   a) How many groups of students are there? Model the problem with counters, skips on a number line, or repeated subtraction.
   b) Write the division sentence that goes with your model.

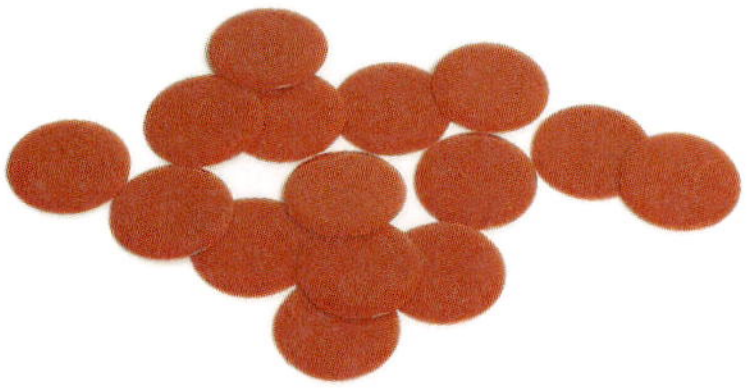

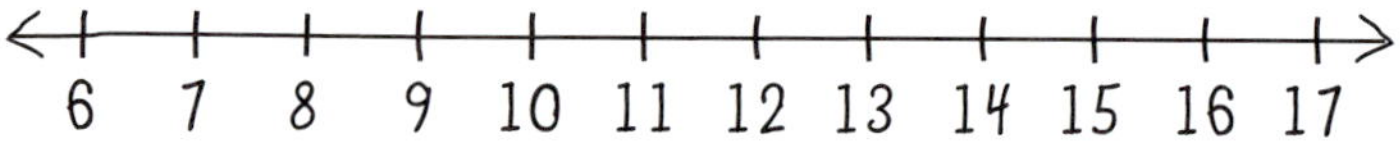

3. Divide. Show your work using pictures and numbers.
   a) 14 ÷ 7 = ■
   b) 45 ÷ 5 = ■
   c) 6 ÷ 1 = ■
   d) 42 ÷ 6 = ■
   e) 8 ÷ 8 = ■
   f) 49 ÷ 7 = ■
   g) 27 ÷ 9 = ■
   h) 36 ÷ 9 = ■

4. Choose one of your pictures from Question 3. How does your picture show multiplication?

5. Sometimes the quotient is the same as the number you divide by. Write 4 other division sentences where this happens. Model with counters or a number line.

   4 ÷ 2 = 2

3

6. Solve this problem. Explain your steps.

   Nisha has 38 bottles.
   A carton holds 6 bottles.
   How many cartons does she need?

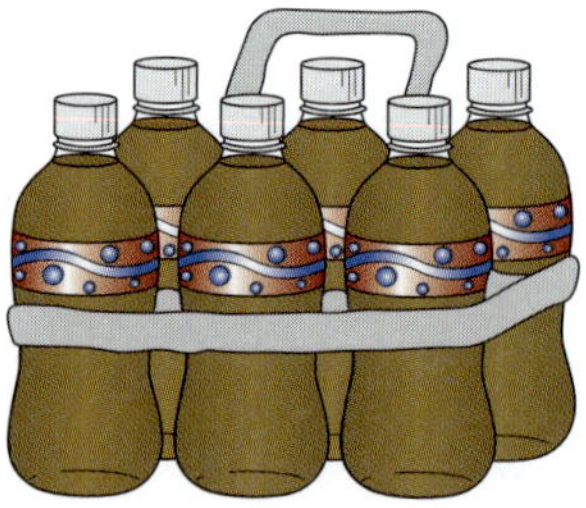

7. 33 oranges are shared equally by 6 children. Draw a picture. Explain your solution.

Fill-a-Row Division

Number of players: 2 or 3
How to play: Calculate quotients and place number cards on division strips.

Step 1 Choose a division strip.

Step 2 Shuffle the cards and place them face down in a pile.

Step 3 Take turns drawing a card from the top of the pile. If the number shows the quotient for a division on your strip, say the division sentence. Then place the card on that part of your strip. If there is already a card on that spot, place the card at the bottom of the pile.

Play until a player has covered a whole strip.

You will need

- 3 sets of number cards (1 to 7)

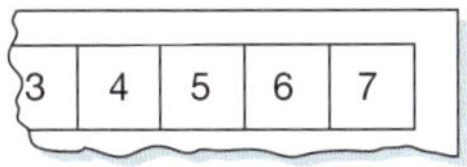

- division strips

- counters

- a number line

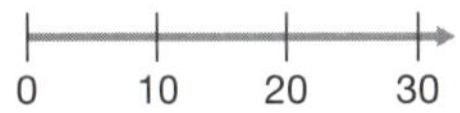

4 Exploring Division Patterns

Goal **Identify, describe, and extend division patterns.**

You will need

- a 100 chart

1	2	3	4
11	12	13	14
21	22	23	24

- pencil crayons

? What pattern is used in each list?

Nicola's pattern	Robin's pattern	Mo's pattern
100	100	100
90	95	98
80	90	96
70	85	94
■	■	■
■	■	■

A. Extend each pattern to 0. Write each pattern rule.

B. Colour each pattern on a 100 chart. Use a different colour for each pattern.

C. Describe the patterns on your 100 chart.

D. Nicola's pattern shows numbers that are all **divisible** by 10. What do you notice about the numbers?

E. Which patterns show numbers that are all divisible by 2? What do you notice about the numbers in each pattern?

F. Which patterns show numbers that are all divisible by 5? What do you notice about the numbers in each pattern?

divisible

Can be divided with nothing left over

$40 \div 10 = 4$
40 is divisible by 10.

Reflecting

1. Which of these numbers are divisible by 10?
   30 35 77 80
   How do you know?

2. a) Which numbers in the patterns are divisible by 2 and also by 5?
   b) The numbers in part a) are also divisible by 10. Explain how you know.

Using Equal Groups

Keisha used multiplication to find her score in a game.

Keisha's Multiplication

5 + 5 + 5 + 5 + 6 = ■

I have 4 fives.

4 × 5 = 20 and 6 more makes 26.

I have a score of 26.

A. Rachel said, "I thought of 5 × 5 = 25 and 1 more makes 26." Explain her thinking.

B. Show how Keisha and Rachel would calculate this:
4 + 4 + 4 + 4 + 4 + 3 = ■

Try These

1. Use multiplication to calculate each score.

a)

b)

2. Calculate each amount.

a) 2 + 2 + 2 + 2 + 2 + 1 = ■

b) 5 + 5 + 6 + 5 + 5 + 5 + 5 = ■

c) 3 + 3 + 3 + 2 = ■

d) 4 + 4 + 4 + 8 + 4 + 4 = ■

e) 5 + 5 + 5 + 2 + 2 + 2 = ■

f) 2 + 3 + 3 + 3 + 3 = ■

5 Patterns in Tables

Goal **Solve division problems using patterns.**

You will need

- grid paper

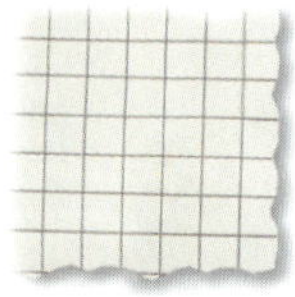

- a calculator

- counters

Sukan is going to a rodeo in 42 days.

? How many weeks away is the rodeo?

Sukan's Table

Sukan started a table with the number of weeks and the number of days.

Number of weeks	1	2	3	4			7
Number of days	7			28	35	42	

A. Complete Sukan's table. Explain your method. Use a calculator or counters to check.

B. How many days are in 3 weeks? Write the multiplication sentence. Explain how the table shows this.

C. Write 2 other multiplication sentences for the table.

D. How many weeks does Sukan need to wait? Write the division sentence. Explain how the table shows this.

E. Write 2 other division sentences for the table.

Reflecting

1. Write a multiplication problem that you can solve with Sukan's table. Solve your problem.
2. Write a division problem that you can solve with Sukan's table. Solve your problem.
3. How can you use the table to find out about how many weeks are the same as 26 days?

Checking

4. Barbara started making a table about books of tickets for a rodeo. Each book has the same number of tickets.

Number of books	1	2		4	5	6
Number of tickets		16	24	32		

a) Use a calculator or counters. Complete the table.

b) Barbara sold 48 tickets. How many books of tickets did she sell? Write the number sentence.

c) Alex sold 5 books of tickets. How many tickets did he sell? Write the number sentence.

Practising

5. Rose started this table for rodeo souvenirs. Each bag has the same number of souvenirs.

Number of bags	1	2	3	4	5	6		8				12
Number of souvenirs		8		16		24	28		36	40	44	48

a) Complete the table. Explain your method.

b) How many souvenirs are in 8 bags? Write the number sentence.

c) How many bags would Rose need to buy to get 36 souvenirs? Write the number sentence.

6. a) Show a multiplication pattern in a table like Rose's.

b) Write 3 division sentences for your table.

7. Each flag pole at the rodeo has the same number of flags. Max recorded the number of flags on some poles.

Number of poles	6	10	16	8		22	
Number of flags	12	20	32		22		50

a) A number pair in Max's table is 6 and 12. List 2 other number pairs for the table. Complete the table.

b) Write 2 number sentences for the table.

c) How many flags are on each pole? Explain.

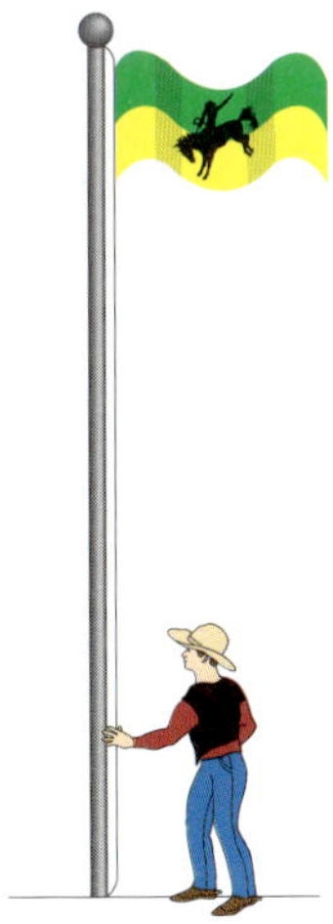

6 Estimating Quotients

You will need

- play coins

Goal Solve division problems using estimation.

? **About how much does each poster cost?**

Lyn's Estimate

I'll get 6 posters for \$25.

$25 \div 6 = \blacksquare$, so I can work with $6 \times \blacksquare = 25$.

I know $6 \times 5 = 30$. That's too high.

I know $6 \times 4 = 24$. That's too low, but close.

So $25 \div 6$ is about 4.

Each poster will cost a little more than \$4.

I'll check my estimate by modelling with loonies.

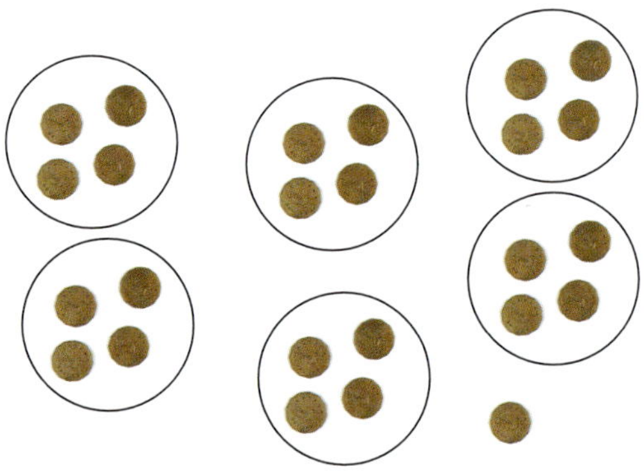

There are 4 loonies in each group with 1 left over.

So my estimate makes sense.

Reflecting

1. Why does Lyn try to think of a number she can multiply by 6 to get close to 25?
2. a) Why would you say "about 4" to answer $25 \div 6$?
   b) Give another example of when you might use an answer of "about" when dividing by 6.

Checking

3. Estimate. Use "about" in your answers. Model with coins. Explain your answers.
   a) $16 \div 3$ b) $46 \div 4$
4. a) 5 students are buying a gift for $22. About how much does each student need to pay? Model with coins. Show your work.
   b) The cost of the gift, gift wrap, and tax is $27. About how much does each student need to pay? Model with coins. Show your work.

Practising

5. Estimate. Write the number sentence you used for each estimate.
   a) $17 \div 5$ c) $40 \div 6$ e) $21 \div 6$
   b) $34 \div 7$ d) $50 \div 9$ f) $43 \div 8$
6. Estimate. Model with coins. Sketch your model. Explain each estimate.
   a) the number of weeks in a month with 31 days
   b) 44 pencils shared by 6 children
   c) $48 to buy 7 posters
7. 3 teachers share 25 posters. About how many posters does each teacher get? Draw a picture to show your work.

Skills Bank

LESSON

1

1. Copy and complete each picture to show equal sharing. Write the division sentence.

a)

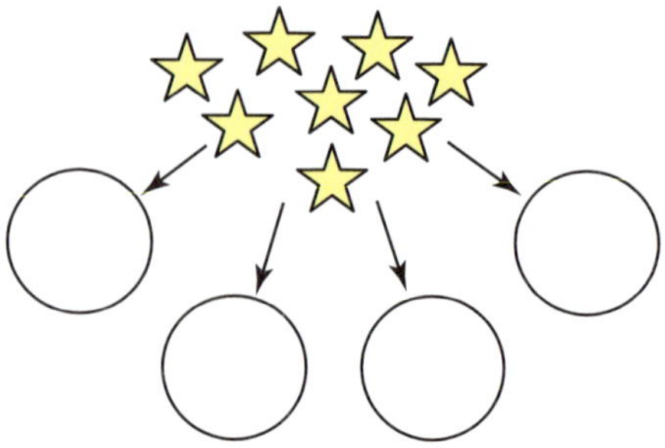

b)

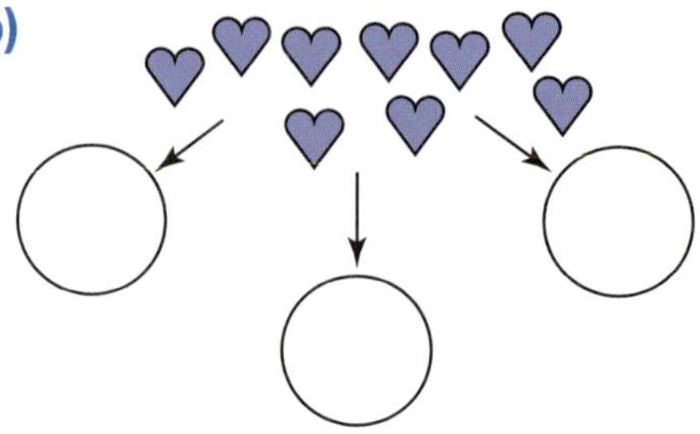

2. Model each for equal sharing. Write each division sentence.
   a) 20 tickets are shared by 5 people.
   b) 27 tickets are shared by 9 people.
   c) 7 tickets are shared by 7 people.
   d) 6 people share 18 tickets.

3. Divide. Use pictures, numbers, and words.
   a) $28 \div 7 = ■$
   b) $27 \div 3 = ■$
   c) $40 \div 8 = ■$
   d) $35 \div 5 = ■$
   e) $49 \div 7 = ■$
   f) $48 \div 6 = ■$
   g) $32 \div 8 = ■$
   h) $45 \div 9 = ■$

2

4. Write a division sentence for each model.

a)

b)

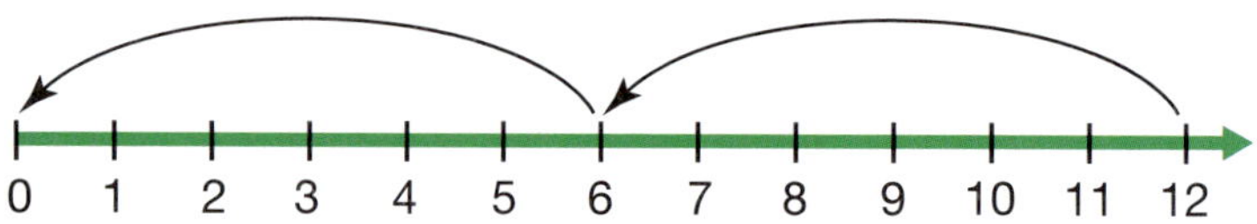

5. A clown is giving out groups of balloons. How many children can get balloons? Model each division. Write a division sentence for each.
   a) 15 balloons in groups of 3
   b) 24 balloons in groups of 8
   c) 42 balloons in groups of 7
   d) 30 balloons in groups of 6

6. Divide. Model the problems with number lines or counters.
   a) $24 \div 6 = ■$
   b) $35 \div 7 = ■$
   c) $32 \div 8 = ■$
   d) $5 \div 5 = ■$
   e) $28 \div 4 = ■$
   f) $3 \div 1 = ■$
   g) $36 \div 2 = ■$
   h) $44 \div 4 = ■$

2 **7.** Solve. Model each division.

a) How many hands make 30 fingers?

b) How many packs of 6 can you make with 36 boxes?

c) 6 tickets cost $42. How much is each ticket?

d) There are 4 seasons in a year.
How many months are in a season?

4 **8.** Which of these numbers are divisible by 2?

14 9 98 49

Explain your answers.

9. Which of these numbers are divisible by 5?

29 45 5 60

Explain your answers.

10. Which of these numbers are divisible by 10?

14 90 75 100

Explain your answers.

5 **11.** Devon put the same number of stamps on each postcard. He made this table to show the number of stamps on some postcards.

Number of postcards	1	2	3		5	6		8
Number of stamps		12	18	24			42	48

a) Complete the table.

b) How many stamps did Devon put on each postcard?
Explain how the table shows this.

6 **12.** Estimate. Write the number sentence you used for each estimate.

a) $7 \div 6$

b) $13 \div 2$

c) $19 \div 6$

d) $24 \div 5$

e) $29 \div 5$

f) $44 \div 9$

g) $43 \div 7$

h) $50 \div 8$

13. About how many weeks are in 32 days?
Draw a picture to show your work.

LESSON

Problem Bank

1 **1.** There are 6 posters.
How many children can share the posters equally?
Find all the ways.

2 **2.** Each car holds 4 people.
13 people are going. How many cars are needed?

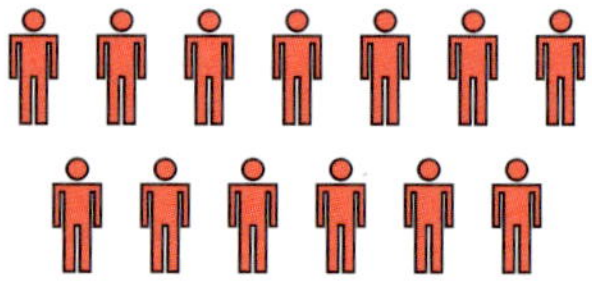

3. Make 3 division sentences. Use each number only once.

2	3	4	5	6	7	10	12	42

4. Flowers cost \$6 a bunch.
How many bunches can you buy for \$40?
Show your work.

3 **5.** Tiffany bought 3 boxes of muffins.
Each box had 1 dozen muffins.
She put the muffins in bags of 3 to freeze them.
How many freezer bags did she use?
Model with counters. Write the number sentences.
Explain your solution.

6. Create your own problem like Question 5.
Draw a picture to show how to solve your problem.

5 **7.** Ben wants 41 stickers that are all the same.
He found stickers sold in these packages.

- 4 rodeo stickers or
- 6 clown stickers or
- 7 sports stickers

Ben wants as few stickers as possible left over.
Which size of package should he buy?
How many packages should he buy?

LESSON

Chapter Review

1 **1.** Show 2 ways to solve 20 ÷ 5 = ■.
Use pictures, words, and numbers.

2 **2.** Marlene's class is going camping.
5 students will be in each tent.
How many tents do they need for 25 students?

3. Divide. Show your work using pictures, words, and numbers.

a) 40 ÷ 8 = ■ **b)** 36 ÷ 9 = ■ **c)** 48 ÷ 3 = ■

4. Maggie's book has 48 pages. She reads 6 pages each day. How many days will she take to finish the book?

5. Evan's book has 48 pages. He plans to finish the book in 6 days by reading the same number of pages each day. How many pages does he need to read each day?

6. How are Questions 4 and 5 the same?
How are they different?

7. Divide.

a) 35 ÷ 5 = ■ **c)** 42 ÷ 6 = ■ **e)** 28 ÷ 7 = ■ **g)** 21 ÷ 3 = ■
b) 14 ÷ 2 = ■ **d)** 4 ÷ 1 = ■ **f)** 24 ÷ 4 = ■ **h)** 49 ÷ 7 = ■

3 **8.** How can you find out if 7 people can share 44 tickets equally? Explain your answer. Use a model.

4 **9.** My house number is between 39 and 49.
It is divisible by 2 and by 5.
What is my house number? Explain how you know.

5 **10. a)** Complete this table to show equal groups.
Use counters or a calculator.
b) Write a division sentence for the table.

1		3	4	5	6			9	
	10	15		25		35	40	45	50

6 **11.** Estimate 34 ÷ 6. Write the number sentence you used.

Chapter Task

Dividing a Recipe

Malik wants to make a batch of fruit punch to share with friends. If he follows the recipe, he will have too much punch.

Fruit Punch

12 cups of apple juice
16 cups of grape juice
8 cups of ginger ale

? How can Malik make a smaller batch of punch?

Part 1

A. Suppose Malik decides to divide the recipe by 2. How many cups of each ingredient will he need? Show your work. Check that you are right.

B. How many cups of punch will he make altogether? Show your work.

Part 2

C. Malik can divide the recipe another way instead of by 2. He still uses only whole cups of each ingredient. Show how he can do this. Check that you are right.

Task Checklist

- ☑ Did you show all your steps?
- ☑ Did you use math language?

CHAPTER 11

3-D Geometry and 3-D Measurement

Goals

You will be able to

- describe and name prisms and pyramids
- compare and sort 3-dimensional (3-D) objects
- relate rectangle-based prisms to their nets
- identify congruent 3-D objects
- explore perpendicular, parallel, and intersecting lines
- estimate, measure, and compare capacity
- solve measurement problems
- estimate, measure, and compare mass

Measuring and baking

CHAPTER 11

Getting Started

Describing 3-D Objects

You will need

- 3-D models (2 matching sets)

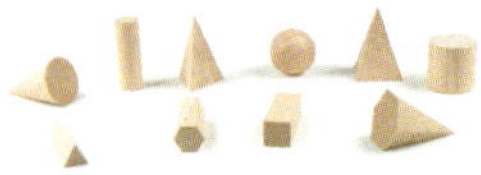

- a divider

In Follow the Leader, one player describes a structure so another player can copy it without looking. The players have matching sets of objects.

Follow the Leader

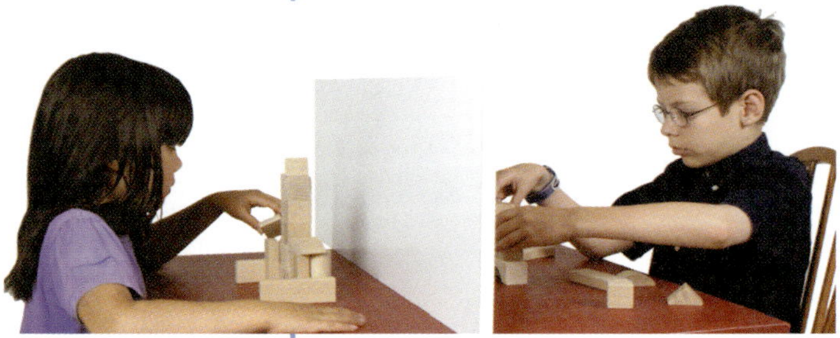

Step 1 Put a divider between you and your partner.

Step 2 Use 2 or 3 objects to build a structure on your side of the divider.

Step 3 Describe your structure so your partner can copy it without looking.

Step 4 Look at your partner's work. If your partner's structure is different from yours, give more clues.

Step 5 Play until the 2 structures look the same. Then switch roles and play again.

? How can you explain how to build a structure?

A. Play Follow the Leader with a classmate. As you play, list all the math words that you use. Include **position** words.

B. Which math words did you use most? Why?

C. Tell about one time when using a math word helped your partner understand your directions.

Do You Remember?

1. Match each name with an object.
   a) sphere
   b) cube
   c) pyramid
   d) cone

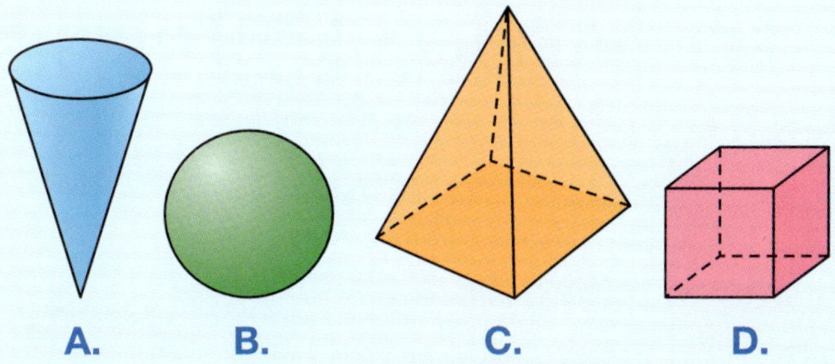

2. Use 3-D models.
   a) Find all the models that have squares.
   b) Trace a square from one of the models. Trace another square that is **congruent**.

3. List the objects in order from heaviest to lightest.

stapler

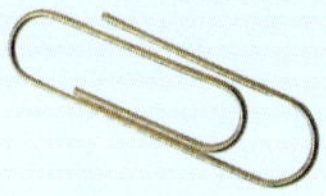
paper clip

crayon

4. a) Which container do you think holds the most? Explain your answer.
   b) Which container do you think holds the least? Explain your answer.

drink box

juice carton

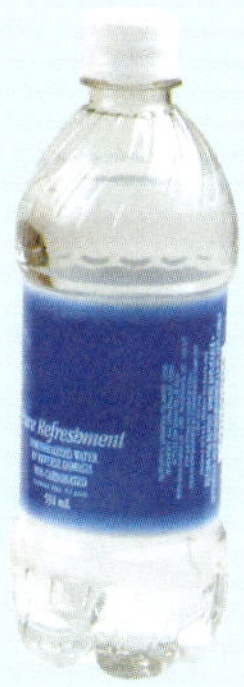
water bottle

milk carton

1 Stacking Blocks to Make Prisms

You will need
- pattern blocks

Goal **Describe and name prisms.**

Rashad was watching his sister play with a toy puzzle. He noticed that 2 of the 3-D objects had 6 **faces**.

face
A 2-D shape that is a flat surface of a 3-D object

? Which objects have 6 faces?

Rashad's Model

I can stack triangle pattern blocks to make a model of the object that fits through the triangle hole.

My model has 5 faces.

It is a triangle-based **prism**.

The **base** faces are triangles.

The other faces are rectangles.

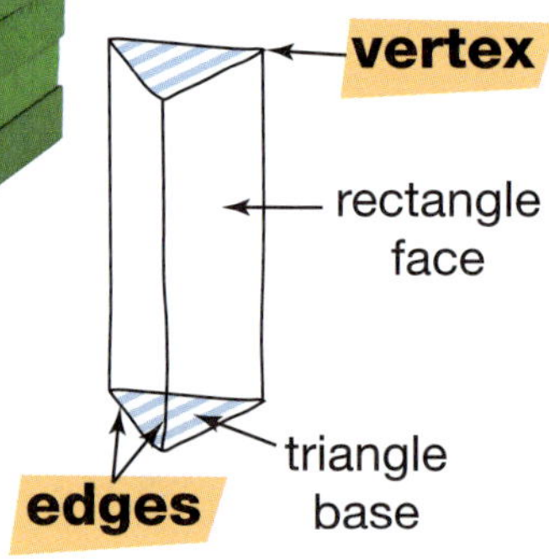

prism
A 3-D object with congruent ends called bases. The other faces are 4-sided.

base
The face on which a 3-D object rests

vertex (vertices)
The point at a corner

edge
The line where 2 faces meet on a 3-D object

A. How many vertices does Rashad's model have? How many edges does it have?

B. Stack pattern blocks to model the objects that fit in the other holes of the toy.

C. Are your models prisms? How do you know?

D. Find the models that have 6 faces.
  a) Name the 2-D shape that is the base for each.
  b) Name each 3-D object.
  c) Count the vertices and the edges for each 3-D object.

E. Find an object that is not a prism.
Explain how you know it is not a prism.

Reflecting

1. Pattern blocks are prisms. Which pattern blocks have 6 faces? What do you notice about the bases of these pattern blocks? What do you notice about the other faces?
2. A prism is named by its base. Explain with examples.

Checking

3. Name these prisms.

a) 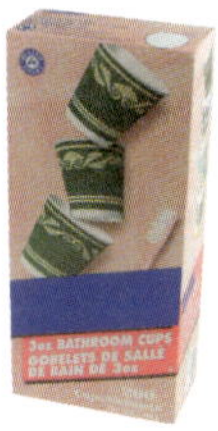

b) 

c) 

Practising

4. Name the prism you could make with each base.
Describe each prism.

a) 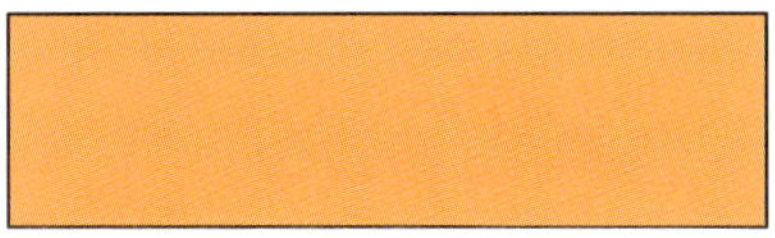

b) 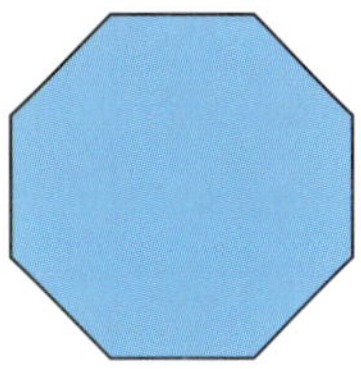

5. Which are prisms? Explain how you know.

a) 

b) 

c) 

d) 

CHAPTER 11

2 Identifying Faces of Prisms and Pyramids

You will need

- models of prisms and pyramids

Goal **Compare, sort, and name 3-D objects.**

Rose's Mystery
I have a mystery 3-D object.
• It has 5 faces.
• Some of its faces are triangles.
What could it be?

? What is Rose's mystery object?

Nisha's Solution

First I looked at all the models. Then I sorted them to make a group with triangle faces.

These are the models that have triangle faces.

I found only 1 prism, but I found lots of **pyramids**.

I sorted the models to find those with 5 faces.

Then I traced the faces.

Name	Faces
triangle-based prism 	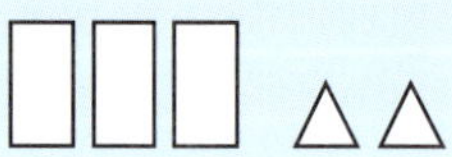
square-based pyramid 	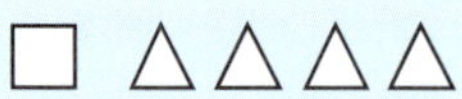

Rose's mystery object could be a triangle-based prism or a square-based pyramid.

pyramid

A 3-D object with a flat base. The other faces are triangles that meet at a vertex.

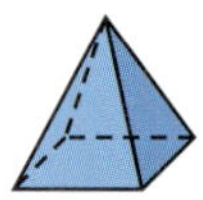

square-based pyramid

Reflecting

1. When Nisha first sorted she had only 1 prism and several pyramids. Why?
2. Use faces, edges, and vertices. How are pyramids and prisms alike? How are they different?
3. A pyramid is named by its base. Explain with examples.

Checking

4. Sharleen has a mystery object.
   a) Use Sharleen's 1st clue to sort the models. Record the models that fit the 1st clue. Use the chart.
   b) Use the 2nd clue. What is Sharleen's mystery 3-D object?

Sharleen's Mystery
I have a mystery 3-D object.
• None of its faces has 4 sides.
• The shape has 7 faces.
What could it be?

Name	Faces

Practising

5. What prisms or pyramids fit Ian's clue?

Ian's Mystery
I have a mystery 3-D object.
One of its faces looks like ☐.
What could it be?

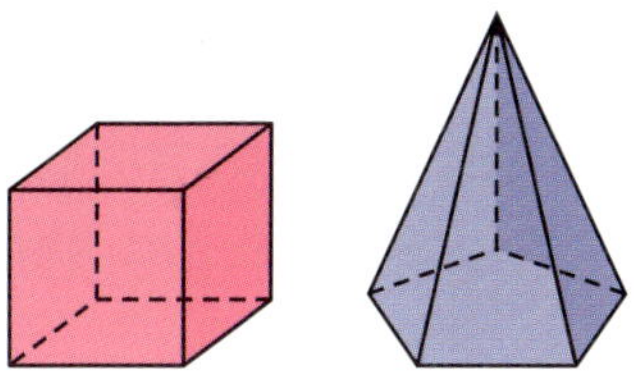

6. a) Name each 3-D object.
   b) Use faces, edges, and vertices. How are they different? How are they the same?
7. Sort at least 6 prisms and pyramids. Write your sorting rule.

3 Using Nets for Rectangle-Based Prisms

Goal Relate rectangle-based prisms to their nets.

You will need

- boxes for rectangle-based prisms

- scissors

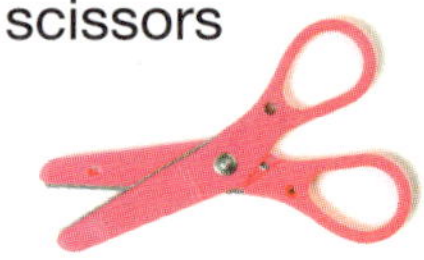

- tape

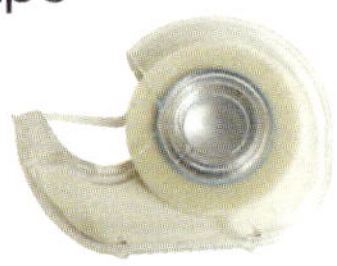

- nets and shapes

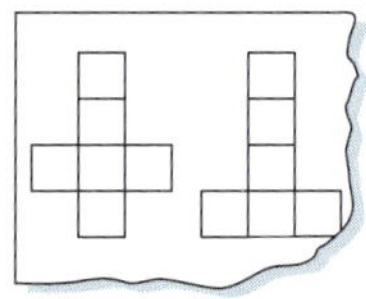

Kindergarten children are building with boxes.

? What does the net of a box look like?

net
A 2-D shape that can be folded into a 3-D object

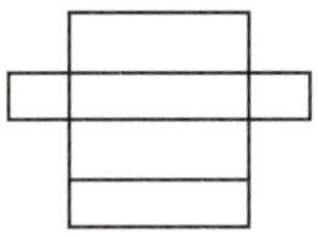

net for a rectangle-based prism

A. Look at some boxes shaped like rectangle-based prisms. What is the same about the shapes of the boxes? What is different?

B. Choose a box. Cut along some edges and flatten the box to make a net.
How many faces does your net have?

C. Do any of the faces look congruent? Which ones?

D. Look at other nets for boxes that your classmates have cut. What is the same about all the nets?
What is different?

E. Fold your box back together.
Record the number of faces, edges, and vertices.

Reflecting

1. Is it possible for a rectangle-based prism that is a cube to have any different faces? Explain.
2. Is it possible for a rectangle-base prism to have different nets? Use one of your boxes to explain your answer.

Checking

3. What 3-D object do you predict you can make with each net? Explain why you think this. Check your predictions.

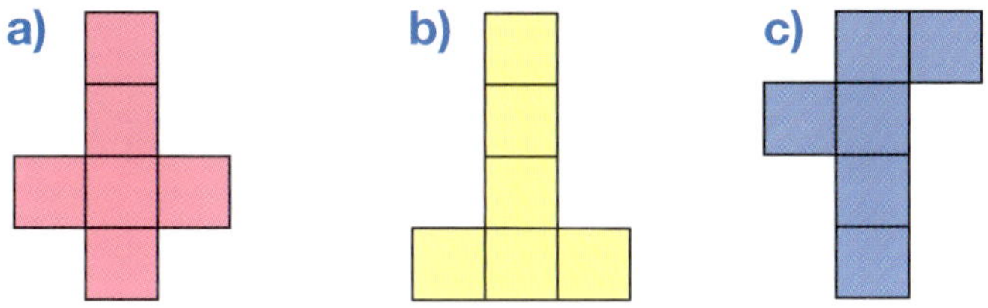

Practising

4. Predict which of these shapes you can use to make a cube. Explain why you think this. Check your predictions.

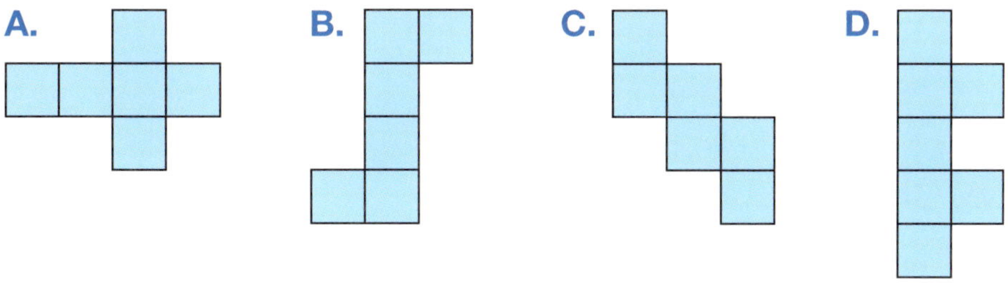

5. Explain how you can predict whether a 2-D shape can be folded to make a rectangle-based prism.

6. What is the same about all nets for rectangle-based prisms? Explain why this makes sense.

4 Describing Congruent Objects

Goal Find and describe congruent objects.

? How do you decide whether objects are congruent?

Amit's Boxes

The boxes for Crispy Crackers and Corn Crunches are the same shape and the same size.
That means they are **congruent**.

The box for Cracklies is not congruent to another box.
The box for Snappy Snacks is not congruent to another box.

A. How do you know the Cracklies box is not congruent to another of Amit's boxes?

B. How do you know the Snappy Snacks box is not congruent to another of Amit's boxes?

C. Find 2 congruent objects. Name the objects. How do you know they are congruent?

D. Find 2 objects that are not congruent. Name the objects. How do you know they are not congruent?

E. Find 2 objects that someone might think are congruent, but they are not congruent. Name the objects. Why might someone think they are congruent? How do you know they are not congruent?

Reflecting

1. Can a small cube be congruent to a large cube? Explain your thinking.
2. These are the bases of 2 triangle-based prisms. What other information do you need to decide whether the prisms are congruent?
3. How do you decide whether objects are congruent?

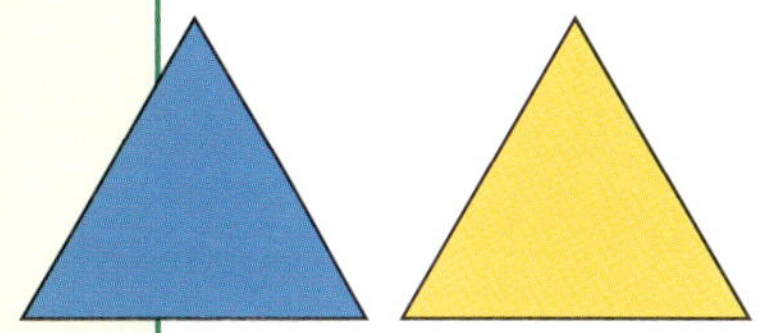

Curious Math

Predicting with Patterns

You will need

- models of prisms

If you know the shape of the base of a prism, you can predict the number of faces, edges, and vertices.

1 Complete this chart for these prisms.

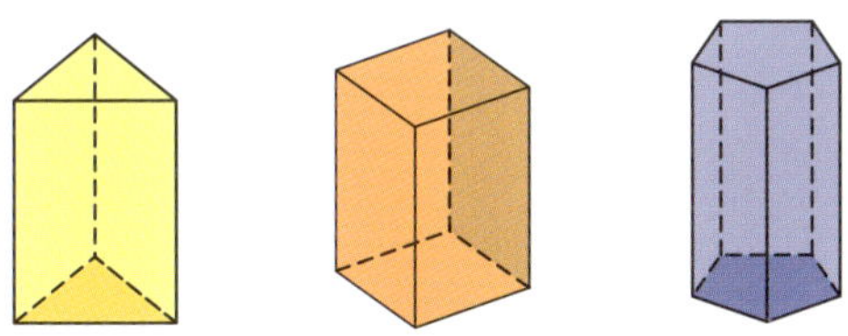

Base of prism	Number of faces	Number of vertices	Number of edges
triangle			
square			
pentagon			

2 Describe the pattern for each.

a) the number of faces for a prism
b) the number of vertices for a prism
c) the number of edges for a prism

3 Predict the number of faces, vertices, and edges for each. Use models to check your predictions.

a) hexagon-based prism
b) octagon-based prism

5 Exploring Lines

Goal Explore intersecting, perpendicular, and parallel lines.

You will need

- a box

- pencil crayons

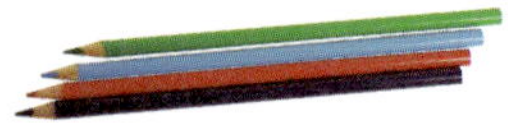

? Where can you find intersecting lines, perpendicular lines, and parallel lines?

Jessica's Box

The **purple** and **yellow** edges of Jessica's box are **intersecting** lines.
They are also **perpendicular** lines.

The **purple** edges of Jessica's box are **parallel** lines.

intersecting
Intersecting lines cross or meet at a **point**

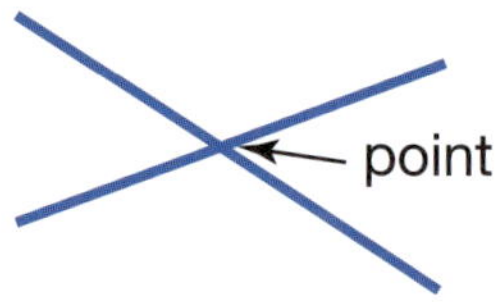

perpendicular
Perpendicular lines intersect to make a square corner

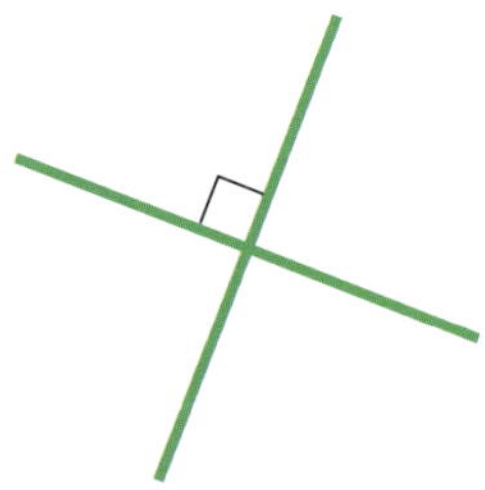

parallel
Parallel lines never intersect

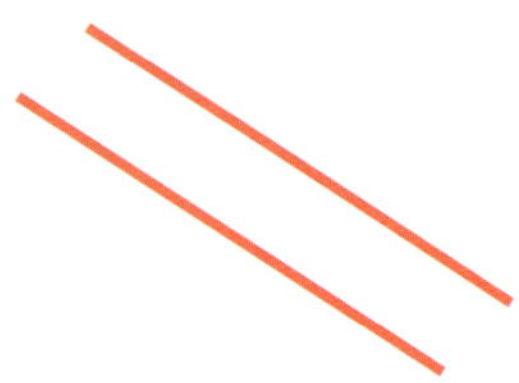

A. **a)** Explain how you can tell that the **purple** and **yellow** edges of Jessica's box are intersecting lines.
b) Explain how you can tell that the **purple** and **yellow** edges are perpendicular lines.
c) Explain how you can tell that the **purple** edges are parallel lines.

B. Are the **yellow** edges of Jessica's box parallel lines? How do you know?

C. Find an object with edges that are intersecting lines. Sketch the object. Use **blue** to show 2 intersecting lines. How do you know they are intersecting?

D. Find an object with edges that are perpendicular lines.
Sketch the object.
Use **green** to show 2 perpendicular lines.
How do you know they are perpendicular?

E. Find an object with edges that are parallel lines.
Sketch the object.
Use **red** to show 2 parallel lines.
How do you know they are parallel?

F. Choose a box that is a rectangle-based prism.

a) Point out edges that are intersecting lines.
How do you know?

b) Point out edges that are perpendicular lines.
How do you know?

c) Point out edges that are parallel lines.
How do you know?

G. Faces of a box can be intersecting, perpendicular, or parallel.
Use your box.

a) Point out faces that are intersecting.
How do you know?

b) Point out faces that are perpendicular.
How do you know?

c) Point out faces that are parallel.
How do you know?

Reflecting

1. Perpendicular lines are intersecting lines.
Sketch an object to show this.

2. Some intersecting lines are not perpendicular lines.
Sketch an object to show this.

3. Parallel lines are not intersecting lines.
Sketch an object to show this.

6 Building with 3-D Objects

Goal **Build a structure with 3-D objects.**

You will need

- 3-D objects for building
- scissors

- tape

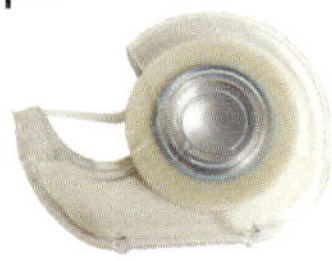

? What can you build with 3-D objects?

A. Plan a structure that you can build with 3-D objects.

B. Build your structure. Use tape if necessary.

C. Describe your structure.
Use names of 3-D objects.
Describe faces, edges, and vertices.
Use geometry words such as congruent, parallel, perpendicular, and intersecting.

D. Explain how you built your structure.

Reflecting

1. Is it easier to build with objects that are shaped like prisms or like pyramids? Why?
2. Are any of your objects not prisms and not pyramids? How do you know?

Math Game

I Spy

You will need

- 3-D models or packages

Number of players: 2

How to play: Guess the object that another player "spies."

Step 1 The 1st player says, "I spy…" and gives a clue about a 3-D object.

Step 2 The 2nd player asks yes-or-no questions to guess the object.

Play until the guesser figures out the object. Then switch roles and play again.

LESSON

Mid-Chapter Review

1 **1.** The stacks of signs make 3-D objects. Name each 3-D object.

a)

b)

c)

2 **2.** Name and describe each 3-D object.

a)

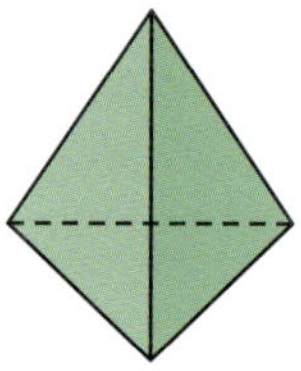

b)

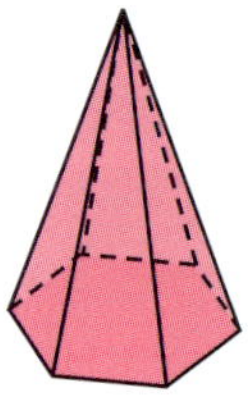

c)

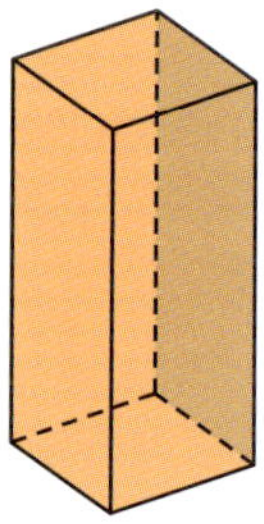

3. A pyramid has exactly 4 triangle faces.
What 3-D object might it be?

3 **4.** Which shapes are nets for a prism? Explain how you know.

A.

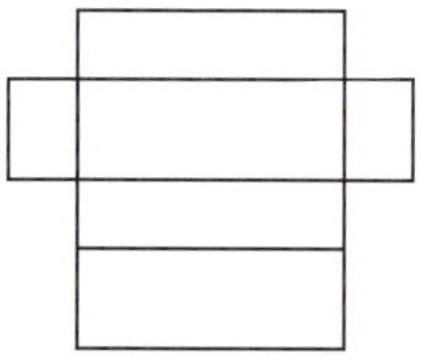

B.

C.

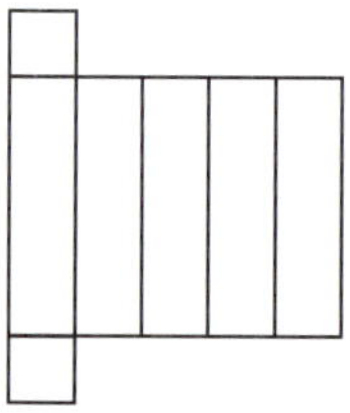

D.

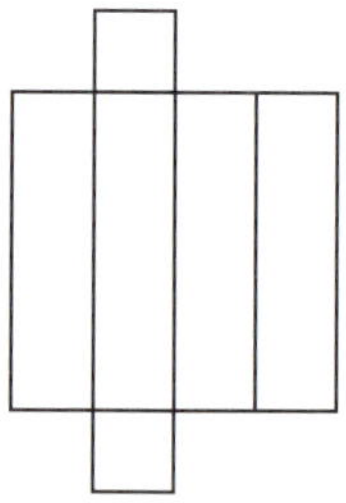

4 **5.** Can a small rectangle-based prism be congruent to a large rectangle-based prism? Explain your thinking.

5 **6.** Look at the 3-D objects in Question 2.

a) Does the object in part a) have perpendicular edges? How do you know?

b) Which object has parallel faces? How do you know?

Estimating by Comparing

A. Lyn is pouring the apples from the bowl into the pail. She thinks she would need to fill the bowl 3 times to fill the pail with apples. Explain why she thinks this.

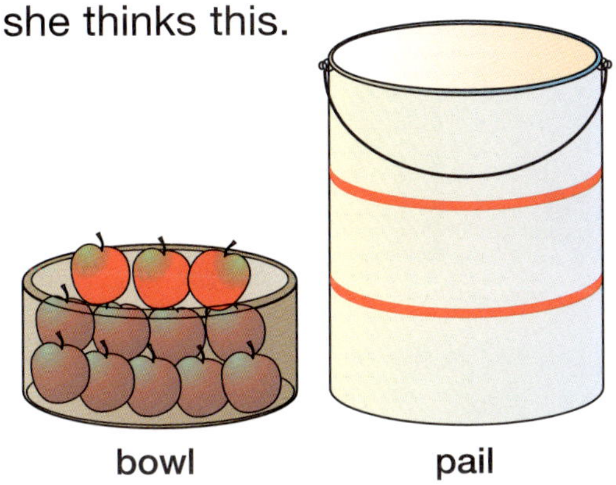

B. About how many small glasses of water would fit into the large glass? Explain your thinking.

Try These

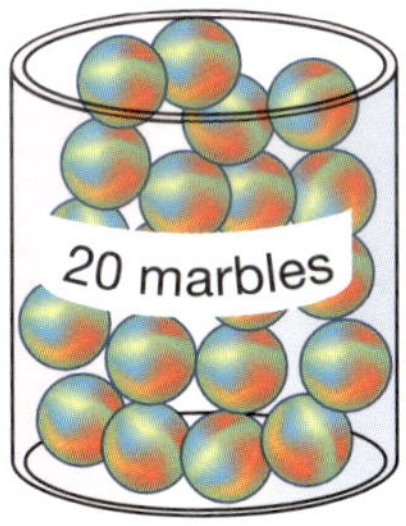

1. About how many marbles will fit into each container? Explain your thinking.

a)

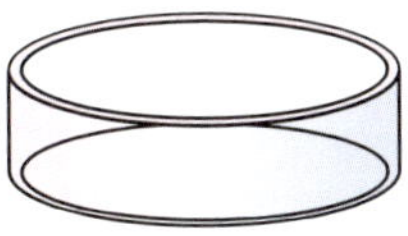

b)

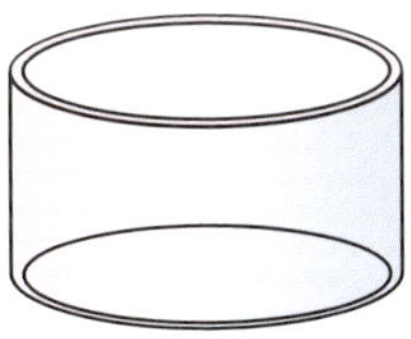

2. The small carton holds 1 glass of milk. How many glasses of milk does the larger carton hold?

7 Estimating and Measuring Capacity

Goal **Estimate, measure, and compare the amounts containers can hold.**

You will need

- water
- small containers such as spoons, cups, or pop cans
- large containers such as bowls, pails, or jugs

Lyn has 3 water jugs.
She wants to take the jug that holds the most water on a hike.

? How can Lyn choose the jug that holds the most water?

Lyn's Plan

The jugs look like they have about the same **capacity**.
I'll find out how many mugs of water it takes to fill each.

capacity The amount a container can hold

A. Explain why a mug is a reasonable unit for Lyn to use to measure capacity.

B. Choose 3 containers that you predict have about the same capacity. Choose a small container such as a mug for measuring the capacity of your containers. Explain your choice of unit.

C. Estimate the capacity of one of your containers. Record it in a chart.

Container	My estimate	Measurement
bowl	10 mugs	

D. Measure the capacity. Record it in your chart.

E. Repeat parts C and D for your other containers.

F. Which of your containers has the greatest capacity?

Reflecting

1. Suppose Lyn did not have a small container such as a mug. How could she figure out which jug has the greatest capacity by pouring water from one jug to another?
2. Sharleen used a jar to measure the capacity of 2 jugs. She used a mug to measure the capacity of another jug. What is wrong with comparing the capacities?
3. How can you use your estimate to check whether a capacity you measured is reasonable?

Checking

4. Which would you use to measure each capacity: a spoon, a mug, or a pail? Explain your choices.
   a) a paint can b) a cup c) a wading pool

5. Choose 2 large containers.
   a) Choose a small container for the unit of measurement. Estimate the capacity of each large container.
   b) Measure the capacity of each large container. Which has a greater capacity?

Practising

6. a) Choose 3 large containers. Predict their order from least to greatest capacity.
   b) Choose a small container for a unit of measurement. Explain your choice.
   c) Measure to check your prediction.

7. a) Choose a large container. Measure its capacity twice. Use a different small container for the unit of measurement each time.
   b) Is the number of units the same each time? Explain why this makes sense.

CHAPTER 11

8 Using Litres

Goal **Estimate, measure, and compare capacities in litres.**

Gabe and his sister are making vegetable soup. The recipe calls for 1 L of water.

You will need

- water
- a 1 L container

- large containers with different capacities
- a small container for pouring

? How can you find containers with a capacity of about 1 L?

Gabe's Plan

I'll look at a measuring cup for one **litre**, or 1 **L**, and find the mark for 1 L.

First I'll estimate the capacities and sort my containers.

Then I'll measure to check.

litre (L)
A unit of measurement for capacity

A. Look at the mark for 1 L on a 1 L cup.
Place the 1 L cup beside several containers that have different sizes and shapes.
Estimate to sort your containers into 3 groups: less than 1 L, about 1 L, and greater than 1 L.

B. Measure with the 1 L cup to check your sorting.

C. Use your containers that have a capacity greater than 1 L. Pour 1 L of water into each of these containers. Does the water go to the same height for each container?

Reflecting

1. a) Explain your strategy for finding containers with a capacity of about 1 L.
   b) What other strategy could you have used? Explain why it would work.
2. Why do you think Gabe's recipe calls for 1 L of water instead of 1 bowl of water?
3. a) Why does the measuring cup have a mark for 1 L?
   b) Why does 1 L of water go to different heights for different containers?

Checking

4. a) Choose 2 containers that you estimate have a capacity greater than 2 L. Without using a 1 L cup, estimate as you pour water into each container. Stop pouring when you think you have poured about 2 L.
   b) Check by measuring the water you poured.

Practising

5. a) Choose 3 large containers. Estimate the capacity of each in litres.
   b) Measure the capacity of each in litres.
   c) Order the containers from least to greatest capacity.
6. Pour exactly 1 L of water into a large container.
   a) Estimate the capacity of the container in litres.
   b) Measure to check your estimate.
7. Repeat Question 6 for a different container.
8. Why would you measure capacity using litres instead of using a mug or can?

9 Solve Problems About Combinations

Goal **Solve problems using a chart to record combinations.**

Marcus and Asha are helping Julia take water for the horses.

? What different amounts of water can the children carry to the horses on 1 trip?

Charlie's Solution

Understand the Problem

1 child, 2 children, or all 3 children can take water.

I need to find all the amounts of water they can take.

Make a Plan

I can use a chart to find all the combinations.

Carry Out the Plan

Water Taken by 1 Child

Name	Total capacity
Marcus	1 L
Asha	2 L
Julia	8 L

Water Taken by 2 Children

Names	Total capacity
Marcus and Asha	1 L + 2 L = 3 L
Asha and Julia	2 L + 8 L = 10 L
Marcus and Julia	1 L + 8 L = 9 L

Water Taken by 3 Children

Names	Total capacity
Marcus, Asha, and Julia	1 L + 2 L + 8 L = 11 L

The children can take 1 L, 2 L, 3 L, 8 L, 9 L, 10 L, or 11 L of water to the horses.

Reflecting

1. How can you tell that Charlie has found all the possible combinations?
2. Why is it helpful to use a chart to solve a problem like this?

Checking

3. Suppose these pails are used. What different amounts of water can 3 people take to the horses on 1 trip?

Practising

4. Lee has these bowls. What possible amounts can he measure without refilling the bowls? Show your work.

5. Ari has these vases. How many different measures can he make without refilling the vases? Show your work.

6. Shin is in a contest to fill a barrel by pouring water as few times as possible. The barrel holds exactly 24 L. He must use 2 of these containers to pour the water. He can use each of the 2 containers any number of times. Which containers should Shin choose?

CHAPTER 11

10 Estimating and Measuring Mass

Goal **Estimate, measure, and compare the masses of objects.**

The cost of the raisins Michael buys at the grocery store depends on their **mass**. Michael wondered if his class should use mass to decide on prices for a junk sale.

? Would measuring mass be a good way to decide on prices for a junk sale?

You will need

- balance scales and masses

- books and other objects to measure
- counters

- a clear plastic bag

mass
How heavy an object is. Mass can be measured in **grams (g)** or **kilograms (kg)**.

1000 g = 1 kg

Michael's Measuring Tools

I can use balance scales to measure the mass of a bear. The price in cents will be the number of **grams**.

I found that the mass of the bear is 30 **g** (grams).

That's a lot less than one **kilogram** (1 **kg**).

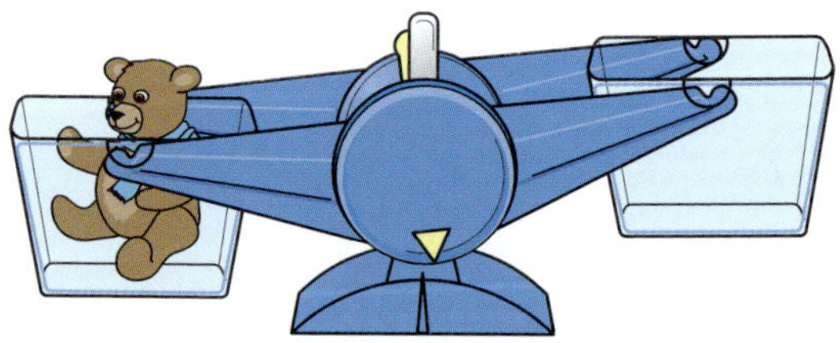

A. Find things you could use for a junk sale like Michael's. Predict their order from least to greatest mass.

B. Measure the object you think has the least mass. Record the mass in a chart. Record the price.

C. Estimate the mass of the next object.
Measure to check your estimate. Record the price.

D. Repeat part C for your other objects.
Use the chart to check your predicted order.

Object	My estimate	Measurement	Price
book	500 g	580 g	$5.80

E. Do you think measuring mass is a good way to decide prices? Explain your thinking.

Reflecting

1. How can you use the mass of one object to estimate the mass of another object?
2. How did you decide whether to measure the mass of an object in grams or kilograms?

Checking

3. a) Make a stack of books that you estimate has a mass of about 1 kg. Measure to check.
   b) Make a stack of different books that you estimate has a mass of about 3 kg. Explain your estimation strategy. Measure to check.

Practising

4. Find 4 objects to measure the mass.
   a) Record your estimates and measurements in a chart.
   b) Order the objects from greatest to least mass.

Object	My estimate	Measurement

5. a) Put counters in a plastic bag until you estimate the mass is about 250 g. Measure to check.
   b) Use the bag of counters to estimate how many counters have a mass of about 100 g. Explain your estimation strategy. Measure to check.

Skills Bank

LESSON

1 **1.** Name each 3-D object. Describe it.

a)

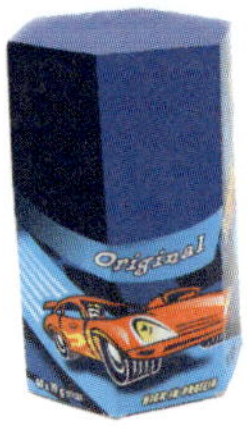

b)

2 **2.** Name each 3-D object.

a)

4 faces

b)

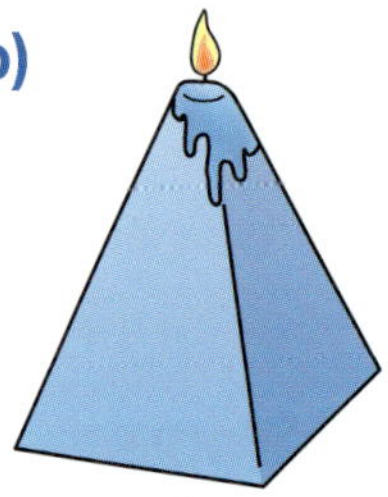

5 faces

3. Name the 3-D object that has these faces.

a)

b)

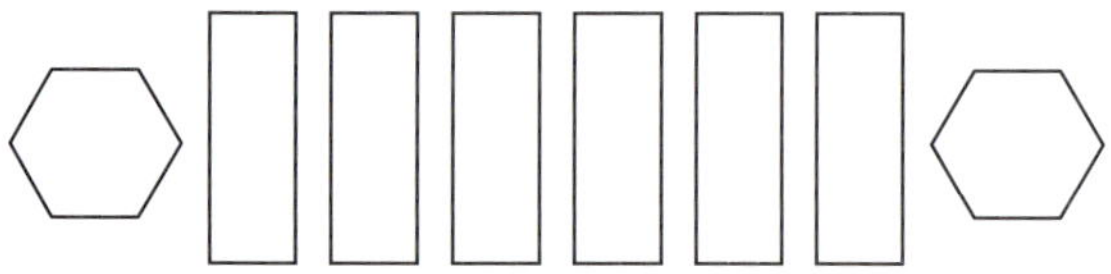

4. **a)** Choose a prism. Record its name.
Trace each face. Name the 2-D shape for each face.

b) Repeat part a) for a pyramid.

5. What is each mystery 3-D object?

a) I am a prism.
I have 2 faces that are pentagons.
What am I?

b) I am a pyramid.
I have 6 faces that are triangles.
What am I?

6. I am a prism. Write 2 things you know about me.

7. I am a pyramid. Write 2 things you know about me.

3 **8.** What is the same about all rectangle-based prisms?

4 **9.** **a)** Does the green lid fit on the yellow box?
How do you know?
b) The red and yellow boxes are congruent.
Does the yellow lid fit on the red box?
How do you know?
c) The pink and yellow lids are congruent.
Does the pink lid fit on the yellow box?
How do you know?
d) Are the pink and yellow boxes congruent?
How do you know?

7 **10.** **a)** Which unit would be best to fill a pail with water:
a cup, a spoon, or a jug? Explain why.
b) Use the unit you chose. Measure the capacity of a pail.

8 **11.** Choose the best estimate.

a)

2 L
10 L
20 L

b)

1 L
10 L
100 L

10 **12.** Choose the best estimate.

a)

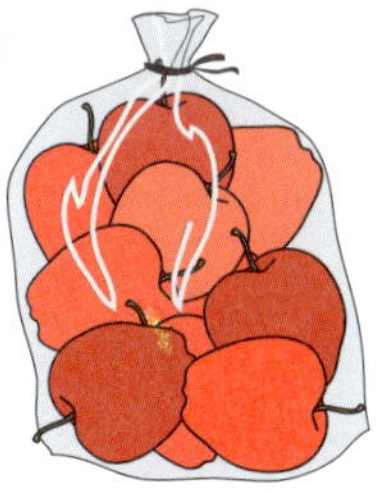

3 kg
3 g
300 g

b)

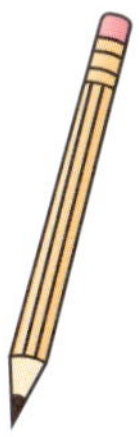

5 kg
50 kg
5 g

c)

3 kg
3 g
300 g

13. Grocery store clerks pack lighter food on top of heavier food.
a) Which should go on the bottom?
b) Which should go on the top?

LESSON

Problem Bank

2 **1.** I am a pyramid with 9 faces. What does my base look like? Explain how you know.

3 **2.** Where can you draw the face that completes this net of a box? Show more than one answer.

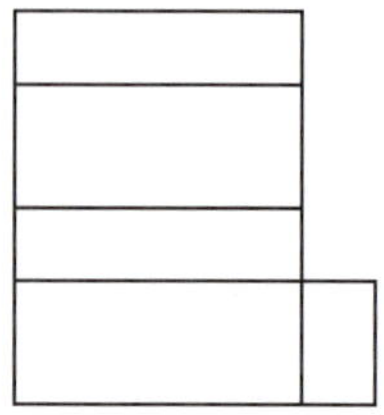

3. Make 5 different nets for a cube.

8 **4.** You have a 2 L container and a 9 L container. How can you measure 5 L by pouring water from one container to another?

5. You have made 5 L of punch for a party. About how many small paper cups of punch could you pour? Explain your strategy.

9 **6.** 3 friends could use these pails to bring each amount of water to the horses at once.
1 L 2 L 3 L 6 L 7 L 8 L 9 L
What is the capacity of each pail? Explain your strategy.

10 **7.** About how many of each item would balance 4 containers of cheese? Explain your thinking.
a) loaves of bread
b) soup packages
c) bags of rice

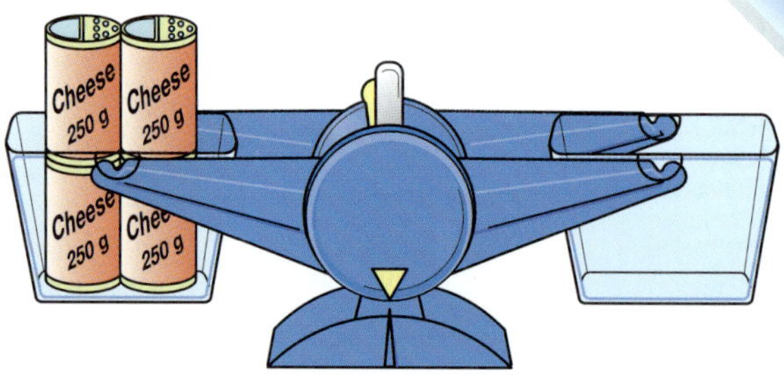

Chapter Review

LESSON

1 **1. a)** Name each 3-D object.
b) What is the same about the objects?
c) What is different about the objects?

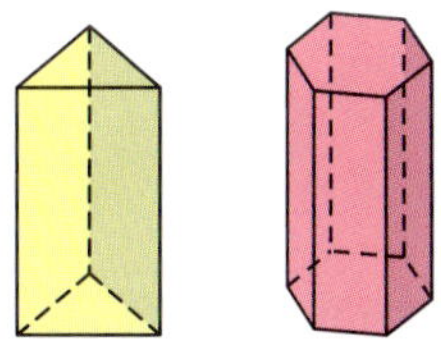

2 **2.** Brady isn't sure if her object is a prism or a pyramid. What can you ask to help her find out?

3 **3.** Will this shape make a rectangle-based prism? Explain your thinking.

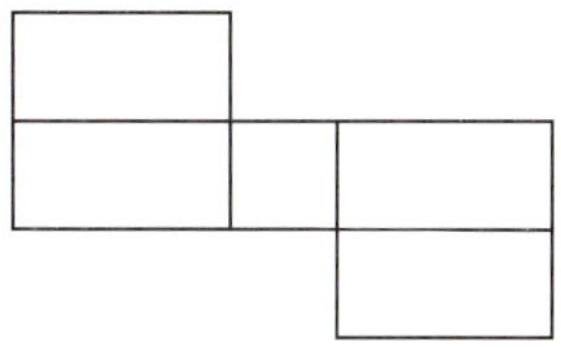

4 **4.** If 2 prisms have congruent bases, must the prisms be congruent? Explain your answer using words or pictures.

5 **5.** Look at a group of 3-D models.
a) Which models have at least 1 pair of parallel faces?
b) Describe the models from the group that you did not name for part a).

6 **6.** Use as many geometry words as you can.
a) Describe a table in your classroom.
b) Explain how the table is like a classroom door.
c) Choose 2 other objects. How are they the same? How are they different?

8 **7. a)** Choose a large container. Estimate its capacity in litres.
b) Measure to check your estimate.

9 **8.** Use these 3 pails. What different amounts of water could you measure without refilling any pails? Give all the possible combinations.

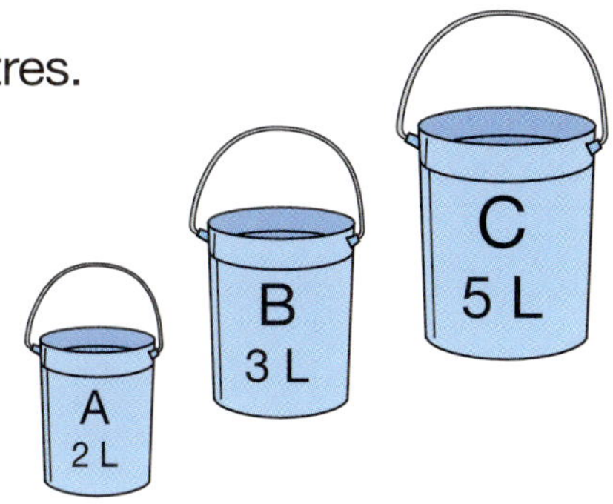

10 **9. a)** Fill 3 cans of different sizes with sand or counters. Measure the mass of one can in grams.
b) Estimate the masses of the other cans in grams.
c) Measure to check your estimates.

Chapter Task

Making Pets

This is Rachel's pet pyramid.

? What pet pyramid or prism can you make?

Part 1

A. Use some dough to make your own pet pyramid or pet prism.

B. Name your pet.
Make an identification tag for it.

C. Describe your pet's shape and any special features, such as faces, edges, and vertices.

Part 2

D. After the dough dries, estimate the mass of your pet.
Then measure the mass of your pet.
Explain how you measured.

E. Compare the mass of your pet with the mass of a classmate's pet.
Which mass do you think is greater?
Check by measuring.

Pet-Maker Dough

Choose a small glass for measuring.
Use the same glass for each measurement.

all-purpose flour	20 glasses
salt	10 glasses
water	10 glasses
vegetable oil	1 glass

Mix together and knead until smooth.
To dry, bake at 160°C for 45 minutes or leave out in the air for 24 hours.

Task Checklist

- ✓ Did you include a diagram?
- ✓ Is your description clear?
- ✓ Did you record the measurements?

Cumulative Review

Cross-Strand Multiple Choice

1. Ken is walking south.
Which direction is at his left?

A. north **B.** south **C.** east **D.** west

2. Which division has the greatest answer?

E. $30 \div 6 = ■$ **F.** $42 \div 7 = ■$ **G.** $36 \div 6 = ■$ **H.** $35 \div 5 = ■$

3. Which number sentence represents counting the spaces on the grid?

A. $4 + 3 = ■$
B. $3 \times 4 = ■$
C. $4 + 4 + 4 + 4 = ■$
D. $3 + 3 + 3 = ■$

4. Which division sentence matches this array?

E. $12 \div 6 = ■$
F. $18 \div 3 = ■$
G. $10 \div 2 = ■$
H. $14 \div 2 = ■$

5. Which measurement doesn't make sense?

A. a cooking pot: 3 L
B. a bottle of pop: 1 L
C. a jug of milk: 2 L
D. a mug: 4 L

6. Which shape is a triangle-based pyramid?

E.
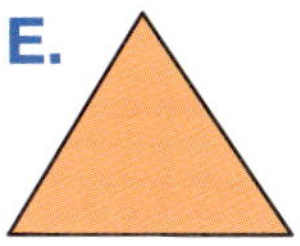

F.
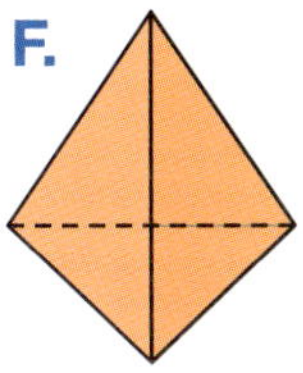

G.
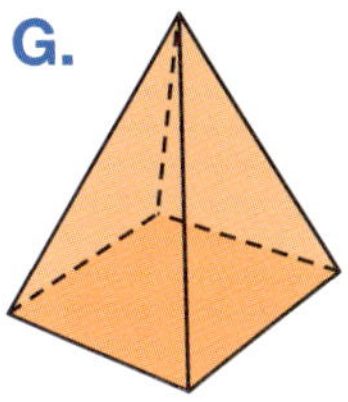

H.
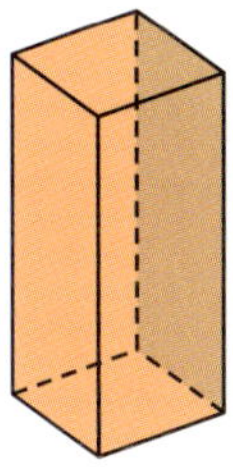

Cross-Strand Investigation

Building Structures

7. You can build models of skyscrapers with blocks. One storey of a skyscraper is shown.

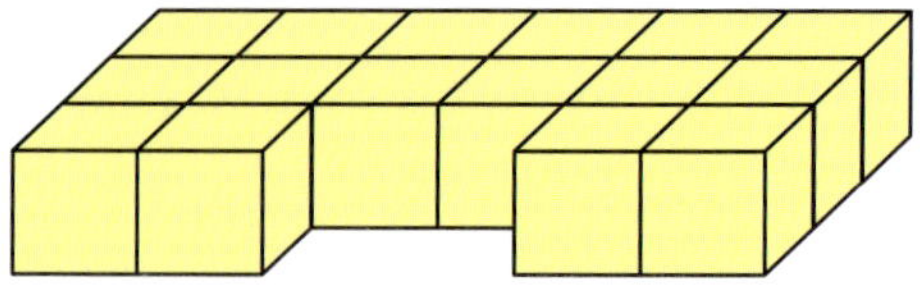

   a) How many blocks would be in a 10-storey skyscraper? Show your work.
   b) Which grid models the floor of the skyscraper?

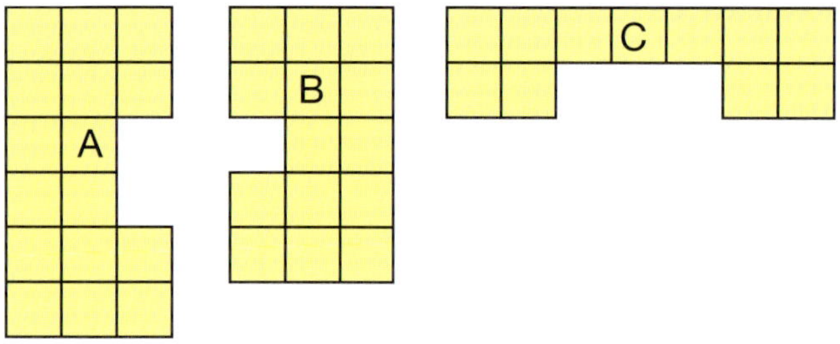

   c) Find the area of the floor of the skyscraper.

8. Choose some 3-D objects you could use to build a skyscraper that looks unusual.
   a) Name your 3-D objects and sort them using 2 attributes: type of 3-D object and number of faces.

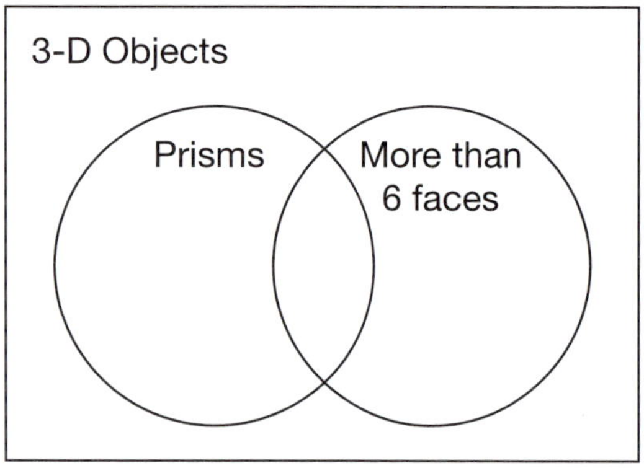

   b) How do you know which 3-D objects are prisms and which are pyramids?
   c) Build a skyscraper using 3-D objects.
   d) Describe the steps you took in making your skyscraper.

CHAPTER 12

Fractions

Goals

You will be able to

- **represent and describe fractions**
- **represent and describe equal shares**
- **communicate about fractions using drawings**

Favourite collections

Getting Started

Common Fractions

? How can you show $\frac{1}{2}$, $\frac{1}{3}$, and $\frac{1}{4}$ of something?

You will need

- counters

- fraction mats

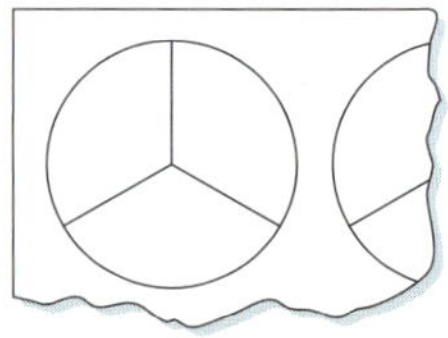

A. What fractions do the plates of food show?

B. What fractions do the drinks show?

C. What fractions describe the people at the table?

D. What is a fraction?

E. Use counters to show $\frac{1}{4}$.

F. Find examples of the fraction $\frac{1}{2}$ in the picture.

G. Use fraction pieces or counters to show $\frac{1}{2}$.
Explain how each shows $\frac{1}{2}$.

Do You Remember?

1. Which picture shows $\frac{1}{3}$ blue?

A.

B.

C.

D.

2. Show each fraction using fraction mats or coloured counters. Sketch your fraction model.

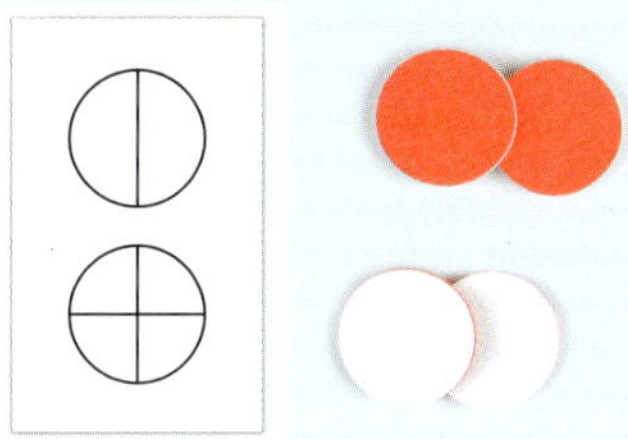

a) $\frac{1}{2}$ **b)** $\frac{1}{4}$ **c)** $\frac{3}{4}$

3. What fraction of each rectangle is green?
What fraction of each rectangle is white?

a)

b)
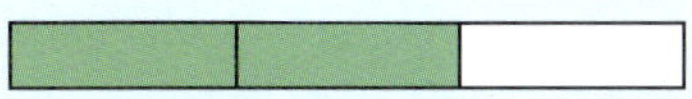

1 Fractions as Parts of a Set

You will need

- counters

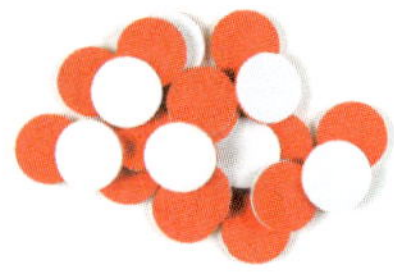

Goal Use fractions to describe parts of a set or a group.

? **How can you describe parts of a group?**

Brady's Fractions

In this group, 2 out of 5 students have long hair.

I can say two fifths of the students have long hair.

I can use counters to model the students.

$\frac{2}{5}$ 2 ← **numerator**; 5 ← **denominator**

A. How do the counters model that $\frac{2}{5}$ of the students have long hair?

B. What other way can you complete this sentence?
$\frac{2}{5}$ of the students ________.

C. Represent some or all of the students using 3 different fractions. Use counters. Write the fraction for each model.

numerator
The number above the bar in a fraction that shows the number of parts the fraction represents

denominator
The number below the bar in a fraction that shows the number of parts

Reflecting

1. Look at each fraction you modelled in part C.
   a) What does the denominator tell you?
   b) What does the numerator tell you?

2. a) What fraction of the students are children?
   b) What fraction are adults?
   c) Explain how you know the fraction in part b) by looking at the fraction in part a).

Checking

3. What fraction of each group are children? Explain.

a) 

b) 

Practising

4. a) Model $\frac{2}{3}$ using red counters and white counters and a sketch.
   b) What fraction is *not* red?

5. A kennel has 10 animals. $\frac{3}{10}$ of the animals are cats.
   a) Model the animals with counters and a sketch.
   b) What fraction are not cats?

6. $\frac{3}{5}$ of a group are girls.
   $\frac{3}{5}$ of the same group have black hair.
   a) Represent the group using counters.
   b) How many are girls? How many are boys?
   c) How many girls could have black hair?
   d) Suppose a boy with red hair joins the group. Represent the new group with counters and fractions.

CHAPTER 12

2 Fractions as Parts of a Region

Goal **Use fractions to describe parts of a region or a whole.**

? What fraction of the pizza is left?

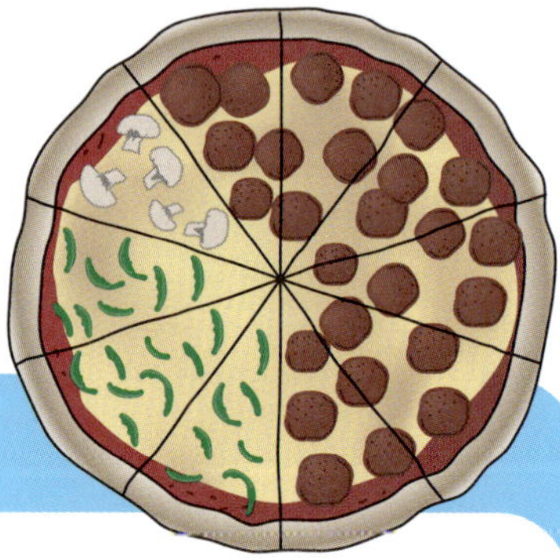

You will need

- pencil crayons

- fraction mats

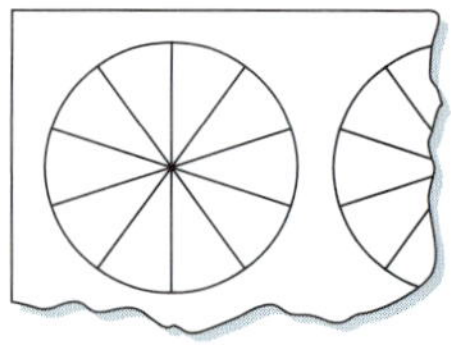

- pattern blocks

Ian's Pizza

I modelled the pizza toppings with a fraction mat.
I ate the pepperoni part of the pizza.
That's 6 out of 10 slices.
I can write $\frac{6}{10}$, or six tenths.
Only $\frac{4}{10}$, or four tenths,
of the pizza is left.

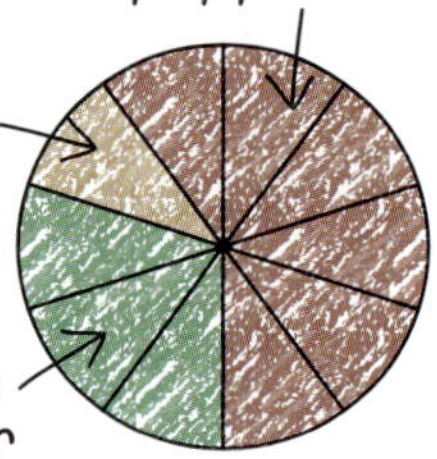

A. Brady ate the part of the pizza with green pepper. What fraction of the whole pizza did she eat?

B. What fraction is left after Ian and Brady eat?

C. Lee ate the part of the pizza with mushrooms. What fraction of the whole pizza did he eat?

D. What fraction of the pizza is left after all 3 children eat?

E. What fraction of the pizza did all 3 children eat?

F. Model your own pizza with 5 slices.
Use 2 toppings. Cover each slice with only 1 topping.
Use fractions to describe your pizza.

Reflecting

1. a) Why are all the denominators for the parts of Ian's pizza the same?
   b) Why are the denominators for the parts of your pizza different from Ian's?
2. a) The whole number 0 describes the pizza in part D. Explain why.
   b) The whole number 1 describes the pizza in part E. Explain why.
3. Suppose $\frac{1}{2}$ of a pizza is covered with tofu. Do you know how many slices it has? Explain with an example.

Checking

4. a) Colour a fraction mat so that $\frac{7}{10}$ of a pizza has pineapple.
   b) What do you know about $\frac{3}{10}$ of the pizza?
5. What fraction is coloured?

a)
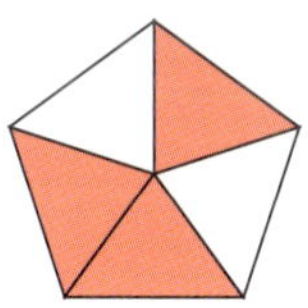

b)
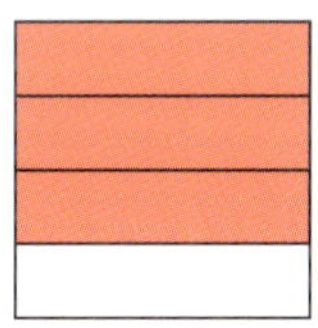

c)
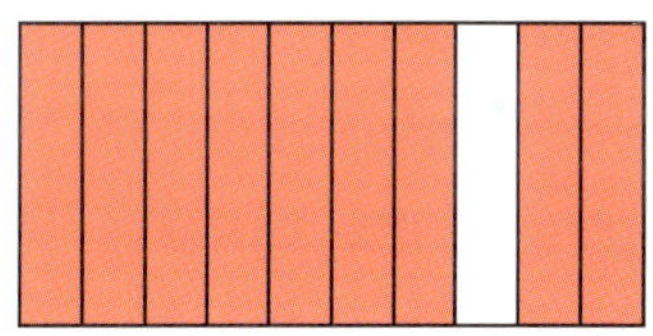

Practising

6. Use a fraction mat for each pizza. Write a fraction for the part that is not covered.
   a) Cover $\frac{2}{3}$ with mushrooms.
   b) Cover $\frac{5}{5}$ with green pepper.

7. Place pattern blocks on the yellow hexagon. What fraction of the hexagon is each?
   a) 1 blue rhombus b) 1 red trapezoid c) 5 green triangles

3 Exploring Fair Shares

You will need

- pattern blocks

- pencil crayons

Goal **Use fractions to describe fair shares.**

Keisha's class is studying First Nations crafts.

Keisha, Devon, Sharleen, Jack, and Ben are sharing this piece of material equally for making a quilt.

? How can you figure out fair shares?

A. Use one type of pattern block. Place pattern blocks on the material to figure out the fair share for each of the 5 students.

Trace the pattern block that represents a fair share. Colour the shape **purple**.

B. Keep tracing the pattern block to sketch the whole piece of material. Colour each share a different colour.

C. One fifth, or $\frac{1}{5}$, describes each share.

a) What does the denominator mean?

b) What does the numerator mean?

$\frac{1}{5}$

one fifth

D. Write a fraction that describes the part left after 1 student takes a share.

a) What does the denominator mean?

b) What does the numerator mean?

E. Tiffany and 9 other students are sharing this piece of material fairly.

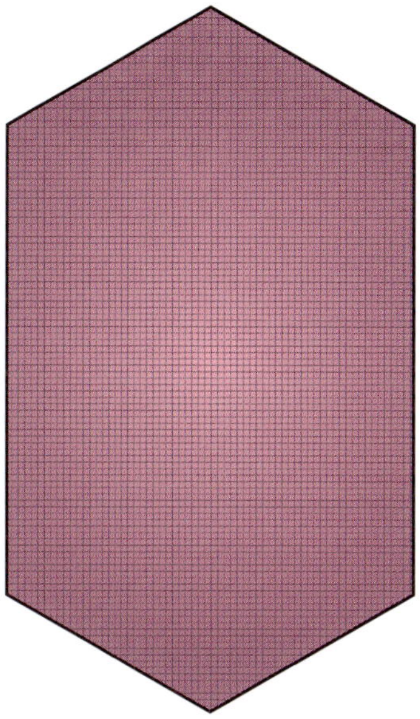

a) Use one type of pattern block.
Place pattern blocks on the material to figure out the fair share for each student.

Trace the pattern block that represents a fair share. Colour the shape **blue**.

b) Keep tracing the pattern block to sketch the whole piece of material.

c) Colour 2 shares **green**, 3 shares **red**, and the other shares **yellow**.

d) Write a fraction for each colour.

F. Write the fraction that describes the whole piece of material Tiffany and the 9 other students shared. What does the numerator mean?

Reflecting

1. **a)** Describe your strategy for figuring out fair shares.
   b) Why would you use only one type of pattern block for each piece of material?

2. Fair shares are equal shares. Explain why this is true.

3. **a)** This is Lee's plan for cutting a piece of material into 3 equal parts. What is wrong with Lee's plan? How could you help him?
   b) Sketch a piece of material cut into 4 parts that are not fair shares. Explain why the shares are not fair.

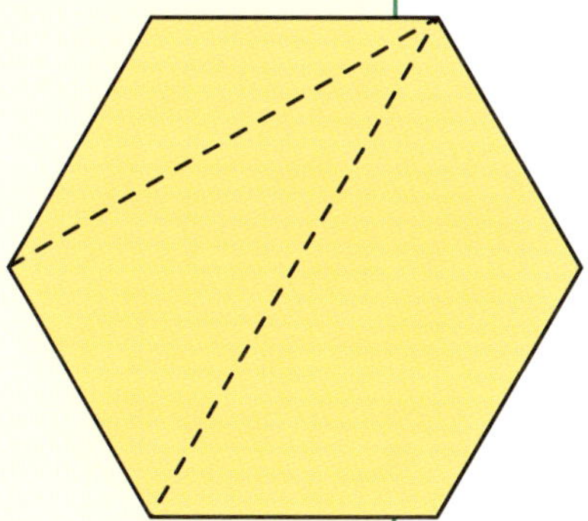

4. Explain why you can use a whole number to describe each whole piece of material that is shared.

4 Communicate Using Drawings

You will need

- scissors

Goal Represent and explain fractions using drawings.

Juan is sharing a Saskatoon berry pie with 3 friends.

? How can Juan model the pie and explain how to make fourths?

Juan's Instructions

Step 1 Make a circle to model the pie.

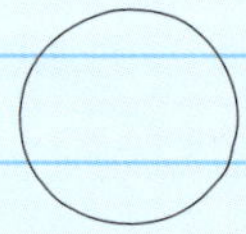

Step 2 Fold the circle in half twice.

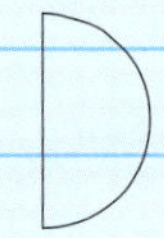

Step 3 Unfold the paper to show fourths.

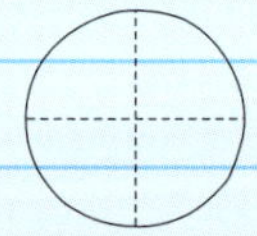

The drawings helped me to understand.

Did I show enough detail?

Communication Checklist

- ✓ Did you show all the steps?
- ✓ Did you put the steps in order?
- ✓ Did you show the right amount of detail?
- ✓ Did you include drawings?

A. Which parts of Juan's instructions were unclear?

B. Which parts can you improve? Explain using the Communication Checklist.

C. Trade your work with a classmate. Test the instructions by making a pie model. How can you improve the instructions?

Reflecting

1. Why is each of these important in instructions?
   a) the order of the steps
   b) details about what is supposed to happen in each step
   c) drawings for each step
2. Why is it a good idea to give your instructions to someone else to test?

Checking

3. Juan wants to share the pie with 7 friends.
   a) Write instructions for modelling a pie cut in eighths.
   b) Which parts of your instructions were unclear?
   c) How can you improve your instructions?

Practising

4. Sharleen needs to cut a potato casserole for a family of 6.
   a) Write instructions for modelling a casserole cut in sixths.
   b) Trade your work with a classmate.
   Test the instructions by making a casserole model.
   c) How can you improve the instructions?

5. Rashad is cutting this cake into 6 equal pieces.
   a) Write instructions to explain how to cut the cake.
   b) How are these instructions like the ones for Question 4?
   How are they different?

Math Game

Fraction Concentration

Number of players: 2
How to play: Turn over cards to find matching fractions.

Step 1 Mix up the cards.
Arrange them face down in an array.

Step 2 On your turn, turn over 2 cards.
If the fractions match, keep both cards and take another turn.
If the fractions don't match, turn them back over.

Step 3 Take turns. Play until all the cards are gone.

The player with the most cards wins.

You will need

- fraction concentration cards

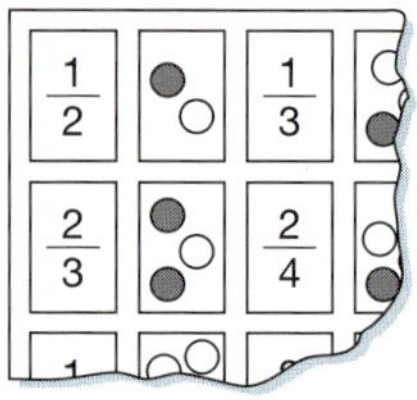

Fraction Neighbours

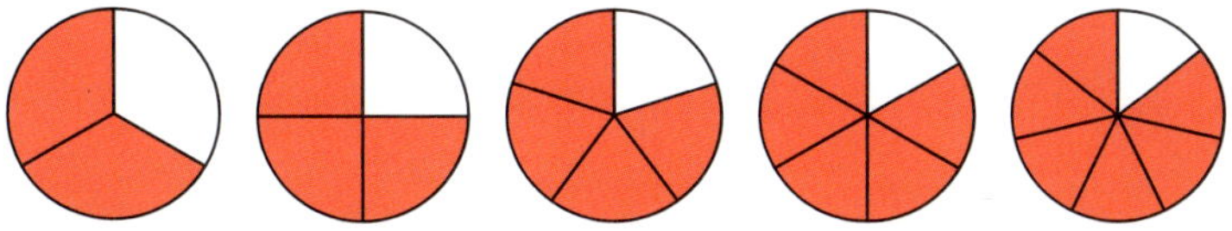

$\frac{2}{3}$ $\frac{3}{4}$ $\frac{4}{5}$ $\frac{5}{6}$ $\frac{6}{7}$

1 Which circle has the largest coloured area? Which has the smallest?

2 Which circle has the largest white area? Which has the smallest?

3 Complete the chart to describe the fraction circles.

Fraction coloured	$\frac{2}{3}$	$\frac{3}{4}$	$\frac{4}{5}$	$\frac{5}{6}$	$\frac{6}{7}$
Fraction not coloured					

4 Look at each column in the chart for Question 3. What do you notice?
How could you predict this by looking at the numerators and denominators of the fractions?

5 Predict which circle would have a larger area coloured: a circle showing $\frac{8}{9}$ coloured or a circle showing $\frac{9}{10}$ coloured. Explain your prediction.

Building Fractions

This drawing represents $\frac{1}{3}$ of a sandbox.

$\frac{1}{3}$

This drawing represents the whole sandbox.

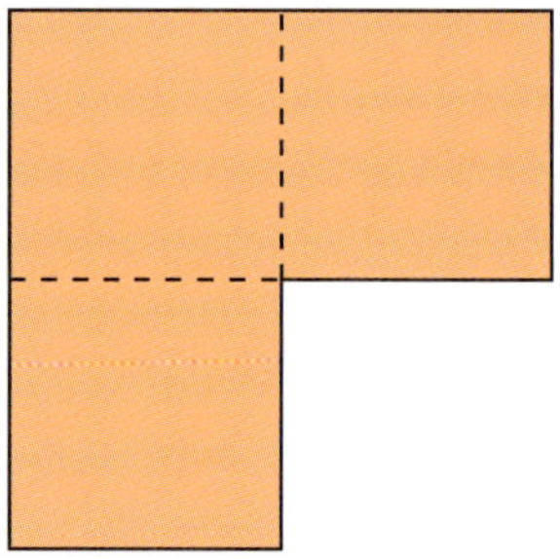

$\frac{3}{3}$

Try These

1. Each drawing represents part of a sandbox. Sketch the whole sandbox for each.

a) 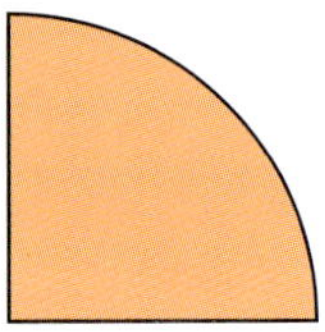

$\frac{1}{4}$

b) 

$\frac{1}{2}$

c) 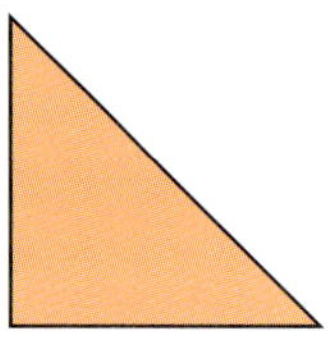

$\frac{1}{5}$

d) 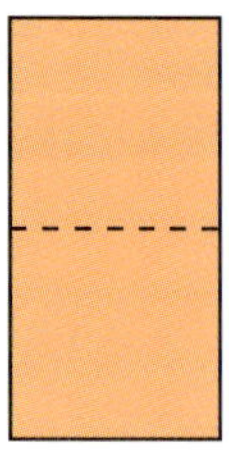

$\frac{2}{3}$

e) 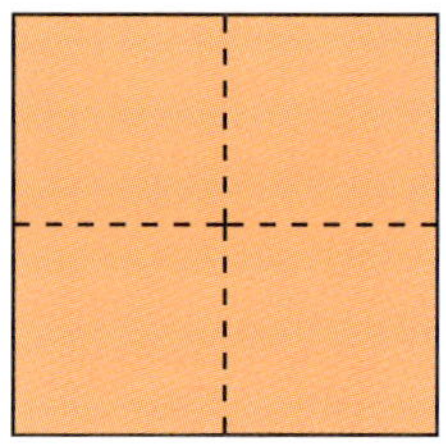

$\frac{4}{5}$

f) 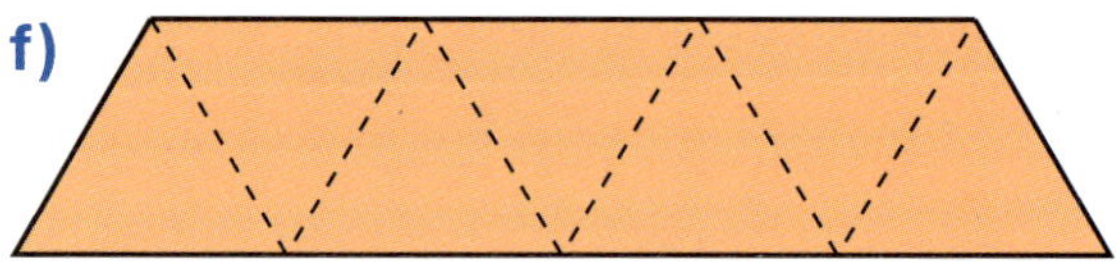

$\frac{7}{10}$

Skills Bank

LESSON

1

1. What fractions are shown by each group?

a)

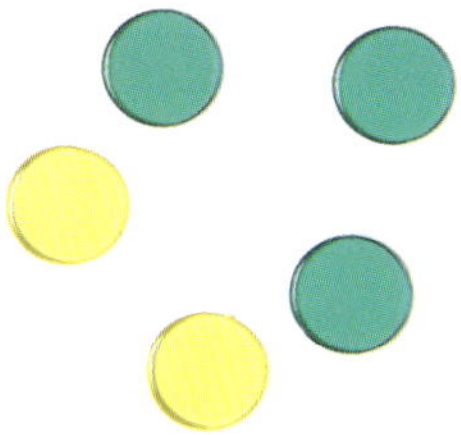

b)

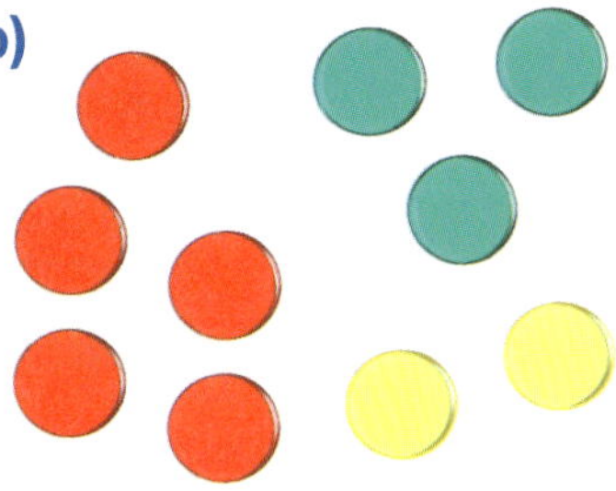

2. Model each fraction using coloured counters. Sketch your model.

a) $\frac{4}{5}$ b) $\frac{1}{2}$ c) $\frac{7}{10}$

3. Describe a group of people to match each fraction. Model the group. Sketch and colour your model.

a) $\frac{3}{5}$ b) $\frac{6}{10}$ c) $\frac{3}{4}$ d) $\frac{1}{3}$

4. a) What fraction of the coins are pennies?
   b) What fraction of the coins are dimes?

5. $\frac{4}{5}$ of the hats are black. What fraction of the hats are *not* black?

2

6. What fraction is left? What fraction has been eaten?

a)

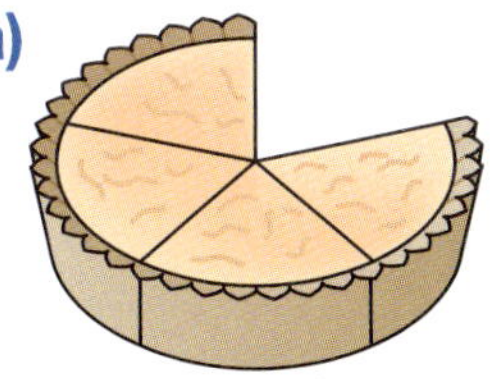

b)

2 7. a) Sketch a sandwich. Colour $\frac{4}{4}$ of it.

b) Sketch a granola bar. Colour $\frac{2}{3}$ of it.

8. What fraction of each shape is blue?

a) 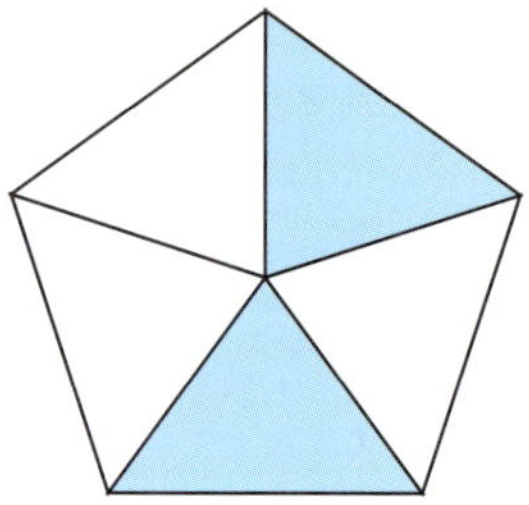

c) 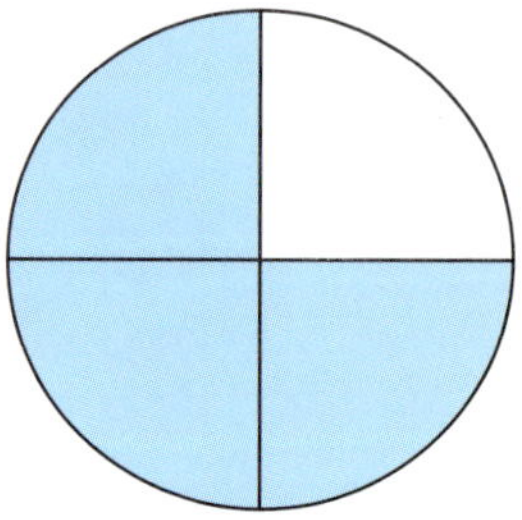

b) 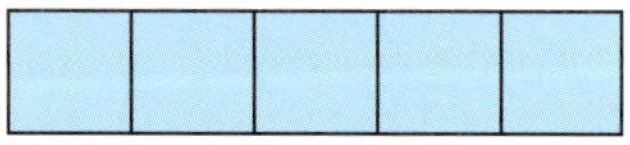

d) 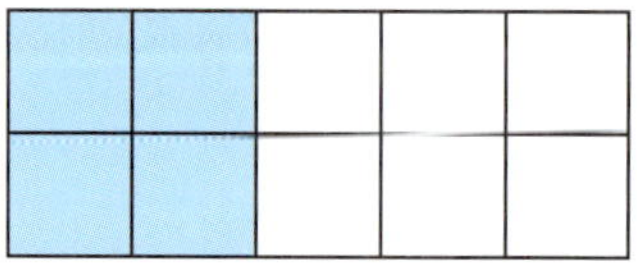

9. What fraction of each yellow hexagon is covered?

a) 

b) 

c) 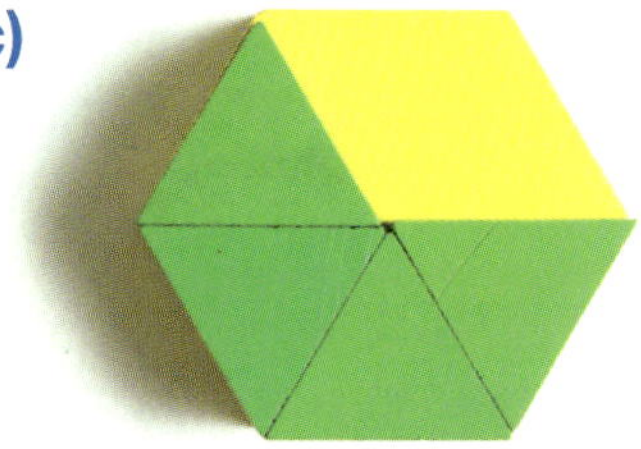

3 10. 5 students are sharing this piece of material fairly.

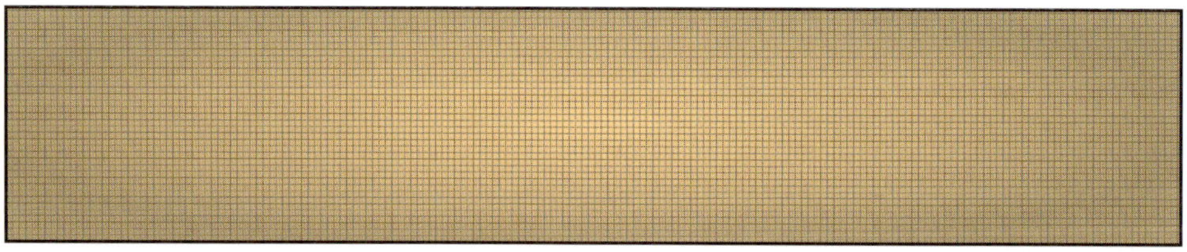

a) Trace the pattern block that represents a fair share. Colour the shape **purple**.

b) Write a fraction for 1 share.

c) Keep tracing the pattern block to sketch the whole piece of material.

d) Write a fraction for 2 shares.

e) Write a fraction and a whole number for 5 shares.

LESSON

Problem Bank

1 **1.** $\frac{4}{5}$ of the basketball team members are very tall.
$\frac{2}{5}$ of the team members are excellent dribblers.
How many of the tall members of the team could be excellent dribblers? Is there more than one answer? Explain why.

2. April has some coins with a total value of 32¢.
What fraction of the coins could be pennies?
Show different possible answers.

3. Write 10 three-letter or four-letter words.
Tell something that is true about $\frac{4}{10}$ of the words.

4. Michael had a collection of badges.
He put $\frac{4}{10}$ of his badges in a bag.
Nisha took $\frac{1}{4}$ of the badges from the bag.
There are 3 badges left in the bag.
How many badges did Michael have in his collection? Show how you know.

2 **5.** Copy this quilt square.
Colour a design so that $\frac{1}{2}$ is yellow, $\frac{1}{4}$ is blue, and the rest is green.
What fraction is green?

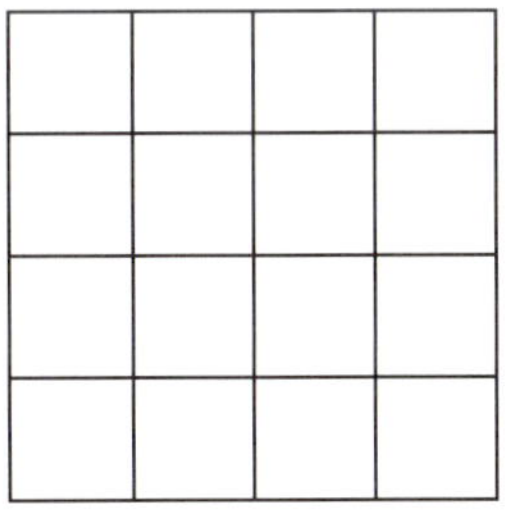

6. Use a geoboard to make a square like this.
Find at least 4 ways to show $\frac{1}{2}$ of the square.
Draw what you did on dot paper.

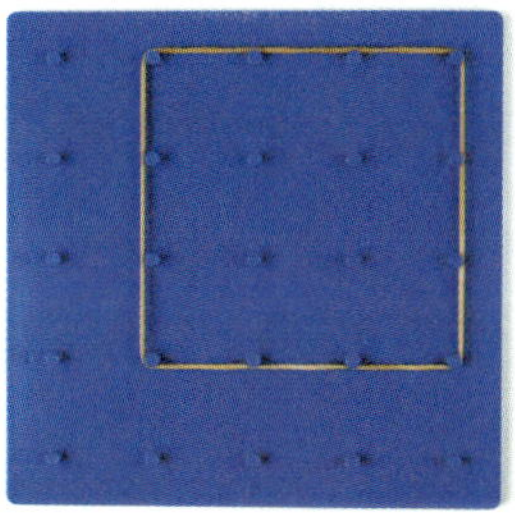

LESSON

Chapter Review

1 **1.** Use fractions to describe the houses.

2. Model each fraction using counters. Sketch each model.

a) $\frac{2}{3}$ of the apples are green.

b) $\frac{2}{5}$ of the children have glasses.

c) $\frac{10}{10}$ of Jessica's fingers have rings.

d) $\frac{1}{10}$ of the children have blond hair.

3. Can you use counters to represent $\frac{0}{10}$? Explain your thinking.

4. These sentences describe the same group of shapes.

- $\frac{3}{5}$ of the shapes are rectangles.
- $\frac{1}{5}$ of the shapes are circles.
- $\frac{2}{5}$ of the shapes are blue.
- $\frac{1}{2}$ of one of the shapes is green.

a) Sketch a group of shapes to make the statements true.

b) Show a different answer.

5. Keenan was asked to model this fraction with counters, but ink covers part of the fraction. Explain why he needs more information to model the fraction.

2 **6.** What fraction of the pizza is covered with each topping?

a) pepperoni b) green pepper c) mushrooms

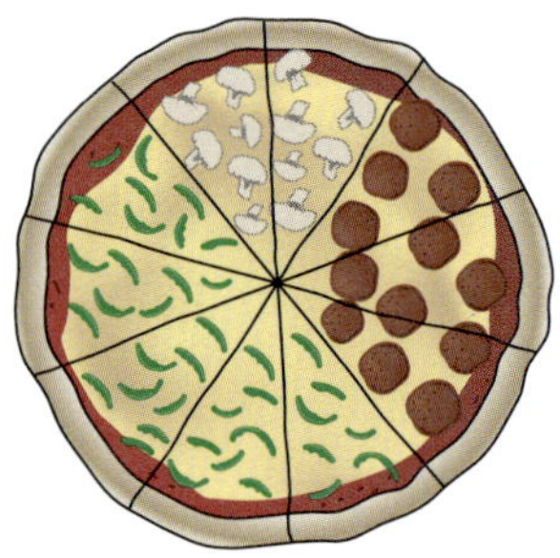

7. Look at the pizza in Question 6.
Write a fraction and a whole number for each.

a) the whole pizza

b) none of the pizza

2 8. Model each fraction as part of a rectangle. Sketch each model.

a) $\frac{1}{3}$ of a cake has been eaten.

b) $\frac{3}{5}$ of a blanket is yellow.

9. For each model, tell what fraction is blue and what fraction is not blue.

a)

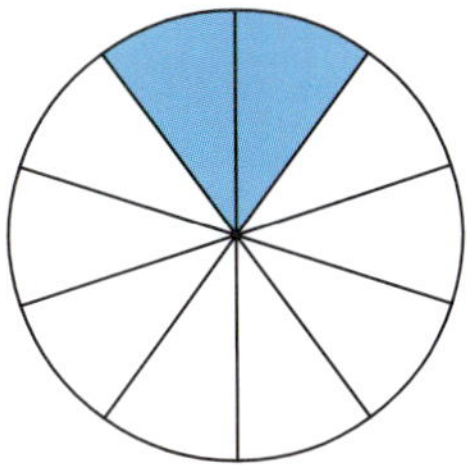

b)

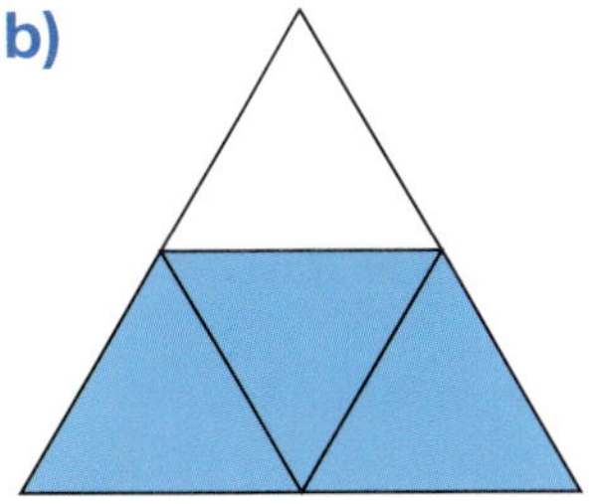

3 10. Nisha and some friends are making a quilt. Nisha, Charlie, Rose, Jay, and Michael are sharing this piece of material fairly.

a) Trace the pattern block that represents Jay's share.

b) Write a fraction to describe Jay's share.

c) Keep tracing the pattern block to sketch the whole piece of material.

d) Write a fraction and a whole number to describe the whole piece of material.

4 11. a) Write instructions for dividing a strip of paper into thirds.

b) How can you improve your instructions?

Chapter Task

Designing a Storage Closet

Keiko must find spaces for her toys and games.
She needs

- $\frac{1}{10}$ of the closet for toy trucks and cars
- $\frac{4}{10}$ of the closet for board games
- $\frac{5}{10}$ of the closet for other toys

? How can you use fractions to design a storage closet?

Part 1: A Closet for Keiko

A. Design a rectangular closet that fits Keiko's needs. Colour it to represent each fraction.

B. Could the closet have only 2 shelves? Explain.

C. How many shelves could the closet have? Explain.

Part 2: A Closet for You

D. Write different fractions for storing your toys.

E. Design a closet to fit your fractions.

Task Checklist

- ✓ Did your diagrams show equal parts?
- ✓ Did you explain your thinking?

CHAPTER 13

Probability

Goals

You will be able to

- predict results of probability experiments, conduct experiments, and describe conclusions
- use probability language
- model and solve probability problems

Collecting posters

CHAPTER 13

Getting Started

Probability Situations

Ian and Rachel are conducting a **probability** experiment. They put 4 **red** and 2 **blue** tiles in a bag. Ian thinks it is **likely** that he will draw a **red** tile from the bag.

? What do you think the results will be?

A. Place 4 **red** tiles and 2 **blue** tiles in a paper bag.

B. Don't look. Draw a tile from the bag.

C. Record the colour of the tile.

D. Put the tile back in the bag. Mix up the tiles.

E. Repeat parts B, C, and D 10 times.

You will need

- red and blue tiles

- a paper bag

- pencil crayons

- a die

F. Count the number of **red** tiles and the number of **blue** tiles you drew from the bag.

G. Did you draw more **red** tiles or **blue** tiles from the bag?

H. You are asked to draw 1 more tile from the same bag. Which sentence is a better description about what you might expect?

- You are likely to draw **red**.
- You are **unlikely** to draw **red**.

Explain your answer.

Do You Remember?

1. Use likely or unlikely to describe each situation.

a) When a coin is flipped 10 times, it will land on heads every time.

b) When it is autumn, leaves will fall from the trees.

c) When a die is rolled, the number will be greater than 2.

d) When a die is rolled, the number will be 6.

e) When it is July in Canada, it will snow.

2. Draw a picture or describe something that is likely to happen.

3. Draw a picture or describe something that is unlikely to happen.

1 Conducting Experiments

You will need

- spinners

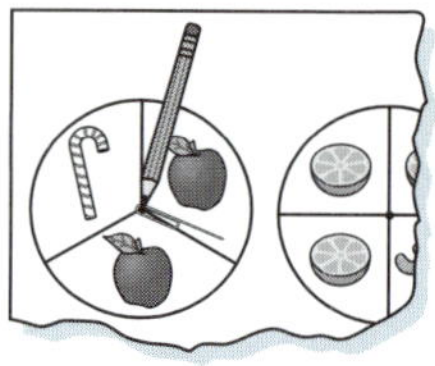

- a paper clip

Goal **Make predictions and conduct experiments with spinners.**

Sharleen's mother says she can have candy for a snack some days, but not too often. The other days, Sharleen must have a healthy snack, such as an apple.

Sharleen made this spinner to choose her snack each day.

? How likely is it that Sharleen will spin a healthy snack?

Sharleen's Experiment

I spun the spinner 7 times.

Each time I recorded the results on a tally chart.

Healthy	Unhealthy
𝍸	||

A. Make a prediction: How many times do you think Sharleen would spin a healthy snack in 12 spins?

B. Spin 12 times and record your results.

C. How many times did you spin a healthy snack? How many times did you spin candy?

D. Which **probability** word best describes the **chance** of spinning a healthy snack? Explain.

impossible **unlikely** **likely** **certain**

impossible
A result that cannot happen

certain
A result that will always happen

Reflecting

1. Why might you expect more healthy snack spins on Sharleen's spinner?
2. a) What would a spinner look like if it were certain to spin a healthy snack every time?
   b) What would a spinner look like if it were impossible to spin a healthy snack?

Checking

3. a) Predict the number of times that you will spin a healthy food in 15 spins of this spinner.
   b) Spin 15 times. Keep a tally chart.
   c) What probability word best describes the results of your 15 spins? Explain your choice.
   impossible unlikely likely certain

Practising

4. a) Predict the number of times that you will spin a healthy food in 15 spins of this spinner.
   b) Spin 15 times. Keep a tally chart.
   c) Use a probability word to describe the chance of spinning a healthy food. Explain your choice.
   d) Which probability word describes the chance of spinning an unhealthy food? Explain your choice.

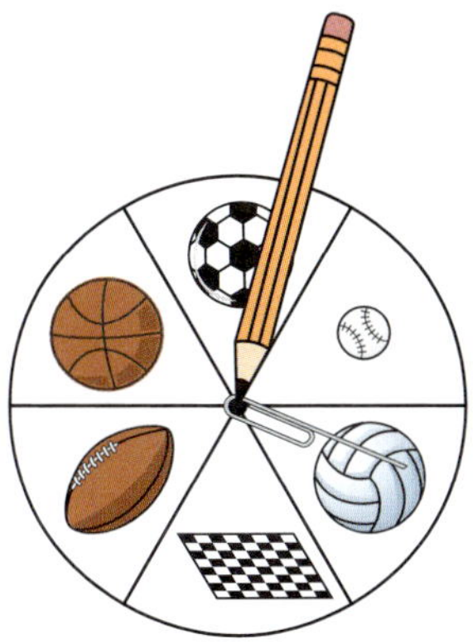

5. Vasco and his friends made this spinner to help them decide what game to play.
   a) Predict the number of times Vasco will spin a ball game in 15 spins. Explain your prediction.
   b) Spin 15 times. Keep a tally chart. Explain your results using probability words.
   c) Make a new spinner so that it is likely to spin a board game. Experiment with your spinner.

2 Communicate About Probability

Goal **Use math language to describe probability.**

Juan made a list of what he might do tomorrow.
Each item on his list is called an **event**.

Juan's Events	
A	I will ride a horse tomorrow.
B	When I roll this die, the number will be greater than 6.
C	I will breathe tomorrow.
D	When I roll a die, the number will be less than 3.
E	When I drop a penny, it will land on its edge.

? How can Juan describe the probability of each event?

Juan's Description

The probability words I know are impossible, unlikely, likely, and certain.

Event A is unlikely because I am not near a horse.

I'll place event A on a **probability line**.

I'll mark A closer to impossible than to certain because it is unlikely.

Event B is impossible because …

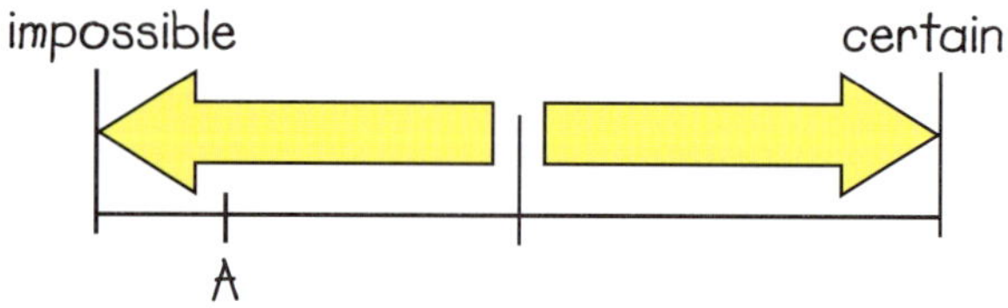

A. Finish describing the probability of event B. Place event B on the probability line.

B. Continue for events C, D, and E.

Reflecting

1. Did Juan consider both questions in the Communication Checklist? Explain.
2. a) How did the Communication Checklist help you describe the probability of events B to E?
   b) How did you decide where to place events B to E on the probability line?
3. Juan described the probability for event A. Why do you think it was important for him to explain his thinking?

Communication Checklist

- ☑ Did you explain your thinking?
- ☑ Did you use math language?

Checking

4. Lyn made an event list about this spinner. Describe the chance of each event.

Lyn's Events	
A	I will spin a number less than 3.
B	I will spin a number greater than 6.
C	I will spin a number greater than 1.
D	I will spin a number less than 7.

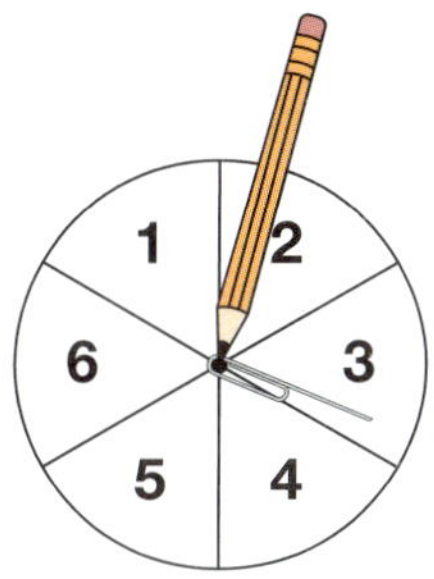

Practising

5. Make a list of 5 events that might or might not happen at school tomorrow. How probable is each event? Explain your choices of probability words.
6. Label your events for Question 5 with A, B, C, D, and E. Draw a probability line. Place your events on it.
7. You are drawing beads from this bag without looking. Describe the probability of each event. Use the Communication Checklist.

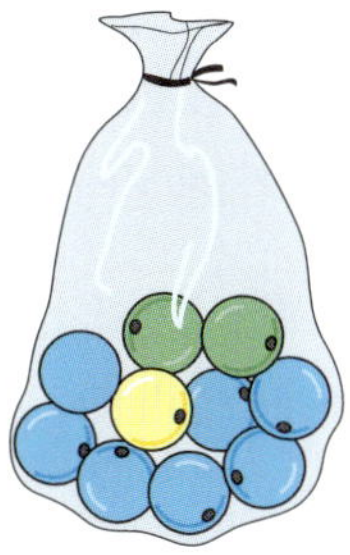

   a) You will draw a blue bead.
   b) You will draw a purple bead.
   c) You will draw a green bead.
   d) You will draw a coloured bead.

CHAPTER 13

3 Making Predictions

Goal **Make predictions, conduct experiments, and describe conclusions.**

You will need
- a die 
- 3 nickels 

Jack and Ben are trying to decide who will go 1st in a game. They decide to roll a die.
If they roll a number less than 4, Jack will go 1st.
If they roll a number greater than 4, Ben will go 1st.
If they roll 4, they'll roll again.

? Who is more likely to win the roll, Jack or Ben?

Jack's Prediction

Possible **outcomes**: 1, 2, 3, 4, 5, 6
Numbers less than 4: 1, 2, 3
Numbers greater than 4: 5, 6

I predict we will roll a number less than 4 more times than a number greater than 4.

I think I'm more likely to go 1st.

We'll conduct an experiment.

outcome
A single result that can happen in a probability experiment

A. Make a prediction: Is it more likely to roll a number less than 4 or a number greater than 4? Explain why.

B. Conduct an experiment: Roll a die 20 times. Record the outcomes.

C. Compare your results with your prediction.

D. Describe your conclusion: Who is more likely to go 1st? Explain how you know.

Reflecting

1. If you did the experiment again, would you change your prediction? Explain.

Checking

2. Tiffany and Sukan are rolling a die.
   If they roll 1 or 3, Tiffany wins.
   If they roll an even number, Sukan wins.
   a) Make a prediction: Is it more likely to roll 1 or 3, or to roll an even number? Explain why.
   b) Conduct an experiment: Roll a die 20 times.
   c) Compare your results with your prediction.
   d) Describe your conclusion: Who is more likely to win? Explain how you know.

Practising

3. Rashad and Keisha are tossing 3 coins at once.
   There are 2 ways the 3 coins can land.
   - The same: all heads or all tails
   - Different: at least 1 head and at least 1 tail

   If the coins are the same, Rashad wins.
   If the coins are different, Keisha wins.

   a) Make a prediction: Is it more likely for a toss to be the same or different? Explain why.
   b) Conduct an experiment: Toss 3 coins 20 times.
   c) Compare your results with your prediction.
   d) Describe your conclusion: Who is less likely to win? Explain how you know.

4. a) Make up 2 choices for winning rolls of a die or tosses of a coin. Which do you think is more likely?
   b) Conduct an experiment and describe the results.
   c) What is your conclusion? Explain your thinking.

Off to the Races

Number of players: 2
How to play: Roll sums and move counters on a game board.

Step 1 Pick a start number on the game board. Put a counter on that number.

Step 2 Take turns. On your turn, roll 2 dice. Add the numbers. If the sum is the number you chose, move your counter up 1 row. If it is not the number you chose, leave your counter where it is.

Step 3 At the start of any turn, you may place a new counter on another start number. When you roll the dice, you may play any of your counters.

Continue playing until a player gets to the top row.

You will need

- Off to the Races game board

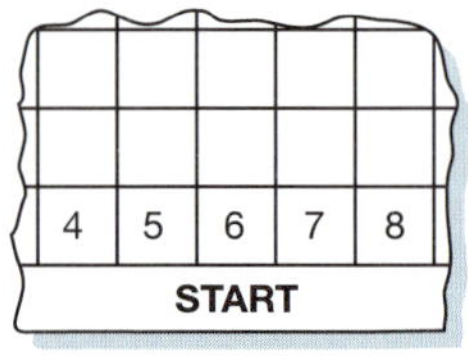

- counters

- dice

Number Cubes

You will need

- a die

- construction paper

- scissors

- tape

Devon made a number cube out of construction paper.

Jessica imagined folding this net to see if it would make Devon's number cube.

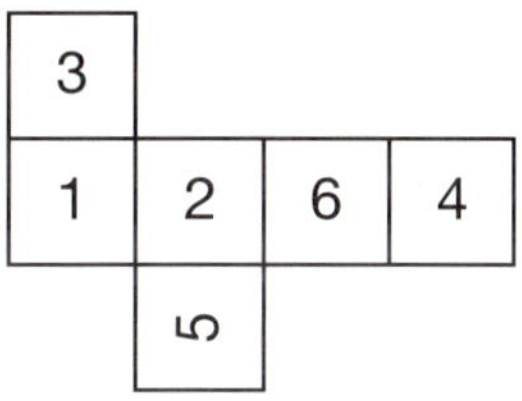

A. How does Jessica know that 6 and 1 will be opposite each other?

B. How does she know that 4 and 2 will be opposite?

C. How is Devon's number cube different from a die?

Try These

1. Will this net make Devon's number cube? Explain.

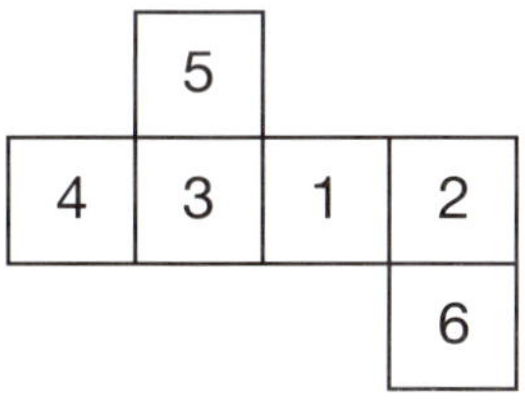

2. Copy and complete this net to make Devon's number cube.

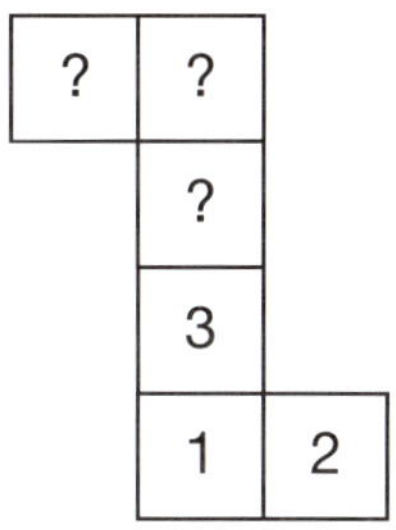

3. Make a net that will fold to make a die.

4 Probability Models

Goal **Use a probability model to solve an everyday problem.**

You will need
- coloured tiles

- a paper bag

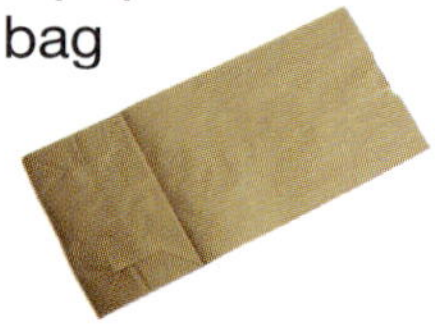

Nisha wants to know how many boxes she will need to open to get all 4 action figures.

? How can you use probability to solve Nisha's problem?

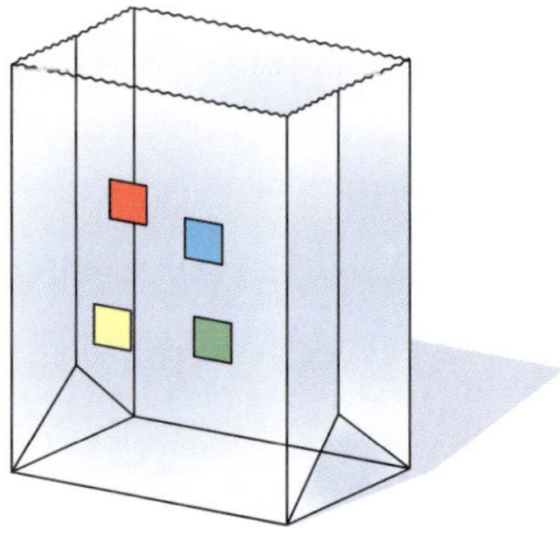

A. Put 4 different coloured tiles into a paper bag. You can model Nisha's problem by drawing 1 tile at a time from the bag and putting it back.

a) What does drawing a tile represent?

b) Why do you need to draw a tile of each colour to model the problem?

B. Make a prediction: How many times will you have to draw a tile from the bag to get all 4 colours?

C. Conduct an experiment: Draw a tile from the bag. Record the colour in a tally chart and replace the tile. Continue until you have drawn all 4 colours.

Red	Green	Yellow	Blue

D. How many times did you need to draw a tile to get all 4 colours?

E. Repeat the experiment 5 times. Make a prediction each time. Make tally charts.

F. Compare your results with others in your class.

Reflecting

1. Did you change your predictions as you repeated the experiment? Why or why not?
2. a) Is it possible to get all 4 colours in 4 draws? Explain.
   b) Is it possible to draw a tile 20 times and not get all 4 colours? Explain.
3. Can this model be used to find out *exactly* how many boxes Nisha needs to open? Explain.

Curious Math

Spinning Red

You will need

- spinners

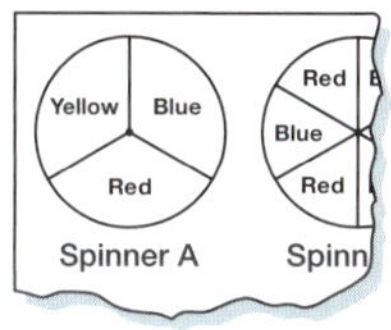

- a paper clip

Do you think spinning **red** is more likely on Spinner A or B? Or is it equally likely? Test your predictions by spinning.

Suppose you are playing a game with 1 other player. You win by spinning **red**. The other player wins by spinning **blue**. Do you have a fair chance? Explain.

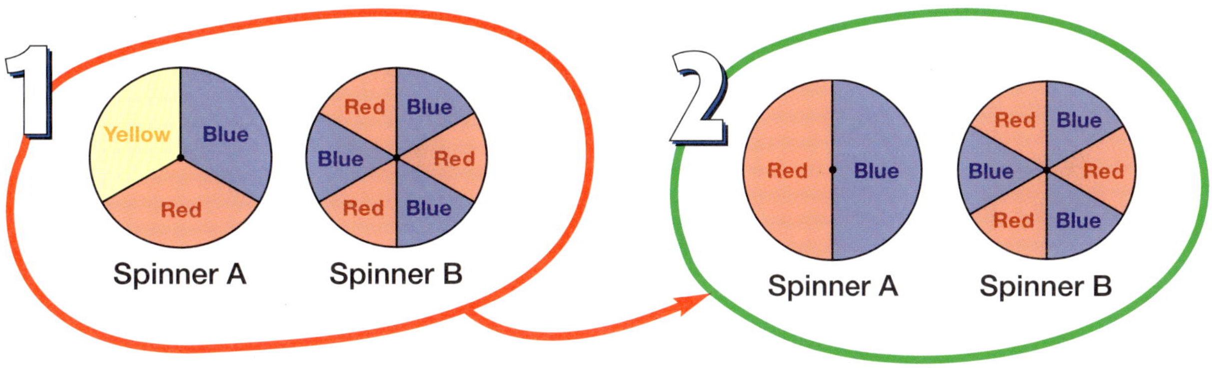

LESSON

Skills Bank

1

1. What is the chance of spinning each?
Use these probability words:
impossible, unlikely, likely, certain.

a) 1
b) red
c) a number less than 5
d) a number greater than 4
e) a number less than 4
f) yellow
g) an even number

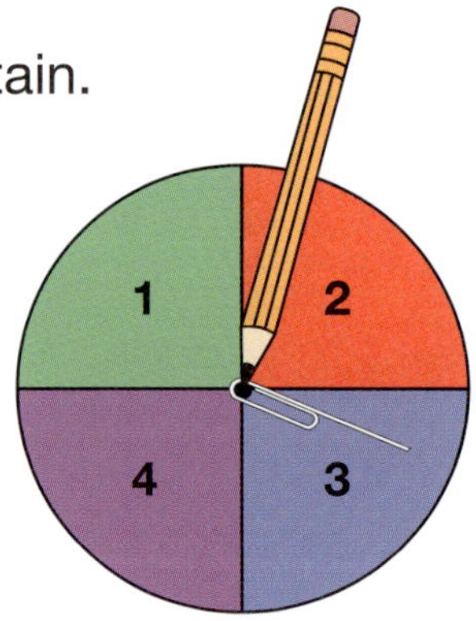

2. What is the probability of spinning each?
Use probability words.

a) a dog
b) a cat
c) a puppy
d) an animal
e) a fish

2

3. Describe the probability of each event.
Use these probability words:
impossible, unlikely, likely, certain.
Explain your thinking.

a) In August, there will be a snowstorm where I live.
b) I will throw a ball so high that it won't come down.
c) When I toss a coin 10 times, it will land on heads every time.
d) I will ride my bike to school 1 day this week.
e) When I roll 2 dice, the sum of the numbers will be 1.
f) I will ride a snowmobile to school tomorrow.

3 4. For each experiment, predict which outcome is more likely. Conduct the experiment. Record your results in a tally chart.

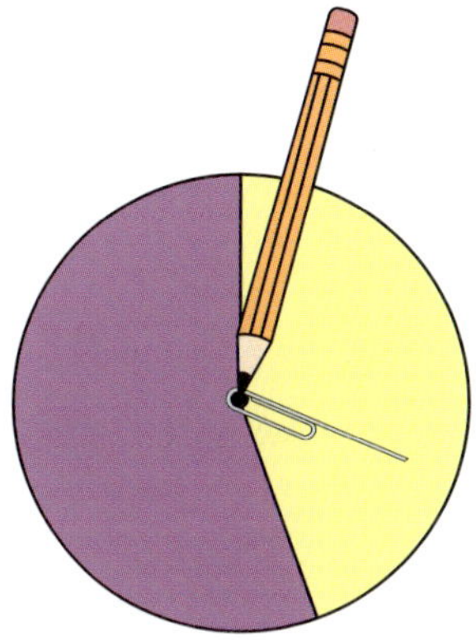

a) spinning purple or spinning yellow

b) rolling 6 or rolling an odd number with this die

c) drawing a green tile or drawing a yellow tile from this bag

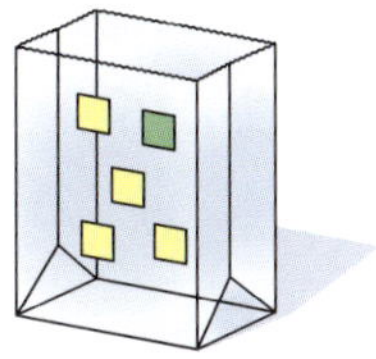

5. 2 coins are spilled from a can. The coins could land in these ways.

a) Draw a diagram to show each way.
- both heads
- both tails
- 1 heads and 1 tails

b) Make a prediction: If you spill 2 coins from a can 20 times, what outcome is most likely? Explain why.

c) Conduct an experiment: Spill 2 coins from a can 20 times. Record the outcomes.

d) Compare your results with your prediction.

e) Describe your conclusion: What outcome is most likely? Explain how you know.

6. Predict which outcome is more likely.

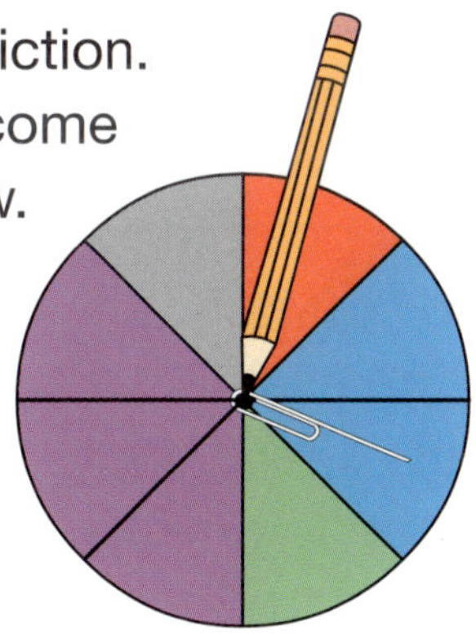

a) spinning purple or spinning blue

b) spinning blue or spinning red

c) spinning purple or spinning grey

d) spinning blue or spinning grey

4 7. A restaurant includes a toy with each child's meal. There are 6 different toys. Amit is wondering how many meals he will need to order to collect all 6 toys. How could you model this problem using dice?

LESSON

Problem Bank

1

1. Do you think Rose used Spinner A or Spinner B? Explain your answer.

Rose's Results

Triangle	Square	Circle
||||	~~||||~~ |	~~||||~~ ~~||||~~

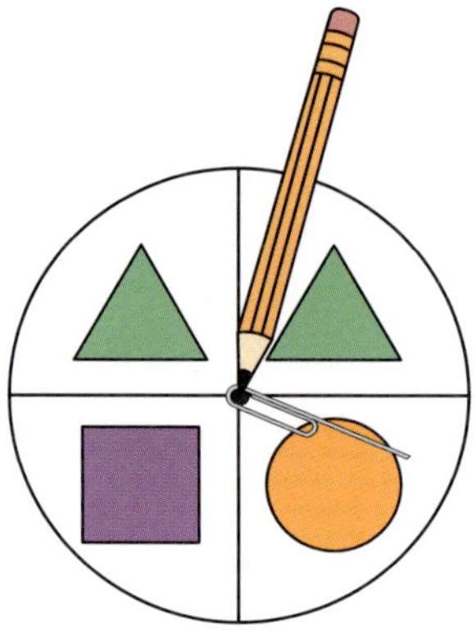
Spinner A

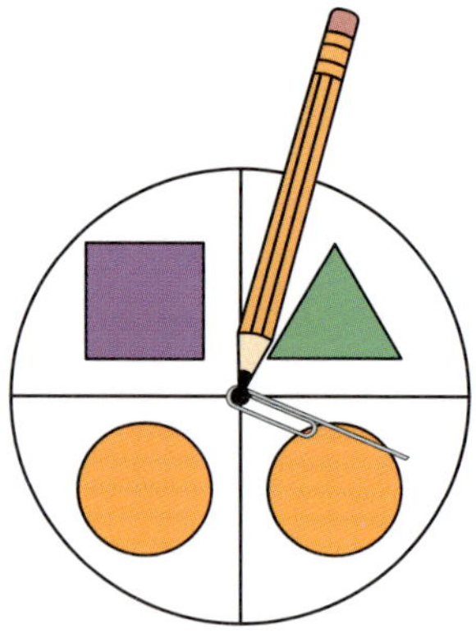
Spinner B

3

2. Chieko rolls 2 dice and calculates the product of the 2 numbers. Which outcome do you think is most likely?

A. The product is less than 5.

B. The product is more than 6.

C. The product is odd.

Test your prediction by experimenting with dice. Keep a tally chart.

$2 \times 3 = 6$
The product is 6.

3. Use 6 coins to make 42¢. Include nickels. Sketch your coins.

a) Suppose you point to 1 of the coins without looking. Do you think it is more likely to be a nickel or a penny? Explain your answer.

b) Conduct an experiment to find out which is more likely: pointing to a nickel or pointing to a penny. Keep a tally chart.

4

4. Juan took 6 blue socks and 6 white socks off the clothesline. He wonders how likely it would be to pick 2 socks of the same colour without looking.

a) How could you model this problem?

b) Experiment with your model. Keep a tally chart.

LESSON

Chapter Review

1

1. Describe the chance of spinning each shape. Use a probability word.

a) a yellow shape

b) a red shape

c) a flat shape

d) a cube

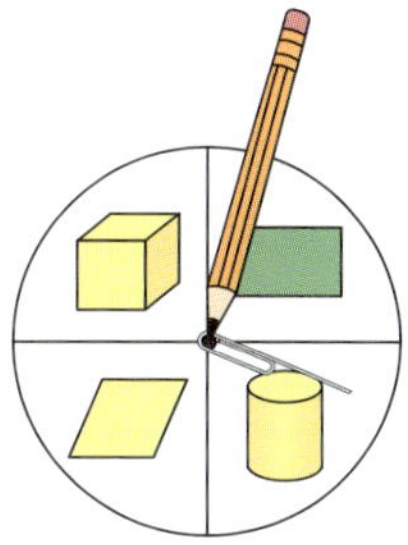

2

2. Draw a probability line.
Place the letters for these events on the probability line.

A. I will read a book about dogs this week.

B. I will spin yellow.

C. July will be the month after June this year.

D. A horse will fly.

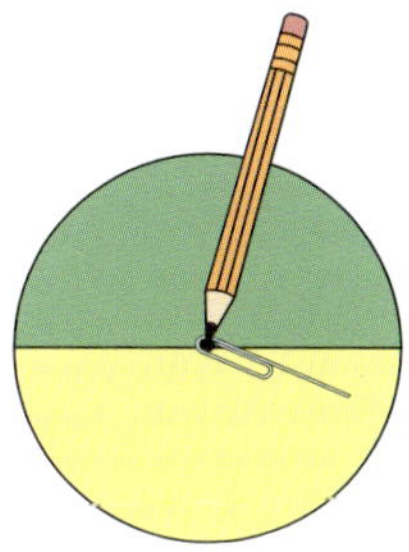

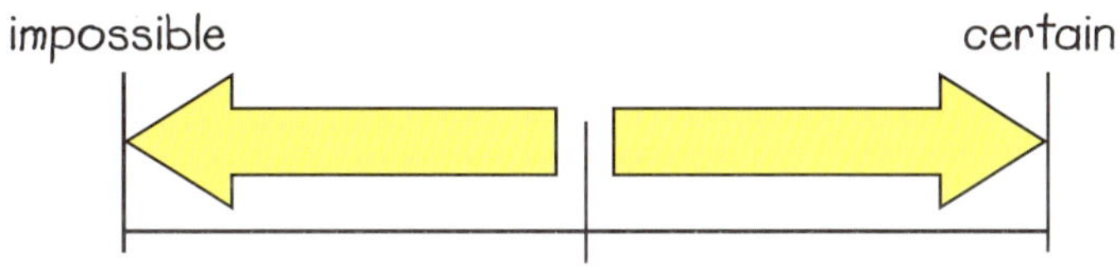

3

3. Eric and Rashad are playing a game with a die.
Eric needs to roll a number greater than 4 to win.
Rashad needs to roll an even number less than 4 to win.
Who is more likely to win? Explain.

4

4. Keisha is playing a fish pond game with 3 possible prizes. This spinner is a model for the prizes.

a) How many times do you think she will need to spin to win all 3 prizes?

b) Conduct an experiment.
Make a tally chart.
Stop when you've won all 3 prizes.

c) How many times did you need to spin to win all the prizes?

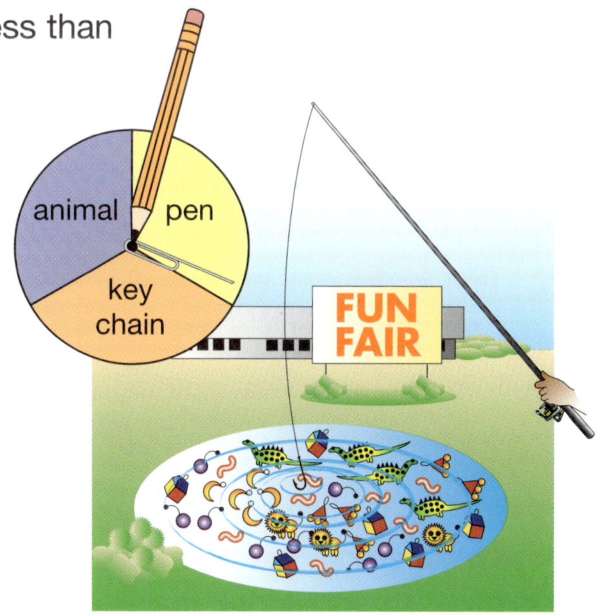

Chapter Task

Designing Spinners

Chelsea is inventing a board game.
Here are her rules.

- There will be 2 spinners.
- The players need to go to all of the places on the board before reaching Finish.
- On each turn, the player can choose which spinner to use to move forward or back on the game board.

? What do the spinners look like if they match these descriptions?

The spinner is more likely to land on "forward" than "back."	**The spinner is unlikely to land on "forward." It is likely to land on "back."**

Part 1

A. Make each spinner.

B. Make a prediction: How many times do you think each spinner would land on "forward" in 20 spins?

C. Test your spinners.
Compare your results with your predictions.

D. Explain how each spinner matches its description.

Part 2

E. Play the game. Did you use both spinners?
For each spinner you used, give an example of when you chose it and explain why.

Task Checklist

- ✓ Did you include tally charts?
- ✓ Did you explain your thinking?

Cumulative Review

Cross-Strand Multiple Choice

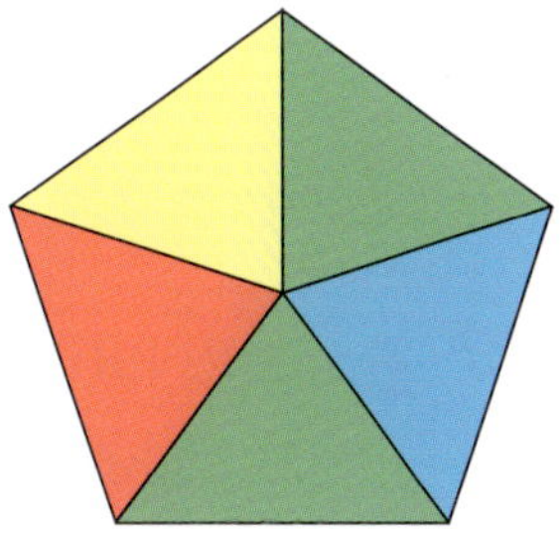

1. Which fraction of this shape is green?
   A. $\frac{2}{6}$ **B.** $\frac{2}{5}$ **C.** $\frac{3}{5}$ **D.** $\frac{3}{4}$

2. Which describes the 10 in $\frac{3}{10}$?
   E. numerator
   F. fraction
   G. denominator
   H. part of a whole

3. Which fraction is represented by the juice boxes?
   A. $\frac{3}{5}$ **B.** $\frac{2}{3}$ **C.** $\frac{3}{4}$ **D.** $\frac{4}{5}$

4. Choose the probability statement that does not make sense.
   E. You are unlikely to drink 100 L of milk today.
   F. It is likely that you can lift 100 pennies.
   G. You will certainly eat 100 kg of potatoes for breakfast.
   H. You are likely to write at least 100 words today.

5. Choose a probability word to describe the chance of spinning red with this spinner.
   A. impossible
   B. unlikely
   C. likely
   D. certain

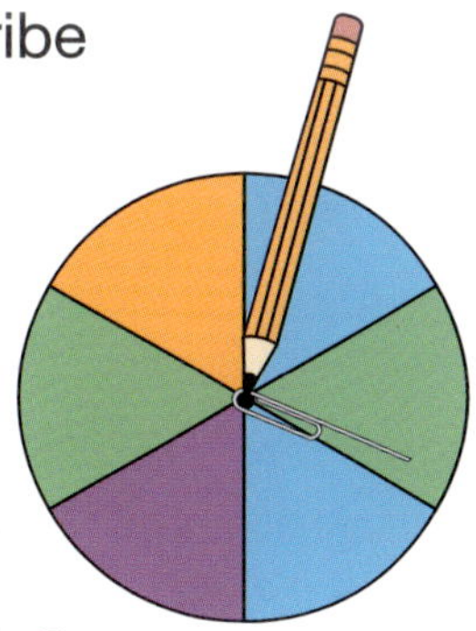

6. Which statement is true with this die?
   E. A number greater than 5 is likely to be rolled.
   F. It is impossible to roll an even number.
   G. A number less than 7 is certain to be rolled.
   H. A number greater than 1 is unlikely to be rolled.

Cross-Strand Investigation

How Words Look

Dawn and Marcus used letter cards to show their names.

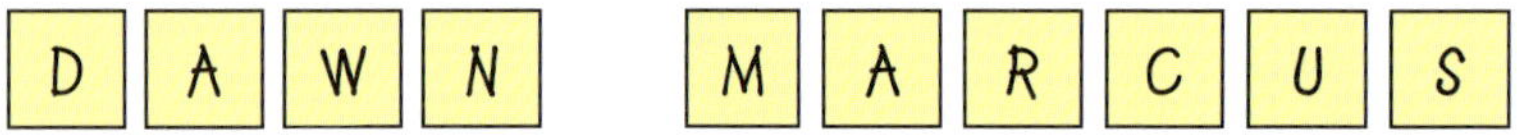

7. a) Marcus made $\frac{5}{6}$ of the letters of his name **purple**. Show what this looks like.
   b) Dawn made $\frac{1}{2}$ of the letters of her name **green**. Show what this looks like.
   c) What fraction of the letters in Dawn's name are vowels?
   d) Use grid paper. Draw a rectangle and show the fraction of the letters in Dawn's name that are *not* vowels. Colour the part that represents this fraction **blue**. Write the fraction.
   e) Repeat parts c) and d) for Marcus's name. Use **red**.
   f) Do you think most names have a greater fraction of vowels or consonants? Explain your thinking.

8. Marcus put the letters of his name on a cube and rolled it once.
   a) Use probability words to describe the chance Marcus will roll a vowel. Explain.
   b) Dawn put the letters of her name on a cube. Is Dawn more likely or less likely to roll a vowel than Marcus? Explain.

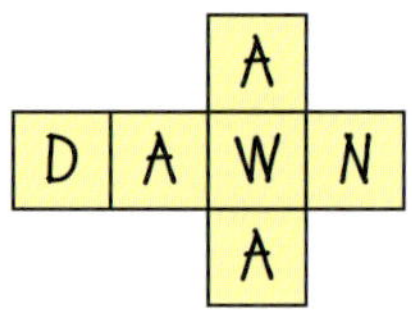

9. Dawn and Marcus put the letters of their names on a spinner. Use probability words to describe the chance of each event.
   a) spinning A
   b) spinning a letter in Marcus's name
   c) spinning Z
   d) spinning a letter in either Dawn's name or Marcus's name

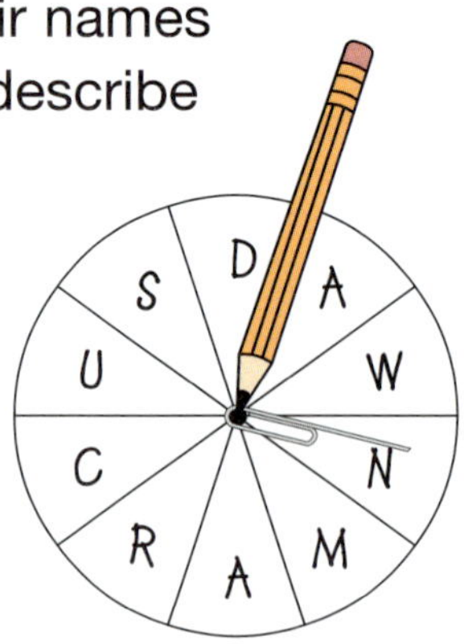

Glossary

Instructional Words

C

calculate: Figure out the number that answers a question; compute

classify: Put things into groups following a rule and label the groups; organize into categories

compare: Look at 2 or more objects or numbers and identify how they are the same and how they are different (e.g., Compare the sizes of the students' feet. Compare 2 shapes.)

construct: Make or build a model (e.g., Construct a structure using boxes.)

create: Make your own example

D

describe: Tell, draw, or write about what something is or what something looks like; tell about a process in a step-by-step way

draw: 1. Show something in picture form (e.g., Draw a diagram.)
2. Pull or select an object (e.g., Draw a card from the deck. Draw a tile from the bag.)
3. Make a decision (e.g., Draw a conclusion.)

E

estimate: Use your knowledge to make a reasonable decision about an amount; make a reasonable guess (e.g., Estimate the length of a bus in metres. Estimate 217 + 89.)

explain: Tell what you did; show your mathematical thinking at every stage; show how you know

explore: Investigate a problem by questioning, brainstorming, and trying new ideas

extend: In patterning, continue the pattern

L

list: Record thoughts or things one below the other, or one after the other

M

measure: Use a tool to describe an object or determine an amount (e.g., Use a ruler to measure the perimeter of a shape. Use balance scales to measure mass. Use a measuring cup to measure capacity.)

model: Show an idea using objects and/or pictures (e.g., Model a number using base ten blocks. Model a division problem using counters.)

P

predict: Use what you know to work out what is going to happen (e.g., Predict the next number in the pattern 2, 4, 6, 8, ….)

R

record: Set down work in writing or pictures

relate: Show a connection between objects, drawings, ideas, or numbers

represent: Show information or an idea in a different way that makes it easier to understand (e.g., Draw a graph. Make a model.)

S

show (your work): Record all calculations, drawings, numbers, words, or symbols that make up the solution

sketch: Make a rough drawing (e.g., Sketch a picture of each step.)

solve: Develop and carry out a process for finding a solution to a problem

sort: Separate a set of objects, drawings, ideas, or numbers according to an attribute (e.g., Sort 2-D shapes by the number of sides.)

Glossary

Mathematical Words

A

addend: A number that is added to another number

algorithm: A series of steps to carry out a procedure (e.g., add, subtract, multiply, or divide)

area: The number of square units needed to cover a surface

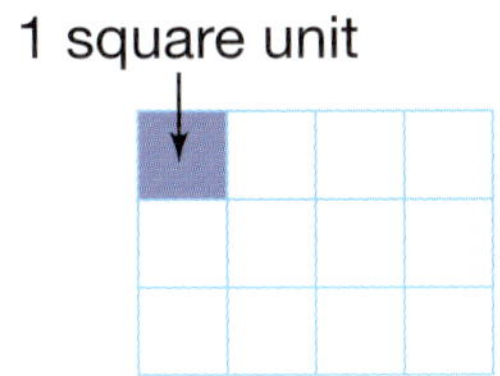

The area of this shape is 12 square units.

array: A rectangular arrangement of objects or pictures in **rows** and **columns**

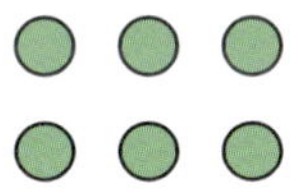

attribute: A feature that you can use to describe and compare things (e.g., Some attributes of shapes are size, colour, and number of sides.)

axis (plural is **axes):** A line in a graph, labelled with words or numbers to show what the bars or symbols in the graph mean

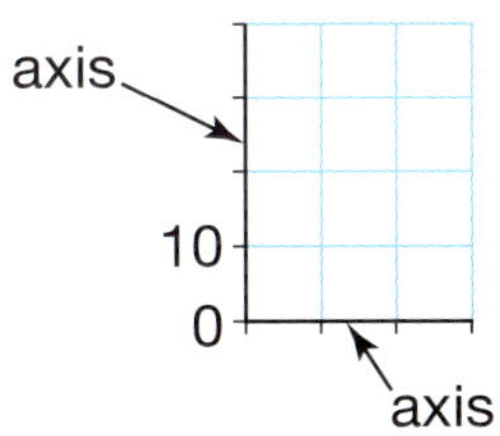

B

bar graph: A **graph** that uses bars to represent data

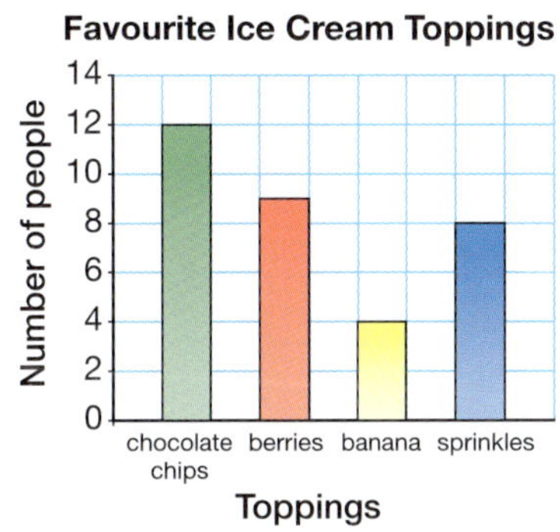

base: 1. In a 3-D shape, the **face** on which it is resting
2. In a prism or pyramid, the face that determines the name of the prism or pyramid

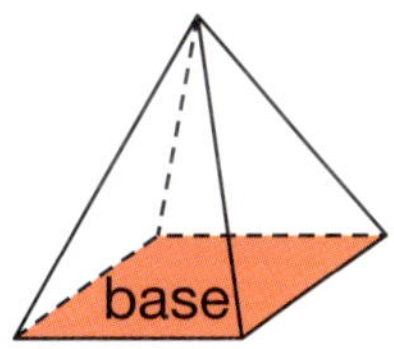

rectangle-based pyramid

base ten blocks: Blocks that represent numbers as ones, tens, hundreds, and thousands

Hundreds	Tens	Ones
3	5	4

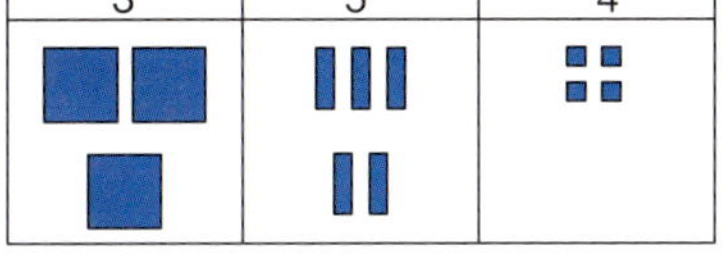

C

capacity: The amount a container can hold; capacity can be measured in **litres (L)**

centimetre (cm): A unit of measurement for **length** (e.g., A fingertip is about 1 cm wide.); 100 cm = 1 m

certain: A result that will always happen (e.g., If you roll a die with a 3 on every face, rolling a 3 is certain.)

column: Objects or pictures lined up going up and down (See also **row**.)

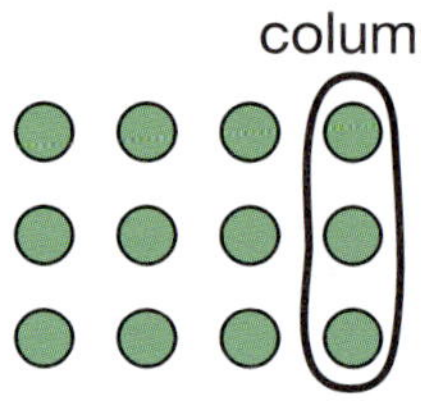

congruent: The same size and shape

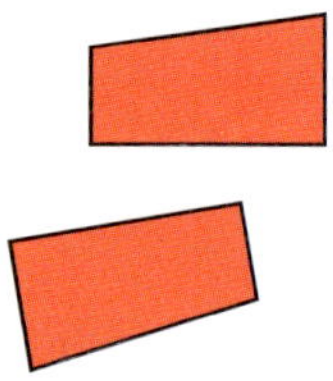

These shapes are congruent.

cube: A 3-D object with 6 **congruent** square faces

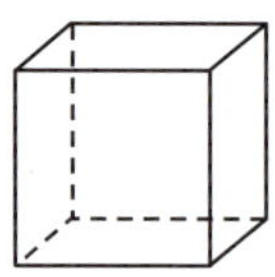

D

data: Information collected in a survey, in an experiment, or from other sources (e.g., Data can be in words like a list of students' names, in numbers like lengths, or in pictures like drawings of pets.)

decimal point: A dot used to separate the dollars from the cents

degree Celsius (°C): A unit of measurement for temperature (e.g., Water freezes at 0°C and boils at 100°C.)

denominator: The number below the bar in a **fraction** that shows the number of parts in the whole or in the group (See also **numerator**.)

$\frac{3}{4}$ ← denominator

difference: The result when you subtract; the amount by which one number is greater than or less than another number

$$\begin{array}{r} 93 \\ -45 \\ \hline 48 \end{array}$$ ← difference

digit: A number symbol (e.g., The digits are 0, 1, 2, 3, 4, 5, 6, 7, 8, and 9. For 890, the digits are 8, 9, and 0.)

dimension: A way to describe how an object can be measured (e.g., A line has only length, so it is 1-dimensional. A rectangle has length and width, so it is 2-dimensional (2-D). A cube has length, width, and height, so it is 3-dimensional (3-D).)

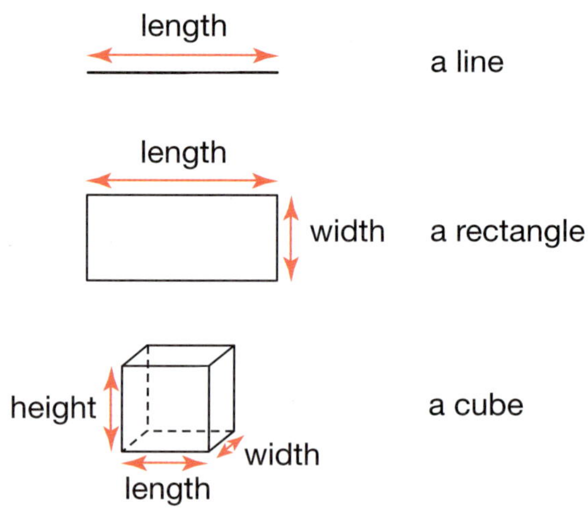

divisible: Can be divided with nothing left over (e.g., 30 is divisible by 5 because you can make exactly 5 groups of 6 from 30.)

division: Equal sharing or grouping
$18 \div 3 = 6$
18 objects shared by 3 people is 6 objects each.
18 objects grouped in 3 groups is 6 objects in each group.

double: Multiply a number by 2

E

edge: The line where 2 **faces** meet on a 3-D object

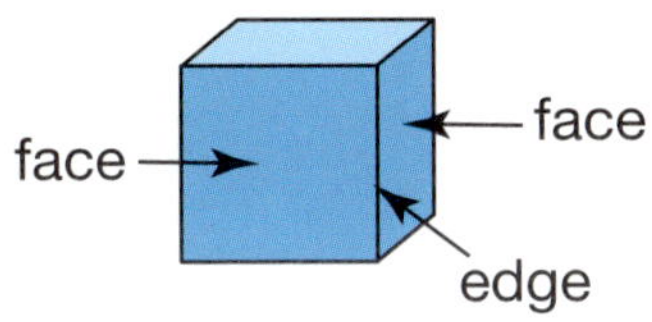

equally likely: Results that have an equal chance of happening (e.g., When flipping a coin, heads and tails are equally likely.)

estimate: A reasonable guess about a measurement or answer

even number: Any number you can reach by skip counting by 2s starting at 0

event: Something that could happen

expanded form: A way to write a number that shows the value of each digit (e.g., In expanded form, 365 is 300 + 60 + 5.)

F

face: A 2-D shape that forms a flat surface of a 3-D object

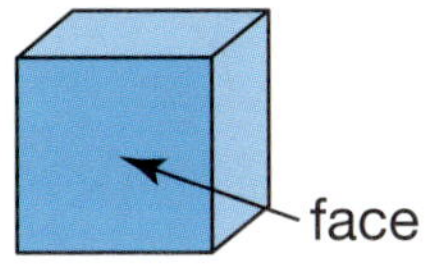

fact: An addition, subtraction, multiplication, or division sentence (e.g., $9 + 9 = 18$)

fact family: A set of number facts that use the same numbers

A fact family for 2, 3, and 5:

$3 + 2 = 5$ $5 - 3 = 2$
$2 + 3 = 5$ $5 - 2 = 3$

factor: Numbers you multiply

$2 \times 6 = 12$

factor factor

fraction: Numbers used to name part of a whole or part of a group (See also **numerator** and **denominator**.)

(e.g., $\frac{3}{4}$ is a fraction.)

G

gram (g): A unit of measurement for **mass**; 1000 g = 1 kg

graph: A way of showing data so it is more easily understood. A graph can be concrete (e.g., apples in one line and oranges in another), a **pictograph** (e.g., symbols to show apples in 1 row and oranges in another), or a **bar graph** (e.g., 2 bars to show the number of apples and oranges)

Favourite Fruits

Favourite Fruits

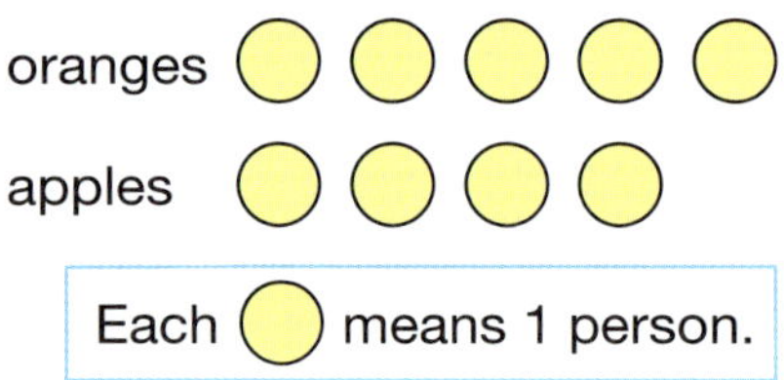

Favourite Fruits

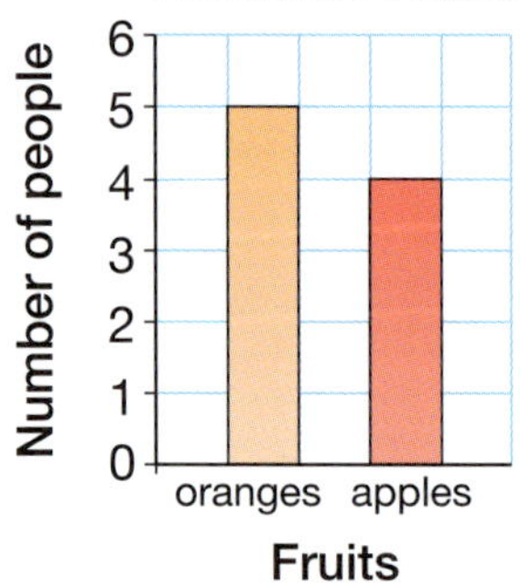

H

hexagon: A polygon with 6 sides; a 2-D shape with 6 straight sides

I

impossible: A result that cannot happen (e.g., If you roll a die with a 3 on every face, rolling a 5 is impossible.)

intersecting: Intersecting lines cross or meet at a **point**

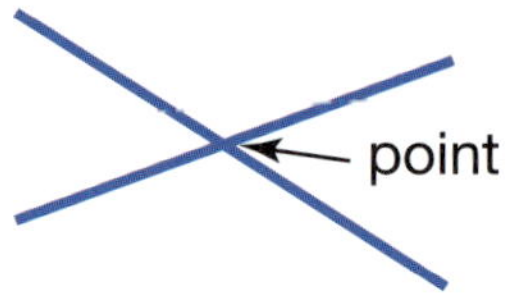

K

kilogram (kg): A unit of measurement for **mass** (e.g., A math textbook has a mass of about 1 kg.); 1 kg = 1000 g

kilometre (km): A unit of measurement for **length**; one thousand metres; 1 km = 1000 m

L

length: The distance from one place to another; length can be measured in **centimetres**, **metres**, and **kilometres**

likely: A result that can easily happen (e.g., If you roll a die with a 3 on all the faces but one, rolling a 3 is likely.)

litre (L): A unit of measurement for **capacity**

M

mass: How heavy an object is; mass can be measured in **grams (g)** and **kilograms (kg)**

metre (m): A unit of measurement for **length** (e.g., 1 m is about the distance from a doorknob to the floor.); 100 cm = 1 m and 1000 m = 1 km

multiplication: Repeated addition
$2 + 2 + 2 + 2 + 2 = 10$
$5 \times 2 = 10$
5 groups of 2 is 10.

N

net: A 2-D shape that can be folded into a 3-D object

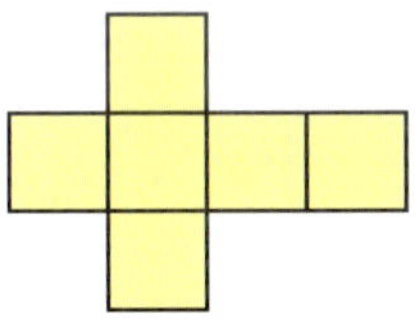

This is a net for a cube.

nonstandard unit: A unit of measurement that is not part of a measurement system (e.g., A desk is about 5 juice cans wide.) (See also **standard unit**.)

number line: A diagram that shows ordered numbers or points on a line

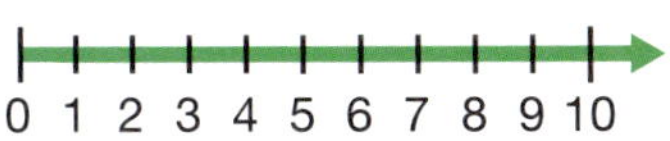

number sentence: A mathematical statement that shows how 2 numbers are related (e.g., $3 + 8 = 11$)

number word: The written word for a number (e.g., The number word for 65 is sixty-five.)

numeral: The written symbol for a number (e.g., 4 and $\frac{3}{4}$)

numerator: The number above the bar in a **fraction** that shows the number of parts the fraction represents (See also **denominator**.)

O

octagon: A polygon with 8 sides; a 2-D shape with 8 straight sides

odd number: Any number you can reach by skip counting by 2s starting at 1

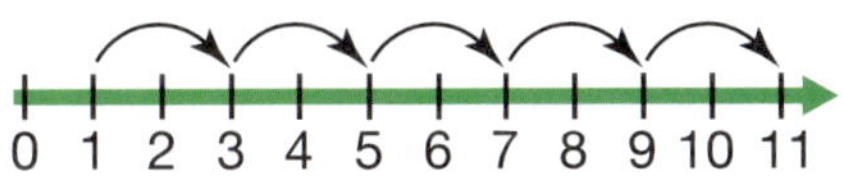

3, 5, 7, 9, and 11 are odd numbers.

ordinal number: A way of describing order (e.g., 1st, third, 15th)

organized list: The problem-solving strategy of following an order to solve a problem

outcome: A single result that can happen in a probability experiment (e.g., If you roll a regular die, the possible outcomes are 1, 2, 3, 4, 5, and 6.)

P

parallel: Parallel lines never **intersect**; always the same distance apart

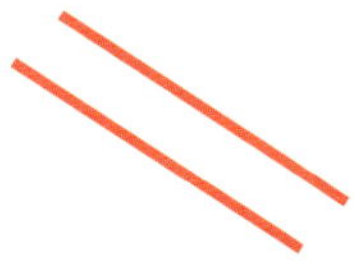

parallelogram: A 4-sided shape with **parallel** opposite straight sides (e.g., A **rhombus**, a **rectangle**, and a **square** are all parallelograms.)

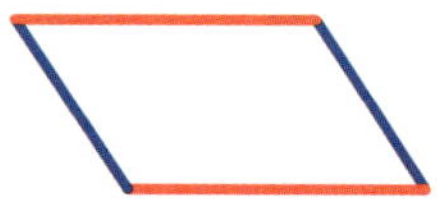

pattern: Something that follows a rule while repeating or changing

pattern rule: A description of how a pattern starts and how it can be extended

pentagon: A polygon with 5 sides; a 2-D shape with 5 straight sides

perimeter: The distance around the outside of a shape

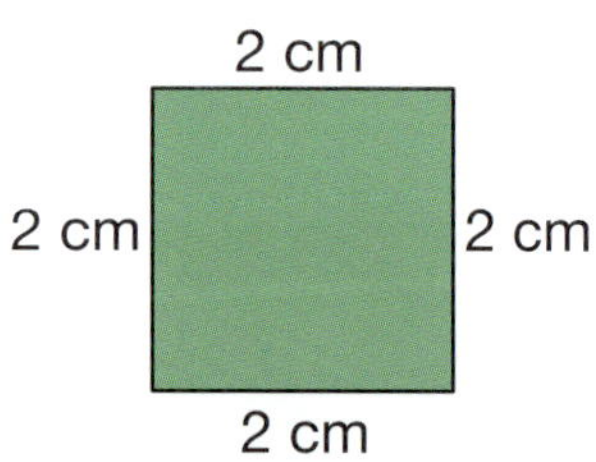

The perimeter of this square is 8 cm.

$2 + 2 + 2 + 2 = 8$

perpendicular: Perpendicular lines **intersect** to make a square corner

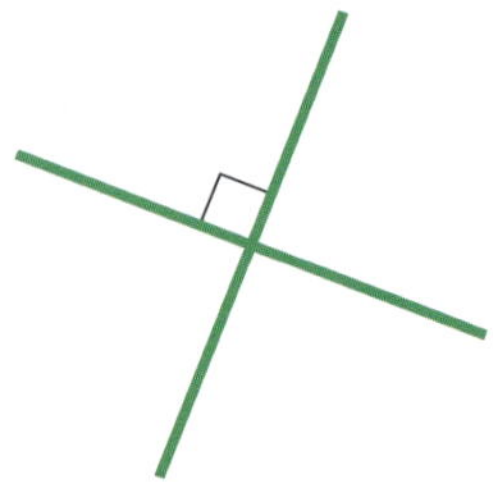

pictograph: A **graph** that uses pictures or symbols to represent data

place value: The value given to a digit shown by its position in a number (e.g., The 3 in the number 237 represents 3 tens.)

point: Where **intersecting** lines cross or meet

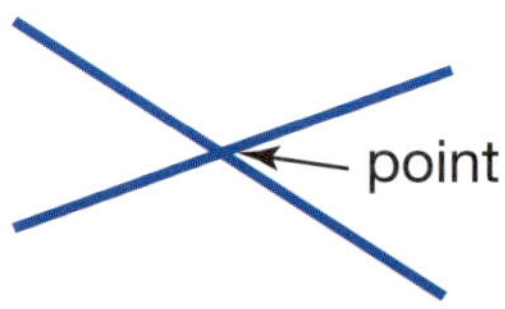

polygon: A 2-D shape with sides that are straight lines

position: A place or location (e.g., beside, on top, to the right)

possible: Any result that can happen (e.g., If you roll a regular die, the possible outcomes are 1, 2, 3, 4, 5, and 6.)

prism: A 3-D object with **congruent** ends called **bases**; the other faces are rectangles (e.g., a triangle-based prism)

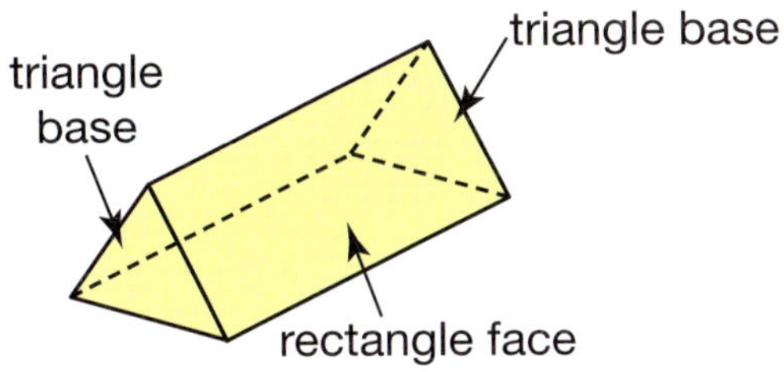

probability: How likely it is that a result will happen

probability line: A way to show probabilities

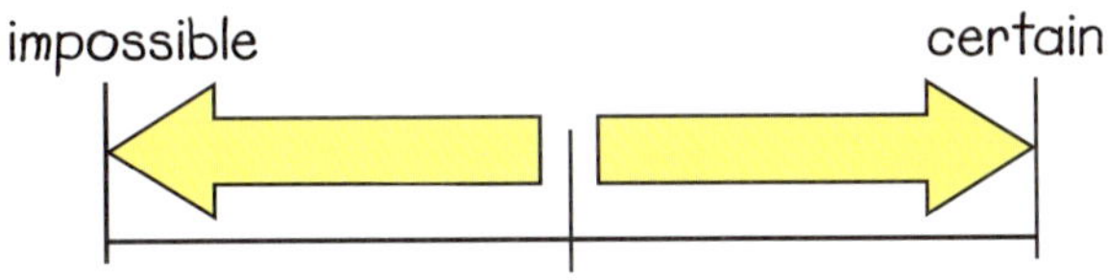

product: The result when you multiply

$$2 \times 6 = 12$$

↑ product

pyramid: A 3-D object with a flat **base**; the other faces are triangles that meet at a **vertex** (e.g., a rectangle-based pyramid)

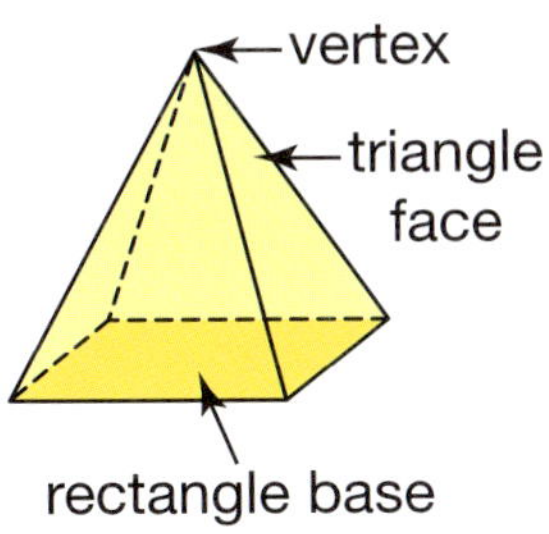

Q

quotient: The result when you divide

$$12 \div 6 = 2$$

↑ quotient

R

rectangle: A polygon with 4 sides and 4 square corners; a 2-D shape with 4 straight sides and 4 square corners

regroup: Show the same number in a different way by trading 10 smaller units for 1 larger unit or 1 larger unit for 10 smaller units

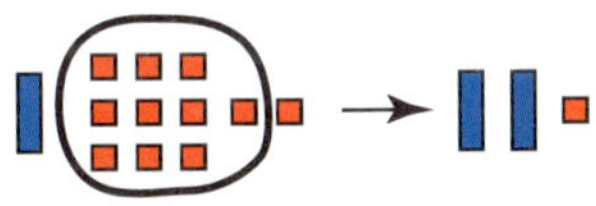

represent: Mean, stand for, show (e.g., A symbol in a graph represents a certain number of items.)

rhombus: A 4-sided shape with 4 equal straight sides

round: Estimate a number to a given place (e.g., 327 rounded to the nearest hundred is 300.)

rounding to the nearest hundred: Estimating a number to the closest number of hundreds (e.g., 83 rounds up to 100.)

rounding to the nearest ten: Estimating a number to the closest number of tens (e.g., 83 rounds down to 80.)

row: Objects or pictures lined up across (See also **column**.)

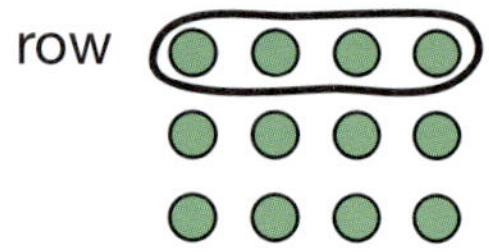

S

scale: 1. The number of items represented by each symbol in a pictograph
2. The number of items represented by each square in a bar graph

shape: The **attribute** that describes a geometric form (e.g., Circles have a round shape.)

side: One of the lines that forms a 2-D shape

skip count: To count forward or backward by the same number each time

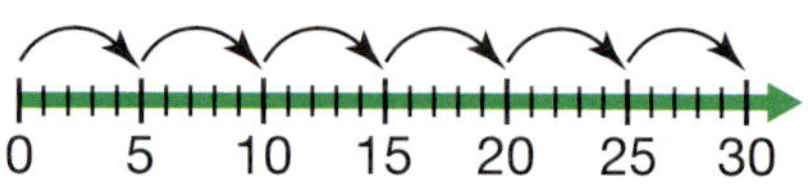

skip counting by 5s

square: A polygon with 4 equal sides and 4 square corners; a 2-D shape with 4 equal straight sides and 4 square corners; a rectangle with 4 equal sides

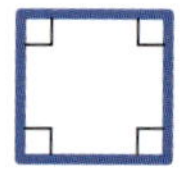

square corner: A vertex that makes a square (e.g., Squares and rectangles have 4 square corners.)

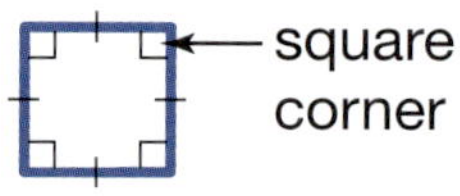

square unit: A **nonstandard unit** shaped like a square for measuring **area**

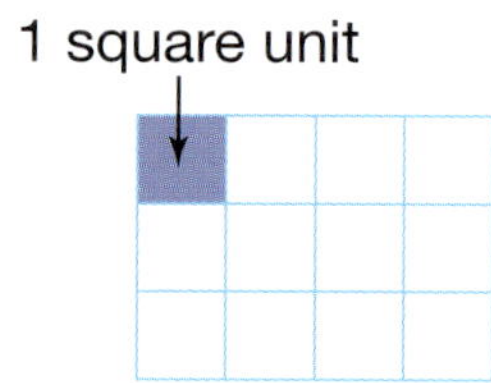

standard form: The usual way in which we write numbers (e.g., 365 is written in standard form.) (See also **expanded form**.)

standard unit: A unit of measurement that is part of a measurement system (e.g., **Metres**, **kilograms**, and **litres** are all standard units.) (See also **nonstandard unit**.)

sum: The result when you add

$14 + 37 = 51$

↑ sum

survey: 1. A set of questions asked to obtain information directly from people
2. To ask a group of people questions

T

2-D shape: A shape that has the 2 **dimensions** of length and width; a 2-dimensional shape

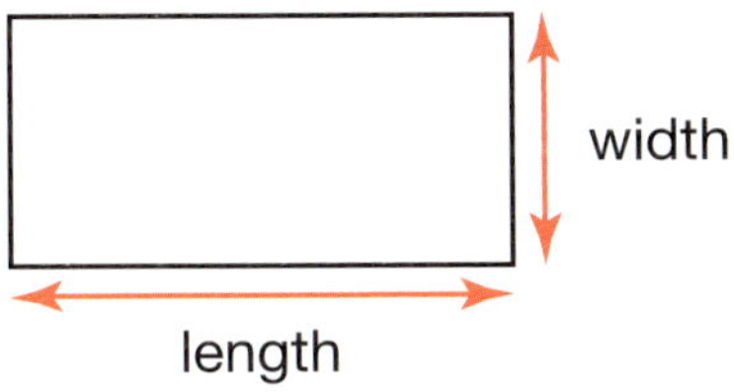

3-D object: An object that has the 3 **dimensions** of length, width, and height; a 3-dimensional object

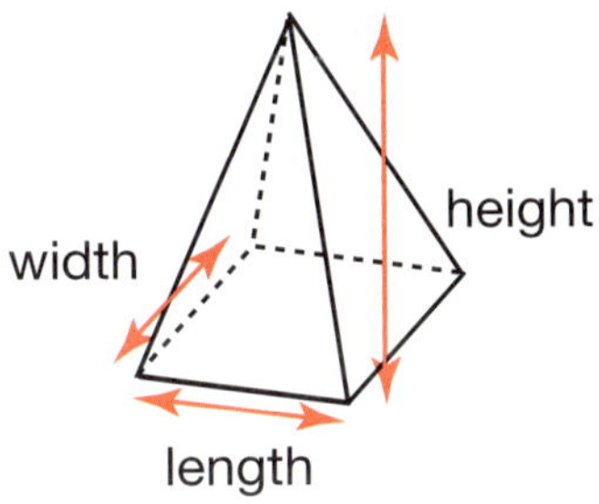

tally: A way to keep track of data using marks

𝍸 𝍸 |

tally chart: A chart that uses tally marks to count **data** (e.g., If you are surveying students about favourite flavours of ice cream you can use a tally chart.)

Favourite Ice Cream Flavours	
vanilla	𝍸 𝍸 |
chocolate	𝍸 𝍸 𝍸 𝍸 |||
strawberry	𝍸

t-chart: A way to organize **data** in a chart with 2 columns; both sides of the t are labelled

Number of weeks	Number of days
1	7
2	14
3	21

trapezoid: A 2-D shape with 4 straight sides and only 1 pair of **parallel** sides

triangle: A polygon with 3 sides; a 2-D shape with 3 straight sides

U

unlikely: A result that has little chance of happening (e.g., If you roll a die with a 3 on all the faces but one, rolling a number other than 3 is unlikely.)

V

Venn diagram: A diagram that uses circles and a rectangle to show relationships for objects, shapes, or numbers

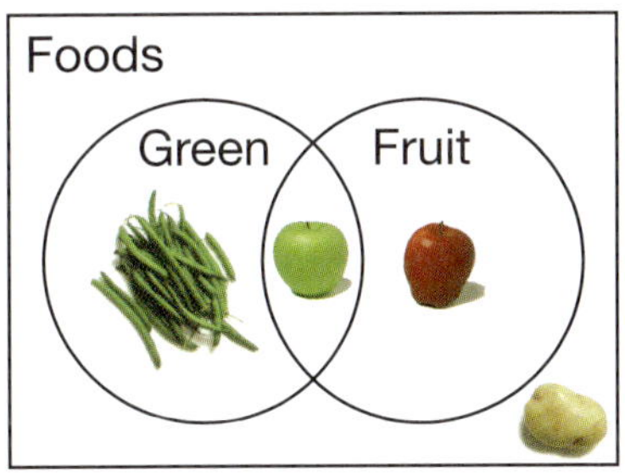

vertex (plural is **vertices**)**:** The point at the corner of a shape or object (e.g., A triangle has 3 vertices. A cube has 8 vertices. A cone has 1 vertex. A rectangle-based pyramid has 5 vertices.)

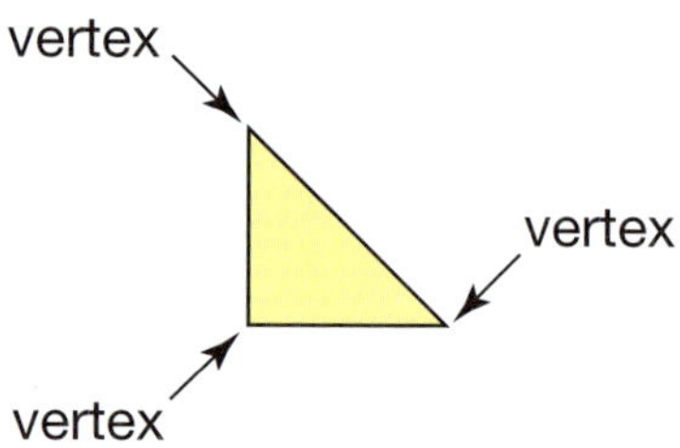

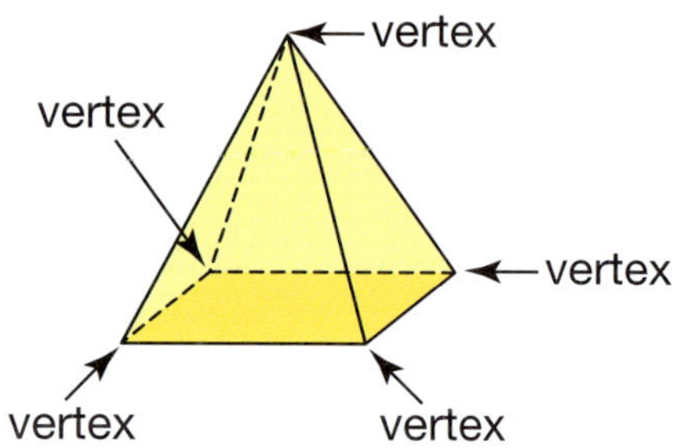

W

whole numbers: The counting numbers that begin at 0 and continue forever; 0, 1, 2, 3, …

Index

C

M

N

O

P

Q

R

S

U

V

W

Credits

Front cover: T. Kitchin/First Light

Back cover: Alan and Sandy Carey/Photodisc Green/Getty Images

Contents Page ix left: © Stewart Tilger/Corbis/Magma, right: © Ian McKinnell/Taxi/Getty Image; x: © Bonnie Kamin/Photo Edit; xiii: © Roman Soumar/Corbis/Magma

Chapter 2 Opener Page 22: © Pablo Coral/Corbis/Magma; Page 26: © Wally McNamee/Corbis/Magma; Page 32: Jim Stringer/CP Picture Archive; Page 40: C Squared Studios/Photodisc Green/Getty Images

Chapter 3 Page 57 top row, left to right: bottom row, left to right: C Squared Studios/Photodisc Green/Getty Images, © Robert W. Ginn/Photo Edit, ThinkStock LL/Index Stock; bottom row left to right: C Squared Studios/Photodisc Green/Getty Images, © Felicia Martinex/Photo Edit, © Tony Freeman/Photo Edit; Page 74 top row, left to right: Duncan Smith/Photodisc Green/Getty Images, Corel, G.K. and Vikki Hart/Photodisc Green/Getty Images, bottom row, left to right: Corbis/Magma, Corel; Corbis/Magma; Page 77 left: Thomson Nelson photo, right: © Spencer Grant/Photo Edit; Page 78 top row, left to right: Corel, Corel, Jack Star/Photolink/Getty Images, bottom row, left to right: Corel, Corel, Corel, Corel

Chapter 4 Page 86: *Where My Clothes Are* by Bruce Lansky from POETRY PARTY, published by Meadowbrook Press. Reprinted with permission of the publisher and the illustrator, Stephen Carpenter; Page 105: Digital Vision; Page 107: © Felicia Martinez/Photo Edit

Chapter 5 Page 122: Dr. Edward S. Ross; Page 134 top: C Squared Studios/Photodisc Green/Getty Images, bottom: © Michael Prince/Corbis/Magma

Chapter 6 Opener Page 145: Corbis/Magma; Page 148: Ataboy: The Image Bank; Page 149 top: Zefa Visual Media/Index Stock, bottom: Ian McKinnell; Page 151: © Dave G. Houser/Corbis/Magma; Page 152: © H.D. Thoreau/Corbis/Magma; Page 154: Dick Hemingway; Page 157: © Stewart Tilger/Corbis/Magma; Page 158: © Paul A. Souders/Corbis/Magma; Page 164: © Frank Siteman/Photo Edit; Page 166: T. Kitchin/First Light

Chapter 7 Page 182: Courtesy of Christine Thresh

Chapter 8 Opener Page 203: Al Harvey/The Slide Farm; Page 214: © Bonnie Kamin/Photo Edit; Page 217 top to bottom: Gary Vestal/Index Stock, Photodisc Collection/Photodisc Blue/Getty Images, Chase Jarvis/Photodisc Red/Getty Images, Jim Schabel/Index Stock, Jeremy Woodhouse/Photodisc Green/Getty Images, Canstock Image/Index Stock, Corbis/Magma; Page 221: Joel Rogers/Stone/Getty Images

Chapter 9 Page 235: Superstock

Chapter 10 Page 255: Yvette Cardoz/Index Stock; Page 263: C Squared Studios/Photodisc Green/Getty Images; Page 263: © Tony Freeman/Photo Edit

Chapter 11 Page 271 left: Ryan McVay/Photodisc Green/Getty Images, centre: C Squared Studios/Photodisc Green/Getty Images, right: C Squared Studios/Photodisc Green/Getty Images; Page 273 bottom left to right: Stefano Biancetti/Corbis/Magma, TRBfoto/Photodisc Green/Getty Images; Page 286 left to right: Corbis/Magma, Corbis Magma, Stockbyte/First Light

Chapter 12 Page 308: Rouman Soumar/Corbis/Magma; Page 310: Spike Mafford/Photodisc Green/Getty Images; Page 311: David Roth/FoodPix/Getty Images

Chapter 13 Page 323 left to right: Corbis/Magma, First Light; Page 334: Corel